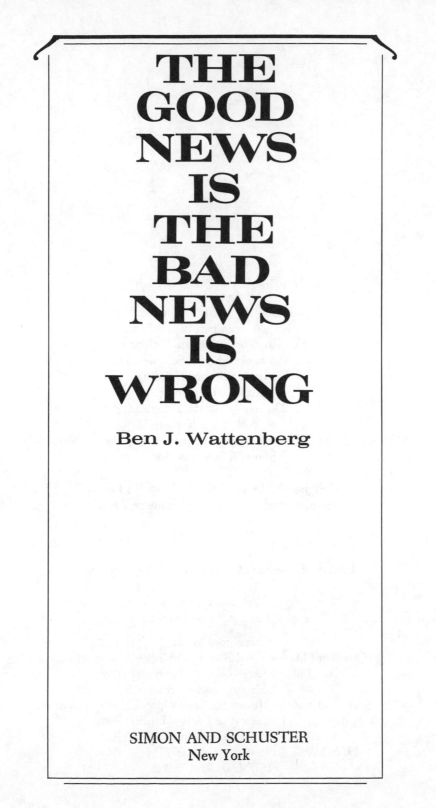

THE GOOD NEWS IS THE BAD NEWS IS WRONG

Ben J. Wattenberg

SIMON AND SCHUSTER
New York

Copyright © 1984 by BJW, Inc.
All rights reserved
including the right of reproduction
in whole or in part in any form
Published by Simon and Schuster
A Division of Simon & Schuster, Inc.
Simon & Schuster Building
Rockefeller Center
1230 Avenue of the Americas
New York, New York 10020
SIMON AND SCHUSTER and colophon are registered trademarks of
Simon & Schuster, Inc.

Designed by Jennie Nichols/Levavi & Levavi
Manufactured in the United States of America

1   3   5   7   9   10   8   6   4   2

Library of Congress Cataloging in Publication Data

Wattenberg, Ben J.
The good news is the bad news is wrong.

Includes index.
1. Quality of life—United States—Addresses, essays, lectures.
2. United States—Social conditions—1980–
—Addresses, essays, lectures.
3. Social indicators—United States—Addresses, essays, lectures.
4. Cost and standard of living—United States—
Addresses, essays, lectures.   I. Title.
HN60.W37   1984   306'.0973   84–10574
ISBN: 0-671-47545-2

Acknowledgments

The following Acknowledgments are gratefully made:

To Holt, Rinehart and Winston, Publishers, for the quotation "POSSLQ," from "There's Nothing That I Wouldn't Do If You Would Be My POSSLQ," by Charles Osgood, Copyright © 1981 by CBS, Inc.

To Mr. Tom Lehrer, for the lines from his song "Pollution."

FOR DIANE

Contents

CHAPTER 1

Cameo: Cocktails at Claude's

PRELUDE

Welcome to Claude Cleeshay's cocktail party!

The big living room is beginning to bustle. The waiters thread their way from group to group, moving the canapés. Swirling ice cubes, still with square edges, sound a muted clatter.

The brightest, most knowledgeable, most articulate people in the realm of public affairs are already here: an aggregation of economists, a pride of anchormen, a conglomeration of businessmen, a clutch of lobbyists, a spectral selection of columnists, an assembly of activists, a universe of sociologists, a gaggle of gossips, a pack of journalists—not to mention politicians, labor leaders, bankers, think tank fellows, consultants, authors and sages.

Come on over, meet some folks. Here's an interesting group.

"Well, what would you expect?" an economist is saying. "We've been on a long binge—and we had to pay the piper." His colleagues nod.

A politician grimaces. "Easy enough for you to say," he mumbles, tapping cigarette ashes on Claude's oriental rug. "But I've got to face the voters. How long are they going to stand for paying the piper?"

"It's been a long time," says an anchorman. "A dozen years and nothing but inflation, a big recession, stagflation, another big recession, more inflation, a huge recession—biggest since the Depression—high interest rates, big deficits, high unemployment. And now—" the anchorman pauses, "now, the question is: will the recovery last?"

"The high interest rates will abort the recovery," says a columnist.

"What's hurting the economy is too much government," says a businessman. "Too much spending, too much regulation. Big deficits."

"We encourage consumption and punish investment," says a young supply-side economist.

"Words, abstractions, generalities," a sociologist says. "You don't understand the agony behind those abstractions. There are real people out there. Unemployment for teenage blacks is at 50 percent! That's an incendiary situation—they're in a culture of poverty, a tangle of pathology, they'll never get real jobs . . ."

"Well, that's what I mean," says the economist, "we're paying the piper, we've been wringing it out . . ."

"We?" asks the sociologist archly, "Not *we—we're* fine. *They're* paying the price. Female-headed households are paying the price, unemployed steelworkers in the Frostbelt are paying the price—their jobs will never come back. Old people on the scrap heap are paying the price—Social Security and Medicare are busted. Poor people are paying the price, blacks are paying the price—the safety net has been shredded!"

The room is filling up now. Here's Claude Cleeshay himself, surrounded by a pair of pundits, a coterie of commentators, a cluster of canapés.

"The economy has been a shambles; the American dream is over," says Claude. "Young people haven't been able to buy a home. The polls show that young people don't think the future will be as good as the past. They've seen that the standard of living has fallen."

"Of course the standard of living is falling," says an environmental activist. "We've got too many people for our resource base. And we still keep taking in more immigrants!"

"It's not just the standard of living—it's the quality of living," says Claude, "it's the quality of life that's eroding . . ."

"It's eroding because we're degrading the environment," says another activist, "and we're paying for it. We keep gobbling up farmland to make more tacky suburbs. And dioxins. Dioxins are carcinogens. Dioxins are a disaster. They're everywhere."

"And the national parks," says a liberal columnist. "The national parks are a disgrace. We're selling them off. It's disgusting; they've turned into piles of rusting beer cans."

"Beer cans—alcoholism," says a conservative columnist. "Alcoholism is an epidemic in this country. It's even worse than drugs."

"It's all part of the permissiveness of our time," says a young man from a conservative think tank, gesticulating with his glass of Scotch. "Alcohol. Drugs. Pornography. Homosexuality. Divorce. Illegitimacy."

"It's an erosion of values," says Claude Cleeshay.

A psephologist has joined the group. "It may be values. All I know is that the gays are in politics in a big way. They're activitists. They hold the balance of power in a lot of elections."

"Just one more special interest," says Claude. "Our politics are being taken over by special interests."

"The Democrats are being taken over by special interests," says the conservative columnist. "Gays, feminists, minorities, unions, environmentalists, abortionists. And freezeniks and peaceniks. We're disarming unilaterally. We're being pushed around. The Soviets are on the move."

A liberal columnist edges his way into the group. "At least they're all voters," he says. "The Republicans have been taken over by special interests that talk for big money, not for voters. Corporate power. Oil companies. Chemical companies. Fat cats. Businessmen. Political action committees."

"Our politicians can't be bought—only rented," says Claude, drifting away to another group.

"Nothing has worked right recently," says a sociologist in the new group.

"It's a time of transition," says an author.

"People are upset," says a pollster.

"Well," says Claude Cleeshay, "who can blame them? The economy has been a mess. Our values are eroding. The quality of life is eroding. Our politics don't work. People don't respect America any more. It's a mess."

CHAPTER 2

Neon Numbers
Fighting
Typhoid Mary

THE THESIS AND PLAN OF THE BOOK

Indeed, it often seems as if we are living in a desperate moment. Just think of what we have been hearing in recent years:

Many conservatives tell us mournfully that our values have become permissive. Sex and crime are everywhere!

Many liberals maintain that the quality of life is eroding. I have on my desk, so help me, a clipping about dioxin in gefilte fish.

All across the political spectrum, from socialist to supply-sider, almost everyone seems to agree that for a dozen or so years the economy was in a shambles in America, in Europe, and in much of the rest of the world. As this book goes to the printer in the spring of 1984, there is an economic upswing going on, but there remains a haunting fear that we will soon reenter the realm of economic chaos, as high deficits and high interest rates mug the recovery.

We are told that our politics are unresponsive, unraveling, venal, and often just plain immoral. The popular political press suggests that the recent American presidents have been—in sequence—a liar, a crook, a bumpkin, a sanctimonious yokel, and a vapid movie actor.

It is said that American power and influence have diminished in a world that is drifting into uncharted and unpleasant waters.

All that, at least, is the story that seems to come to us along the web of modern communications. It is a story often sparked by intellectual panic-mongering (sometimes purposeful). It is a story connected to overheated political rhetoric. It is pushed along its way by the print media. And, finally, it is a story puffed up and ultimately dominated by television, which has in the past few years vastly expanded the amount of attention it pays to public affairs.

My view is that these messages of despair and failure are wrong, and more than that, dangerous. For, in a sense, the messages we get are presorted and hand-delivered by Typhoid Mary: something unpleasant can happen to you after you've been exposed.

I believe we live in a nation that in most respects—excuse the expression—never had it so good. While there is (as always) some countervailing statistical evidence, some of it quite serious, I believe this never-had-it-so-good proposition is clearly demonstrable. I believe it is important that we appreciate this, lest we do some silly things and fail to do some wise ones.

One further thought at the outset: Although this book appears in a highly charged election year, the progress I am talking about has come about under Democrats and Republicans, liberals and conservatives—perhaps because of them, or in spite of them. But *America* has moved forward. Conservatives may find it hard to accept that we moved ahead during the "Carter years" or during "big-spending Democratic congresses"; liberals may find it hard to swallow that there was progress in America even as Ronald Reagan was President. Alternatively, liberals may claim that this book validates the Welfare State; conservatives may say it proves that free enterprise makes us great. But something good happened. *America* has moved ahead.

=====

So—as a first task—this book attempts to assess our present circumstance.

I begin by asking, *how are we doing?* That is, what do these last dozen or so years look like without all the hothouse rhetoric and media exaggeration? Particularly, what do these years look like when one steps back and views them statistically? What might a man from Mars think about us if he thumbed through the pages of the *Statistical Abstract of the U.S.* starting with 1970 and going up to early 1984?

I try to do this by looking mostly at data that deal as directly as possible with our human condition, that is, data about people and how they have fared. The reader will not find here a discussion of items that, while important, have only a second- or third-order impact on the citizenry. Nothing here about "the potential disintermediation effects of high budget deficits," or other such arcana.

I try here to answer some very personal questions: how healthy are we? How much money do Americans make? Are we well educated? How are women doing? Blacks? Do we live in surroundings that we find pleasant? Do we find meaning in our lives? Are our values permissive? Are our families intact? Are our businesses thriving? Are our politics responding to our desires? That political question is less susceptible to a data-oriented answer than some of the earlier ones, but nonetheless yields an important glimpse of our American condition.

I believe that many of the answers to these questions are quite interesting—and not what most of us have been led to believe. Did you know, for example, that 1.1 million young blacks are now in college—a 400 percent increase in just the last two decades?

So, first, I see this work primarily as a book of reportage about some of the interesting and important trends of our time that are often misreported or unreported. In explicating the data, I try to keep the body of the text as simple as possible. It is too easy in this trade to get pulled into a statistical swamp. Sometimes it seems as if there is a contrary datum for every statistic a poor author tries to lean on. But I am dealing here with major trends over a period of a number of years. The numbers, I believe, typically speak for themselves. Where there is an argument about how to measure big trends over time, I try to present the opposing view, allowing the reader to choose his poison. (See, for example, chapter 22, dealing with income, and chapter 23, dealing with poverty.)

Partly to keep the reader out of a numerical morass, but mostly because I have become fascinated with it, I offer up in this volume the Doctrine of Super Numbers.

Our society puts forth a prodigious barrage of data. Row after infinite row, the numbers tumble out of high-speed computer printers. Accordion folds of printouts stack up into mountains of statistics. The United States government spends $1.4 billion per year to generate numbers; 6,000 books of government statistics are published annually. In addition, there are data emanating from the private sector, also mountainous.

Many of these numbers can be dismissed by the general observer: they confirm existing trends, or announce facts that do not dazzle. Are you interested to know that the industrial consumption of wood turpentine declined slightly during the decade of the Seventies?

But some numbers fascinate: 6.5 million Americans traveled abroad in 1970, and in 1982 the number was 10.3 million. During the same time the number of foreign travelers to the U.S. went up from four million to eleven million. I find such numbers interesting and important. Later in this volume they will form part of a mosaic that depicts our present circumstance in an unaccustomed way. Question: how do those numbers square with the idea of the "global recession" we've heard so much about?

And then, beyond the dull and beyond the fascinating, there are the Super Numbers. Every so often, it seems to me, some statistics jump out of the computers as if encased in neon and surrounded by exclamation points. Such numbers seem to do for the study of contemporary life almost what Copernicus's observations about the sun and the earth did for astronomy—and for religion.

Quite simply, the world we know after seeing these Super Numbers is not quite the same world we knew before we saw them. They fly in the face of received wisdom; they cause us to search for corollaries for confirmation; they ultimately push us toward reevaluating our opinions. The classic case of such a Super Number occurred after the census of 1890, when historian Frederick Jackson Turner examined some obscure data and announced quietly that the American frontier was closed. Talk about a Copernican revelation!

In recent years, I suggest here, some new Super Numbers have emerged. When possible, I concentrate on them in this work. They are of great importance in their own right; they must be dealt with, no matter how interpreted. Taken together, augmented by some other material offered here, I think these Super Numbers sketch out a fairly broad view of what has happened to us recently. And while a few are negative, I believe most of them are clearly positive—some of them sensationally so—and tend to confirm the thesis I am presenting here.

═══

If we're doing so well, that leads inexorably to some big questions that form a second facet of this book: how is it that we are always laboring under the misperception that nothing seems to be working out? Where is all the bad news coming from?

The American press corps (print and electronic) is probably the best in the world. American journalists have more access to events and to government than do journalists anywhere else in the world. We have high professional standards; there is little corruption. Our journalists have often shown a great deal of moral and physical courage. Our public affairs coverage on television is surely the most prolific, most interesting, most technically proficient in the world.

Further caveats, for the record: a free and vigorous press is indispensable to a democracy. I oppose censorship. I am against governmental force-feeding of good news. Senator Daniel P. Moynihan has it right when he says, "If you come into a country and all you see in the paper is good news—then all the good people are in jail."

But still, after all the caveats, something is wrong. There is even something wrong about the way the media are usually criticized. The harsh words are often about technical matters: the body count in

Lebanon was wrong, someone rehearsed a television interviewee, someone taped a phone interview, a columnist helped a candidate, this fellow in poverty would have been there even without the Reagan program cuts. You're getting the story wrong, we seem to be saying to the reporters.

But that's not the real problem with the media. The problem is that they are missing the biggest stories of our era—about progress—and missing them regularly, consistently, structurally, and probably unwittingly. It's not that they are often getting the story wrong. They are often getting the wrong story.

And that is too bad, because as we shall see, it may be distorting the whole system.

═══

A personal note that has some bearing on this work: This is by no means my first attempt to use data in a book about America. The first was *This U.S.A.* (in collaboration with Richard M. Scammon), which concentrated on data from the 1960 census. On a more political theme, but also with a statistical core, I coauthored *The Real Majority* (also with Scammon). That was published in 1970. In *The Real America* (written alone) I looked at the American situation up through to the mid-1970s.

Working on each of these earlier books offered me a great reward: a sense of seeing firsthand some startling changes in the panorama of American life.

And so too in this volume. There have been remarkable changes. The new data, typically starting in 1970 and often running up to early 1984, raise some ideas that were simply not plausible earlier. I could never have guessed twenty years ago that I would be writing about a birthrate so low as to yield a declining population. Or about booming immigration. Or about people moving to, not from, the country. Or about blacks moving to the suburbs at a faster rate than whites.

But it is not only the statistical substance of this book that makes it different from the earlier ones. Here I try to go further into realms where numbers can't tell the whole story. In none of the earlier volumes did I engage in much media-baiting or future-mongering. It was difficult enough to attempt a look at the message, let alone the messenger; difficult enough to try to assess the present, let alone the future.

I track my argument further this time, for a reason. I am an optimist, a congenital optimist, convinced that, in our country at least, optimism is realism. I haven't changed. But this time around I sense that there could be some stormy waters ahead unless we are careful. The bad news syndrome may prove to be self-fulfilling. In order to visualize that possibility—in order perhaps to help prevent it—one must, alas, try to speculate about the future. I do that here.

I think things will work out all right, but I am not sure of it.

PART I

QUALITY
OF
LIFE

CHAPTER 3

Us as Enemy

THE ENVIRONMENTAL ARGUMENT

If you visit American city,
You will find it very pretty.
Just two things of which you must beware:
Don't drink the water and don't breathe the air.

Chorus: Pollution, pollution—you can
use the latest toothpaste,
And then rinse your mouth with
industrial waste.

It may seem like only yesterday to the middle-aged, but that was sung, to a calypso beat, by satirist Tom Lehrer two decades ago, in 1965. By then, the nation had already started grappling afresh with the altogether proper and age-old issue of "the quality of life."

If it seems cavalier to date the advent of a serious movement from a strumming guitar, then perhaps the recent, much publicized wave of concern about environmental degradation can be said to have been well begun with the publication of Rachel Carson's best-selling *Silent Spring* in 1962.

Carson maintained that chemicals, particularly pesticides, particularly DDT, remained in "the food chain," unbalanced the ecosystem, and caused grievous harm to plants, animals, and human beings. She was also making a more general point, which has taken on a life of its own: that modern life could be spinning out of control and that we'd better do something about it, and quickly.

It is upon that central beam—the possibility of runaway modernism—that a great castle of ideas has been constructed during the last generation. It is a castle with many rooms. It is an argument with many strands.

I recall it here because "environmentalism," as the big argument has come to be called, has become one of the potent engines of popular thought and action in the world today. From the Clean Air Act to Love Canal, from Three Mile Island to dioxin at Times Beach, from carcinogens to ozone depletion, much of the argument concerns the sad effects of modern living on our health. But from that starting point it goes almost everywhere. From small Japanese cars in American garages to "Green" political parties in Europe, from OPEC gas lines to saving the whales, from the population explosion to the era of limits, from suburban sprawl to acid rain, the idea of environmentalism is omnipresent. In terms of specifics, the concept often yields programmatic guidance that is both correct and valuable. But as a comprehensive vision of our time—one that says the Quality of Life is eroding—the environmental view is, in my judgment, dead wrong and damaging.

The environmental notion that the Twentieth-Century-May-Be-Bad-For-Your-Health—and just plain bad—is one of the backdrops against which this book is written. It is an idea that has grown in importance in large measure because, at its core, it is a bad news argument. Accordingly, it has attracted the red eye of the TV camera: Meltdown at Three Mile Island! Cancer at Love Canal! Mercury in your tuna fish! We're running out of oil!

And so, to properly put forth the case that we are moving ahead, not backward, that the bad news is often the wrong news, it is necessary to start out by remembering and recounting the twisting strands of the environmental argument.

First strand: *pollution*. From Carson's account of DDT in the food chain, the general idea of pollution spread broadly to include water pollution, air pollution, radiation (a most malign and insidious kind of pollution), and a host of specific sources such as mercury, toxic waste, oil spills, Kepone, and a list of carcinogens long enough to lead the evening news on any day that nothing else was happening, and even on some days when other things were happening. Indeed, there were some environmentalists who said that our entire economy could be best described as a new kind of GNP—a "Gross National Pollution."

Second strand: *consumerism*. If runaway modernism creates unhealthy pollution, it also creates unhealthy products, such as unsafe drugs and plastic fabrics and stepladders that collapse when you step on them.

If modernism is the beast that tears at the quality of life and puts us at risk, it must be tamed. Scrubbers and catalysts could help tame pollution, but what could tame the *products* of modern life that were harming us? Consumerism could. And so it was demanded that sugared cereal must not be advertised; that nitrites must be purged from bacon; that certain new drugs must be kept off the market; that cyclamates must not sweeten soft drinks.

Behind each demand was a much publicized horror story: this caused cancer, that caused cancer, babies were burning up in inflammable nightshirts, or being contaminated by chemically treated nonflammable nightshirts. Night after night we saw it on television—plenty of bad news about our unhealthy society.

Third strand of the bad-news quality-of-life argument: *the population explosion*. Unlike pollution and consumerism, this is not directly a proposition about health, although it ultimately leads there. After World War II, population growth rates soared. World population jumped from 2.5 billion in 1945 to 4.7 billion in 1983. Neo-Malthusians shuddered: we were told that famine, pestilence, ecocatastrophe, and war would follow the population explosion. Man the lifeboats!

In the United States, from roughly 1945 to 1965, we experienced the "Baby Boom." Eighty million infants were born in the U.S. during that period, an apparent tidal wave of humanity.

It was said that "the population bomb" was ticking, and America would not be spared by the explosion. America, we were told, was "overcrowded." The big cities, it was said, had slums that were "overcrowded" and created crime and tension.* California was "overcrowded." Watch out: if we didn't do something about it, Colorado and Oregon would soon be Californicated. Moreover, a new tide of immigrants, mostly Hispanic and Asian, swept across the land, adding still more people. All this, we were told, diminished the quality of our lives.

It was maintained that population growth exacerbates the pollution problem. More people means more pollution: more cars, more particulates, more sewage, more industrial waste. After all, it was said that "the enemy is us," and if there were more of us, that must mean more trouble.

The idea of a population explosion blended easily with a fourth strand of the quality-of-life argument: *running out of resources*.

More people, obviously, use more resources. In 1972, using computer models, the Club of Rome published "The Limits to Growth." It was a work, seen to be seminal, that declared that the physical world within a hundred years would no longer be able to provide the resources necessary to maintain a high standard of living. (Only years later did the Club publicly retract and disown some of its findings and methodology.)

---

* In fact, the slums—inner cities—were losing population.

In 1973, the Arab states of OPEC embargoed oil exports to the United States. The ensuing dislocations caused high prices, spot shortages—and provided a rocketlike boost to the idea that our resources were disappearing. All this was intensified by nightly television news clips of less than even-tempered motorists, with odd-numbered license plates, seeking a fix at the pump.

And soon, also on television, the voice of the environmental pundits could be heard across the land, saying, "We live in an era of limits." Oil was limited, and so were other nonrenewable resources, such as natural gas, coal, strategic metals, and everyday metals too.

It wasn't only the nonrenewables; we were told there were problems with renewables too. There would be shortages of water, of farmland to produce our food—after all, it was said we could see with our own eyes that farmland was being paved over every day into suburban malls for as far as the eye could see.

All this too was laid at the doorstep of runaway, reckless modernism. An underresourced, overcrowded, polluted world would surely be one that imparted less "quality" to its inhabitants. That, of course, reverberated in media land: our echo system covers the ecosystem.

There is an aesthetic aspect to the quality-of-life argument as well. Strand five: *gluttony, antinatural materialism, ugliness.* Americans, said many in the environmental movement, consumed too much. They drove big gas-guzzling cars. They lived in big, detached, single-family houses, each with an energy-consuming air-conditioning plant. All this meant a still greater demand upon finite resources and still more pollution, and therefore a worsening quality of life. We were, said Paul Ehrlich, an "effluent society."

Moreover, and more deeply, it was also understood that America's concentration on material values was not just bad in terms of resources or pollution, it was its own punishment. All that materialism not only despoiled the air, it took us far away from nature and defiled our souls. Our children were hooked on quadrophonic rock 'n' roll and fast-food hamburgers. What kind of a future could we hope for?

You could see the problem outside any American city, mile after concrete mile: McDonald's, used-car lot, Burger King, loud teenager with dual exhaust hot rod, discount carpet emporium, gas station, Shakey's Pizza, health spa, gas station, Toys 'R' Us, gas station, Seven-Eleven with cold six-packs, Arthur Treacher's.

Ugly! Loud! Visual pollution! Aesthetic pollution! Artificial, commercial, unnatural, stress-inducing—all corroding the quality of life.

So then, a vast constellation of ideas pointing toward a single thought: things are in a bad way. Our health is harmed. Our resources are strained. Our lives are crass and ugly.

Bad news. And all of it reported, directly and indirectly, night after night in living rooms across the nation as never before.

======

Such, briefly, is the case. I sketch it here in perhaps harsh strokes, with too few shades of gray. After all, no sane people are antienvironmental; we are all for improving the quality of life. No one proposes to swim in polluted waters; no one gobbles carcinogens just for the hell of it. Wise people know that at some point, exponential population growth will, and should, stop. And while there was much exaggeration, surely some of the alarm bells that have sounded do point to real problems: asbestos can cause cancer, Kepone did harm people, thalidomide has caused deformed infants. There is much merit in the old argument, "better safe than sorry." When dealing with nature, a modern industrial society must mind its manners.

But that is not the point. The point is that much environmental thinking in recent years has been directed toward the idea that the overall quality of our lives was poor or deteriorating, and would likely get worse.*

Such a view is incorrect, as I hope to demonstrate now, strand by strand. Moreover, such a mind-set is not only wrong, it is probably harmful in its own right. I hope to show here that if we come to believe the vision put forth by the Quality-of-Life movement and trumpeted by the media, we may well diminish our quality of life.

Can it be that environmentalism may be bad for the environment?

---

* The official environmental view surfaced in 1980 in the *Global 2000 Report to the President*. In its first paragraphs the study makes the moderate claim that "if present trends continue, the world in 2000 will be more crowded, more polluted, less stable ecologically . . . the world's people will be poorer . . . life for most people on earth will be more precarious. . . ." The late Herman Kahn referred to it as "Globaloney."

CHAPTER 4

Cameo: An Epidemic of Life

CANCER RATES

What about health?

We begin here a run of six short chapters that look at our health situation from several points of view, and which address, among other things, two issues in the environmentalist quiver—pollution and consumerism.

To begin, consider cancer, surely the most feared disease. It is also the disease that seems most closely linked to the quality of life. Radiation, nuclear power, food additives, air pollution, toxic chemicals, Agent Orange—the all-star team of environmental horrors—have all been at least loosely linked to cancer.

More specifically, there is the scientific theory that a large percentage of cancers are caused by "environmental" factors. This idea is generated from data that reveal that the incidence of specific sorts of cancer varies greatly from nation to nation and from culture to culture. The assumption is that the "environment"—diet, workplace hazards, life-style, modernism, if you will—causes the difference between the lowest and the highest rate of a specific cancer in different areas of a given country as well as between nations.

There has been, moreover, a dreaded sense of futility about cancer: "Mr. Jones died after a lingering illness." That sense has been mirrored, until recently, by a generally pessimistic view within the scientific community. "Cancer is not one disease," it was said by experts, "it's a hundred diseases, and we may be years away from being able to deal with it."

Finally, there has been a personal sense, shared by many, that these days we somehow know more people who are afflicted with cancer. All this has led to the thought, rather widely held, that there is "a cancer epidemic."

Wrong. The late Dr. Philip Handler, former president of the National Academy of Sciences, a man of wisdom who could turn a phrase, had a more accurate way of putting it. "What we have," he said, "is an epidemic of life."

The difference—and the link—between "cancer epidemic" and "epidemic of life" is rather surprising. It works out this way: the chances are you do indeed know more people who have cancer. One big reason for this is that cancer is a disease whose incidence increases as a person's age goes up. It is "age specific." Now if people are living longer these days, as we will see in the next chapter, then it is also apparent that more people are "at risk" of getting a disease whose incidence increases with age. More older people equals more cancer.

But when the data are corrected to account for increased longevity—when they are "age adjusted"—there has been no increase in the incidence of cancer. In fact, during the twenty-four-year period from 1947–48 to 1969–71 the age-adjusted rate for cancer in all sites of the body actually *decreased* by 3.9 percent. Furthermore, a closer examination of the data shows that the overall incidence rate would be even lower were it not for a sharp increase—more than a doubling—in lung cancer.

But much lung cancer is regarded as "self-induced," linked to cigarette smoking. Those lung cancers induced by cigarettes are not imposed on innocent citizens by the pell-mell effects of modernism on the quality of life. Cigarette smoking, after all, is a voluntary act. If one looks at the cancer incidence rate as a function of our *involuntary* exposure to the environment around us (that is, deducting lung cancers), the rate is down by *11.3* percent over the roughly twenty-year period.*

There is yet another big reason why cancer seems more apparent these days. Consistent with our sense of it, we are indeed more likely to know more people with cancer. That is because more people who have it remain alive.

In the early part of this century, relatively few cancer victims had much expectation of long-term survival. By the 1930s, the data show that the five-year survival rate for cancer patients was about one person in five. By the 1940s it had climbed to one in four. In the 1960s and 1970s it was one in three. These days it is better than half, according to the National Cancer Institute.

* Data from "Cancer Incidence and Mortality Trends in the United States: 1935–74," by Susan S. Devasa and Debra T. Silverman, *Journal of National Cancer Institute,* vol. 60, no. 3 (March 1978). The study is generally regarded as the definitive study of cancer incidence, involving about 146,000 cases.

Cancer experts are no longer chronic pessimists. The same ones who were saying it would take decades to deal with cancer have now starkly revised their estimates. The distinguished physician, researcher, and author, Lewis Thomas, recently said:

> Predictions were made in the early 1970s, when the arguments were stridently held about the wisdom of the conquest of cancer program. Several eminent scientists protested that the program shouldn't be launched at that time because we were 50 years away from being able to ask really significant questions about cancer. And one of the eminences who made that kind of prediction told me a few weeks ago that he's revised it. Now it's two years, in his own laboratory, anyway. Things are moving very fast.*

Strange, but true: the fact that people live longer and that more people are cured of a dread disease gives the impression of greater misery. What we sense as a "cancer epidemic" is in fact directly attributable to an "epidemic of life."

* Interview on Public Broadcasting Service (PBS) series "Ben Wattenberg At Large," 1981. Program title: *Medical Progress.*

CHAPTER 5

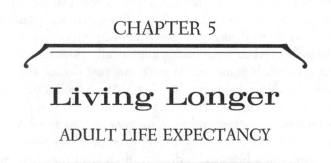

Living Longer

ADULT LIFE EXPECTANCY

An epidemic of life? Let us investigate.

Here is our first simple set of Super Numbers. Reader: look at these data carefully. They are important to the society as a whole. And they are important to you specifically because these are not your run-of-the-mill, life-expectancy-at-birth data. These numbers deal with how long adults—like you—are likely to live.

AVERAGE EXPECTATION OF LIFE IN YEARS, AT AGE 40

	Years Remaining	Increase from Previous Decade
1940	31.0 years	—
1950	32.8 years	1.8 years
1960	33.8 years	1.0 years
1970	34.6 years	.8 years
1980	36.7 years	2.1 years
1982 (provisional)	37.2 years	2.6 years (1970–1982)

Source: U.S. National Center for Health Statistics.

These are Super Numbers. Understood correctly, they should begin to change the view we hold of our time. They should also help change the view of those who believe the quality of life has deteriorated in our time.

The key fact in the table is this: *Since 1970, adult life expectancy went up faster than at any time in recent American history.* In fact, probing further, one finds that adult life expectancy went up faster in the 1970s than at *any time* in American history, going back to 1900, when such data were first systematically collected!

What on earth is going on? Wasn't this past decade the very same one when headlines were proclaiming that air pollution was frying your lungs, radiation was corroding your innards, carcinogens were everywhere, even popping up in your genetic structure? Wasn't this the same decade when Rachel Carson's grim prophecies were supposed to come true, when low-level radiation, high-level radiation, eutrophic water, and floating particulates were about to cut our time short? After all, the premise of the whole environmental legislative thrust—clean air, clean water, and so on—was that our health was in grave new danger, that the quality of our lives was eroding.

The evidence of the Super Number says that was not so. Exactly the opposite was true. We have been leading healthier lives; that is, if you accept the idea that longer life equates with healthier life. (If you don't accept that, in subsequent chapters it will be shown that in other ways our lives are indeed healthier.)

Moreover, this jump in adult life expectancy was not anticipated.

Until very recently, it was held that increases in the adult life span would proceed very slowly. Most experts were predicting a "plateau" in the rates, as human beings bumped up against what was seen to be their "natural" physiological limits.

Now life expectancy rates are obviously not trivial data, and they are not trivial to the argument of this book. After all, they go to the heart of the value we hold most dear: survival. It would be hard to seriously support the enhancement of the "quality of life" without noting that the supreme quality of life involves continued living. It is hard to make the case that modern society is harmful to your health if, collectively, we live so much longer and the gains have been so great, so recently.

Consider the numbers in some greater detail: they deal not only with the Seventies, but with the last four decades—with the modern, mostly postwar world. The gain in life expectancy for middle-aged adults has been about six years. Back in 1940, a typical forty-year-old American could expect to live to almost age seventy-one. But by 1982, that typical American could expect to live to a bit more than seventy-seven. That works out to a 20 percent increase in life expectancy. That's a lot. (If, perhaps, you think that a six-year extension of life at age seventy-one is trivial, you might test out that notion on your favorite seventy-year-old.)

It should also be explained why it is so important to note that these data do not deal with "life expectancy at birth." Those rates too have been soaring—in fact, almost twice as fast as the adult rates shown here. (From 1940 to 1981, life expectancy at birth has jumped by eleven years.) But such gains are only miraculous, not uncommon. Life expectancy rates "at birth" can jump quickly because infant and child death rates typically decline rapidly due to things we now take for granted: the advent of modern obstetric practice, childhood disease vaccines, and other public health measures.

But historically, the prolongation of life for adults has been a much harder, slower, more tortuous process. The statistical circumstance and the historical data bear this out.

After all, everyone dies of something, and the older you get the sooner it comes: save an eighty-year-old man from death by heart disease and he may die the next year of cancer, yielding little in the way of statistical gain.

Consider the history. The turn of the century is as far back as the national data go, but there are age-specific life-expectancy rates for Massachusetts going back as far as 1850. From 1850 to 1950, life expectancy at birth in Massachusetts went up by 30 years—from a life expectancy of 39 years to one of 69 years. During that same hundred years, life expectancy at age 40 went up only 4 years!

So the six-year adult gain since 1940 is major by any standard.

Furthermore, brace yourself, the immediate future looks as bright as the recent past. Professor Eileen Crimmins, a gerontologist at the University of Southern California, says, "We have entered a new era of mortality decline, one concentrated at the older ages."

Look now at the situation, not from age forty as we have done, but from age sixty-five, the time of retirement. Today, a person aged sixty-five can expect to live to age eighty-one. Professor Crimmins, having examined the data and the likely course of medical progress, says that an American aged sixty-five in the year 2000 can expect to live to age eighty-seven. (The author applauds: God willing, he will be sixty-five in 1998.)

Professor Crimmins is neither alone nor necessarily on the optimistic side of such futurology. The highly respected dean of French demographics, Jean Bourgeois-Pichat, says that a typical person sixty-five years old, living in a Western country in the year 2000, should expect to live almost to age one hundred. I myself doubt that; but then again, it was gloomy doubters who said that adult life expectancy had begun to plateau in the mid-1960s.

Finally, if the reader would, by some chance, like to make the case that this increase of life is something that has been disproportionately granted to the power structure—rich, white, males—the reader could not be more wrong. Women live longer, and their survival rates have been climbing faster than men's. Blacks, disproportionately poor in America and starting from a lower base, have in recent years seen a faster rise in life expectancy at all ages than have whites. Blacks are still behind, but by less than before: about five years behind whites at birth, about three years at age forty, about even at age sixty-five.

========

What can we learn from the first set of Super Numbers?

First, in fairness they do not tell us conclusively that the quality of life is getting better—only that people are living longer and healthier lives. Longer life is important, but by no means a conclusive rebuttal to the quality-of-life argument, which deals with more than just longevity or health. More evidence is required to make the point that the quality of our lives has improved, and more will be offered.

But these data should provide, at the least, a first gonglike warning that all may not be as it has been described.

These numbers serve to call into question at least one rhetorical premise of recent years: that we live in an unhealthy society, probably getting unhealthier. The data demonstrate we live in a healthy society, getting healthier.

So what? Did we only muff a big fact? That might be only of passing journalistic interest.

It is more than that. Clause One in the Speechwriter's Code reads: Rhetoric Yields Reality. A society with wrong-headed rhetoric, based on wrong-headed premises, will often pursue a wrong-headed course of action. Bad assumptions yield bad policy.

For, if nothing else, our politics are highly responsive. If we come to believe that our planet is being poisoned, that toxic wastes are causing mutant children, that a nuclear power plant may blow up one fine night, why, our politicians will give us legislation that responds to just those perceptions.

A case in point: would the Clean Air Act amendments of 1970 have been passed in the form they eventually were if lawmakers hadn't been pressured by environmental activists who were hit-listing the "dirty dozen" legislators, while predicting that a silent spring of poisonous degradation was just over the smoggy horizon? Would they have passed in that form if, stirred by television reportage, the public had not come to believe the worst about the quality of life in the U.S.? Probably not.

Now surely a modern society needs solid laws to establish clean air standards. Surely such laws may help make our society—which is getting healthier—even more healthy.

But *that* law?

The Clean Air Act is estimated to cost the public and private sectors about $30 billion per year. It has had the effect of raising prices across the entire economic spectrum—for poor people as well as others. There is a case to be made that it contributed to a process whereby American heavy industry became less competitive with foreign producers, costing us jobs.

Yet there is an incredible unpublicized fact about clean air legislation. Eminent scientists, in and out of government, are asking an extraordinary question: is there *any* good evidence of important gains in health or life expectancy due to the clean air regulations that come anywhere near justifying the expenditure of $30 billion every year, year in and year out?

Is that really possible? After all the hoopla, after all these years, is it really possible that there is still no solid evidence that cleaner air makes us substantially healthier, or that dirty air makes us less healthy? Yes it is. That was the personal view of the late Dr. Philip Handler, then the president of the National Academy of Sciences, whose agency had investigated the issue in great depth.

A bit of confirming history: Pittsburgh cleaned up its air decades before the rest of us. A good thing, too, if for none other than aesthetic reasons. But there is no medical evidence that the once-smokey city has improved its health any faster than the rest of the United States.

Now $30 billion is a lot of money, probably too much to shrug off by saying, "better safe than sorry." After all, might not some, or much, of that money have been better used to accelerate, say, the search for a cure for cancer? Or to provide school lunches for poor children? Or to provide for the hungry and homeless? Would we have been less healthy if the clean air standards had been enacted, but were not quite so strict, not quite so wedded to the idea of a poisoned planet?

In a climate of near-hysteria, those are the sort of questions that don't get asked, or if asked, get answered in a less than wise manner. In an overheated climate, we end up getting public policy that is over-done; not necessarily wrong, mind you, but injuriously excessive. Bad news that is wrong can harm us.

How did so many of us come to believe all the bad news about an eroding quality of life?

Well, there was—and is—an articulate body of opinion makers holding such views. There is probably not a sentence in the preceding analysis that will not be challenged by someone in the environmental community.

Someone trying to pull a fast one may say the increase in longevity is due to environmental legislation like the Clean Air Act. That won't wash. The big increase of life expectancy happened *before* the effects of environmental laws could have been felt; for example, the sections of the Clean Air Act that deal with pollution abatement were only passed in 1970, and the process of implementing the most important health-oriented sections has stretched out for a decade and beyond.

Smarter environmentalists will say, well, all these diseases caused by pollution may take 30 or 40 years to develop. They may indeed, although if that were the case it is likely that by now we would have seen such evidence in our older industrial cities, which we have not.

On balance, the general environmental argument probably comes down to a complicated cost-benefit calculus between avoiding unknown amounts of potential harm versus engendering unknown amounts of potential progress.

It's something to argue about.

Within the intellectual-humanist community generally, it may well be that environmentalist views are in the majority. But it is also likely that in the scientific community, the hard-core environmental views are in a minority. What we know is that there are responsible alternative views on the issue.

Question: have those alternative views been given proper exposure? Has the nightly news given us a sense that there are valid arguments to suggest that we are a healthy society, getting healthier? Has television, for one example, stressed with any real vigor or continuity the story that the most basic barometer of health—survival—has been moving in a positive direction? It has not.

Why don't we regularly hear the good news? Given the choice between an ongoing story of progress or an ongoing story of danger, pollution, and catastrophe, why did we get bad news almost exclusively night after night: radiation, mercury poisoning, toxic wastes, little seagulls covered with oil, beer causing cancer?

How serious is this? Bad news not only yields faulty public policy. We can, and do manage to live pretty well with faulty policy. But crisis-mongering yields a more cosmic symptom: a mentality out of touch with reality.

So then, many questions for the media about real problems. We shall be discussing these ideas at greater length and depth later on. For now, I offer only one word of solace. If you look at the Super Number, you will see that most of us should have many extra years to think about these matters.

CHAPTER 6

Cameo: The Other Drug Culture

PHARMACOLOGICAL PROGRESS

While we are thinking about health, consider the tale told by Dr. Lewis Thomas, the distinguished physician and former director of Sloan Kettering Memorial Hospital, whom we first heard from in chapter 4.

Thomas was born in 1913. He recently recounted to the author the story of his father, also a doctor, who was born in the latter part of the last century and graduated from medical school in 1905:*

> In my father's day, it was expected that some members of every family would die at an early age. The thing that was most frightening, in somewhat the same sense that cancer is frightening today, was tuberculosis. And there was absolutely nothing to be done about it. Tertiary syphilis was the other major illness feared by everybody, and it was the cause of more insanity than any other disease.

It was not that there had been no progress in medicine during the early career of the elder Dr. Thomas. There were indeed major gains, but most were attributable to public health measures: clean water, vaccinations, and so on. But the medical usefulness of old-fashioned doctors was extremely limited and typically futile. The younger Dr. Thomas recalls his father's frustration:

> . . . the only science that existed and had any effect on what he did with his professional life was in the process of making an accurate diagnosis. But he used to tell me, over and over again, that he did not believe that anything that he had to offer from the black bag that he carried around on house calls had any measurable effect on illness.

* Interview on Public Broadcasting Service (PBS) series "Ben Wattenberg At Large," 1981. Program title: *Medical Progress.*

The younger Dr. Thomas, however, became a physician at a very different moment. He recalls an exciting time:

> I was a medical student and a house officer in the late 1930s when a
> big upheaval occurred . . . the introduction of first, sulfanilamide
> and then penicillin and the other antibiotics.

The results of that pharmacological upheaval are well known. Rather suddenly, the infectious diseases came under a large measure of control: not only the dreaded tuberculosis and syphilis, but also rheumatic heart disease, mastoid infection, food poisoning, osteomyelitis, influenza, pneumonia, meningococcal meningitis.

For the first time in history—a history going back millennia and ranging from Hippocrates in ancient Athens, to witch doctors in jungle villages, to early twentieth-century physicians—doctors finally had something in their black bags to cure people. To put this in perspective, consider what Dr. James G. Hirsch, dean of graduate studies at Rockefeller University wrote in 1980:

> The conquest of bacterial infectious diseases is without a doubt the
> most impressive advancement in the entire history of medical science.

With all that, these drugs had a major drawback. They tended to affect the entire human system. That meant "side effects." The antibiotics could kill an infection, but if large dosages were required, they could sometimes kill the patient as well. That is not regarded as sound medical practice.

And so, pharmacological progress began colliding with side effects. Just a few years ago, it was being said by experts that what had come to be called "The Pharmacological Revolution" was over. Any future gains, it was said, would be slow in coming and of limited effect.

That view turned out to be wrong. Be it noted that during this time when we have been told that our health is threatened we are also right in the midst of what is being called "The Second Pharmacological Revolution." Instead of aiming at *human beings,* drug researchers are now targeting *human cells.* The change has been compared to the difference, in warfare, between using cannonballs and laser beams.

The new drug technologies include the use of "monoclonal antibodies," "enzymes," and other unfathomables. The drugs are new, but their goal was accurately described by the German microbe hunter Paul Ehrlich long ago: the creation of "magic bullets." The new drugs tend to bypass many of the earlier side effects. They enter the body boldly, announcing, "Take me to your gall bladder."

Cimetidine is one such new medicine. It has dramatically lowered the rate of surgery for peptic ulcers. The new "beta blockers" are increasingly effective in treating many cardiovascular diseases: angina, high blood pressure, abnormal heart rhythms, and subaortic stenosis. They also help prevent second heart attacks. Another new set of drugs, "calcium channel blockers," which are now being tested and studied further, have already been effective in preventing coronary artery spasms, and many researchers believe they will be quite effective in treating hypertension.

Other remarkable new pharmaceuticals are on the way, according to drug industry and medical sources. These include substances that will deal with certain forms of cancer, and with asthma, arthritis, Parkinson's disease, obesity, a broad range of mental disorders, glaucoma, epilepsy, gallstones, menstrual cramps, birth control, and fungus infections. New painkillers, emulating the body's natural opiates, are being investigated.

People who will not suffer from these diseases, or who will suffer less from these diseases, may be assumed to have an enhanced quality of life.

CHAPTER 7

Living Healthier

CONSUMERISM, DANGER, NEW PRODUCTS

That's quite a story Lewis Thomas tells about his father. And it's quite a list.

To universalize the point, it would be nice at this juncture to introduce, with a flourish, another grand Super Number. Ideally, it would deal with health in its broadest sense, combining several of the intertwined strands of the quality-of-life argument that have so concerned environmentalists and consumerists: new drugs and other medical techniques, the effects of allegedly dangerous products and procedures, the effects of new nonmedical products on risk and health in our society.

"Aha," this author would then write, "careful measurement has determined that we live in a healthier, *less* dangerous world. The Health/Danger Index number used to be 78.6, and it is now only 57.9! Hooray!"

Instead of "aha!" one can only offer "alas." Beyond the broadest measure—the life expectancy data discussed in chapter 5—there seems to be no such number available covering health and risk in its many modern forms.

However, if there is no Super Number for health and risk, there is a mountain of anecdotal evidence. Thus, if we cannot talk about "all products" with any scientific certainty, we can talk about certain specific products. If we cannot talk about "all environmental dangers," we can talk about certain specific environmental dangers. And with enough anecdotes, one begins to gain a sense, if not a certainty, of what is happening.

So our angle of attack here is *lists*. Four of them.

LIST ONE: NON-HORRIBLE HORRORS

First comes a list of products that *we have been told were dangerous— and aren't*, at least not under conditions of normal use, or in anywhere near the severity that was originally reported.

Fluorides. We forget that the first big objection to chemicals in the water was mounted not by environmentalists but by the far-out right wing in America. We were told that adding fluorides to the drinking water, ostensibly to reduce tooth decay, was not only a communist plot, but would cause cancer.

Today, 123 million Americans drink water to which fluosilicic acid, or an equivalent, has been added. In large measure because of this procedure, the incidence of tooth decay dropped by 33 percent from 1971 to 1980, according to a study by the National Institute of Dental Research.* Another federal study shows no linkage of fluoridation to cancer rates and no adverse effect on overall health.

---

* The town of Antigo, Wisconsin, population 8,600, stopped its fluoridation program in 1960. In the next four years tooth decay among preschoolers went up by 92 percent!

There is some evidence, in fact, that fluoridation may be related to the steady decline in deaths from heart disease. Funny—there may be some fringe types running around out there opposing fluoridation who would be long dead from heart disease had fluoridation not come along.

Agent Orange. It has been charged that this herbicide—which contains dioxin—has been responsible for a wide variety of health defects among individuals exposed to it in Vietnam. However, no study has established a cause-and-effect relationship between Agent Orange exposure and any symptoms of ill health other than a temporary skin rash resembling acne, know as chloracne.

Upon the direction of Congress, the National Academy of Sciences conducted a study of the health effects of herbicides in South Vietnam. This study was "unable to find adequate data upon which to reach any conclusions concerning a causal effect between exposure to herbicides and health effects, including birth defects," according to the Congressional Research Service report on Agent Orange. Similar studies conducted in the early 1980s came to similar conclusions.

A 1984 Air Force study of veterans directly involved in spraying Agent Orange—presumably the group most heavily exposed—found less cancer than in the general population.

The *Journal of the American Medical Association* in May of 1984 reported that 204 workers exposed to dioxin in a 1949 manufacturing accident in West Virginia "showed no higher rates of heart disease, liver disease, kidney damage, nerve problems, reproductive problems or birth defects than did unexposed workers. Also, no higher rates of cancer were found in the exposed workers." A tracking of another dioxin accident in Seveso, Italy, in 1976 has shown similar results, according to the American Medical Association Council on Scientific Affairs.

Love Canal. Several scientific panels have conducted investigations to determine whether the chemicals dumped from 1942 to 1953 by the Hooker Chemical and Plastics Corporation near Niagara Falls, New York, caused deleterious health effects among the residents of a housing development later built on the site.

A physicians' panel appointed by New York Governor Hugh Carey concluded, in 1980, that the initial studies that had indicated possible serious health damage "were not scientifically warranted." Another state report in 1981 also discounted the early warnings of a "great and imminent peril" to the public. The director of the New York

State Health Department's Cancer Control Bureau, Dr. Dwight Janerich, reported on June 11, 1981, that "there wasn't any evidence of an increased cancer rate associated with residence at Love Canal." A later report by the Federal Center for Disease Control concurred. And on July 14, 1982, a report by the Environmental Protection Agency and the Public Health Service, in cooperation with other federal agencies, found that the neighborhood around Love Canal was habitable, and that outside of the immediate area of the canal (within one and a half blocks), which has been carefully capped and drained, the levels of soil and water contamination are comparable to those in other parts of Niagara Falls and in other industrial areas around the United States.

DNA. In the mid-1970s, a fierce national debate raged over the safety of recombinant DNA research. Critics argued that the technology could not be adequately handled and controlled. A serious accident, they said, could literally imperil the human race. For a time, the city council of Cambridge, Massachusetts, actually banned DNA experimentation within municipal limits. Strict national research restrictions were promulgated, then relaxed.

Today, the controllability and safety of DNA research are generally no longer questioned. And its benefits, actual and potential, are almost universally accepted as enormous.

Three Mile Island/Nuclear Power. No one was killed during the reactor accident at the Three Mile Island nuclear plant in Pennsylvania in 1979. No one was injured. Five years have now gone by and there is no report of an increase in any radiation-induced illness in the Harrisburg, Pennsylvania, area. That is no surprise, for the additional radiation exposure for area residents was less than 100 millirems, well below medically acceptable levels. (A standard diagnostic X ray produces between 45 and 75 millirems.) Put another way, Three Mile Island's local residents had a combined natural and accidental radiation exposure roughly equivalent to the amount normally absorbed by residents of Colorado, where "background" radiation is slightly higher than in Pennsylvania.

Indeed, the data concerning safety in the nuclear industry are remarkable. In America, nuclear plants have now been operating commercially since 1957, a total so far of over 600 plant years. Not a single civilian death by accident or radiation has been caused directly by the operation of the nuclear part of a civilian nuclear power plant.*

The comparison of coal plants to nuclear plants is interesting. A review of recent major studies done for Congress by the Library of Congress maintains that, based on the "most probable" of many disputed estimates, a coal plant as currently operated and equipped may cause 25 to 257 deaths each year. The comparable "most probable" estimates for a nuclear plant might range from about .6 to 4 deaths each year, including the effects of both normal plant operations and the estimated impact of plant accidents.†

The Pill. After decades of criticism, scientific and unscientific, the birth control pill is now being viewed in a more positive light. A review of more than 700 studies of "pill" use, released by Johns Hopkins University in July 1982, concluded that the pill not only does not cause cancer, but actually helps provide protection for the user against ovarian and uterine cancer! Other possible (and unexpected) health benefits of the pill listed by the review include the following:

- suppression of acne
- substantial protection against toxic shock syndrome
- protection against rheumatoid arthritis
- protection against ectopic pregnancy
- protection against pelvic inflammatory disease
- menstrual benefits, including reduction of iron deficiency anemia

The Food and Drug Administration is now making arrangements to add an entire new section on "beneficial effects" to labels on oral contraceptives.

The Johns Hopkins review also concluded that there is no documentable link between pill usage and breast cancer, infertility, birth defects, or melanoma (skin cancer). And previous fears of gall bladder disease, benign liver tumors, cervical cancer, and circulatory problems seem to have been greatly overstated or confined largely to certain high-risk populations, such as smokers or women over thirty-five.

---

* On January 3, 1961, in the very early days of nuclear power, three *military* technicians were killed at an *experimental* reactor testing station in Idaho Falls, Idaho.

† *Coal and Nuclear Power Policies: Seeking Protection From Uncertain Risks,* Langdon T. Crane, 8—140 SPR, Library of Congress, August 1, 1980, pp. 7–8.

The findings of the review were "unexpected and much broader than originally thought," according to one of the report's compilers, and indicate that the benefits of taking the pill "clearly outweigh the risks."

And finally, a word from an expert about the pill and the media: "I find it amazing that every negative claim against the pill makes headlines rapidly while reports of the positive benefits of the pill, evidence that has been steadily accumulating for ten years, are largely ignored by the press," said Dr. Howard Ory, director of a major new study on the safety of the pill now underway at the U.S. Centers for Disease Control.

More. Such an anecdotal recitation of non-horrible horrors could be vastly expanded. Contrary to some original reports:

- Mercury levels in fish today are no higher than in some ancient fish fossils, nor higher than in certain 100-year-old pickled fish now reposing in the Smithsonian Institution.
- The advent of supersonic aircraft (including the Concorde) has not led to sonic booms yielding insanity, nor to an increase in skin cancer, nor an accelerated greenhouse effect that will parboil the world.
- Saccharin is not dangerous at quantities consumed by humans.
- Lake Erie is not dead from eutrophication.
- Nitrites are apparently not carcinogenic; the Food and Drug Administration has decided against a ban.
- Coffee drinking isn't linked to birth defects.
- Urea-formaldehyde insulation is not dangerous at levels in an average affected house.
- EDB is not the potent danger it was portrayed as during the scare of 1983–84.

LIST TWO: HARDLY NOTICED
HEALTH ENHANCERS

Well, that's one list—of things that were alleged to be terrible for the quality of our lives, but apparently aren't.

But we need another list. Most new products and procedures get little attention, because there is nothing wrong with them. Most new products and procedures are never tried in the court of public relations. By the time they reach the marketplace they will have been thoroughly tested and found useful. Apparently because there is little risky or dangerous about such products, they are not deemed very newsworthy. And so, the popular media frequently pay little attention to some of the biggest news of our era: the development of products and procedures capable of bringing better health and longer life to more people.

We have seen the beginning of a list of such developments in our discussion of the second pharmacological revolution in chapter 6. But of course, it is not only new drugs that help us medically.

- What about laser surgery that prevents blindness caused by disorders of the retina?
- What about plastic surgery—not for a droopy eyelid—but to treat victims of severe burns, allowing them, in fact, to survive?
- What about the new techniques which pulverize kidney stones using sound waves and shock waves, often curing one of life's most painful afflictions without major surgery?
- What about the kidney dialysis machines, a bizarre idea a relatively few years ago, now keeping 60,000 Americans alive?

(One good exception comes to mind. A good deal of media attention was paid to the development of open-heart bypass surgery, once the scariest imaginable operation, today almost a commonplace health enhancer.)

Or think beyond the realm of medicine. Consider all those non-medical products, systems, and procedures that make our lives safer than in earlier generations.

For example, with all the remaining problems, it is safer by far to fly in a commercial airliner today than it was only a few years ago. In fact, the accident rate is about one-third what it was a decade ago (1972 *v.* 1983).

Or think about satellite weather forecasting. It often provides early warning of floods, tornadoes, hurricanes. If you are able to move to high ground before a flood hits, if you are able to find shelter before a hurricane strikes, your life is less risky than it would be without such weather forecasting capability.

What about those simple little smoke detectors? They smell out fires early and save hundreds of lives each year.

What about new building construction techniques that have made earthquakes less feared in the U.S. and around the world?

What about new coal-mining techniques that reduce the possibility of cave-ins?

Mine disasters, earthquakes, fires, floods, transportation accidents. As it happens there are statistics on "deaths by catastrophic accident," compiled by the National Center for Health Statistics. There were almost 14,000 Americans killed in the 1950s in "accidents yielding five or more deaths." In the 1970s, in a much larger population, the number was about 10,000.

And what about that "911" emergency telephone number now in use across the country? It's a nice thing to have in place if you're having a heart attack.

What about those new ground fault circuit interrupter outlets that reduce the risk of electrical shock?

Finally, and probably most important, consider the changes in diet that have come about in recent years, as nutritionists and the medical profession have jointly trained their eyes on the relation of food to health, and as food manufacturers and processors have adapted (sometimes resentfully, sometimes under customer pressure) to new knowledge about dietary dangers. The incidence of heart disease has dropped dramatically in the U.S. in recent years. New knowledge about diet and new products using that knowledge have apparently been one major cause of the decrease.*

LIST THREE: HARDLY NOTICED QUALITY-ENHANCERS

The above list dealt with salutory developments concerning health/ danger/risk. But our story here is about the quality of life, which goes beyond that. Surely we need a third list dealing with all those new things, services and conditions—not related directly to health or risk— that have added a bit of quality to some lives.

- Have those contact lenses made a near-sighted girl feel prettier?
- What about new drugs that cure severe acne? Might that help a desperate teenager?

* The natural food movement was dealt a psychic blow in 1983, however, by the sad news from University of California biochemist Bruce Ames that alfalfa sprouts, mushrooms, celery, figs, parsley, herb teas, beans, nuts and vegetable oils, among other staples of natural living, contain a (natural) toxin that is potentially carcinogenic. Is nothing sacred?

- Has *in vitro* fertilization helped a barren couple have a baby?
- What about having your mother's voice on an audio cassette long after she is gone?
- What about those word processors? Not a bad device for a legal secretary who would otherwise have to wholly retype that long contract after every new draft. Not a bad device for Mary Buena and Susan Irvings—who used a word processor for the many, many drafts of this manuscript.
- What about the fun of seeing the instant replay on the football game?

The new product list goes on: cable television brings video reception to remote areas and increases the selection of available programming for all. The video cassette recorder (VCR) lets you save what television you like, to see what you missed, to buy what you want to see again and again.

And what about direct-dial telephoning, which has allowed long distance phone rates to come way down. Does this add to the quality of life? Only if talking to your grown children in Denver does, only if your grandfather wants to feel that he's in on the family action, only if—as the Bell folks say—you want to reach out and touch someone.

The list goes on and on: music in stereo, self-regulating cameras, and the great unsung invention of our time, air conditioning, about which more will be said later in this volume.

LIST FOUR: REAL DANGERS

Lists of publicized health dangers that were not dangerous. Lists of health enhancers. Lists of quality enhancers.

But, of course, one list is missing. There are some much publicized dangers that really are dangerous. These include:

Thalidomide. This German sedative did indeed cause tragic malformations in the fetuses of pregnant women who took it. Thalidomide was never approved for general prescription use in the United States, although a small number of patients took the drug under a testing program.

Kepone. This ant and roach insecticide caused trembling and memory loss and possibly, other ill effects among an estimated sixty production workers in Virginia. All have since been pronounced cured. Kepone has been linked to liver cancer in test animals, but seems to have mostly neurological effects on humans. It is no longer produced. Its former manufacturer, Allied Corporation, was fined $5 million for water pollution by the federal government. Allied also paid the Commonwealth of Virginia and the town where their plant was located $5,250,000 for cleanup, established an $8 million nonprofit endowment fund to cleanse the James River, provided employee compensation totaling about $3 million, and funded research at the Medical College of Virginia to study the effects of Kepone poisoning.

Asbestos. Asbestos is known to be associated with lung and gastro-intestinal disorders, including asbestosis, lung cancer, mesothelioma, and gastrointestinal cancer. Actual rates of incidence and magnitude of asbestos effects are difficult to determine, but it is generally believed that 1–3 percent of the 6–8 million Americans exposed to asbestos could suffer ill-health effects. Lacking a precise notion of how much airborne asbestos fiber is hazardous, federal agencies have banned its use in friable form (that which can be readily turned to dust), recommended that in other applications substitutes be used whenever possible, and set recommended low exposure standards.

The list obviously could be expanded. There is at least some evidence to indicate some harm from items such as: lead, formaldehyde, environmental arsenic, polybrominated biphenyls (PBB), agricultural and industrial dusts, benzene, banned food dyes, carbon tetrachloride, and PCBs.

=

Lots of lists.

Question: if a total compilation were available—which it isn't—would there be more items, and more important items on the healthy side or unhealthy side of these lists?

Because it cannot be proven, I will assert: most of the highly publicized dangers have turned out either to be not dangerous or much less dangerous than originally described. Most of the health-enhancers work fine. Therefore: better health.

But I will assert further, appealing now to logic, that whether the "dangerous" list or the "nondangerous" list is greater, the basic case made in this chapter is bolstered.

Figure it out for yourself. If the health-enhancing list is greater, then our world is safer than you've been led to believe. If the "dangerous" list is larger—then what? Society has almost invariably acted on the danger. Just try to get a prescription for thalidomide. Or some asbestos wallboard for your new playroom. Or some Kepone to knock out those pesky ants.

This leads us to a strange thought—at least strange for this book. Environmentalism and consumerism, for all their alarmism and exaggeration, for all their contribution to distorted priority-setting, have led in many ways to a healthier America. If that sounds like an author seeking to carry water on both shoulders—pro and antienvironmental, pro and anticonsumerist—so be it. That's why we have two shoulders. I will explain.

CHAPTER 8

What We've Done

ENVIRONMENTAL PROGRESS

The theme of this section of the book is that the quality of life in America has been improving in recent years. In the course of this discussion it has been noted, in many ways and many places, that the people who were saying the quality of life is deteriorating or endangered were wrong. Great progress was going on, as we've seen, in longevity, health, safety, as well as in the accumulation of labor-savers, grace notes and amenities. As described so far, this has come about for the most part without the efforts of environmentalists and consumerists. The drug companies, for example, are not generally seen to be part of the consumer movement.

But it would be both unfair and misleading to suggest that the various aspects of the Quality-of-Life movement have not played a role in improving the day to day quality of our lives. They have. The movement may specialize in gloom-and-doom-pronouncements, but despite its millennialist rhetoric, it is also activist—very activist—and is always suggesting remedies (although sometimes expensive ones for problems that hardly exist).

Moreover, one does not have to be an expert in public opinion to understand that environmentalism and consumerism have built up a huge political following in America. It is apparent that such political clout has been used to make things happen—often positive things.

This book sets out to show that many very good things are happening in America. It is entirely consistent, then, to applaud all quality-of-life advances, including those engendered in part by people who erroneously believe that the quality of life is deteriorating.

Here are some examples, not anecdotal as in the previous chapter, but data-oriented:

The consumerists have paid a great deal of attention to accident prevention—everything from unsafe stepladders to shatterproof glass.

The National Center for Health Statistics compiles the number of annual deaths from accidents of all sorts: transportation, falls, drownings, fires, firearms, electrical shock, explosions, hot and corrosive liquids, radiation, poisoning, asphyxiation, choking, medical complications, and all other means. The time line looks like this:

DEATHS FROM ACCIDENTS AND OTHER ADVERSE EFFECTS

Year	*Deaths per 100,000 population*
1910	85
1950	61
1960	52
1970	56
1980	47

Source: National Center for Health Statistics.

That is a 17 percent drop in the last decade, just the years when consumerists were doing their thing. It would appear that consumerist scare-mongering may have helped save lives.

Some of those nondead Americans have been enjoying the rapture of nature, which, it is said, enhances the quality of life. In large measure because of environmentalist pressure, the areas available for nature loving have increased dramatically:

PUBLIC PARK, WILDERNESS AND WILDLIFE AREAS

1949	57 million acres
1959	61 ″ ″
1969	81 ″ ″
1978	98 ″ ″

Source: U.S. Department of Agriculture.

During the tenure of Secretary of the Interior James Watt the rate of acquisition of such lands for future use diminished—amid much consternation. Watt, however, offered justification. There were so many people using the existing parks that conditions had deteriorated in the parks, and (he felt) this was the time to spend money getting them into better shape. I take no position on that strategy, but Watt was right about the number of people using the areas:

USE OF FEDERAL RECREATIONAL AREAS

1970	345 million visits/visitor days
1980	533 ″ ″ ″ ″
1982	567 ″ ″ ″ ″
1983	559 ″ ″ ″ ″

Source: Combination of National Park Service and Forest Service data.

The 1970–83 increase was 64 percent! (One may assume the 1982–83 dip was recession-induced, or Watt-induced, as political preference dictates.)

Nowhere have the environmentalists been more successful than in attacking pollution. One may argue, as I have at the end of chapter 5, that *some* of the monies thus spent may have been unnecessary or mis-directed. One may argue, as I do throughout this volume, that environmentalists have been guilty of great gloomy exaggerations about the effects of pollution, and that such exaggerations cast a shadow across our national soul. But neither of those arguments takes away from the fact that some very big things have happened recently on the environmental front.

For instance, federal expenditures for environmental programs went from $3.7 billion in 1973 to $11.8 billion in 1982.

But federal expenditures are only a small part of the pie. Federal environmental laws typically mandate that other people (mostly businesses) spend money. Data compiled by the Bureau of Economic Analysis show that in the nine years from 1972–81 total national annual expenditures for pollution abatement rose from $18 billion to $60 billion. Most of these dollars are capital expenses—a total of $198 billion in 10 years!

There have been some stunning success stories owing to such expenditures. Consider the case of water pollution.

As environmental awareness increased, as legislation took hold, scores of additional cities began treating their sewage.

POPULATION SERVED BY MUNICIPAL SYSTEMS WHICH TREAT WASTEWATER

1960	40 million
1970	86 million
1980	157 million

Source: Environmental Protection Agency.

Prodded by government, American industry has also acted. In 1982, industry removed 12.6 million metric tons of suspended solid pollutants, 3.4 million tons of biochemical oxygen demand, 4.0 million tons of chemical oxygen demand, 3.7 million tons of oil and grease from their discharges into water bodies.*

The results of these developments are visible throughout the country. Lake Erie, after being considered virtually dead, now supports extensive recreational use. Salmon fishing thrives on Lake Ontario for the first time in decades. The director of the District of Columbia's

* There have also been some substantial reductions in the amounts of "toxic residues in humans" from 1970 to 1979. DDT, dieldrin and BHCs are way down. Levels of PCBs, oxychlordane, and heptachlor expoxide have plateaued.

environmental program says that "we are within a few years of assuring that it's okay to swim in the Potomac."

Air pollution is a more controversial matter, mostly because evidence is scanty about whether dirty air causes much harm. Still, there is an aesthetic argument, and a "better safe than sorry" argument.

And there has been change in the air:

CHANGE IN AIR POLLUTANT LEVELS,
1975–1982

Particulates	down 15%
Sulfur dioxide	down 33%
Carbon monoxide	down 31%
Nitrogen dioxide	unchanged
Ozone	down 18%
Lead	down 64%

Source: Environmental Protection Agency.

Another form of pollution that is way down is radioactivity. As measured in milk, the level of strontium 90 has receded from 17.6 pico curies per liter in 1965 to 2.3 in 1983. The comparable data for cesium 137 is 58 in 1965 and 1.4 in 1983. This is a result of cessation of atmospheric atomic weapons testing.

Perhaps the greatest contributor to decreased air pollution has been the increased mileage of new cars sold in America:

FUEL ECONOMY OF NEW AUTOS, 1970–81

1970	14.9 miles per gallon
1975	15.8 " " "
1980	22.4 " " "
1982	27.4 " " "

Source: U.S. Department of Transportation.

Fewer gallons of gasoline used means less air pollution. The federal regulations that mandated more mileage per gallon came about partly because of the OPEC oil heist and partly because of environmental pressure. So on the surface, it would seem that we ought to applaud environmentalists one more time.

But hold on. The story is not quite so simple. Let us examine some recent heroes and villains in the eternal quest for quality of life.

CHAPTER 9

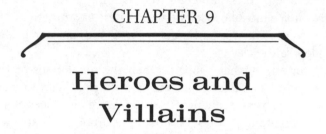

Heroes and Villains

CASE HISTORIES: CARS, ALCOHOL, SMOKING

Our lives are healthier and safer.

This leaves us only with some comments about the strategic questions of why it happened, how best to keep it up, who caused it, and one tiny little additional list that reminds us all, even your oddly optimistic author, that not everything works out for the best. Sometimes things get all screwed up.

First, consider strategy. If we accept as a given the fact that everyone wants to continue to minimize risk and increase quality in our society, how should we go about it?

There seem to be two general approaches. The first says, scrutinize, scrutinize; ring the alarm bell whenever a hint of danger appears. That makes some sense, and we may offer a bouquet to consumerists, environmentalists, and their media megaphones for raising alarms that keep us all on our toes when it comes to safety.

The second strategy says: Dare! Modernism rewards! Let the human intellect roam freely, let there be a cascade of new procedures, new products, and we will all be the better for it. That too makes sense.

The problem, of course, comes about when these two legitimate goals, progress and safety, come into conflict. The usual view, typically seen on your television news program, is that the consumerists hold the moral high ground on this argument: better safe than sorry. The producers, in the conventional view, are profit-hungry and prepared to risk our safety for their bank accounts.

Actually, the democratic orchestration of these two points of view has yielded both progress and safety in recent years. That's what both the lists and the data have shown us here.

But what about the argument at the margin? Which way does one go when a choice must be made between safety and progress? My sense is that an irony is at work: the quest for a safer society has at times yielded a less safe society.

That, after all, is what happens when the regulations of the Food and Drug Administration make the cost of producing a new drug vastly more expensive than necessary. In some instances it then becomes diseconomic to produce another new drug at all, and we never even know what we're missing. In some instances the drug is produced, but it gets to market years later than it might have if somewhat less stringent regulations had been in effect. Question: is the sick person who is denied access to a potentially useful drug living in a less risky world than he or she would be if regulations allowed that drug to get to market? This is not an idle speculation: drugs do get to market in England and Germany more quickly than they do in the U.S. Those are not primitive countries without a sense of regulatory control.

It is of such pieces that the great risk-and-regulation argument is constructed.

═══

So who are the real heroes in the quest for quality and safety? Our last list tells us that it's not a simple question.

Most of the dangers we hear about concern the *involuntary* aspects of our life. If your child goes to a school with a flaking asbestos ceiling, he or she is endangered *in the normal course of events*. If you buy a ladder and it collapses while you're cleaning the gutters, *it's not your fault*. If a nuclear plant releases radiation into the air and you get sick, *someone else did it to you*.

Yet the three biggest product-oriented dangers in our lives are mostly *voluntary*:

- About 42,000 Americans per year are killed in automobile accidents; another 5 million are injured. (1983 data. Many of these deaths and injuries come about due to unsafe driving practices—voluntary behavior—particularly drinking, and failure to use seat belts.)

- Although the data are contested by the tobacco industry (but hardly anyone else), the surgeon general maintains that cigarette smoking (a voluntary act) causes 340,000 deaths per year. It is estimated that a smoker typically cuts five years from his or her life expectancy.

- The National Institute for the Abuse of Alcohol estimates that drinking kills from 60,000 to 95,000 people each year. About 10 million Americans are thought to have a drinking problem.

These basically *voluntary* dangers far and away surpass anything mentioned on any of the previous danger lists and quite possibly surpass *all* the items on *all* the lists.*

Two points: First, it is hard to blame "society" or the "environment" or "modern life" for dangers we assume voluntarily.

Second, as these dangers are the greatest ones we place upon ourselves, it is interesting to assay how well consumerists and environmentalists—risk-reducers by their own definition—have done in combating these biggest risks.

On smoking, they've done well. Consumerists, environmentalists, call them what you will, have played a role in publicizing the dangers of tobacco. Their activity has helped save lives.

On drinking, until very recently, they did very little. The anti-alcohol crusade was pretty well dominated by traditionalist and religious groups, typically from the right of the political spectrum. Booze, they said, is "the devil's plaything."

On cars, the picture is mixed and fascinating, lending further clarification to the who-has-the-moral-high-ground argument.

Consumerists have championed the cause of safe automobiles. Ralph Nader's book *Unsafe at Any Speed* took on the automobile industry. Consumerists pioneered the push for safety belts, safety windshields, collapsible steering columns, mandatory headrests, crash-resistant bumpers, childproof door latches and window openings, and for "passive restraint" legislation, mandating that each new car sold in America would provide for an *automatic* method to protect the driver from injuries due to collision.

---

* The levels are dreadful, but the trends are salutary. Auto deaths per mile driven are down, as are total auto deaths. The rate of people who smoke and/or drink is down, most strikingly among youth.

Well and good. But the consumer/environmental lobby, in its many manifestations, also argued for smaller, lighter American cars. It was said that the "gas guzzler" was a symbol and a symptom of the American gluttony that drained the world's finite resources, while fouling the air. Big cars were bad! And it happened. Cars got smaller.

Of course, the sharp increase in oil prices during the 1970s had a lot to do with the down-sizing of the American automobile. A big, heavy car obviously uses more gasoline per mile than a small one. But the Congress, pushed by consumer/environmental lobbyists, decided to push the market. Legislation was passed. Car sizes came down from an average weight of 3,968 pounds in 1974 to 3,099 in 1981.

Did this save oil? Yes, and that made geopolitical as well as economic sense. But one thing was forgotten: small cars are dangerous.

A 1982 study conducted by the Insurance Institute for Highway Safety shows that death rates in small cars are substantially higher than death rates in large cars. In 1979 small cars were involved in 55 percent of all fatal crashes, although they were only 38 percent of the cars on the road. Studies show that the occupant of a small car is two to eight times more likely to die in a crash than is the occupant of a large car, depending on the type of accident. In the years to come, tens of thousands of Americans will die because they are driving in smaller, lighter cars—cars demanded by the people who had seized the moral high ground of risk abatement!

More Americans by far will die from accidents in small cars than from the combined effects of nuclear radiation, artificial sweeteners, mercury in fish, toxic wastes, air pollution, and Kepone put together. More by far!

Now, it didn't take a genius to know it would come to this. A course in high school physics will tell you that a passenger gets more protection in a big car than in a small car, if that car should, say, go off the road and roll over, or crack into a truck or a lamppost.

Perhaps it was worth it, perhaps it was necessary. The oil crisis was real, or perceived to be real. But where was the balanced approach? Where was the expression of the trade-off: oil for lives? Did consumerists talk about death in a small car? They did not. The consumerists went into the tank on that one.

The felony was later compounded by the other side. In 1981, the National Highway Traffic Safety Administration announced that the regulations mandating passive restraints would be delayed. The Reagan administration really believes in libertarian risk.

Well, the consumerists/environmentalists got their way. They have put people in small, light cars. The Reagan ideologues got their way. No intrusive government is forcing us today to have an air bag or a mandatory harness. Everyone got his way except all those people who will die because ideology overruled real risk assessment on both sides of the political spectrum. What happened was bipartisan, multi-ideological, involuntary manslaughter.

I close the lists with this somber reminder: even we optimists, convinced about progress in the modern world, have retained a capacity for consumerist outrage.

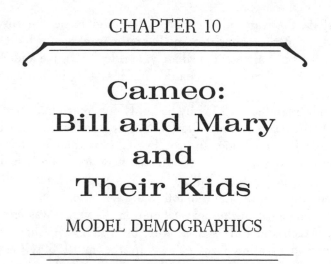

CHAPTER 10

Cameo:
Bill and Mary
and
Their Kids

MODEL DEMOGRAPHICS

If health, broadly seen, is probably the greatest concern of the environmental/consumerist quality-of-life movement, then "resources" is probably next in line.

And central to the resources situation is the change in population growth patterns. We begin here a sequence of five chapters that explore that situation, which, as we shall see, is monumentally important—replete with a dazzling Super Number.

When all is said and done, a nation is made up only of people. People come from families. To see what has happened we begin, in microcosm, with a tale of an American family.

During the 1930s, Bill and Mary got married. Times were tough;

the Depression unemployment rate reached 25 percent. The young couple delayed having children; Mary was able to get a part-time sales clerk job for a while. Soon, despite hard times, they decided to have a family. They had *two* children, the first of whom was a boy named Charles. (The "total fertility rate" in 1933 was 2.17 children per woman, which was then the lowest level in American history.)

Bill had a younger brother, Joe, who came of age at a very different time. He was graduated from high school in the early 1940s, and was drafted into the army. As he left on the bus for basic training, he waved goodbye to Rose, his high school sweetheart. While Joe was away, in combat on the European front, Rose had a full-time job, plus overtime, in a war plant.

In 1945, the war ended, and G.I. Joe and Rosie the Riveter got married. Soon they bought a small house in a newly built suburb. They had a baby almost immediately, and by 1950, Joe and Rose had *three* children, Thomas, Richard, and Harold (1950 total fertility rate: 3.09).

It can be said that Joe's family had only one more child than Bill's— three children versus two children. Surely, that is the way Bill and Mary, and Joe and Rosie, and the five cousins thought about it. But demographers did not think about it that way. Joe's family had 50 percent more children than Bill's. That is a striking fact. Still, it was expected; high fertility tends to follow a war.

What happened in the next generation, however, was entirely unexpected. Consider Bill's son Charlie, born in 1933. Almost immediately after graduating from college in the mid-1950s, Charlie got married, found a good job, moved to a new suburban home, had a baby, and another one, and then another one, and one more! (The total fertility rate in 1957 was 3.8 children per woman.)

The phrase "Baby Boom" was born. *Four* children per family in a modern industrial society was almost unheard of. A fertility rate of four children per woman means that the total population of a modern nation will likely double in only 35 years. Thus, with America's population in 1950 at about 150 million, if the birth rate had stayed at about four children per woman, then U.S. population would have been about 300 million by 1985, and about 1.2 billion by 2055, which was not so far away. That was a scary calculation.

The high U.S. fertility rates of the 1950s (coupled with the even sharper growth rates in other parts of the world) soon yielded a frightening phrase that said it all: "the population explosion."

It was a good phrase to describe what it meant to describe: uncontrollability. Something was going on that seemed to have a dynamic of its own. Population growth was described as "malignant." It was from such numbers, phrases, and images that the too-many-people strand of the quality-of-life argument grew.

But a funny thing happened on the way to the Explosion. The 1960s arrived. Now it was G.I. Joe's three children who had reached adulthood.

Tom married in the mid-1960s and had *three* children (the total fertility rate in 1964 was 3.2 children). That was one fewer than Cousin Charlie's four kids, but by any recent American standard, three children per family was plenty. The Baby Boom was still on.

The continued high rates kept the explosionists worried. At about this time, population growth was blamed for crime, war, famine, poverty, pollution, and racism. A famous, or infamous, newspaper advertisement financed by population activists sought to raise funds with a full-page picture of a man being strangled, and the caption asked, "Have You Been Mugged Today?" The remedy for mugging, it was explained in the ads, was fewer babies. A Stanford University biologist named Paul Ehrlich turned his attention from the reproductive habits of fruit flies to the reproductive habits of human beings and claimed that, just as fruit flies will multiply uncontrollably, so will human beings. His book, which ultimately sold millions of copies, was called *The Population Bomb*.

Strangely, while the rhetoric about malignant population growth continued, the birth rate kept falling. We can see it through the life story of G.I. Joe's next son, Richard, called Dick.

He was born in 1949. He graduated from high school in 1967. He was drafted and served for a year in Vietnam. He entered college in 1969. His girlfriend said she wanted to have a career. She took birth control pills. In college, their professors told them the world was overpopulated, that the environment was being raped, that we were running out of resources. America went into one recession, then another. Inflation rates climbed. Jobs were not so easy to come by (remember, Dick was a Baby Boom baby and was competing for jobs with huge cohorts of fellow Boomers).

Dick graduated from college in 1973 at age twenty-four. He didn't get married until age twenty-six; his wife was twenty-five. She went to work. They didn't have their first child until she was twenty-seven. They thought about not having a second child, but decided to go ahead. Dick's wife was thirty when her second child was born. She went back to work when the child was age two, and announced firmly that she didn't want to go into labor, or leave the labor force, ever again.

A *two*-child family. In the early 1970s the U.S. total fertility rate reached 2.0, lower than during the depths of the Great Depression.

And now we have Harry. That's G.I. Joe's youngest son, born in 1950. He got married in 1976, by which time the U.S. fertility rate had dropped well *below* two children, 1.738 children per woman, to be exact. He and his wife didn't have their first baby until 1980. It remains to be seen whether they will have a second child. What demographers call "expectation" data reveal that the rate of women who say they want just *one* child, or none, is at an all-time high.

The demographic saga of the two brothers, Just Plain Bill and G.I. Joe, of Just Plain's son Charlie, and of Joe's three sons, Tom, Dick, and Harry, is the story of an incredible half century in American life. Consider the rollercoaster fertility patterns that the family embodies:

1930s	Bill	2 children
1940s	Joe	3 children
1950s	Charlie	4 children
1960s	Tom	3 children
1970s	Dick	2 children
1980s	Harry	1 child (so far, with a fraction more to come.)

One archetypical family. But families make nations. When these family numbers are played out on a national canvas, we get a Super Number that fully satisfies our criteria: it is contrary to general impression; it should change the way we look at our world. Moreover, it devastates a key pillar of the quality-of-life argument.

CHAPTER 11

The Birth Dearth

FERTILITY

Here is the Super Number that reflects all those intimate family decisions of the last half century:

U.S. TOTAL FERTILITY RATE AND
INTRINSIC RATE OF NATURAL INCREASE
1945–1979

Year	Total Fertility Rate*	Intrinsic Rate of Natural Increase Per Year†
1930–34	2.1 children per woman	0%
1935–39	2.0 " " "	−.2%
1940–44	2.5 " " "	+.5%
1945–49	3.0 " " "	+1.2%
1950–54	3.3 " " "	+1.7%
1955–59	3.7 " " "	+2.1%
1960–64	3.4 " " "	+1.9%
1965–69	2.6 " " "	+.8%
1970–74	2.1 " " "	.0%
1975–79	1.8 " " "	−.7%

---

* Expressed as lifetime births of children per woman.
† The annual rate at which a population will grow or shrink if given fertility and mortality rates remain in effect over a long period of time.

Source: U.S. National Center for Health Statistics.

The data are clear. If there was a population explosion in America, it is long over. In the twenty years from the late 1950s to the late 1970s, the total fertility rate has been cut in half!

Charlie had four kids; Tom had three; Dick had two; statistically speaking, Harry may not even have two. The Baby Boom has become a Birth Dearth. This development, even when subject to some caveats to be mentioned in a few moments, will change the nature of our nation forever.

Is this good news? Is this big news?

Well, surely in terms of the quality-of-life argument as originally raised, it is very good, very big news indeed.

After all, if it was bad news that our population was exploding, big news that extra population polluted our environment and gobbled up our resources, then surely it must be big good news when such a threat is removed or diminished.

Accordingly, we might have expected to hear the environmental community announce that fact with vigor. Nor would it be unfair to expect that such developments would have been explained in our newspapers and on our television sets. It was not.

How big is this story that the media missed? How good is the good news?

It is, in my judgment, the biggest story of our era, in America and around the world. It is mostly good news for the short and inter-mediate term. But after that, we shall see. I hate to be a messenger of bad news, but unless some trends turn around, it may prove to be a major long-term problem in America and disaster in certain other industrialized countries.

In a modern society a total fertility rate (TFR) of 2.1 children per woman roughly equals "replacement," that is, the rate required to keep a population at a stable level over an extended period of time. The key line in the Super Number table is the one in the late 1970s, when the TFR dips below 2.1 children per woman and when, accordingly, the "pluses" change to "minuses."

The Super Number shows that unless something changes, over time America will be *losing* population. There is an important quali-fication to that statement—regarding immigration—which will be out-lined in chapter 14. Still, it is a very big story for a nation whose history has been predicated on vigorous population growth.

At the root of the magnitude of the change is the nature of the total fertility rate. If the TFR is *above* the replacement level of 2.1 children per woman, a population will (other factors being stable) not only *grow* over time, but grow *geometrically*. Similarly, when the rate is *below* replacement, the population not only *declines* but declines *geometrically*.

Reverend Thomas Malthus noted long ago that population changes are exponential in nature, and he pointed out the incredible potency of that fact. Of course, he concentrated on the up-side of such changes.

Consider a husband and wife who have four children. All the children survive to adulthood, and each of them produces four children. All of the ensuing children do the same. By only the fifth generation, at that rate, the original couple will have 1,024 descendants! Such calculations put meat on the bones of the concept of a "population explosion."

But we have now entered the world of "Suhtlam"—that's Malthus spelled backward. What Malthus did not stress is that if population decreases, it also decreases geometrically. Consider 1,024 husbands and wives. If each couple has only one child, not four, after five generations there will be only thirty-two new potential parents left!

Geometric population change can proceed up or down.

This is not a trivial matter. Look at West Germany. A study by demographer Carl Haub of the Population Reference Bureau shows how quickly negative geometry can work. The West Germans now have a total fertility rate of 1.4 children per woman. If that low rate continues, West Germany's population will shrink, slowly at first, from today's 62 million to about 57 million by the year 2000 (that decline has already started). By the middle of the next century, if rates stay as low as they now are, the German population would decline to about 40 million people and then sink with a rush to about 9 million by the end of the twenty-first century! To get even more preposterous about it, at current fertility rates, the number of Germans would go down to about a quarter of a million people by the year 2500. That is roughly the population of Anaheim, California.

Or consider Latvia. Demographers look at its very low fertility rates, coupled with Russian in-migration, and speculate that Latvia is "going out of business."

It's a very big story.

Now the American situation is not the German situation, and even the German situation is not set in concrete. People can change their fertility patterns. But America, like Germany, and like most of the developed world, has what demographers call a "negative replacement rate." Absent a catastrophe, like the Black Death, *such a condition has never before existed for many nations over a period of time.*

Is this good?

From the environmentalist view, it should be deliriously good news. In fact, we all should share a portion of their unstated, unpublicized joy. It is important to know that population rates can go down as well as up, that we are not locked into an ever upward demographic spiral, that our great-great-grandchildren will not live in an environmentalist nightmare, "packed like sardines in a can," as they used to say.

But it would be less than honest to leave it at that. There are some distressing aspects to this new development. These will be mentioned here briefly, and will crop up again later in this volume.

There is a global situation to consider, of which America is very much a part. "Suhtlam" is at work in the developed, industrial nations, where the total fertility rate averages 1.9 children per woman. But it is not (yet) operative in the less developed countries (LDCs), nor will it be for a long, long, time. Although their rates are coming down in a heartening manner (see chapter 15), the LDCs still have a very high fertility rate—of 4.1 children per woman, which is well more than twice that of the developed world.

Try this projection on for size: Today, people in the LDCs out-number the industrial nations by about three to one. By the end of the next century, according to the UN's "medium" series of projections (which assume a continuing decline in LDC fertility), that ratio will rise to about eight to one!

Should these projections come true, the economic, racial, cultural, and geopolitical implications are staggering. In brief: the nations that are rich, technological, mostly European, mostly white, mostly liberal and democratic—will shrink demographically.

What will the world be like when massive labor shortages hit the industrial world? Will democratic values survive in a world where the current democratic nations become a tiny minority? Might there be turbulence about changing racial balances?

Of course projections aren't necessarily predictions. All this could change if birthrates go up again in the Western world. Sooner or later that will happen, because it must. The only trouble is that reversing a Malthusian spiral—up or down—takes a long, long time. Until it happens, and while it happens, the nature of the planet changes, perhaps permanently, perhaps in ways that we or our descendants will live to regret.

There is also the American economic situation to think about. As will be shown later, the near to intermediate term is very positive. All those Baby Boom babies are becoming productive young adults. They are having few children. That temporarily lessens the burdens of support on both parents and state.

But what happens when, in a few years, it is the Birth Dearth babies who start becoming young adults? What happens over time, if our population should really start declining? The environmentalists say our problem is too many people. It may be just the opposite.

Will there be labor shortages in the U.S.? Will there be too few young and middle-aged people around to pay for their parents' pensions via Social Security? Will there be millions of vacant houses? Will there be a Depression?

Some glancing blows will be struck at these questions as we go along. We are not locked in; we can shape our future, if we are wise. There are several factors to consider.

First: it seems likely that we will retain a low birthrate. It's not likely to change. What has happened is not just a short-term wiggle in the line. Although hardly anyone bothered to notice it at the time, America went to negative replacement in 1972, and we have stayed there for a dozen years already.

Reasons? Improved contraceptive technology has contributed to lower birth rates. Further improvements are expected in the years to come. The trend of women active in the labor force shows no signs of reversing. Women at work are likely to end up having fewer children than nonworking counterparts. Housing costs and tuition costs have soared, each related to the perceived costs of rearing a child. Prospective parents shudder over estimates that it will cost $200,000 to raise a child to adulthood.* The number of legal abortions is at a very high level. Young women these days say they want to have small families in the future. The age of marriage has gone up; the number of months between marriage and first child has gone up. An old demographic axiom states: "fertility delayed is fertility denied."

Second: none of the possible negative effects of the Birth Dearth is upon us *yet*. Because of what demographers call the "echo effect" of the earlier Baby Boom, our population will be growing for a while before it may start leveling off and then declining.

Third: It is only our natural fertility rates that yield negative population growth rates. It takes a while to play out the scenario, but if there were no immigration, our population would level off within a couple of decades, remain stable for a while, and then start tumbling rapidly, at a rate of a loss of about eight million Americans per decade by the middle of the next century!

But immigration at varying levels can make those rates less negative, or stable, or positive. It can provide a population policy that even an environmentalist could applaud.

* Lawrence Olson, *Costs of Children* (Boston: Lexington Books, 1983).

Immigration will provide us with a new Super Number.

Immigration is wonderful except for one small fact. Americans don't like it and don't want it. We shall see that after some brief interludes with Jews, Mormons, and Koreans.

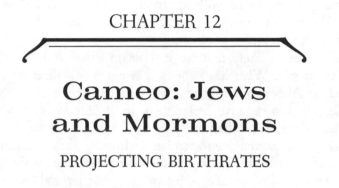

CHAPTER 12

Cameo: Jews and Mormons

PROJECTING BIRTHRATES

Macro and micro. We talk about "total fertility rates," we talk of "geometric rates of decline," but what happens in America is only the totality of what happens to Just Plain Bill, to G.I. Joe and Rosie the Riveter, to Tom, Dick, and Harry, and to the rest of the individuals in the nation.

What happens in America may also be seen as the totality of what happens to various *groups* within America. The changing tide of fertility we have witnessed in recent years, the ferocious undertow of negative replacement rates, has not, and will not, affect all groups equally. To gain a fuller sense of the power of these demographic developments, it is useful to look at two groups in America that are quite similar in many ways, but very different demographically.

Consider Jews and Mormons.

Today there are six million Jews and three million Mormons in America. Twice as many Jews as Mormons. But Jews in America face a demographic nightmare. Mormons are in demographic clover. If that is not entirely apparent today, just wait a hundred years.

Judaism is an exercise in survival. Jews have been working at it for almost four thousand years. They do only moderately well at it. It is estimated that two thousand years ago Jews comprised 2.2 percent of the world's total population. Today they comprise 0.3 percent. But they are still around.

America today has by far the largest number of the world's Jews. But American fertility, as we have seen in the Super Number, has gone way down. And Jews in America in recent decades have always had much lower fertility rates than the rest of the population.

It was no particular problem when America had high fertility and Jews somewhat lower fertility. Both "all Americans" and "Jews" were "growing" populations, although at different rates. But today, total American fertility is at levels below replacement. And every estimate of Jewish fertility remains well below national rates—below 1.5 children per woman according to some studies—the lowest rate for any group or subgroup in the United States. It is so low that if played out over the next century, it will reduce the Jewish population in America from almost six million to about "three to four" million Jews, according to one estimate, or to "about one million" according to another. If one arbitrarily chooses a mid-range figure—three million—that means the Jewish population will still be *halved* (!) by the end of the next century.

Curious: many young Jews have been attracted to the ideas of the "Zero Population Growth" movement. The world is overcrowded, say the ZPGers, we're running out of resources, there's too much pollution, there's a population explosion, there are too many people, and all of that erodes the quality of life. Therefore, the ZPGers say, people ought to have fewer children.

Jews too? Jews whose population was diminished by a third in the holocaust? Jews in America, whose fertility rate will lead to a population headed for geometric decline?

Of course, it is true that in the world as a whole, population is climbing. But as Milton Himmelfarb points out, when a fat person comes to a doctor, he is counseled to reduce. When an emaciated, malnourished person comes to the same doctor, he is advised to gain weight.

There is more bad news for Jews, and some good news, too. The bad news is that the American Jewish demographic situation is roughly replicated in all the nations of the Diaspora with major Jewish populations: the Soviet Union, France, England, Argentina, and others. Simply put, unless fertility rates change markedly, as the years go on there will be fewer and fewer Jews in all these countries.

The good news is that in Israel fertility is moderately high, and in an interesting way: the Israeli Sephardic Jews (today, mostly of Asian and African ancestry) have reduced their fertility from very high levels.

At the same time, Ashkenazi Jews in Israel (of European ancestry) have higher fertility rates than they used to and higher rates than Jews in Europe or America. Fertility rates for Sephardic and Ashkenazi Jews have converged toward a total fertility rate of about 2.7 children per Jewish mother in Israel. That rate yields a growing population. That rate is also one of the highest national fertility rates in the "developed" world.

So: it can be done. "Modern" people, well educated, in urban circumstances—as in Israel—can have growing populations, if they have the will to do it.

No one understands this better than Mormons in America. Although high birthrates are normally associated around the world with poverty and lack of education, that is clearly not the case with Mormons in America, who are generally well-to-do and well educated. The Mormon religion encourages high fertility and Mormons have been acting on their beliefs. The Mormons have the highest birthrate of any religious group in America, about four children per woman. As noted earlier, at that rate a population doubles itself roughly every thirty-five years.

If the Mormon population really were to double every thirty-five years, then there would be six million Mormons in the United States by roughly the year 2020, about twelve million Mormons by the year 2055 and about 24 million Mormons in the year 2090, near the end of the next century.

Today there are twice as many Jews as Mormons: six million to three million. By the end of the next century, if one projects current rates, there will be eight times as many Mormons as Jews. Twenty-four million Mormons. Three million Jews.

That probably won't happen. Straight-line population projections don't go on forever. Some demographers at Brigham Young University believe the Mormon birthrate will start diminishing in the relatively near future.

Nor is it likely that Jews will continue to behave like lemmings. Sooner or later Jews will begin having babies again. They will, perforce, remember that if the biblical injunction to "be fruitful, multiply" is not heeded, then geometric demographic halving leads, simply, to no more Jews.

There is, however, a great momentum effect in demographics. It takes a long time to turn a trend around. Thus, the babies born in a boom will reproduce when they reach adulthood. But all the babies *not born* in a period of low fertility are simply not around later on to rebuild a population. That means long-lasting change. America will end up with lots of Mormons, few Jews.

Well, it is said, all that doesn't matter. Some Jews, as well as the ZPG movement, say "raw numbers" don't really count in the modern world. "Quality is what really counts," they maintain.

Don't believe that. Raw numbers, for one example, will count a great deal if Jews expect to remain an important political force in the U.S. Democracy, at its soul, is a numbers game. There's more voting clout for Jews with six million than with three million. There's more voting clout for Mormons at twenty-four million than at three million.

Raw numbers count in little things, too—like whether it will be possible to support a synagogue in Charleston, West Virginia. And as we shall see in chapter 14 (about immigration), raw numbers count in some other very big ways in this world.

CHAPTER 13

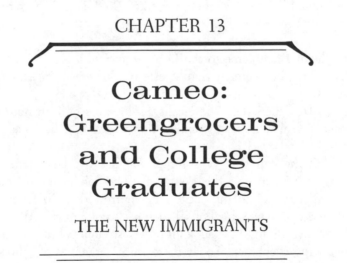

Cameo: Greengrocers and College Graduates

THE NEW IMMIGRANTS

As a key part of the population puzzle—a key part of the quality-of-life puzzle—we shall be talking next about immigration, with another Super Number coming up.

Before beginning, it might be wise to remember once again that behind all the numbers are individual people.

There is a small grocery in New York City, in the West Seventies, owned and operated by a family of Korean-Americans. The store opens early in the morning, but even earlier its owner is at the Hunts Point Market in the Bronx, where he bargains for fresh vegetables. The store closes late at night.

The little store operates seven days a week, and it is taken for granted in the neighborhood that it will be open. One day, however, shoppers strolled by and saw that the door was shut tight. And there was a sign: "Closed Sunday Afternoon. Son Graduating from Princeton."

The immigration statistics suggest that the owners of the store are likely to be recent immigrants to the U.S. Our accurate immigration data begin with the year 1820. From then to 1950—that's 130 years— less than ten thousand Koreans came to the U.S.

But in the decade of the 1950s alone, there were 6,000 legal Korean immigrants.

In the Sixties, there were 35,000!

And from 1971 to 1980 there were 267,000! That high rate is continuing into the 1980s.

Mr. Jhoon Rhee came to the U.S. from Seoul, Korea, on November 21, 1957. He entered Southwestern University in San Marcos, Texas.

"In my freshman year," he recalls, "it took me half an hour to read one page of English." By the end of that year, Mr. Rhee made almost straight A's.

In 1962, he came to Washington, D.C., to take a summer job teaching martial arts at the Pentagon. The job never materialized. Mr. Rhee had $47 in his pocket. He borrowed $400 from Korean friends and opened a school of self defense in downtown Washington.

Almost overnight, he had a hundred students. His business has been growing ever since. Today there are 21 branches of "Jhoon Rhee Institute of Tae Kwon Do." Mr. Rhee also owns a factory that makes safety equipment for use in sports. His business grossed several million dollars in 1983.

Jhoon Rhee is probably the most prominent man in Washington's Korean community. Because he came to the U.S. earlier than most Korean immigrants, Mr. Rhee has a certain perspective about the flow of things.

"Twenty-five years ago," he recalls, "I had a student who owned a grocery store and was a member of a small grocery store association in the Washington area. There were 125 members, of whom 124 were Jewish people. But most of their children became doctors and lawyers. They don't have to run grocery stores anymore. I know the Jewish people are very ambitious. But when it comes to work, the Koreans are one of the most ambitious people in the world."

Jews have indeed left the small grocer trade in Washington. The two predominantly Jewish small grocers associations in Washington disbanded in the late 1960s. In the early 1970s, the Korean Businessmen's Association of Greater Washington was formed, composed mostly of small retailers. There are about 1,000 members today, and about 85 percent of the District's neighborhood grocery stores are Korean-owned.

Not only the closed-for-Princeton-graduation signs, but the Census Bureau now provides evidence that the Koreans followed the Jews, not just into grocery stores, but into universities as well. The bureau gathered detailed data for Koreans for the first time in the 1980 census. It showed Korean-Americans with more education and higher incomes than the average American!*

Mr. Rhee likes this development. In 1983 he started a foundation to help send still more youngsters to college.

Rhee says, "It was my dream to come here. Can you see how much I fell in love with America? This will be my great tribute to America—to try to build the patriotism of American young people."

---

* Median school years completed: for Korean-Americans, 13.0 years, for total population, 12.5 years. Median family income: for Korean-Americans $20,459, for total population, $19,917.

CHAPTER 14

The First
Universal Nation

IMMIGRATION

Population can only grow in two ways: by "natural increase" (births exceeding deaths) or by immigration. It's a short list, but that's all there is.

As we have seen, the rate of natural increase turned negative in America in the early 1970s, has stayed negative, and shows every sign of remaining negative. This creates a very new situation: over the long term, immigration will be the key to continued American population growth—or loss. Turned one way the key yields population growth. Turned the other way, we will have population decline in the not-too-distant future.

Our next set of Super Numbers deals with immigration. It is different in a critical respect from the first two Super Numbers. Few, if any, will argue that longer life is anything but good. A lower birthrate is more controversial, surely at a negative replacement level, but the basic idea of a decline from the peak rates of the Baby Boom would be saluted by most Americans.

Things are different with our immigration Super Numbers. They are Super Numbers all right, but many Americans would deny that they're any damn good at all.

There are three of them, and they will be presented in reverse order of the displeasure they engender among the citizenry.

After the passage of the restrictive immigration law of 1921, the Per Centum Limit Act, it was generally thought that the robust and monumental tale of American immigration was mostly over, relegated to a footnote of American history. After all, during the peak decade of 1901–1910, a total of 8,795,000 legal immigrants arrived in the U.S. Nothing like that could ever happen again—could it?

Well, not quite. But look what did happen: immigration went way down, and it was thought it would stay down. It hasn't, and that is the first of the immigration Super Numbers:

LEGAL IMMIGRATION (BY DECADES)

1931–1940	528,000
1941–1950	1,035,000
1951–1960	2,515,000
1961–1970	3,222,000
1971–1980	4,493,000

Source: Immigration and Naturalization Service.

Immigration today is way up, in part because of liberal provisions of the 1965 Immigration and Nationality Act Amendments. Still, the numbers are nowhere near the proportional levels of the earlier boom decades.

But look beneath the surface to the second Super Number:

ESTIMATED ILLEGAL IMMIGRATION (BY DECADES)

1931–1940	.5–1.5 million
1941–1950	.5–1.5 million
1951–1960	.5–1.5 million
1961–1970	1–3 million
1971–1980	3–5 million

Well, then, when *illegal* immigration is added to *legal* immigration, there was about as much immigration to the U.S. in the Seventies as there was at any other time in American history!

Now that is true only as an absolute number, not as a ratio to existing population. The last big wave of immigrants came to an America that was only about one-third as populous as America today. But no matter how it is calculated, the estimated 7.5–9.5 million immigrants in the last decade are a lot of folks. In fact, during this time America took in more immigrants than were taken in by all the other countries of the world put together. Talk about Super Numbers! This is the third one:

PERCENT OF U.S. IMMIGRATION FROM EUROPE (LEGAL)

1820–1960	82%
1960–1970	34% (!)
1970–1980	18% (!!)

Source: Immigration and Naturalization Service.

That is just the legal immigration. But a disproportionate share of the illegals are non-Europeans (mostly Mexican). In all likelihood, the European share of our total recent immigration is only about 10 percent.

Tale of the three Super Numbers: *Suddenly, there are many more immigrants, and they aren't coming from where most of the rest of us came from.*

Is this good or bad for America, salutory or detrimental to our quality of life?

I argue: good for America, salutory for the quality of life.

I make this case with full understanding that Americans these days are turned off by the new wave of immigration. A 1982 Roper poll showed that 66 percent of Americans wanted legal immigration cut back, and only 4 percent wanted an increase. The feeling against illegals is even greater: Roper showed 91 percent of the public agreeing that the U.S. should make an all-out effort to halt the flow of illegal immigration.

What do Americans have against immigration?

There is, first, an economic fear. It is said that immigrants take away American jobs, lower the wage scale, gobble up welfare payments.

There is, second, a racial and ethnic bias that is not often talked about, but hard to ignore:

Question: Here is a list of some different groups. (Card shown respondent.) Thinking both of what they have contributed to this country and have gotten from this country, for each one tell me whether you think, on balance, they've been a good thing or a bad thing for this country?

	Good thing for country	Bad Thing
English	66%	6%
Irish	62	7
Jews	59	9
Germans	57	11
Italians	56	10
Poles	53	12
Japanese	47	18
Blacks	46	16
Chinese	44	19
Mexicans	25	34
Koreans	24	30
Vietnamese	20	38
Puerto Ricans	17	43
Haitians	10	39
Cubans	9	59

Source: The Roper Organization, 1982.

White Europeans way on top, although Japanese, blacks and Chinese get substantially favorable ratings. Other Orientals and all Latins are seen negatively.

And there is, third, the more intellectual case that we started out with many pages ago: it is said that further population growth (of which immigration is the key determinant these days) is harmful because it erodes the quality of life.

Let us deal with each of these negative arguments in turn: economics, race and ethnicity, and quality of life. In the course of rebuttal, with a few interesting digressions, a positive case will be advanced to make the point (with some caveats) that the recent immigration increase, as reflected in the Super Numbers, has been, and will be, beneficial to us.

The economic case is the easiest to deal with.

Regarding "taking jobs away" and "wage depression": immigration may indeed be painful on a personal level for a small number of people for a relatively short period of time. Blacks in the Miami area complain that Cuban immigrants take away the lower-level jobs that blacks used to get. Gulf Coast fishermen in Texas complain that Vietnamese refugees fish in their waters, depleting the potential catch. (There has been violence, including murder, connected with this conflict.) Yet a major 1984 study by the Urban Institute concluded that "growth in the Mexican and other Hispanic population . . . has not caused unemployment rates among other minorities to rise."

Indeed, when one takes a macroeconomic perspective over a long term, immigration is not much of a problem, and in fact probably helps the economy and the U.S. generally.

It is easy to be cavalier about someone else's job. If an immigrant, particularly an illegal one, came to America and quickly wrote a book about how bad news has been big news—and if such a book were an immediate best seller and eliminated the market for this volume— this author might not be so blasé in reiterating what is, however, a truth: over a period of time the number of jobs in a nation like the United States is not finite. Jobs that are "taken away" are also "re-created."

Thus: an immigrant gets a job. A million immigrants get jobs. They then can buy food, which requires more farmers and more people to make the bottles to put ketchup in. They buy clothing, which requires more workers to make more synthetic fiber manufactured by DuPont, which requires still more workers to make more cash registers that go beep-beep-beep in discount stores. Taxes are paid on the monies they earned, which governments then disburse to some additional people who collect the additional garbage. Sooner or later, there may even be a new market for one more book, which I may write.

The point is simple: an American worker displaced by an immigrant has—sooner or later—as good a chance as before of getting and holding a job. Of course, "sooner or later" is easy for cosmic thinkers to visualize, but difficult to bear for those who have lost a job. Fortunately, this experience in America is typically of a relatively short-term nature. Even at the depth of the great recession of 1982, the median length of unemployment was ten weeks (see chapter 24).

In any event, even if every adult legal immigrant who arrived here and was looking for a job took one from an American worker, we would still be dealing with a short-term effect on about 200,000 American workers per year. If illegals are counted, that number might triple, but all that is still only one-half of one percent of the U.S. labor force.

In reality, the effect is even less. Many poor immigrants accept the jobs that, as the popular phrase has it, "no American would take"— agricultural pickers, busboys and dishwashers, live-in domestics.

Who gains from immigrants taking such unpopular jobs?

The poor immigrant has gained. People act in their own self-interest. A Mexican peasant wades across the Rio Grande on a moon-less night. He ends up doing agricultural "stoop labor." We see the tortuous work he performs and his typically squalid living conditions. But what we do not see is the stark rural poverty he left behind, his underfed children, his tired wife. A portion of his earnings, meager, perhaps, by our standards, is sent home and provides food, shoes, per-haps a corrugated tin roof for the family's shanty. It may properly be said of that family that the quality of their life has improved.

Poor immigrants also improve the quality of our lives. Domestic help makes it easier for an American woman to pursue a creative career. The busboy in the restaurant may work for less pay than an American would accept for the same job, but the cost of the meal is reduced somewhat, allowing more Americans to enjoy a meal out at a restaurant.

In short, low wages also make prices lower. Now, by itself, that is a Neanderthal notion. Depressed wages also depress purchasing power, which can lead to unpleasant phenomena such as depres-sions. But when the work involved is "work that Americans won't take," that argument goes out the window. These particular depressed prices haven't depressed any American's wages. There is no loser.

There is another aspect to the "wage depression" argument: *illegal* immigrants are easily coerced to work for less than the minimum wage or under unsafe conditions because their illegality can be used as a club against them. The remedy to this situation, however, is not to eliminate immigrants, but to eliminate illegality. More on this later.

Then there is the further economic claim that immigrants live off the American social welfare system, pushing up costs of government for taxpayers. A careful examination of this proposition, prepared for the Congress by Professor Julian Simon, looks at the balance sheet, comparing the costs (like welfare) that immigrants draw from our society with the monies they put into the system (such as deducted income taxes). His conclusion to an admittedly complicated question:

immigrants put more in than they take out, right from the first year of their arrival.

If you think about it, there is a powerful demographic logic behind such calculations. Most immigrants are adults. The median age of immigrants coming to the United States is 26.3 years. That means they drained *other* societies for the costs of their education and other youth-oriented services, and many of them are indeed highly educated, as will be noted later. They come here as instant taxpayers.

This is important, not just an academic exercise. The American Baby Boom babies will begin to reach retirement age in 2010. That's tomorrow in demographic terms. The number of pensioners accordingly will soar. At the same time, the "producer" class will be shrinking, because of low birthrates in the 1970s and 1980s. That mix is likely to be social dynamite—lots more claimants, fewer providers.

But wait: Is there any way to keep this pension pyramid game going with less tension and better benefits?

Ah . . . if we could only figure out a way to bring in producers who will claim proportionately fewer immediate services and pensions than people already here.

In philosophy there is a term, "the unmoved mover." We need the social welfare equivalent, "the non-tax-eating taxpayer." And—surprise!—they are available in almost any quantity we choose to accept. Such individuals are called immigrants.

===

There is another argument concerning immigration that is much less publicized but potentially much more serious. It is said, correctly, that if immigration continues in its present pattern, it will change the racial, ethnic, and cultural mix of the United States.

That fact is not often stressed on the editorial pages of major newspapers. Publicly talking about race is regarded as racism; assessing the impact of changing ethnic and cultural balances is often regarded as discriminatory.

But whatever may be lacking in public discourse is more than made up for by blunt and passionate talk among plain folks. Immigration has become a big issue. A bumper sticker in Miami reads, "Will the Last American to Leave South Florida Please Take the Flag with You." Tough stuff, bumper-stickering a thought that seems to be growing in America, one that could be expressed something like this: "Our country is being taken away from us!"

Let's look at the race/ethnic situation through four prisms: projections, poetry, peril, and power.

PROJECTIONS

The prestigious Population Reference Bureau has delineated with some precision the magnitude of the potential problem.*

Here is one very simple way to see our racial/ethnic mix as it roughly stands today:

U.S. POPULATION, 1980

Asian (and "other")	2%
Hispanic	7
Black	12
White (non-Hispanic)	79

One can look at those numbers and say, easily, that America is predominantly a "white non-Hispanic" nation.

The PRB study projects what the composition of the United States would be like in the future under different scenarios of immigration. If one looks a hundred years ahead, maintaining the current *legal* level of immigration (about half a million per year), and correcting for projected fertility trends, the picture would look like this:

U.S. POPULATION, 2080, WITH 500,000 PER YEAR IMMIGRATION AT CURRENT RACIAL/ETHNIC MIX

Asian (and "other")	10%
Hispanic	16
Black	16
White (non-Hispanic)	59

(does not equal 100% due to rounding)

* "The Future Racial Composition of the United States" by Leon F. Bouvier and Cary B. Davis, August 1982, Demographic Information Service Center of Population Reference Bureau, Washington, D.C.

Quite a change. The Hispanic share of the population more than doubles. The Asian share quintuples! Still, with somewhat less vigor than earlier, one could say that a hundred years from now, "America would still be mostly a white non-Hispanic nation." After all, 59 percent is more than half.

However, *if* immigration were to proceed not on the basis of the *legal* rate, but rather what the combined legal and *illegal* rate was estimated to be in recent years—and that is a big if—then the picture changes rather starkly. Using a level of *one million* immigrants per year, the PRB projections *show that the "White (non-Hispanics)" become a minority in a hundred years—just 48 percent of the total U.S. population.*

Now, of course, as the PRB points out emphatically, these are projections, not predictions. That is, the numbers merely show what would happen if certain conditions were mechanistically factored into an equation. All or any of these factors could, and almost surely will, change at least somewhat over time.

Still, projection or prediction, the numbers make you think. What they point to is this: *if* present immigration and fertility trends should continue, the ethnic and racial composition of America will change in a big way. It would be a big change, after all, when a heretofore majority group becomes less than a majority.

POETRY

The questions about racial/ethnic change form themselves: will the projections come true? Will what is likely to happen be good for us or bad?

Answers: plenty will happen racially and ethnically, but not as much as the numbers might suggest. What does happen will generally be good for us.

Consider, first, demographic poetry and American poetry.

The unique American proclamation to the world has been political and demographic: we are a free people, and we come from everywhere.

That was not quite so in the past. It took a while for all of us to be free: black emancipation and women's suffrage were not always with us. And we didn't come from everywhere.

By 1960 or so, a perceptive eye looking at the American fabric would have seen that more than 150 million of us were European immigrants and descendants of European immigrants. Another roughly twenty million were blacks, mostly descendants of African slaves. There were, in addition, a few million Americans of Mexican origin in the Southwest, and small pools of Chinese and Japanese, mostly in the West. There were others as well, but viewed broadly they were mere demographic drops in the ethnic ocean. We had, sure enough, many people from many places, but we were not "from everywhere."

And then, suddenly, change. A nation isn't from "everywhere" if it's not from the second largest nation in the world, India. A nation isn't from "everywhere" if it isn't from Iran, the largest country in Asia Minor. A nation isn't from "everywhere" if it isn't from South America. But now it has happend—an explosion of non-European immigrants. Note that one column represents a fourteen-decade span, the other only two decades:

IMMIGRANTS FROM SELECTED NATIONS

Country of Origin	1820–1960	1961–1980
India	14,000	191,000
Iran	3,000	56,000
Egypt	4,000	40,000
Lebanon	5,000	57,000
Jordan	5,000	39,000
Colombia	18,000	149,000
Ecuador	10,000	87,000
Brazil	14,000	47,000
Argentina	20,000	80,000
Peru	8,000	48,000
Korea	15,000	302,000
Vietnam	3,000	177,000
Philippines	20,000	453,000
Cuba	81,000	473,000
Haiti	5,000	91,000
Dominican Republic	11,000	241,000
Guatemala	28,000	42,000

Source: Immigration and Naturalization Service.

Something is happening: *we are becoming the first universal nation in history.*

Holy smoke! The half-true, evolving, poetic proclamation of America is becoming truer and truer: *we are a free people; we do come from everywhere.*

There are some specific potential problems and some specific potential blessings associated with this development, which will be discussed in a moment. But if you believe, as the author does, that the American drama is being played out toward a purpose, then the non-Europeanization of America is heartening news of an almost transcendental quality.

America was the first modern democratic nation. Two centuries ago, four million Englishmen living on a sliver of the East Coast of North America began governing themselves democratically. Today, more than a billion earthlings so govern themselves, in almost every corner of the globe. It is an idea that has become so powerful that even the bloodiest thugs and tyrants are forced to self-certify themselves as "the People's Democratic Republic of Whatever."

The American democracy grew from 4 million to 230 million, in large measure because of immigration, and that immigration taught the world much about democracy. It had been thought that democracy could only work for advanced Anglo-Saxons. But we learned that Poles can live very well under a democratic system in America. More recently we've seen that Cubans participate fully in the democratic process in America. This tells Poles in Poland that there's no internal reason it couldn't happen in Poland. It tells Cubans it could happen in Cuba. As America universalizes, that message goes out to Filipinos, Salvadorans, Arabs, Chinese, Iranians, Cambodians, and to others all over. There is every reason to expect that the American turbulence, begun two hundred years ago among Europeans, will roil the whole world—to its benefit and ours.

PERIL

Surely the process of becoming such a universal nation is fraught with danger. Our last moment of major ethnic change in America—the arrival of Eastern and Southern European non-Protestants to what had been primarily a Western European Protestant land—caused disruption. It would be naïve to rule out the possibility of turmoil this time around.

How dangerous is it?

It is said, for example, that California will become an American version of Canada's Quebec, with Spanish, not French, at issue. That is doubtful. It is not that the Hispanic population of the nation's largest state will not grow. It almost certainly will. Even under the proposed Simpson-Mazzoli immigration law, which is intended to curtail illegal immigration, projections show the Hispanic population in California will grow from 19 percent the state's population in 1980 to 33 percent in 2080.

So what will keep the language wars from California? One simple answer is Asians. For California is the magnet not only for Latin immigrants, but for Asian immigrants as well. By the year 2080, its Asian population will go from 7 to 23 percent. Few of these Asians—Japanese, Chinese, Filipino, Indian, Vietnamese, Korean—speak Spanish. Turmoil? Yes. Quebec? No.

Will it work out? Immigration is never an easy process. Strangers scare natives. But it is an easier process in a scattered nation of immigrants like ours. God shed his grace on America by arranging it so that Italians, Irish, Swedes, Ukrainians, blacks, Germans, and Chinese don't each live in their separate places. It's hard to arrange a civil insurrection when Italian-Americans are scattered from Long Island to San Francisco, when Chinese are dispersed in almost every city across the face of the continent.

This, of course, is quite different from the history of most nations. They absorbed other nations, not immigrants. The Soviets have a monumental ethnic problem, getting worse by the minute, because their nationality groups are typically concentrated in a homeland and would, for the most part, much prefer not to be Soviets. Many Ukrainians in the Soviet Union feel like citizens of a captive nation; the Baltic states of Estonia, Latvia, and Lithuania are indeed captive nations (by U.S. government definition).

To lesser degrees, some Basques in Spain feel that way, so do some Bretons in France, some Irish in Northern Ireland, some Scots in Britain, not to mention the Kurds, the Palestinians, the Moluccans, and scores, if not hundreds, of African tribes.

But American ethnic diversity has not engendered those feelings. If anything, recent arrivals to America may be even more patriotic than natives.

Remember that immigrants, unlike natives, choose to come here. Cross-national surveys (Gallup) show that, all around the world, people are more likely to seek to emigrate to America than to any other place. This is quite remarkable, considering the lurid nature of reporting about America in recent decades. America is portrayed as a society rife with criminality, steeped in drugs, tormented with racial violence, poisoned by pollution, led now by a trigger-happy cowboy President, pursuing a jingoistic foreign policy, and so on. And yet, immigrants come, pursuing the old dream.

They come from Western Europe, although not in the same huge numbers as before. Many are the small entrepreneurs who say America is the best country in the world to do business in, because the government isn't on your back.

Of some of the bigger businessmen—immigrants or absentee investors—it is said that they are "buying up America."

Not so. People who have tried to play economic imperialism in this country have a strange history. They invest and then typically will dispatch a son here to make sure that those barbarian Americans don't do something silly with their money. The son marries an American girl. Grandchildren ensue. Soon the grandchildren wear cut-off jeans and go to football games. Ultimately, the original investor dies leaving much of his fortune to his son. Result: we get both the financial and human capital. It is one of the bonuses America gets from being a place in which people want both to invest and live.

We have been getting great bonuses, economic and otherwise, for a long time from European immigrants and their descendants, from Andrew Carnegie to Albert Einstein. The question today is whether such bonuses are likely to continue to accrue as the Third World immigrants arrive on our shores.

I think so. There is already a new staple television heartwarmer: A Vietnamese girl graduates as her high school valedictorian, though she spoke no English until she was ten years old. (Television does do some good-news stories.) Truer to form, there has been major national attention devoted to Cuban crime in the Miami area, but little attention given to the Cuban business community in Miami. It is vigorous and entrepreneurial, and has helped transform a commercially sluggish area into a booming gateway city linking the U.S. to Latin America. The earlier Mexican immigrations have already yielded stable, religious, family-oriented communities in a broad swath across the southwestern U.S.

And consider the phrase "brain drain." We hear it typically as something negative: "The brain drain is robbing the country of (blank) of its most educated people."

Well, there is at least some truth to that. The U.S. 1965 immigration law gave high priority to immigrants with skills and training: doctors, scientists, engineers, and others. In the last decade, almost 60,000 "professional, technical, and administrative" workers *per year* have emigrated to the U.S. Those professionals, be they Chinese mathematicians, Iranian plastic surgeons, or Indian engineers, trained on someone else's nickel. That is indeed a brain drain for China, Iran, or India. But it is our "brain gain."

There will be problems mixed with the blessings of the new American universalism. Take foreign policy. Every American immigrant group at some point lays claim to a piece of American foreign policy. It is taken for granted that we have "a special relationship" with Great Britain. It is not an accident that when a Falklands Island crisis arises, we end up helping our mother state and mother culture rather than a hemispheric neighbor.

More recent immigrations have yielded other pressures, and other actions. One of many reasons that the U.S. takes a tough stance against the Soviet Union is because of the Soviet conquest of Eastern Europe, subjugating lands from which tens of millions of Americans trace their ancestry.

We are in a continual crisis about arms sales with our strategic NATO ally Turkey because so many Americans come from Greece. Diplomats say there is an "American interest" to such sales. But there is something else always in the equation: "the interest of Americans of Greek descent," who are actively prepared to descend upon their elected representatives if they feel Greece is being harmed by arms sales to the hated Turks.

Most prominently, American foreign policy toward Israel has come under close scrutiny, to find where "the American interest" lies as compared to "the interests of Americans who are Jewish." So too, be it noted, American policy toward black Africa has changed substantially in recent years, as blacks in America have become more politically active.

All this, of course, often bothers the professionals at the State Department. Typically, "the American interest" and "the interests of Americans" coincide or can be made to coincide. When they don't, there is torn fur at Foggy Bottom and on Capitol Hill. The diplomats sulk a little bit about this, but they are for the most part good professionals who have learned to live in the complex world of making foreign policy for a polyglot nation.

They ain't seen nothing yet.

Already we see a foreign policy impact stemming from our new Latin

American immigration. What issue will galvanize the Filipinos in the U.S.? Or Indians? Or Arabs?

We can guess, but only guess. Who would have thought that Jews, Greeks, and Poles—in steerage less than a century ago—would one day play an important part in the formation of American foreign policy in key areas?

Looking toward the future from this hawk's point of view, it surely seems as if Cubans, Vietnamese, Cambodians, Russians, Taiwanese, and many of the Central Americans make a pretty good chorus of firsthand anticommunists. I salute them. But it will be complex and tumultuous. There has never been a universal superpower before. We don't yet know all the ground rules. One thing you can bet on, however: it's not a recipe for isolationism.

POWER

Enough of this sentimental balderdash. Let us think about our current immigration patterns in terms of power. Demography influences power; immigration influences demography.

That idea used to be commonplace. People concerned with American demographics used to think about it in terms of manifest destiny and global power. These days people concerned with American demographics think about it in terms of environmentalism and solar power. That is the wrong way to look at it.

Consider power and demographics over a long sweep of history. It has been said that Zero Population Growth would be a terrific idea for America. Well, what would have happened if America had gone to ZPG a hundred years ago—roughly two children per woman, no immigration?

That would have meant that by 1940 America would have had a stable population of 50 million, instead of the 130 million people who were actually here. Under such conditions what would have become of America's "arsenal of democracy" during World War II? Could we possibly have stood up against the population of 200 million in the Axis nations? Which one of Hitler's protégés would now rule Europe and perhaps the world?

It is said that in a world of nuclear missiles, power is no longer related to population. But think: there may be some big, populous countries that have little power these days, but there are still no small, sparsely populated countries that have much power.

In the industrial world at least, large numbers of people create markets, technology, an industrial base, and economies of scale, all of which yield power and influence. And by the way, a lot of people can pay a lot of taxes, which can buy a lot of military strength.

In the new world of Malthus-upside-down—of negative replacement rates—American population would soon start declining, if it were not for a continued healthy rate of immigration. The shrinkage we are talking about is not trivial. At current U.S. fertility levels, with no immigration, the U.S. population would top out at about 245 million by the year 2000 and drop to about 150 million by the year 2150.

On the other hand, with moderate immigration, the roughly 500,000 we could expect under the proposed Simpson-Mazzoli bill, we could grow moderately to 268 million people a hundred years from now, at which point we will have stabilized our population growth. That's 79 percent more people than in the earlier case.

There is another fact about power: it is not simply linked to absolute demographics. It is relative. That's how power works. Boxer A may be in perfect shape, with a lightning jab and dazzling footwork. But if Boxer B is better, stronger, tougher, Boxer A is a loser.

So we must think about American population in relation to others. We have already noted (chapter 11) that in the world of Suhtlam, the Third World will vastly increase its numbers relative to the industrial world.

What will that mean? We do not know. Perhaps in the fullness of time, the Third World nations will adopt democratic values.

On the other hand, the preeminent working model of a Third World political value system is the General Assembly of the United Nations. That organization, together with its ancillary agencies, is a forum that discourages a free press, pushes for international collectivist economies, applauds genocidal gunmen, punches out democrats for being imperialists, and salutes imperialists for being progressives.

We shall see about the Third World.

A more immediate potential power/demographic problem is apparent relative to the Soviet Union. Suppose that America, the nations of Western Europe, and Japan all maintain their current negative birthrates, and that America takes in no immigrants. Suppose too that the Soviet Union retains its strange, but positive, birthrate (negative replacement in European Russia, very positive in the central Asian, mostly Moslem, areas). Under such circumstances the Soviet Union would be twice as populous as America by the year 2050, which is tomorrow as these things go.

The Soviet GNP would then roughly equal the GNP of the U.S.

Western Europeans would be fewer and fewer, Germany at half its current population within seventy-five years. Could the Soviets then tighten the screws, economically and militarily, forcing the Western Europeans to go neutral, leaving the U.S. alone?

Will things like that really happen?

Truth be told, we don't any of us know. It is doubtful that the world has ever faced such an unusual demographic situation. This is the first time in history that a large part of the world is at negative replacement rates, and the most powerful part at that. We don't know what that will yield, vis-à-vis the Third World or the Soviet Union.

And so, better safe than sorry. We should continue to grow in the U.S., and that means we should continue to accept immigrants, and in fairly good-sized numbers. If we don't, unless we moderately raise our own birthrate,* our adversaries and/or our potential adversaries will become ever more populous than we, and relatively more powerful and influential than they are now. This could have the effect of eroding our ability to defend or promote our values in a world where values are the big issue.

And now, back to our original question, asked a long time ago in this book: is continued population growth dangerous for the U.S. from an environmental point of view?

Over the years, the quality-of-life argument generally maintained that population growth in the U.S. was unfortunate for two basic reasons. First, on its merits: it was said that more people meant more pollution, a drain on resources, and "overcrowding."

Second, it was stressed that the dangers of continued population growth were doubled and redoubled by its uncontrollability and Malthusian momentum. Indeed, the trump card in the antinatalist argument always went like this: "Well, it may be (as some say) that population growth is not dangerous, but just suppose it is. Maybe, just maybe, it leads to ecological disaster, resource depletion, pollution. We know it's very hard to turn off demographic momentum. It's almost uncontrollable. So *why risk it?*"

All that has changed. In the era of Suhtlam, the onus of "why risk it?" now falls upon the Quality of Lifers. There is a risk that if America and the Western nations lose population we will suffer for it. There is a down-side risk.

On the other hand, there is little up-side risk when, as now, the

---

* Which is a very good idea if someone can figure out how to make it happen.

difference between loss of population and gain of population in the U.S. is immigration, rather than fertility. Any additional immigration, after all, is *controllable*. There is less demographic momentum to immigration than to natural growth; there are no necessary new bumper crops of mothers who will have children, and whose children will have children. If you want to curtail further immigration, all you have to do is turn it off.

Provided the immigration is legal.

In recent years much of it hasn't been, and that is a problem that has properly engendered much bitterness. In an earlier time, when noncitizens, in whatever numbers they chose, decided to reside in a country that did not welcome them, a simple word described the process: "invasion." And, of course, invasion is uncontrollable.

So if immigration is to be our control valve on national population growth, if it is to continue to be beneficial, if it is to be at least somewhat palatable to the rest of the nation, it must be legal.

Legislation before the Congress as this is written—the Simpson-Mazzoli bill—addresses the problem in a way both tough and considerate. By use of employer sanctions, the act, if passed in reasonable form, will likely keep illegalism at a low level. But it also allows in a moderate stream of new legal immigrants—not quite enough in this author's view, but not bad either.

Legal immigration has been good for us in the past and should be good for us in the future. It helps our economy, it universalizes our national essence, it makes us more powerful and influential in a tumultuous world that often wishes us ill. It promotes democratic values everywhere, it is controllable and hence is not the kind of population growth that might ultimately harm the quality of life.

Besides, below-replacement fertility rates, without immigration, will lead to snowballing decline. If we don't have immigration we will run out of Americans entirely; we will not have Zero Population Growth, we will have Zero Population.* That will harm the quality of life.

* In about the year 5050, if our native fertility rate remains at 1.8 children per woman and our immigration rate is nil.

CHAPTER 15

Running Out?

RESOURCES

he pattern of diminishing population growth rates should provide a large hint that no further Super Number will be necessary to rebut the idea that an ongoing, escalating depletion of resources is harming, or will harm, our quality of life.

But it is not just population: every element of the running-out-of-resources argument has been turned on its head in the last few years. This should have yielded well-publicized rapture in the environmental/quality-of-life community. Have you heard it?

Recall, in shorthand, just what that case was: there were more people than ever before, there would be still more people coming down the pike, they were already consuming more than ever before, they would be consuming still more—and the combination of more people consuming more meant a rapid depletion of nonrenewable resources. Oil was the publicized case in point.

Occasionally, a weisenheimer would point out that mankind was *always* running out of nonrenewable resources. That was true by definition. Nonrenewable resources are nonrenewable. So what was the big deal?

The rebuttal argument offered by the quality-of-life proponents was that the big deal was the *rate* of resource depletion. That rate, they said, had to be slowed down so that we could develop new and appropriate technologies, preferably "soft" and renewable ones like solar power, before resources would get very scarce, catastrophically scarce. We needed a window of time, it was said.

That argument should now end. It has been overtaken by events: population growth is down, consumption is down, resource use is down. If we needed a window, we have it.

Consider population. In the opening of his book, *The Twenty-*

Ninth Day, Lester R. Brown provided the appropriate metaphor for population alarmism as related to resource sufficiency:

> A lily pond, so the French riddle goes, contains a single leaf. Each day the number of leaves doubles—two leaves the second day, four the third, eight the fourth, and so on. Question: If the pond is completely full on the thirtieth day, when is it half full?
> Answer: On the twenty-ninth day.
> The global lily pond in which four billion of us live may already be half full.

In that part of the world where most resources are consumed, that is, the industrialized world, Mr. Brown's riddle is turning upon itself. We have negative replacement rates. In the advanced countries these days, the right answer to the question "What will the pond look like on the thirtieth day?" is "One-quarter full." Will it be one-eighth full on the thirty-first day? That, after all, is what negative replacement rates mean.

And in the developing world, population growth rates are also falling more sharply than anyone expected (although, of course, the rates are still positive). In the 156 nations categorized by the United Nations as "less developed," population growth has been reduced from an average of 2.4 percent per year during the 1965–70 period to 2.0 percent in 1980–85. That's a drop of almost a fifth. During the same time births per 1,000 population in the less developed countries dropped from 39 to 31, which, as these things work out, means that almost a third of the road to population stability was traversed in about fifteen years.

So if a population growth slow-down was necessary to avert a running-out-of-resources situation, it is already happening.

The other piece of the equation concerned consumption. Scarcity-mongers often took economic growth rates from the most recent full decade for which data were available, the 1960s, and did a few straight-line projections. The world economy in the 1960s grew at an annual rate of 5.1 percent. Now, a 5.1 percent annual growth rate doubles in only fourteen years, and insofar as economic activity equates with consumption, one could say that consumption was doubling every fourteen years.

Well, the rate of worldwide economic growth in the 1970s was substantially less than in the 1960s; it was 3.7 percent, not 5.1 percent. At 3.7 percent the doubling time is not fourteen years but twenty years. Moreover, in the first three years of the 1980s the rate of global economic growth was down to 1.4 percent. At that rate consumption doubles in forty-eight years.

Now this diminishment of economic activity is no damn good. It will be argued in a subsequent section that this slowdown, although much overstated, harms the quality of life. But that it has happened, be it called stagflation or hyperrecession, there is little doubt.

So in the terms established by those who made the running-out-of-resources argument, time has been bought, the period of resource availability has been extended. If economic growth drains resources, then the search for renewable resources and soft technologies can go on for longer than anyone had reason to expect a few years ago.

It is said by some that the recent economic downturn itself actually happened *because* of resource shortage. Oil is a dwindling resource. The OPEC nations, it was said, were able to start hijacking the world in 1973 because oil was in short supply. That's why oil prices went from $3.00 per barrel to $36.00. So goes the tale.

But that is not what happened. There was a hijack all right, but there never was a natural shortage of oil. At the height of OPEC's power, in 1978, those thirteen OPEC nations were pumping only 76 percent of capacity! This means that among the OPEC nations alone there were an extra 8.6 million barrels per day available virtually at the throw of a switch. Some shortage!

OPEC, of course, is a cartel. The shortage was mostly rooted in an act of men, not an act of nature. The cartel took advantage of the fact that oil demand was going up in the world, while at the same time oil in many places was becoming more expensive to get at, as the "easy" sources were depleting.

The cartel was relatively effective for a few years, until the consumer nations started to develop additional supplies and substitutes, as well as conservation measures: nuclear power in France, natural gas in America (at depths of up to 31,000 feet!), synthetic oil from coal in South Africa, gasohol in Brazil, hydroelectric power in Canada, more insulation in homes, smaller cars in Detroit, and more oil and more oil and still more oil almost everywhere—Mexico, Great Britain, Russia, China, India, the Santa Barbara channel, Norway, Canada, in frozen tundras, and Arctic oceans just to begin a very long list. In addition, recession further reduced demand for oil.

If you ever believed that we were running out of oil, running out of resources, all this should be very good news. But you should never have believed it. It is not true and never was. That is the really good news.

Example: in 1973, when OPEC struck, it was said there were 664 billion barrels of proven crude oil reserves left in the earth. Ten years later, after the world had consumed 216 billion barrels, there were more oil reserves in the earth than before: 670 billion barrels.

How could there possibly be more oil in the ground after pumping oil for ten years? Aren't we running out?

Well, no, not in the way it was told. The supreme resource that human beings need to live good lives is not buried beneath the crust of the earth. The only real resource is the human intellect. When unfettered, the human intellect can create all the other resources, sometimes out of thin air!

Once useless rocks became known as "coal," once useless fluids became known as "oil," other once useless rocks became known as "uranium," and all soon became known as "fuel." Using human intellect, that fuel can be used to make an electric toothbrush go jiggle-jiggle when you press a button. It is human intellect that makes ammonia fertilizer out of thin air. And it is human intellect that uses that fertilizer to vastly increase the number of ears of corn that can be produced on an acre of land.

Intellect—unfettered—does more. When tin ore is near the surface and easy to get at, human beings develop machines to scrape it out. When that easy ore is exhausted in a given mine—and worldwide—human beings develop more sophisticated machines to dig out ore from deeper in the earth. This may cost more than mining the easy ore. Human beings, associated in economic enterprises called "markets," will then see to it that the price of tin goes up to cover the cost of mining the more expensive tin.

I observed visual proof of this in the course of making a television documentary on the subject of resources. I visited the open pit tin mines in Malaysia. The record is writ clear on the side of the pits. There is a dark ring around the top of the pit showing where tin was dug many decades ago. When the "easy" tin near the surface was gone, tin from this part of the mine was no longer economic. The pit shut down. Years later, tin prices went up, as "easy" tin was used up worldwide, and the Malaysian miners dug deeper, leaving another mark on the side of the pit. There are dozens of such colored striations visible—a history of supply and demand in the resource business, demonstrating how new resources are "created" by demand.

The more expensive, harder-to-get-at tin is counted as part of "tin reserves" only when it becomes economic to mine and market it. In this way "reserves," or resources, often grow, even as they are "used up."*

If, and as, tin gets really expensive, human beings then begin looking for ways to cut back on the use of tin and also start looking for substitutes that may be cheaper. Would aluminum work in this instance? Would plastic work in that instance?

Moreover, although tin and other resources get more expensive in absolute terms, they have gotten cheaper relatively, as Julian Simon points out in his book, *The Ultimate Resource*. This happens because real income has gone up substantially, and it takes fewer hours of labor to buy a pound of tin than it used to.†

That this process has been going on for quite some time in the tin-mining industry is of only passing interest to most people. It is of greater interest that the same thing is happening in the energy industry, as noted earlier. But the process is the same: more expensive resources yielding more elaborate recovery methods, yielding new and often greater reserves, yielding substitutability, yielding conservation. We can thank OPEC for all this. The cartel stimulated human intellect to oppose the cartel.

And what about OPEC itself? Do you remember Shelley's poem, "Ozymandias"? It is about fleeting fame. The poet approaches a lonely and broken statue in the desert. On it he reads the faded epitaph of a man who somewhere, at some time, had it all. The inscription at the foot of the eroded statue announces grandly: "My name is Ozymandias, King of Kings." And now, Shelley muses, those faded rocks in the desert are all we know about poor old Ozymandias.

Well, now, remember OPEC. Just a few short years ago the cartel was saying, in effect, "My name is OPEC, king of kings, possessor of a mighty 'oil weapon.'" A lot of experts around the world backed them up. Oil went up to $36 a barrel and it was said there was nothing we

---

* From 1950 to 1970, for example, the "known reserves" of iron went up by 1,321 percent, phosphates up by 4,430 percent, potash up by 2,360 percent, chromite up by 675 percent, bauxite up by 279 percent, copper up by 179 percent, lead up by 115 percent, and so on through a long list put together in the *Special Report, Critical Imported Materials* prepared by the Council on International Economic Policy, Executive Office of the President. Only tungsten reserves went down, by 30 percent.

† Not just tin, either. The cost of producing copper (relative to the cost of labor) went down by 87 percent from 1900 to 1970. Iron down 84 percent, zinc down 87 percent, aluminum down 97 percent. (Source: W. D. Nordhaus, in *American Economic Review*, 1974.)

could do except figure out ways to recycle billions of petrodollars while watching the cost of a barrel of oil rise to $50—to $100. All this because we were "running out."

Today we hear different music. There is an oil glut, demand is down, supply is up, the OPEC nations are undercutting each other's prices. Many of them are now borrowing money, and the price of oil is down below $29 a barrel (which is only about $18 a barrel in 1978 dollars) and some say it is headed down even farther. The only weapon OPEC possesses may turn out to be a boomerang. OPEC, like old King Ozymandias, may end up being remembered as a fading rock in the desert.

Overestimated: that we were running out of energy sources, that we lived in an era of limits. We're not, we don't.

Underestimated: that people and societies respond to adversity, and that powerful and technological societies respond powerfully and technologically.

Human intellect is the resource that creates all others, including energy. It is a renewable, unlimited, resource.

Have you heard much about that on the television news?

CHAPTER 16

A New Frontier

GEOGRAPHICAL MOBILITY

Recall the five intertwined strands of the quality-of-life argument.

Two of them, pollution and consumerism, dealt directly and indirectly with health. We have seen that we are living longer, healthier lives; many new products make our lives less risky, others make life pleasanter.

Two of the strands, population and resources, dealt at root with the strains we are putting on the physical world. We have seen that the population boom is receding around the world and is already in reverse in the industrial world. We are not running out of vital resources.

But the quality-of-life argument was never simply an argument about health and demographics. It also dealt with more ethereal ideas. As presented in chapter 2, the final strand of the environmental argument came from a cluster of ideas that included "gluttony," "anti-natural materialism," and "ugliness." The more general rubric would probably be labeled "aesthetics."

Now there is not a whole lot that a book that concentrates on facts and numbers can say about taste and aesthetics, although the next chapter does attempt to strike a glancing blow.

There is, however, one good-sized piece of the argument that is data-related. It will be explored here because it sheds light on the quality argument, but also because it reveals some heartening trends about some more general aspects of the American condition in the 1980s.

There is an ancient argument, heard whenever rural populations move to urban areas, that life is becoming increasingly unnatural. In America, some sorry conditions and unique forms have fueled that view. There was the much-noticed cloud of smog that hung heavy over many urban areas. There was the deterioration of the inner city, often rife with crime—the asphalt jungle. There were those identical gaudy tentacles of commercial highway development that encircled our cities and seemed to extend ever outward, gobbling up the pristine countryside.

Moreover, there has been a sense that urban life—even when and if healthy and elegant—has moved us toward artificiality: a world of apartment buildings, beltways, suburban patios and pools, cute little restaurants that serve ceviche, health spas in office buildings, and ultimately, accountants with bifocals riding a mechanical bronco at a singles' bar bellowing, "Thank God, I'm a Country Boy." Not necessarily bad things, mind you, but regarded as evidence that America has been moving far from the idea that the human species is closely related to the planet it inhabits.

Some of this complaining can properly be judged as romantic nonsense. Environmental aesthetes sip a drink on their apartment balcony and ask, "Where are the good old days when man communed with nature behind a plow and worked by the sweat of his brow?" In fact, those good old days were typically plagued by pellagra, loneliness, ill health, and provinciality.

But at least one part of that where-are-the-good-old-days picture is accurate. Relentlessly, since the establishment of the nation, Americans have been moving from rural areas to urban ones. Our first census of 1790 showed that fully 95 percent of our population lived outside of city areas. By 1970, that percentage had shrunk to 26 percent.

Is it any wonder, considering the vast magnitude of the shift, that there was some sense that we were being cut loose from our natural moorings, with a subsequent bruise on the quality of our lives?

Now there is some evidence of a big change, worthy of Super Numerical status. We have, in fact, two Super Numbers that show it.

The first looks like this:

METROPOLITAN AND NON-METROPOLITAN GROWTH RATES OF THE UNITED STATES:
1950–1980

Period	Metropolitan (Bigger cities and suburbs)	Non-Metropolitan (Rural, small towns)	Metropolitan vs. Non-metropolitan Growth Differential
1950–1960	26%	4%	22%
1960–1970	17%	4%	13%
1970–1980	10%	16%	−6% (!)

Source: U.S. Bureau of the Census.

Reversal. After almost two centuries when the population tilted almost steadily toward the cities, something different apparently happened in the 1970s. It was as if the rink master's whistle blew and people started skating the other way. We seemed no longer to be moving "away from nature."*

* The statistics, it should be pointed out, can get complicated. They reflect only *relative* changes in growth. Thus, despite the changes, America is still a mostly urban nation and will remain that way. Both "suburbs" and "cities" fall under the rubric "metropolitan," and suburbs are still growing, though cities are declining in absolute size. All this is further confused by the statistical procedure

What happened to turn around one of the most sacred and ancient trends in American life?

Migration is an activity that typically involves some balance of both a "push" and a "pull." A person moves because he or she is less than totally satisfied with his or her circumstances—that's the "push." Concurrently, there is typically a "pull"—a new circumstance elsewhere that offers certain attractions.

Consider the "pull" first. To begin, Americans have a residual love of open spaces, of less populated areas. "You can take the boy out of the country," the old saying goes, "but you can't take the country out of the boy."

That sentiment is backed up by public-opinion poll data. For many years most Americans—57 percent according to a recent Gallup Poll—have said that, if given a choice, they would like to live in the country or a small village or town. But the most recent census data show that only 39 percent actually do live in such circumstances. Unrequited love.

The trouble was that, until recently, the romantic "pull" to the country was often short-circuited by reality. As recently as 1950, fully half of the dwellings in rural areas lacked plumbing. Entertainment was nil (*The Last Picture Show*). Education beyond the high school level could typically only be found far away. Over all this was a blanket of provinciality. The boondocks were always in the boondocks ("How're You Going to Keep Them down on the Farm, after They've Seen Paree?"). And most important, as farm mechanization grew more and more sophisticated, the number of jobs in rural areas went down. In 1930, there were 10.5 million Americans employed on farms; by 1982 the number was down to 3.5 million, while our total population had almost doubled.

All that, and more, has changed. By 1980, the percentage of rural homes without indoor plumbing was not the 50 percent of 1950, but 3 percent! Cable television typically came to rural areas before urban areas; rather suddenly there was more video variety in the boondocks than in the cities. The number of college campuses in America, in-

---

of redefining "rural" land as "urban" land once the population in a given jurisdiction begins to grow. Finally, there are some very recent 1980–82 data—administrative estimates, not decennial census numbers as above—that indicate that the rate of non-metropolitan growth has diminished somewhat, quite possibly temporarily due to recessional factors, and probably down to levels just below the metropolitan rate. Still—and this is the critical point—the non-metropolitan growth rates remain substantially higher—somewhat more than double—than the rates of the 1950s and 1960s.

cluding junior colleges, grew from 1,851 to 3,231 during the years
from 1950 to 1980 and many of the new ones were away from big
cities. A fully honored degree from the University of Minnesota
could be earned in Minneapolis, as always, but also in Morris,
Crookston, Duluth, or Waseca.

There's more. Dirt roads are now paved roads. Cross-country high-
ways that used to wend their way through the middle of little towns
so that traffic had to halt at every stoplight have been replaced by
federal interstates. These broad swaths of concrete sterility avoid the
humanity of towns and villages, but they do get a car from here to
there quickly. This vastly expands the plausible range in which to
seek a job or recruit a labor force.

The number of airports in the U.S. has climbed from about 7,000
back in 1960 to about 15,500 in 1981, with many of the new ones far
from big cities. An executive in the boondocks may now be able to get
to a big city faster than another executive can get from one big city to
another.

And jobs came. The search for energy brought jobs to out-of-the-
way places in Kentucky, Colorado, and South Dakota. The search for
leisure-time activities and vacation hideaways brought jobs to rural
Vermont, New Hampshire, Arkansas, Arizona, and of course Florida.
The search for an able labor force and calm surroundings brought
manufacturing plants to rural locales all across the country. And,
finally, almost as a matter of definition, it is apparent that the decline in farm employment must bottom out sooner or later, and it
seems to be happening now. After all, one farmer, even with the
latest air-conditioned John Deere tractor, will not be able to feed all
of America, let alone our huge export markets.

The hegira to the country feeds upon itself. The availability of
better services, recreational activities, and transportation attracts still
more jobs. As the population base grows it can attract a still higher
level of services: an internist, a movie theater, a restaurant. All this further heightens the "pull" of rural living.

Thus, after many years of medical desolation in remote areas, the
number of physicians in rural and small town areas is now going up.*
The presence of medical service makes rural areas more attractive to

* A 1982 study by researchers from the Rand Corporation and the Tufts University School of Medicine found that a major shift of physicians to previously
  unserved rural areas had occurred during the 1970s. By 1979, they reported,
  few towns with 2,500 or more people lacked ready access to a doctor. Further,
  there was a large surge of specialists such as radiologists, ophthalmologists, anes-
  thesiologists, orthopedists, psychiatrists to small towns.

the elderly. And indeed, the data show a sizable number of pensioners among the migrants to nonmetropolitan areas. Pension payments stretch further in country areas, where the cost of living and tax rates have gone up less rapidly than in the city.

Most of all, however, the "pull" to open spaces has attracted young people with children and it is this movement of young people that just about guarantees that the back-to-the-country movement is no flash in the pan. Young families, after all, are the ones that will have children. The fertility rate in nonmetropolitan areas exceeds that of metropolitan areas. This provides natural momentum for continued high relative population growth in the hinterland. The two leading students of the field, demographers Calvin Beale of the U.S. Department of Agriculture and Larry Long of the Census Bureau, agree that the levels of rural growth will remain substantially higher than in earlier decades.

But all this does not come about solely because of a "pull." When parents say, as polls show they do, that they have moved because the country "is a better place to raise kids," that is not just "pulling."

It is also part "push." It reflects a view of urban life as well as of rural life. The escalating price of urban dwellings during the 1970s could easily have pushed a family. If you can't afford a house in a city or suburb, your next step might well be to look for a cheaper and probably bigger home in a rural area.

The pushes go well beyond economic factors. A parent who fears that his child will be exposed to drugs or sexual promiscuity in the suburbs and decides to move to the country is being "pushed" as well as "pulled." Fear of crime is also a push. Perception of racial turbulence is a push. So are perceptions of pollution, noise, and overbuilding.

The perception among some that materialism is rampant, that urbanites have been cut off from their roots, that the stress and pace of urban life leads to a "rat race"—these, too, are "pushes" that have come to be grouped together under the general rubric of the quality of life. I may not believe that some of these complaints are entirely valid, but it is clear that whatever I think, many people have objections to urban life.

All these factors lead to a view in the demographic community that it is not simply "jobs" or "economics" that are bringing people to outlying areas. Demographer Beale, the pioneer student of urban to rural trends, reports that "every survey of newcomers to nonmetropolitan areas has shown that the great majority give social reasons for their move rather than economic reasons."

Now, is all this push-pull move to the countryside a good thing for America?

On a surface level, the pluses seem to outweigh the minuses. Fewer migrants to cities, particularly poor people, relieve some of the social and economic pressure on cities. The long-running migration of rural southern blacks and "hillbilly" whites to big cities created great demands for costly welfare services.

It also helps the hinterland in some ways we may not always think of. For generations now, the adults in small-town and rural America have sadly watched their young people leaving after they have completed their schooling. They have returned, of course, on Christmas or Thanksgiving. But these days, more grandparents will see their grandchildren grow up.

More important is what this city-to-country move tells us about the nature of our society. We apparently live in a land where if people are dissatisfied with the way they live, they go ahead and change the way they live. The fact that there are more people able to do what they want to do is a true measure of an enhancement in the quality of our lives. We often think of life quality in terms of particulates in the air. But we ought to measure how much freedom is in the air; that too is an aspect of quality, and it should not be underestimated.

The importance of changing residence patterns and the thinking behind it should also not be underestimated. As noted earlier, the American historian, Frederick Jackson Turner, changed the way Americans thought of themselves when, after examining the census of 1890, he declared that the American frontier had closed. That perception and the reality it reflected ultimately led to the idea of a maturing America, of an America dealing with finished business rather than unfinished business, of an America more like Europe rather than an America where there was always someplace else to go.

These new data, it seems, suggest something else: the frontier may be reopening.

It is, of course, not the frontier of the nineteenth century. You can get there now in an air-conditioned car on an interstate highway, not in a covered wagon on a rutted trail. You live in a frame house with a big porch, not in a log cabin caulked with mud. Your fuel is natural gas, not buffalo chips. As noted, you have access to a doctor and cable television.

But our frontier was never just a state of nature. It was also a state of mind. If you didn't like it here, you could always go there. That's what's happening now, too. That process, that option, enhances the quality of life of those who choose to move.

===

There is a second Super Number to be addressed here. Unlike some of the others we have dealt with, this one has not been hidden, ignored, deemphasized, or misunderstood. It is called "Sunbelt," a geographical grouping loosely defined, but typically comprising the states of the South and West:

POPULATION OF THE U.S. 1970, 1980 (IN MILLIONS)

		1970	1980	Gain
Northeastern States North Central States } "Frostbelt"		106 million	108 million	2 million
Southern States Western States } "Sunbelt"		98 million	119 million	21 million (!)

Source: U.S. Bureau of the Census.

At the time of the 1980 census, a *majority* (52.3 percent) of Americans lived in the Sunbelt. The proportion continues to grow.

This population shift has enhanced the American quality of life from several perspectives. First, in some ways, it has contributed to a more natural way of life, the sort of life that environmentalist critics have maintained is eroding.

Thus, be it noted that our biggest metropolitan areas, with the greatest densities of population, are typically in the Frostbelt states. If you believe that life closer to the countryside and in sparser surroundings equates with naturalness, then the Sunbelt is where you are more likely to find it. The Frostbelt population density in 1980 was 118 persons per square mile; the Sunbelt density was 45 persons per square mile.

But real quality of life hinges on much more than being close to nature. In earlier times the American southlands were disproportionately our land of poverty, and there ain't much quality in poverty.

Nowadays, the relationship between the South and poverty has been blurred. Back in 1959 the differential between poverty rates in the

South and the rest of the country was 19 percent (a Southern rate of 35 percent versus 16 percent for the rest of the nation). By 1981 the differential had been reduced to 5 percent (a Southern rate of 17 percent versus 12 percent for the rest of the country).

Why did it happen? Many reasons, to be sure, but there is an object lesson here for those who think modernism erodes quality. For the surge of better living in the South and Southwest is in some important measure directly related to the advent of an energy-guzzling, artificial, modernist machine: the air conditioner.

Talk about products which enhance the quality of life. Originally developed by Willis Haviland Carrier in Buffalo, New York, around the turn of the century, the first air conditioners were used to store fresh meat. Soon, the device was cooling live human beings, not dead animals. It was a comfort in upstate New York, but turned out to be a godsend in Texas. (The normal daily maximum temperature in Buffalo in August is 78°. In Dallas it is 96°.)

Statistically, the air conditioning of America looks like this:

Year	Number of Air-Conditioned Houses	% of All Houses
1960	7 million	12%
1970	24 million	36%
1981	48 million	57%

Source: U.S. Bureau of the Census.

Those national data mask major regional differences. In the Northeast only 35 percent of homes are air conditioned. But in the West South Central region (which includes Texas), the figure is 81 percent.

In Phoenix, in July, the normal daily maximum temperature is 105° Fahrenheit. Repeat, normal. In Oklahoma City in August, 93° is a normal day. In New Orleans 91° is normal on an August day.

Those are hot—near tropical—climates; they are hot enough to sap the human spirit. How effectively can you farm your land or drive a truck or work in an office or paint a picture when it's above 90° in the shade day after day? Is it a wonder that until recently, the states in the southern tier of the U.S. were the least productive and consequently the poorest area in the nation?

These areas were close to nature all right, and close to desperation.
Along came the humble air conditioner. Homes were cool, offices
were cool, cars were cool, athletic stadiums were cool. Is it surprising
that simultaneously with the advent of air conditioning, migration to
the Sunbelt increased, businesses relocated, the economy improved,
poverty diminished, educational attainment soared? Does not all that
represent not just an economic advance, but an advance of the human
spirit as well? An aesthetic advance? An advance in the quality of
life?*

* There is no need to carry this point to absurdity in order to consider a dazzling
  thought: is it possible that the air conditioner, of all things, will prove to be
  one of the most revolutionary and most progressive inventions of this era?
     Consider: when all the grand Third World development strategies are ex-
  amined, massaged and analyzed, a good part of the truth at the bottom line is
  climatological. Think of the nature of the world without air conditioning:
  Hot equals poor, poor equals weak. Break that equation—give the intemperate
  zones temperate climates—and the world could change in a most dramatic way.
  It happened that way in America's southern tier. It may well happen that way
  in the rest of the world. As shall be noted later, that process may well have already begun.

CHAPTER 17

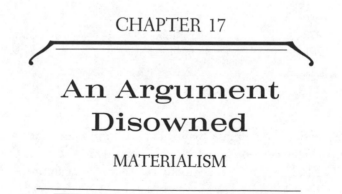

An Argument
Disowned

MATERIALISM

There is a final part of the quality-of-life argument that remains to
be looked at. Deep down, and sometimes not so deep down, there are
some on the Q team who harbor yet another overriding complaint
about American life.

They think we don't got no taste.

Why not? Americans are materialists, say the antimaterialists, because Americans have mindlessly worshiped a glitzy high-growth economy. Americans don't appreciate the finer things in life. They build endless tracts of monochromatic suburban boxes, they want big, flashy, gas-guzzling cars, they turn the music and the air conditioning on high, they scar our scenery with industrial chaos. Too much! Materialism pollutes the soul! The enemy is us! Less is more! Small is beautiful!

Well. There are some conservative economists who believe that a deep recession disciplines our economic circumstance. It drives out the inefficiencies of a fat and sappy marketplace, reintroducing hard-nosed reality. It is tough medicine, say these conservatives, but both useful and necessary.

I take no position on that harsh view of the economic marketplace. But in the intellectual marketplace—let us salute recession! Hard times drive out precious ideas.

Thus, when the economy is bounding along from one new high to another, the idea that national gluttony corrodes the quality of life can become quite fashionable. The politician who notes that we live in an "era of limits" is lionized; planners may lament the gluttonous nature of the "single-family home ethic"; big cars are scorned; we are told to look at "belching smokestacks," not at the steel mill alongside them; the intellectual and political market becomes bullish on the philosophies of no growth, low growth, and slow growth.

But a recession, a deep one like the one we have just lived through, knocks no-low-slow out of the box. It reminds us that voters want the products that some intellectuals see as gluttonous.

And so the Reaganauts offer us a growth philosophy: supply-side economics. Before that, Carter offered us a growth philosophy: re-industrialization. New generations of liberals compete with new labels for old growth philosophies: hi-tech "Atari Democrats" compete with steel-and-cars "Smokestack Democrats" while "Infrastructure Democrats" attempt to bridge the gap with bridges.

Meanwhile, the gluttony-dilutes-quality-idea is quieted. Can you decry the "single-family home ethic" when the public assails the high interest rates that seem to price them out of a cherished goal—the single-family house? How hard can the Q team hit the gas-guzzling automobile culture when automobile workers are out of work? How bad are the belching smokestacks compared to steelworkers out of work because the smokestacks aren't belching?

Of course, an argument about taste cannot be won or lost. One man's glitz is another man's grandeur. But such an argument can be disowned and disinherited, and it has been. No one in public life seems to be in favor of no-low-slow growth any more. Materialism is not much disparaged any more.

The centrally air-conditioned, detached house in a Houston suburb, with two air-conditioned cars in the garage and a boat on a trailer in the driveway may have been seen as gluttony to the Q team, but it is Q to the public. Reflecting recession-scarred public opinion, a wall-to-wall pro-growth coalition now lives in Washington and around the nation.

It is, to be sure, not a foolhardy coalition. It is a consensus that continues to honor environmental intelligence in preserving park lands, keeping beaches safe from oil slicks, enforcing consumer product safety and moderate local zoning ordinances. But it is a coalition that demands that environmentalism not be achieved at the cost of economic growth or at the cost of material well-being that some have denounced as "tasteless."

It has been said that it is the essence of human intelligence to figure out how to have one's cake and eat it too. Such a search is now going on. Its objects are material growth *and* environmental decency, which are not antithetical goals.

When faced with the choice, the American public understood quickly that it was not material growth but the lack of material growth that corroded the real quality of life. This thought will lead us, after an interlude, to the critical question of the second section of this book: Have the economic conditions of the last dozen or so years diminished the quality of life?

CHAPTER 18

Getting the Wrong Story Right

MEDIA AND THE ENVIRONMENT

The five strands of environmentalism have been unbraided and are far weaker when examined separately.

If we are being polluted upon, and subjected to new risks, we are nonetheless living longer, healthier lives. Our population is not exploding, and resources are not disappearing. We have not abandoned nature. We are not a bunch of crass slobs with bad taste, or if we are, we like what we like, and it is not harming us.

The quality of our lives is not eroding. Quite to the contrary, it is being enhanced.

Such, in any event, is the argument of this book so far. Super Numbers support much of the case. But is this being relayed to the citizenry? Are the media doing their job?

I offer the beginning of an answer via a riddle.

Imagine that you are an intelligence agent from Mars. Your mission is to report back to Mars about the nature of American civilization during the last fifteen years, concentrating particularly on the quality of life.

Here are your ground rules, Martian spy: you have only *two* days before your supply of krypton breathing fluid runs out. You may not spend less than one full day at any organization you choose to visit in order to learn about America. When you return to Mars, the Leader will judge your report on the basis of accuracy, completeness, and timeliness. If he is displeased he will cut off your head, or whatever it is you breathe from.

You have landed in Manhattan and are standing on Fifth Avenue at 49th Street, facing north. One block to your left is an office building bearing the name of McGraw-Hill, publishers of such trade magazines as *Chemical Week* and *Information Systems Technology*. One block to your right is Madison Avenue, and the offices of Young and Rubicam, one of America's leading advertising agencies. You are immediately adjacent to Radio City, home of the National Broadcasting Company (NBC), a major television network.

You must choose two (2) from three (3) organizations to get your information: McGraw-Hill, or Young and Rubicam, or NBC.

To which two of these three sources of information about America's quality of life should you go to maximize your chances of survival upon return to Mars?

At NBC (or any other national network) you could review all the old tapes of domestic stories. What would you discover? Many details regarding what John Dean said about Watergate, why Gerald Ford pardoned Richard Nixon, what Koreagate was (what was it?), what Bert Lance did (what did he do?). On the quality-of-life beat you could see pictures of seagulls covered with oil on a Santa Barbara beach. You could see worried faces in Harrisburg, Pennsylvania—worried because it had been announced that each person in the area had been exposed to 95 millirems of radiation (how much is a millirem?). You could hear politicians say that a supersonic airplane will deplete the ozone supply and cause skin cancer. You could hear that the snail darter is an endangered species. You could see good news too, occasionally: Barney Clark with an artificial heart, the space shuttle blasting off, but it would all likely be diluted by flash news about a new development in the Debate-gate scandal.

What could you find at McGraw-Hill (and at other trade and professional magazine publishers)? Undistracted by news about Ed Meese's mortgage or Billy Carter's escapades, you could scan magazine pages and find out that new oil drilling techniques have been developed that allow for oil recovery from beneath the frozen tundra. You could find out that American industries were spending tens of billions of dollars on pollution abatement, all the while complaining bitterly about it, and that pollution was indeed being abated. You could find out that drugs were being developed that will cure some forms of cancer. You could find out that hundreds of thousands of formerly crippled Americans are strutting around on artificial hip and knee joints. You could find out that human corneas can be removed, shaved down, and put back to give sight to the sightless. In trade and professional magazines about sales, you could find out that Americans have been moving to the country—after all, how can you be a marketing man if you don't know that? You could find out that Americans are living longer and that the birthrate is way down—after all, how can you be a marketing man if you don't know that? You could find out about an artificial heart—five years *before* one was put into Barney Clark. You could find out about space shuttle technology—ten years *before* blast off. It's not that network television didn't mention these things, only that their combined coverage was less than that given to whether or not a Congressman had sex with a teen-age Congressional Page. Finally, by reading trade magazines, you would surely not end up reporting back to the Martian Leader that earthlings were running out of resources.

What would you find out at Young and Rubicam and other advertising agencies? You could look at consumer advertising, print and video. You could find out that the cost of stereophonic sound has come down so that most Americans can enjoy it. You could find out that color television has become a commonplace. You could find out that long distance phone rates are down. You could see a man named O. J. Simpson fly through airports, and learn how with a small piece of plastic an average American could quickly gain possession of a $10,000 automobile in one city, drive it to another, and leave it there. You could find out about air conditioners and word processors. (You could also find out more than you want to know about deodorants, cigarettes, and beer.)

Where to go? (Remember, two out of three.)

Author's advice to Spy: if you want to keep your head when you return to Mars, if you want to learn something about American civilization, you probably ought to go to McGraw-Hill, and Young and Rubicam. NBC (or either of the other major networks) would be in third place. Are Bert Lance and snail darters the most important things that have been happening in America?

This is a little sad. Of course, it's only a riddle. Our Martian experiment doesn't yield a definitive judgment that American television viewers should watch the commercials and not the news. Television is not yet a lost cause; there is some solid news about progress on the nightly news, even if it is often swamped by a sea of drivel. Nor is the riddle meant to be a comprehensive indictment of the American media (that comes later). Moreover, certain newspapers and the news magazines do a better job than network television in helping Americans understand their culture. (Our riddle was fixed: it did not offer a visit to *U.S. News & World Report* as an option, nor, on television, a choice of viewing *Nightline* or *MacNeil-Lehrer*.)

Still, the point should be clear, and the "quality of life" is just one broad example. The mass media, particularly television, are often giving us the wrong story.

Why is this happening?

The way the system ends up working, there would seem to be three criteria upon which news judgments are often determined:

1. Bad news is big news;
2. Good news is no news;
3. Good news is bad news.

The first two steps are familiar. The third step is not, and I find it particularly fascinating. All are worth some examples now. Data will be offered later (see Part V).

We may begin our examples where we began this part of the book: with *life expectancy*.

Amid all the TV headlines about the carcinogen-of-the-month, about toxic wastes, about nuclear hazards, about stress, about DDT in food chains, about the ravages of cholesterol, do you recall a major television feature story that dealt with the greatest decade-to-decade increase in adult longevity we have seen in this century? (If you recall one, do you recall two?)

Now the fact that people live longer is not a small story. It may even be as important as Debategate or death by Tylenol.

Well, it may be said, life expectancy is basically a *statistical* story, it happens over a long time, it is hard to get a handle on for news purposes. But suppose life expectancy rates had gone *down* in the last decade as sharply as they have in fact gone up?

Think about it. Would the story of More Deaths be no story because it was statistical? Or would there have been a congressional investigation about it? Would Ralph Nader tell us it was caused by reckless capitalism? Would the environmentalists tell us it was due to pollution and nuclear radiation? Would all this be big news night after night after night on television? Of course it would be. *Bad news is big news. Good news is no news.*

What about the third point: *good news is bad news?*

Here's how it works: there were stories on network television about rising longevity rates—bad news stories!

The increase in adult life expectancy became big news only when the Social Security system was, so it was said, threatened with "bankruptcy." Now, one reason for that revenue shortfall was increased life expectancy. After all, if the elderly misbehave and don't die on time, they keep drawing Social Security payments. It doesn't take much more than that to "break" the system unless, of course, the political apparatus is flexible enough to respond.

So an important part of the big political story of 1982 and 1983 was, in fact, the result of good news. Longer life was instrumental in creating a financial problem. Did a television reporter do a stand-upper in front of the White House or the Capitol and say, "An incredible American success story in the medical system must now be dealt with in the political system?" He did not. What he said was, "Speaker O'Neill said Ronald Reagan doesn't care about old people," or "Ronald Reagan said Democrats will bust the system." *Good news is bad news.**

Another example: consider the way we have dealt with the "population explosion." To be sure, the concept of the "explosion" was treated as bad news and big news. If it was not a staple on the nightly hard-news programs, it surely was a staple on public affairs programs, on documentaries, talk shows, interview programs, Op-Ed pieces, editorials, columns, and magazine features. And what the population explosion caused, we were told, was bad: poverty, overcrowding, environmental degradation, and so on. *Bad news is big news.*

The growth rate of the world's population peaked in 1970 and has declined substantially since then. As has been noted, in many countries—like America—the fertility rates have not only decreased but gone below replacement levels.

Now if the population explosion was bad news and big news, then why is its recessional not good news and big news? Or even good news and small news? But there has been almost no public discussion of the "good news" of the decline in birthrates. *Good news is no news.*

Instead, there has been a great deal of news in America about the side effects—all bad—of the good news. A lower birthrate, for example, causes school closings. That's bad news for some neighborhoods. But after all, what would you expect when the fertility rate declines from roughly four children per woman to two children per woman? School closings, of course, yield teacher layoffs, also bad news. And down the road a bit, believe it or not, there will probably be much talk in America about big problems with labor shortages. All bad news caused by the good news of declining fertility. *Good news is bad news.*

Or look at the coverage of how we were "running out of resources." During the OPEC heist of the 1970s it was said, again and again, that the world "was running out of oil." *Bad news is big news.*

* Headline in the *New York Times*, May 31, 1983: "Longer Lives Seen as Threat to Nation's Budget."

Now that oil prices have come down, now that there is an "oil glut," is there a good news story that the world "is not running out of oil?" There is not. The glut is treated as a disembodied phenomenon unrelated to resources. In fact, it is sometimes said that the decline of oil prices may trigger a depression, because banks won't get their loans repaid by the oil nations. *Bad news is big news. Good news is bad news.*

What about our various lists of risks and quality in chapter 7? How were they covered?

Consider our first list. It dealt with products, systems, and conditions announced as dangerous, but that proved to be not dangerous.

Night after night, the news shows gave us shots of terrorized mothers at Love Canal, worried about birth defects, miscarriage, and cancer. But did the news shows devote equal time, or one-tenth the time, even one-one-hundredth the time to the results of the blue-ribbon investigations that showed no probable harm caused by Love Canal?

The same sort of question could be asked of every item on the list of nondangerous dangers and the answers would be similar. The charge of danger and risk becomes big news as politicians fulminate, public interest advocates raise their voices, editorialists editorialize, and columnists clatter.

Typically, a careful study is then initiated to assess the charge. A year later a report comes out. It is announced that the actual damage from TMI was nil, that nitrites need not be banned, that DNA will not float down the Charles River and create additional mutant species among Harvard students.

Quite unlike the original charges, however, the everything-is-probably-all-right-a-year-later study typically gets a one-day, one-minute spot buried in the middle of a typical nightly news program. Moreover, that same program probably led off with a brand-new danger: hazardous waste disposal is being delayed by government and industry villains! Designer jeans cause cancer!

Bad news is big news. Its repudiation is not.

Of the *Real Danger* list, there is not much to be said. Needless to say, real dangers are covered.

Kepone was in the news for three years. But do you know how many people died as a result of exposure to Kepone? Was it one thousand? One hundred? Ten? It was none.

And consider the list of *Unchallenged Risk Reducers,* medical and nonmedical.

A DC-10 goes down in Chicago, an Air Florida jet goes down at Washington's National Airport, and there is flash news, crash news, news from the site of the accident, survivor stories, rescue stories, next-of-kin stories, funeral stories, accident investigation stories, who-is-at-fault stories. All this, of course, is quite properly "newsworthy."

But was it newsworthy to report that over the two-year period, 1980–81, there was only *one* passenger death—caused by a fall from a gangplank—in nearly 11 million scheduled airline departures covering over 5.5 billion miles? Was it newsworthy that airline travel has become safer and safer over the years? It was not. *Good news is no news.*

On the medical side: was there a big TV hoopla about new drugs that reduce the incidence and risk of ulcers? Or about new drugs to treat arthritis? Was there a big ongoing story about how lasers can be used in eye operations to prevent blindness? There was, to be sure, a mention here and there, but put them all together and they don't add up to one week's worth of stories about dioxin at Times Beach. Of the big medical news, only heart surgery and the development of interferon come to mind as stories that received major and sustained television nightly news coverage.

On the other hand, it is instructive to see how most of the important medical stories moved into the collective American consciousness. New machines, new drugs, new procedures, all cost money. And that became the focus: "Health inflation!"

Good news is bad news.

More attention was surely paid to the *costs* of the CAT scanner, which are indeed high, than to its *value* as a diagnostic tool, which is enormous. More attention is paid to doctors and hospitals that rip off the Medicare and Medicaid payment structure than to the fact that 52 million Americans are entitled to health care under the provisions of these relatively new programs for the poor and elderly. Because these previously undertreated groups are now covered, the costs to the society are raised. Health care as a percentage of GNP has gone up from 4 percent in 1950 to 9 percent in 1980.

Does that trigger "health inflation?" Well, yes. Do doctors and hospitals make out like bandits when health inflation occurs? Well, yes, some of them do. When demand overtakes supply, prices rise, and that is a legitimate problem of medical economics.

But isn't health inflation also an example of a very honorable phenomenon: "reordering of priorities"? Suppose the percentage of GNP going for, say, defense had gone up instead? Would that have been better? Curiously, there are some of us who occasionally think so, but typically not the people who decry health inflation.

What has happened during the last few decades is that the nation has, by conscious design, ordered that more of its wealth be directed to "health"—and we call it health inflation. Not by accident, during the same time, the health of the citizenry has improved. Some bad news!

———

What does all this tell us about how contemporary journalism treats advances in the quality of life?

Good news typically turns into bad news when it touches on politics, economics, corruption, danger, or tragedy. And these, alas, are almost entirely what television news is about, and much daily print journalism as well. But when the news is so transmuted from good to bad, it overlooks what's going on in our civilization.

If our Martian spy returned to his leader with a view of the quality-of-life situation as it was presented on television in the last dozen or so years, he would have interesting material, usually accurate in its specifics, professionally presented, but he would have missed the whole point of what has been going on in America.

It's not that he would have got his stories wrong; he would have got the wrong stories.

Question: if we've been getting the wrong story about the quality of life, is it possible we've been getting the wrong story about other aspects of our modern life?

It is possible.

PART II

STANDARD
OF LIVING

CHAPTER 19

Cameo: Economic Chitchat at Claude's

WHAT'S WRONG WITH THE ECONOMY?

The crowd at Claude Cleeshay's party is getting bigger and louder.

A waiter, once an Iranian air force colonel, elbows his way through the room taking orders for drinks. Another waiter, born in Ghana, now studying electrical engineering in night school, passes a tray of once-puffed-up cheese balls, already soggy and sagging.

An investment banker plucks a cheese ball from the tray, munches on it, and grumbles, "I know what's going to happen. It's going to start all over again. Those clowns in Washington! How can you run an economy with a $200 billion deficit!"

"The problem is they have no plan," says a liberal economist, "that's why it's running out of control again. High interest rates will heat up inflation. Same old story."

"Which will give us one more recession," says a columnist, "and people won't be able to buy houses. How much can we take?"

"It's a problem," says Claude Cleeshay. "We're mortgaging our children's future with those deficits."

"Deficits don't matter," says a supply-side economist. "It's the Fed that will kill the economy with tight money."

"We need a plan," says the liberal economist, "we need a policy."

"Just think of the human capital we're losing," says the commentator. "If our children can't afford to go to college because no student loans are available, how will we compete in microchips? The Japanese and the Soviets train their kids in mathematics and science. But our teenagers are unemployed!"

The pundit moves in. "It's retraining we need," he says. "All those smokestack industries; millions of people out of work. They'll never get those jobs back. We need high-tech training. Unemployment robs us of human dignity and self-worth."

"Right," says a psychologist, "unemployed people think it's their fault they're unemployed—they feel guilty. But it's structural change that's doing it. A husband and wife in Chicago committed double suicide—their note said, 'no jobs.'"

"Old people eating out of garbage cans!" says the public interest lawyer.

"Poverty is going up," says a sociologist, "it's a scandal."

"They've feminized poverty," says the anchorman.

"Blacks and Hispanics take it on the chin," says the sociologist.

"They've cut the safety net out from under them," says Claude.

"And I'll tell you something else," says the sociologist. "It's not just women, blacks, and Hispanics. It's all of us. It's harder to make ends meet than it used to be. People are mad about it."

Like a virus, the talk of economics spreads throughout the room, jumping from white wine to highballs. Off in a corner, the corporate structure huddles.

"It's productivity that's done it," says a chief executive officer. "We weren't innovating or investing, so our productivity rate fell way back."

"The Japanese are innovating and investing," says a lobbyist. "Look what they're doing in robotics."

"That's because they have a partnership of business, labor, and government," says the CEO. "Sunrise industries, sunset industries—that's what does it."

"They plan," says a labor leader who has joined the conversation. "They plan and they cheat. They cooperate to export but they won't let imports in. Planning and cheating."

"Their government is on their side," says the lobbyist. "Ours is working against us—regulations for this, regulations for that. No wonder we can't get things done. No wonder we're not making headway."

Claude Cleeshay has ambled over. "And what about the work ethic?" he asks. "It's eroding."

"You know why it's eroding?" says a young man from a conservative think tank, "I'll tell you why. Because big government is Big Daddy and is breeding dependency."

"And taxes," says the CEO, "taxes are too high. The government keeps getting bigger. Defense spending gets bigger. Entitlements are busting us. We can't plan because they keep changing the rules. No wonder there are so many business failures."

"You're not planning because you're bad managers," says an economist. "American business is only interested in the bottom line and fast profits. There's no pride and no long-distance runners. That's why we get billions for mergers and nothing for investment."

"We're going to end up with a service-only economy," says the labor leader, "an America made up of fast-food joints."

"We need to fix up our bridges and our roads," says a politician, "America is falling apart."

"We're deindustrializing," says the labor leader.

"We need a plan," says the economist, "we need an industrial policy."

===

What a mess!

Or is it?

The indictment laid down at Claude's is familiar, and scattershot. Let's try to organize it.

There are charges against the *economy as a whole*: recession, inflation, and so on.

There are, further, the *effects* these conditions have upon *the population as a whole*: unemployment, diminishment of real income, rending of the safety net.

There are charges about *specific groups* within the population: blacks, women, elderly, college students, and so forth.

And there are charges against *business*: failures, bankruptcies, dried-up research, too much regulation, lack of management skills, and so on.

We shall develop our economic examination according to those loose categories, and ask: how much validity is there in the cocktail party chatter?

CHAPTER 20

Welcome to the World of Ditroi

MACROECONOMIC OVERVIEW

It is surely not my purpose to claim that the American economy has just gone through a dazzlingly good period.

We have lived through a dozen or so years of recession, stagflation, high interest rates, high unemployment, high inflation and high deficits.

Arthur Burns has called the time of the 1970s "The Great Inflation" and says that it and the Great Depression have been the central economic events of this century.

The early 1980s were equally difficult as we experienced what has been described as "the greatest recession since the Great Depression." Indeed, many observers called what happened in the early 1980s "another Depression." Finally, as this book goes to press in July 1984, there is a low-inflation recovery under way. Knock wood. But as the folks at Claude's were saying, it may not last.

How bad was the economic mess? Is it possible that behind all the economic scare talk, the situation wasn't so bad and may actually have been fairly positive?

It is important for all of us to put our recent economic performance in some sort of perspective. If we don't know where we've been, it's hard to guess where we're going. For the purposes of this book such a putting-in-perspective is particularly important. For if we were to find that the years since 1970 (the broad purview of this volume) showed an unrelieved or unusual economic downturn, it would quite simply destroy an important part of the general thesis presented here.

But no such thing has happened. To understand this, let us take a brisk walk across and around the economic landscape.

We begin with a short history lesson: recessions and hard economic times are as American as apple pie. Surely you remember the Panic of 1819, when imports fell by almost a third in a single year, when "manufacturers were in distress; laborers were out of work; merchants were ruined" (in the words of historian Frederick Jackson Turner)?

Or how about the Panic of 1837 and the Depression that ensued, described by economic historian Harold Faulkner as "the worst the nation had experienced"? In May of 1837, all the banks closed. That depression lasted for half a dozen years.

It was followed by the Panic of 1857. Then came the Secession Depression, then the Primary Postwar Depression.

Nor was stability anywhere to be found as the unified nation came back from the abyss of the Civil War. The Crisis of 1873 was a disaster. Historian Allan Nevins wrote of it: ". . . the crisis . . . was pursuing innocent and guilty alike with her vengeance and bringing her heaviest lash upon the backs of the poor—the laboring factory hand, the sweated garment worker, the small savings bank depositor. . . . Unemployment steadily mounted."

We were back in trouble again in the early 1880s and again in the early 1890s. "During 1893," writes Faulkner, "over 600 banking institutions failed. . . . More than 15,000 commercial failures . . . were recorded for 1893. . . . Unemployment, strikes, discontent, and much actual suffering characterized the winters of 1893 and 1894, a period which encompassed the Pullman strike in Chicago and the marching of 'Coxey's Army.'"

So much for the "Gay Nineties."

There were other recessions in the early twentieth century: "the Rich Man's Panic," the "Panic of 1907," the "Crisis of 1914." The end of World War I did not end recessions or make the world safe for stability. In May of 1920, the commodity price index of the Bureau of Labor Statistics was at 247. By late 1921 it was at 140. Banks closed, farmers were foreclosed upon, businesses went bankrupt, unemployment was high.

In all, consider this startling datum to back up the idea that recessions are ever with us: between the end of the Civil War and the advent of the Great Depression, the United States economy was *in recession 45 percent of the time!*

In other words, at any given moment America was about as likely to be in recession as not.

Yet, of course, something else very important was going on in pre-Depression America: growth. Mixed in among all the panics and crises were the "Cotton Boom," the "California Gold Boom," the "Corporate Prosperity," the "New Era Prosperity"—just to pick at random a few of the sexier phrases used by economic historians.

When the dust settled after all the unemployment, the business failures, the bank closings, the booms, and the expansions, it was clear that the growth far outweighed the distress. For example, in only slightly more than a half century (from the early 1870s to the later 1920s), *real per capita gross national product more than tripled,* going from about $500 in the early 1870s to about $1,700 in the later 1920s (expressed in 1958 constant dollars).*

During this time Americans attained the highest standard of living in the world.

We come next to the decade-long shock of the Great Depression. It should not be underestimated. As measured in 1958 constant dollars, the per capita GNP in 1929 was $1,671. Four years later, in 1933, the figure was $1,126!

That is a decrease of 33 percent. (The next time someone tells you that what we're going through is "another Depression," consider that the decrease in real per capita GNP from 1979 to 1982 was 2.6 percent. Moreover, there was no safety net then; there is now.)

From World War II to 1984, the United States has suffered through eight recessions. We no longer seem to put sexy titles on them ("The Frostbelt Fade," "The Precipitous Petroleum Putdown," "The Supply-Side Sinking Spell"), but recessions are still with us, and we have just lived through a big one.

Some questions: are recessions more or less frequent now than at earlier times in our history?

Substantially less. In the years since World War II, America has been in recession for about 20 percent of the time, compared to the 45 percent figure for the pre-Depression era.

Are recessions deeper than they used to be?

They are less deep, whether measured by change in industrial production, change in GNP per capita, or rate of change in number of employed.

Has the recent run of recessions wiped out growth?

That is the critical question. It is far too simple merely to compare pre-World War II economic history and post-World War II history. There are substantial differences *within* the postwar epoch. It is maintained that the period since 1970 has been singularly bad, and the four economic years from 1979 to 1982 absolutely rotten. By the end of that spell, serious people were wondering out loud whether we

---

* Because of rising population, the Gross National Product went up by about ten times during this half century (measured in constant dollars).

were not embarked on a new, sour era of long-term stagflationary economic grief, following a path quite different from the fluctuating but ascendant track of earlier history.

It is that time period, roughly from 1970 to now, that ought to be placed in sharper focus. Recessions may be as American as apple pie, but if in the last dozen or so years the recessionary syndrome has become more and more severe, we may only end up with a very bitter American pie.

It is not easy to measure.

What do you measure? Gross National Product? Gross National Product per capita? Productivity? Per capita income? Family income? Disposable income? Measure from decade to decade? Trough to trough? Peak to peak?

We'll be dabbling with all of the above throughout this part of the book. Some numbers may not appear to be entirely consistent with others; they measure different phenomena, and are affected by a variety of external factors.

But when statistics confuse, it may be useful to begin by looking at another repository of human knowledge: the boilerplate phrase. Sniff out the regnant cliché and then test it against the data.

Quietly, one phrase has come to represent our current economic circumstances. We hear it almost every day, yet think little about its meaning. It deserves further scrutiny: it may indeed turn out to be Super Phrase, a magic collection of dull words that gathers together numbers and Super Numbers and distills the essence of our era.

This candidate for Super Phrase is: "Decrease in the Rate of Increase," or, acronymically, "DITROI."

Welcome to the epoch of DITROI. It is, indeed, our time.

It sounds bad; it's a "decrease." But is it really? Look at our situation through the lens of "the total national economy," that is, the "gross national product." Through such a lens, DITROI is a time when the annual rate of *increase* of real GNP from 1970 to 1980 was 3.1 percent per year, compared to 3.9 percent per year for the prior decade of the Sixties. On the one hand, that doesn't sound like a massive decrease. On the other hand, it is a 21 percent decline in the annual growth rate, which is not trivial.

If one expands the post-1970 period to include the two bad years of 1981 and 1982, the rate of real GNP *growth* declines to 2.6 percent—a third less than the Sixties base decade.

If one looks only at the four bad years of 1979–82, the growth rate was virtually zero, which is not very good. But if one adds in the

comeback year of 1983—in which real GNP was up by 6.2 percent—
the GNP growth rate for 1970–83 is 2.9 percent. (Moreover, economists are predicting that 1984 will provide another solid increase in
real GNP growth.)

Such, then, is one view of the world of DITROI. Things got better,
but at a rate somewhat slower than when things got better faster. In
point of fact "a decrease in the rate of increase" can also be described
more simply: "continued growth."

Of course, it all depends on what your base line is. If you choose
the recession-free 1960s as "normal," then the decrease in the rate of
increase in recent years can be fairly substantial. But suppose you
choose as your base decade not the 1960s, but the 1950s. The annual
rate of real GNP growth in the Fifties was 3.2 percent, quite close to
the 3.1 percent of the 1970s. How much DITROI is there then?

So one can validly argue about how much relative growth there has
been by asking an ancient question: "compared to when?" In words,
rather than numbers, the sequence goes this way: solid but fluctuating
growth from the late Forties to the late Fifties (three recessions); dynamic growth in the 1960s, uninterrupted by recession; back to solid
but fluctuating growth in the Seventies (three recessions); a big twin
recession in the late Seventies and early Eighties, followed now by a
recovery, which may or may not last long. *But always growth.*

DITROI's pattern holds up even if we tighten our focus. The real
GNP rate we have discussed does not correct for population growth.
If population, for example, were growing at a faster rate than GNP,
even a rising GNP would result in GNP *per capita* going down. Such
a result would lend great credence to the bad news view of the world.

But that is not what happened. Real *per capita* GNP went up in
the 1970s by 2.0 percent per year. The comparable figure for the 1960s
was 2.6 percent, and for the 1950s, 1.5 percent.

A thought begins to dawn: what's the big deal? Why all the fuss?
The DITROI (so far) seems so minimal, a few tenths of a percentage
point here, a few tenths of a percentage point there.

Not so fast. A third proper measurement of national economic activity concerns "productivity."

Now by some ways of reckoning, "productivity" is the most sophisticated and most revealing of the national economic indicators. Because it measures "output per man hours," it is the most tightly focused of growth indices.

The numbers go like this:

ANNUAL PRODUCTIVITY INCREASE

1950–60	2.0%
1960–70	2.4%
1970–80	1.3%
1980–82	.9%
1983	3.2%
1984	3.5% (annual rate, first quarter.)

Source: U.S. Bureau of Labor Statistics.

Now, the diminishment of productivity in the 1970s and early 1980s was of major magnitude and was properly a topic for real concern by economists. Many reasons were advanced for the decline: lack of research and innovation, poor business procedure, a decline in the rate of capital formation, too much regulation, the ravages of inflation, labor union practices, OPEC price hikes, changing demographics, and so on. Some of these factors will be examined later.

For the moment, however, the productivity slump seems to have reversed and many economists believe the level will stay up. In a recent Brookings Institution research report Martin Baily maintains that productivity may increase faster in the next few years than it did even during the 1960s. John Kendrick, a leading authority, suggests that the productivity growth rate will continue to average 2–3 percent at least until 1990. That, he says, will ensure a solid boost in real per capita income.

We shall see about all that. For now, however, consider again our original formulation: DITROI means growth. A productivity growth rate of 1.3 percent per year is not 2.4 percent per year (Seventies versus Sixties). But it still doubles itself in fifty-four years. It means your grandson will be twice as well off as you are. That is not a retreat in an economy. It is not a plateau. It is only less growth.

And something else: productivity might not be the best measure. It tells us how much a worker produces. But it doesn't tell us much about who the workers are. The decline of productivity growth remains somewhat of a mystery to experts. But one factor surely concerned the stark change in the nature of our labor force.

Thus, a labor force with 18 percent of its workers aged sixteen to twenty-four (the figure in 1960) is quite different from a labor force with 24 percent in that age bracket (the figure in 1980). Young people are less productive than their elders; they're not well disciplined, they drink and carouse, they tend to quit their jobs, they have less experience, they are less motivated. If the percentage of young workers in the labor force increases by about a third over a twenty-year period, the rate of productivity growth among that labor force will diminish automatically.*

So, too, with women. In 1960, women comprised 33 percent of the labor force. In 1980, just twenty years later, women comprised 43 percent of the labor force.

Let us avoid (at least for the moment) any feminist arguments, by phrasing the next statement as delicately and dully as possible. As a statistical phenomenon, productivity rates tend to go down when the percentage of women in the labor force is rising.

Why? Because women are more likely to be newcomers to the labor force. (That's so by definition: if you sharply increase female participation rates, then while that process is going on, a large percentage of females will be new workers.) Because women are more likely to be in-and-out of the labor force. (They have babies.) Because women are more likely to be working part time than men. (They are still more likely to manage home and children than are their spouses.) All this, seen statistically, reduces productivity in the labor force.

If some of the DITROI in productivity is due to the accommodation of new demographic and social factors (Baby Boom babies coming of age and more women working), is this bad?

It is not bad. It is good. It means more people are working.

Consider this set of incredible Super Numbers against the backdrop of charges of "a sick economy":

* The changing demographic mix of the work force also tends to pull down the statistics regarding hourly and weekly earnings, as will be discussed in chapter 22, dealing with income.

NUMBER OF EMPLOYED PERSONS

1960	68 million
1970	81 million
1976	90 million*
1980	101 million*
1981	102 million
1982	101 million
1983	103 million
1984	107 million (June)

Source: U.S. Bureau of Labor Statistics.
* Political junkies might recall the increase in employment from 1976 to 1980 when considering Ronald Reagan's 1980 campaign line: "Are you better off than you were four years ago?"

From 1970 to 1984, America added 26 million new jobs! (That's more than the *total* number of jobs in Italy in 1984.) Some stagflation!

And a note about the future of productivity: Young people get older. All those extra young people who pulled productivity down in the Seventies will be pushing it up in the latter part of the Eighties, as they mature.

And women? Those tens of millions who have entered the labor force recently will become more experienced, also raising productivity.

In short: the intermediate term looks pretty good. We have (in early 1984) a labor force of about 115 million Americans, of whom 107 million are typically at work at a given moment. As the years roll on this labor force will become better trained.†

There remains a final piece to this discussion of the not-so-sad-as-you-may-have-thought state of the American economy. Most of the preceding comparisons have dealt with decade-to-decade results.

But there was a recession, a shallow one, in 1980. There was then another recession, deeper, starting in mid-1981 and running through 1982. Three bad years.

If, as we've seen, the sorry Seventies weren't so sorry, how bad have the early Eighties been, with all their recessionary flavor?

† In 1983, the Bureau of Labor Statistics projected that the U.S. economy will create another 23–29 million jobs in the next ten years.

It was said as an article of faith that the recent recession was "the worst recession since the Great Depression."

Perhaps. First, consider the 1981–82 recession by itself. The drop in GNP from the previous peak to the trough of the fourth quarter of 1982 amounted to 2.9 percent. Of the eight postwar recessions, three involved sharper drops, while four were milder. (The average drop was 2.7 percent, just a shade less than in 1981–82.)

Or consider a different measure, industrial output. The average drop during the postwar recessions was 10.5 percent, the drop during the recent recession was 12.3 percent. But balanced against that is the fact that "industrial output" was a much greater proportion of the economy then than it is now, with "services" these days comprising a greater part of our economic structure.

In some other respects, however, the 1981–82 recession was worse than other postwar dips. It was longer, lasting seventeen months, a month longer than the 1973–75 recession, and substantially longer than the ten-month average. The rate of business failures was higher, although that has a caveat that will be examined later. (See chapter 33.)

Most important, unemployment was higher in the recent recession—the highest ever since the Depression—peaking at 10.7 percent in December of 1983, compared to the earlier postwar record of 9.0 percent in May of 1975. But again, there is a caveat that will be explored in a later chapter (see chapter 24).

Only by combining the last two recessions, a shallow one in 1980 with a deeper one in 1981–82, can one make a clean case of "the greatest recession since the Great Depression," and then only in terms of length.

But looking broadly at those three bad years, about which we have heard so much, it should be understood that:

- The number of employed people *increased* by 1.33 million.
- The GNP stayed almost steady—a decrease of one percent.
- Personal income per capita, in constant dollars, actually went up, by 1.4 percent.

One thought comes out of all this data: If this has indeed been the "worst recession since . . ." we have been pretty fortunate. What happened since 1970 is not a brand new American story: the statistical valleys are shallow; the statistical hills are relatively high. That is why—over a period of time—Americans make out rather well.

And now, of course, the economy is rising again.

Is it possible—after all the hoopla, all the television interviews on the cheese lines, all the stagflation, all the inflation, the high interest rates, business failures, the deficits—that what we've lived through is just another apple pie blip in the history of a nation that just goes blipping right along, one step backward, three steps forward?

To answer that we should look now not at abstract macroeconomics, but at people.

CHAPTER 21

Cameo: Two Simple Proofs

CONSUMER EXPENDITURES

It has been said (often) that Americans haven't made very much income progress in the last dozen or so years. There are some data (which will be cited in the next chapter) that can be used to back up that notion.

It is said by others (and vigorously in this book) that there has been substantial income progress in the last dozen or so years. There are good data (also cited in the next chapter) to back up that idea. I try, in that chapter, to make clear just why the major-growth argument is much stronger than the minor-growth argument. But, alas, it is a statistically complex question.

How can a layman judge? I offer, in advance, two simple proofs that do not require much more than common sense to understand.

First, I ask you to think seriously about your own life, the lives of your family members, and the lives of your friends and neighbors. If you do, you will probably gain a good sense of how Americans have been faring in terms of income in recent years—a better sense by far than any you will get from the economic news on television, and probably better than you will get from arcane statistical arguments.

Think for a minute. Forget for a moment that you may have been complaining that times are tight, and ask yourself some questions:

Have you or some of your friends bought a video tape recorder? Have you signed up for cable TV?

Are you eating out more often than you were a decade ago? Have you noticed many new restaurants in your community?

Does it seem that you know more young people who are going on to college than before?

Have you been in a traffic jam recently? Does it seem worse than it used to? Are there more cars on the road these days? Have you bought a new car recently?

Does it seem that more people you know are traveling these days? Have you traveled to a national park? Have you been to Europe? Do you have friends who have been to the Caribbean islands? Do you know young people—just out of college, or who have taken a year or two off from college—who have traveled overseas? Do you know some elderly people who have taken a cruise? Is such travel the sort of thing people do when the economy is on the slide, or flat?

=====

Enough questions. Several observations.

First, an answer of "yes" to these sorts of questions would tend to indicate that there has indeed been solid progress on the income front in recent years. This is so despite inflation; we are talking here solely about *additional* goods and services, not merely higher costs. Sending those *extra* kids to college, costs plenty of money; it costs plenty of money to take those *additional* trips.

Second, many American statistics are determined by studying the activity of a sample of Americans rather than collecting data for all Americans. If you, your family, and your friends and acquaintances are behaving in certain ways, that may not be such a bad sample. A few children, a few parents, a few grandparents, a spouse or two, cousins and aunts, business associates, old friends, new friends, friends of your friends—chances are they add up to several hundred people.

Some broad-gauge public-opinion polling is accomplished with samples that small. Such polling can offer a sense of direction, if not precision. Of course, your own sample of several hundred will undoubtedly offer less validity than a scientifically drawn survey. As a hard-cover book reader, you are already part of an American elite; chances are you and your pals are better off than average Americans.

So your sample may well be skewed. But for our purposes, perhaps not as badly skewed as you may think. If your group doesn't represent the whole iceberg, it also doesn't represent merely a stray collection of ice cubes. Remember, all the questions asked above measure *change,* not absolute level. If your sample is going through change, it is almost surely echoing changes going on in the larger society. It is likely that you are not alone, that millions and tens of millions of Americans are also going through change. It is, after all, hard to isolate economic progress; trickle-down economics do trickle down, just as bubble-up economics do bubble up.*

And third: as we shall now see, it turns out that the answers to all those questions just raised—about travel, restaurants, cars, and so on—are indeed "yes," even when viewed on a statistical canvas larger than your own personal sample, in fact on a national canvas.

So we are now going to look at people—plain everyday Americans. Too much of the material offered in the income debate tends to deal with vast economic aggregates and grand trends: gross national product, income cross-tabulated by family composition, the underground economy, noncash government benefits. We have dealt and will continue to deal with all that.

But what about people? What are they up to? Are they changing in the ways your circle of friends and family have been changing? Do those changes reflect growth of U.S. income?

This brings us to our other proof. Offered into evidence is the *Statistical Abstract of the United States.* It is the world's premier national data book.

More so than any other people in the world, Americans are data junkies. The call for a national census is in our Constitution. We grind out numbers, public and private, morning, noon and night. And every year since 1878, the *Abstract* has winnowed not only census and government numbers but a plethora of non-governmental statistics that help sketch our national portrait. The *Abstract* is a big fat book of more than a thousand pages. It should help convince the skeptical reader that things are better than he or she may have thought.

---

* A cross-sectional sample of 2,533 adults was surveyed about income progress in 1983 by Lieberman Research, Inc. for *Money* magazine. The study revealed that most Americans had no doubt that their family was improving its financial situation, at least over the period of a generation. Fully 77 percent of adults surveyed said they thought they were in stronger shape than their parents.

So come along on a waltz through gray pages of numbers. You will learn something about what happened in the U.S. in the years from 1970 to (generally) 1982, a time when our population increased by 14 percent.

The data presented here are from the 1984 *Abstract*:

You will learn in the *Abstract* about greyhound racing. Back in 1970, attendance at the dog tracks was 12.6 million (persons, not dogs). By 1982, that number had climbed to 21.4 million, an increase of 70 percent. When those 21 million attendees go to the track, they typically do one thing: bet money.

Now like the author, you may find greyhound racing somewhat distasteful: hungry hounds chasing robotic rabbits. That, however, is not our topic yet (see Part III, "Values"). Our discussion here merely leads us to ask whether it is likely that so much additional discretionary income would be sloshing around after a dozen years that were characterized by stagflation, recession, and so on.

Losing money at the track can be expensive. That is not to say that attendance at other spectator sports is cheap. A pair of pro football seats went for an average of $26.00 in 1982. Yet, pro football attendance climbed from 10.1 million in 1970 to 14.3 million in 1981. Baseball attendance did even better: 29.2 million to 45.4 million in 1982. Professional basketball is supposed to be the sick sport, yet attendance went from 7.1 million to 10.7 million in 1982, an increase of 51 percent, which, if you're going to be sick, is not a bad way of being sick.

During the worst of those two worst recessions, a strange craze descended upon America. In 1982 alone, it was estimated that Americans, disproportionately young Americans, pumped over one billion dollars (!) into machines called "video games." Now that amount may have been spent in quarters, but it is more than small change. In addition, another $2.7 billion was spent on video games for home use. That total figure of $3.7 billion is equal to the entire GNP of Panama. Where did all that money come from, right in the midst of such a grievous economic period?

Maybe from the same place that golfers and boaters get their money. Golfing and boating are not typically inexpensive recreations. Yet the number of golfers (who played fifteen rounds or more in a year) climbed from 9.7 million to 14.1 million, an increase of 45 percent. The numbers of recreational boats owned went from 8.8 million to 12.9 million—an increase of 47 percent.

And in 1982—a year of deep recession—1.5 million stationary bicycles were sold, worth $136 million. Just imagine: a million and a half Americans, deciding in one depressed year to pedal like mad, going nowhere!

Total spending for all recreation went from $41 billion to $127 billion, an inflation discounted increase of 25 percent in a little more than a decade, almost twice the population growth.

All that does not include lots of other expensive activities, such as foreign travel. During the recessionary catastrophe in America, the total annual number of U.S. travelers to foreign countries climbed from 6.5 million in 1970 to 10.3 million in 1982, an increase of about 60 percent. During the same time period, the number of passports issued went up from 2.2 million per year to 3.7 million, an increase of 68 percent.

Telephones cost money, too. There were 120 million phones in America in 1970—and 182 million phones in America in 1981. Viewed another way, there were 582 phones per 1,000 Americans in 1970—and 789 phones per 1,000 Americans in 1981.

Television costs money, at least cable televison does. During the years of alleged American income stagnation, the number of cable television subscribers increased from 4.5 million to 25 million.

Video Cassette Recorders cost money. From 1978–1984 a total of 16 million VCRs were sold.

Eating out costs money. In 1970 the amount spent in "eating places" was $22 billion. By 1983, the figure was $88 billion, an after-inflation increase of 56 percent.

Sleeping out costs money. The number of rooms rented in hotels and motels went from 464 million in 1970 to 587 million in 1983—a 27 percent increase during a period that included four recessions.

Going to the symphony costs money. The number of Americans who paid money to attend an orchestra performance increased from thirteen million to twenty-two million! Would you believe that not only do Americans go to the symphony more often than to pro football games, but the rate of growth of symphony attendance has been much higher? (A few more Americans watch football on television, however.)

Cars cost money. There were eighty million in use in 1970, and 109 million in 1983. That's a 36 percent increase while the adult population was increasing 26 percent. There are many more households today with two or three vehicles than with one.

Going to college costs money. As we shall see in chapter 30, the rate of Americans going on to college is up substantially.

What a strange catastrophe! What a remarkable economic disaster! All those downtrodden people going to the dogs!

Is it possible that they are going to the dog races instead? And to pro football games? And to restaurants? And that they play golf and go to the symphony? (Could Beethoven putt?) And travel in America, and overseas? All this, more often than ever before?

That is what the numbers say, and that, if I may guess, is likely what you know about your friends and family as well.

Of course, even with all the cars and restaurants and symphonies, it could conceivably be that economic progress is merely taking place for a few of us: the hundred million plus with cars, the fourteen million golfers, the twelve million American young people in college at any given moment. Is it conceivable that the rest of America is in a different boat, mired in the economic mud, going nowhere?

Unlikely. Real poverty rates are down from 1970. Safety net expenditures are up, not down. All this will be seen in later chapters.

The bad news has been wrong. There has been income progress in America. The reader knows it by thinking personally about how he or she and family and friends live these days. The data from the *Abstract* concerning the goods and services that people purchase show that. Next, we will see the logical corollary—that the broad general income data reflect these trends as well.

All this, in fact, is fairly obvious, known to most of us despite the fact that we hardly ever see it, hear about it, or read about it, on television, radio, or newspapers. Maybe we all ought to read a few pages of the *Statistical Ashtract* every morning while we're riding our stationary bicycles.

CHAPTER 22

Measuring Apples and Lizards

INCOME

By looking at the growth of the gross national product, we have seen that the *economy* has been doing better.

By looking at the *Abstract,* we have seen the *effects* of a strong economy on people: video games, boats, cars, orchestras, foreign travel, greyhound racing, telephones, and restaurants. Moreover, other effects of more wealth will be noted in subsequent chapters. It will be seen that Americans are living in bigger, better dwellings, that old people never had it so good, that the safety net is holding, that there are fewer people in poverty, that women are doing better than ever before, and so on.

For all this to be true—and I believe it is clearly and demonstrably true—*Americans must be making more money today than before.* If not, it would be hard, for example, to account for an upgrading of the housing stock, a diminishment of poverty, better conditions for the aged, and so on.

It should come as no surprise, then, to see that many direct measurements of income show that Americans *do* make more money today than before. In constant 1972 dollars, personal income per capita in the United States went from $4,276 in 1970 to an all-time high of $5,483 in 1983, making a 28 percent increase over a thirteen-year span.* Not bad. Or, as Herbert Stein has noted about the rise in these sorts of data, "in the perspective of history, it is enormous. At that rate, our grandchildren would have twice our present income well before they reach our age."

---

* In addition, current estimates indicate that the recovery year of 1984 will yield a year-to-year per capita income-growth rate of from 3 percent to 5 percent.

It would be nice to end this chapter right here. A 28 percent increase in real income in thirteen years would seem to be clear evidence that individual Americans—consistent with the other indicators we have examined—are doing better financially. That case is, in fact, bolstered, as we shall see later, by other factors, particularly the growth of the "underground economy" and of non-cash transfer payments. It's probably worth a Super Number.

Alas, such a claim cannot be made without an argument.

For statistical combat rages. The terminology is almost impenetrable to a layman. One fellow will tell you that the Gini coefficient can be imputed cross-sectionally. His opponent will demand that you consider the longitudinal parameters of the covariant structure of the proxy responses.

Boiled down, which is not easy to do, the argument is about how to measure income. It is a fascinating argument and an important one, because it tells us something not only about income and statistics, but a great deal about America.

One team says we should measure the income of social units: families and households. The other team says, somewhat more simply, measure the income of individual people.

The variation in the results of these two sorts of measurements is rather broad. Neither team says that real income has gone down. But the proponents of the "social unit" approach argue that income has remained essentially flat in the past dozen or so years, although with a healthy up-tick in the recovery years of 1983 and (so far) 1984. The "individual people" team says there *was* a substantial increase in real income in the past dozen years, *and* there was an additional big up-tick in the recovery years of 1983 and (so far) 1984.

So the argument is "flat" versus "up."

The most comprehensive, up-team number was already given: up 28 percent from 1970–83. That number comes from the Bureau of Economic Analysis. It is a straight per capita measurement: the amount of income divided by the number of people in America.

The Census Bureau, when it wears its up-team hat, measures income of people in a somewhat different way. Their per capita series for 1970 to 1980 shows an increase of 16 percent. It is estimated that the 1980–83 period was about flat, and if one tossed in a 1984 estimate of about 3 percent the whole 1970–84 per capita income growth would equal something under 20 percent. In short, up substantially, even if not as much as the 1983 BEA measurement of 28 percent.

But the Census Bureau, when it wears its flat-team hat, provides the "social unit" numbers as well. If one measures median *family* income, from 1970 to 1980, it is just about flat, an increase in ten years of only .4 percent. If one traces median *household* income rather than family income, the figures actually decline a bit—minus 4 percent. (In 1981 and 1982, the income numbers receded farther under the lash of the recession, but bounced back in the 1983–84 recovery.)

Needless to say, it is this flat view of America—and worse—that has been the story presented regularly to the American public. This is not just the fault of the media. It is never just the fault of the media.

When Ronald Reagan—the same fellow who today pleads for stories about good news—ran for President in 1980 he liked to tell Americans that we were already in a depression, not a recession mind you, but a depression. What could the press do but report what candidate Reagan said?

When candidate Edward Kennedy said again and again in 1980 that economic conditions had been getting worse and worse in America, what could the press do but report what he said?

When labor union leaders, looking for political support, said that workers were worse off; when business leaders, looking for political support, said that businesses in America couldn't make any money anymore; when black leaders, looking for political support, said that blacks were doing worse than ever; when feminist leaders, looking for political support, said that economic conditions for women were retrogressing; when pollsters, looking for a headline, said the American dream was over; when academic stars, often looking for a theory worth a raised eyebrow, said that America was on the skids; when all agreed that times were tough and getting worse, what could the media folks do but report such views with vigor and gusto?

All that, by the way, was said prior to the advent of the recession of 1981–82. After that began, of course, the data really interfaced with the fan.

It should be apparent that there is a vested interest in bad news, in this clear instance, the choice of the "flat" view over the "up" view of income. After all, people generally believe "if it ain't broke, don't fix it." Accordingly, it is incumbent on anyone who wants to do anything in the public arena—get elected, cut taxes, raise taxes, support a program, cut a program, or make a public splash—to demonstrate that, whatever it is, it's broke.

Question: who speaks for success?

The answer is almost no one, except perhaps the incumbent President running for reelection (like poor Jimmy Carter in 1980), and who on earth would believe an incumbent President in an election year? The television version of a politicized income story would begin with a stand-upper: "Visiting Elmira today in an attempt to shore up his sagging support among middle-class voters, the President said you never had it so good, but many voters didn't agree." Cut to factory worker: "We've never had it so tough, cost of living being what it is, we can't keep up anymore."

In any event, here, roughly, is the case made by the honorable but misguided people who hold the flat-earth view of income in America.

People typically live in families or households, not in solitary limbo. A wife and husband typically pool earnings; two roommates pay one rental fee, not two. Most important, say the social unit advocates, one big reason for the increase in per capita income is because birthrates have fallen, pulling down the size of households and families. Fewer babies lower the numerator of the fraction in the per capita income formula. This raises per capita income, but it does so in a skewed way. Consider a $20,000 a year family with five people. It has a per capita income of $4,000. If one child should run away from home, the same family would have a $5,000 per capita income, an increase of 20 percent. But that rise is statistical, not real. Mortgage payments remain the same, car payments remain the same, cable television fees remain the same, and so on.

It is a complicated situation, the Flattists admit. But on balance, they maintain, the fact remains that people do live in social units. By that measure, income growth has been flat. And that, they conclude, is because the economy as a whole has been flat.

The case that income has gone up is different but potent. On the surface, the argument sounds statistical, but it is much more than that.

First, consider the nature of our "social units," that is, the "families" and "households" that are measured in many income statistics.

For a comparison of social units over a period of time to be valid, they should be at least somewhat similar: if one compares a bushel of apples in 1970 to a bushel of apples in 1982, it is fair to ask how many apples are in each bushel, how big they are, how ripe, and so on. But if one compares a bushel of apples to a bushel of oranges, the comparison becomes somewhat more difficult, although valid statements still might be made about "bushels of fruit." But suppose the switch is not from apples to oranges, but from apples to lizards?

That is almost what has happened to the structure of our social units in America in just the past decade or so.

At least five major structural changes in social units have taken place. These days families and households

- are older
- are younger
- are smaller
- are more likely to have two earners
- are more likely to be female-headed.

Statistically speaking, one could describe all this drily as the "changing structure of social units." But let us understand that in our real world these apples-to-lizards changes represent a turbulent period in American history, when behavior, sociology, technology, economics, and demography changed quickly and starkly.

There are so many more *older* people in America today because of (a) medical developments that have prolonged life, and (b) a high birthrate and high immigration (with many young children) in the early part of this century. And as we will see in chapter 29, more of these older people are living alone instead of with their children—creating many additional, separate, "social units."

There are so many more *young* adult households today because of the high birthrate following World War II—the Baby Boom. The young brats of the Fifties are the adults heading households today.

Families and households are *smaller* today because for the past fifteen or so years, young people have been living as singles longer, marrying later, and having fewer children.

That development was intertwined with several changes in the role of women in America. These days, American married women are much more likely to be engaged in paid work. That, obviously, increases the percentage of *two-earner* families in America.

And these days, too, there is also a higher divorce rate. The higher divorce rate, of course, raises the level of *female-headed* families.

In short: a swirling change through the society in the 1970s. The magnitudes have been truly remarkable. In the baker's dozen years from 1970 to 1983, the following occurred:

- The average size of the American family went from 3.6 persons to 3.3, down 8%.
- The average size of the American household went from 3.1 persons to 2.7, down 13%.
- The proportion of families headed by women went from 10% of all families to 15%.
- The proportion of all households whose heads were in prime working ages (35–64) declined from 55% to 49%.

- The proportion of married couples where both the husband and the wife work has gone up from 46% to 52%.
- Moving beyond averages and proportions, look at the data this way: the number of households headed by women went up by 68%, the number of households headed by young people (under 35) went up by 27%, the number of households headed by older persons (over 65) went up by 41%, the number of non-family households (most of them singles) went up 89%, while the number of two-earner families went up by 21%.

All this, mind you, has happened just since 1970!

Talk about apples and lizards!

Talk about the foolhardiness of using a social unit standard to measure income! Comparing social units over time is like comparing the life-style of Dagwood Bumstead with Mary Tyler Moore!*

It is important to note that, of the *five* big structural changes in family and household composition, *four* of them clearly work toward *understating* the real increase in American income.

Thus: the middle-age years (thirty-five to sixty-five) are the ones when people typically earn the most money. These days, middle-aged Americans are people (like your friendly author, a Depression baby) who were born during an era of low fertility. As a result, there are relatively few of them to load the statistics with high income earners.

On the other hand, it is the young and the old who make the least money. The young people are just getting started, the old folks are retiring. These days their numbers are swelling unnaturally, loading the income statistics with comparatively low earners.

Or consider the decrease in family and household size. Suppose—to make the case overly obvious—you compared a 1970 household, with a husband and wife and two young children, to a 1980 household, with a single man living alone. Suppose both men are earning, say, $20,000. Who's living better? Yet a measure of income by *household* would detect no change; in each instance a household existed with $20,000 in income.

The female-headed family, too, pulls down the social unit measure. A mother with children and without a husband typically has a big set of problems. Alimony and child support, even in the best of circumstances, never quite seem to equal the prior earnings of the previously

* For young readers: Bumstead was Blondie's husband, when "Blondie" was a family comedy not a rock band. The Bumstead household was a traditional one, with two adult parents, of different sexes, and two children. Ms. Moore's television household had one person—Ms. Moore.

"intact" family. In many cases, the female head of household cannot work full time, or at all, because of the demands of young children.

In short, the shift of a family from "intact" to "female-headed" typically adds one low-income family to the universe of all families, once again depressing the aggregate social-unit income level.

That is a statistical downer, but curiously, the total income of all the involved family members is often likely to go up. Figure it out for yourself. Typical case: husband-wife-two kids—splitsville. Husband retains job, pays some alimony and child support, but not enough. Woman goes back to work—or if she cannot, gets some aid in cash (Aid to Families with Dependent Children) or in noncash (food stamps, Medicaid, rent supplements, and so on). Mathematically at least, while neither of the two new social units—the new female-headed family or the one-person household of the husband—is making any more money than the previous unsplit social unit, the aggregate income of all the members of the original family is up. The husband makes the same as before; the wife has new cash and/or noncash sources.

Of the five great recent structural changes in the American family, only one—the increase in two-earner families—tends to inflate the family income numbers. (The number of such two-earner families increased by 5.4 million from 1970 to 1982.)

So: four factors artificially lowering the trend line of social-unit income—one factor boosting it.

Conclusion: the apples of 1970 cannot be compared with the lizards of 1980. The family-income standard disguises and hides real income progress. The more valid standard in a time of great social flux is the per capita standard, and that, recall, went up by 28 percent in real uninflated dollars from 1970–83, according to the BEA.

But even that is understatement. There are other major factors working against the recognition of major income gains in recent years.

Consider the underground economy. It is regarded, properly, as a national scandal. Growing numbers of people earn growing portions of their money "off the books"—paying less than legal amounts of tax, or paying no tax at all. Politicians denounce it. "60 Minutes" does a feature on it, finding tax evaders ranging from wealthy gangsters to poor waitresses.

Scandal, right?

Right indeed; the rest of us are paying more taxes because those cheaters aren't. But hold on. Along with the scandalously growing underground economy comes a bonus—and a big one at that. All those cheaters are making money—real, live, green, United States money.

Remember that phrase, "the growing underground economy." As Groucho Marx used to announce: "Say the magic word and you win $100!" The magic word is "growing." If the amount of the underground economy were large but remained proportionately constant to a growing GNP it would not be of great consequence to our argument. The GNP figures would then be wrong, but wrong in a constant way. But if the error is *growing*, and it is not accounted for, then the statistics are misleading.

By its nature, of course, there is no precise measurement of the underground economy. But while there is wide disagreement about its actual level, there is wide agreement that it is *growing*.

Why?

Consider some recent trends in our society that would tend to *increase* sharply the amount of underground economic activity:

- Increased illegal immigration. Not only won't illegals report earnings to the nice census lady who asks for information for the current population survey, they won't even be around to talk to the nice census lady.
- Increases in crime, particularly drugs and theft.
- Increases in means-tested transfer payments. Every person getting a check from the government who might not get it if his or her income was higher, is a good candidate for nonreporting of income. This very much includes some very upright elderly citizens between the ages of sixty-five and seventy whose Social Security payments are reduced if they earn more than minimal levels.
- Increases in taxes. Some people ultimately say, "to hell with it, I'm paying enough already," and don't report income to IRS, or to census, or to anyone else.
- Increased self-employment. As will be noted later, this has gone up substantially in recent years, rising 30 percent faster than total employment since 1970. This includes the Avon lady, the Tupperware lady and sidewalk vendors. Statistically, self-employment and tax evasion go together like love and living together. One IRS study showed that 47 percent of workers who classified themselves as independent contractors *did not report ANY earnings for income tax purposes*! Also contributory: a sharp increase (44 percent from 1970–80) of

people who were "moonlighting in own business" and of people working at home (11 percent of the workforce in 1983), typically tempting situations from which to stash a few bucks out of harm's way.

- Increased inflation—the cost of living went up by 156 percent from 1970 to 1983. People feel squeezed, even if their incomes have increased correspondingly. They are pushed into higher tax brackets ("bracket creep") and resist by evading taxes, and then don't like to report their evaded income to census takers.
- Increased interest rates. The IRS says a large proportion of interest income is never reported (up to 32 percent). As rates went up, a disproportionate amount of money was paid out in interest—and not reported.
- Increased burden of regulatory licensing and labor laws which have to be complied with by above-board workers.

And so on. How much all together?

Plenty. And growing.

The estimates of the size of the underground economy span a wide range. There was an official estimate made back in 1978 by the Bureau of Economic Analysis of "only" $100 billion per year.

As the years rolled on, the estimates went up. On the high side is economist Edgar Feige's estimate of $775 billion in 1981. That was 27 percent of GNP, and if tax had been paid on it, the huge federal deficit would have totally disappeared overnight. There are a cluster of estimates in the neighborhood of 10–15 percent of GNP—about $300 to $450 billion in 1982. Perhaps the most notable of these is the one computed by the Congressional Research Service, using a method devised by economist Peter Gutmann and based on Commerce Department and Federal Reserve data. That analysis placed the magnitude of the underground economy at $420 billion in 1981, about 14 percent of the Gross National Product. (That figure was well more than twice the size of the defense budget!)

As noted, most analysts seem to agree that the underground economy is *growing*. Thus the Congressional Research Service/Gutmann study shows that during the Sixties the underground economy averaged 4.5 percent of GNP, while during the Seventies it averaged 10 percent. Even that understates what's been happening. That 10 percent breaks down this way: during the first five years of the Seventies, the underground economy averaged 7.5 percent of GNP, while in the last five years it was 12.5 percent! (And in 1981, as mentioned, it was about 14 percent.)

One general view of the matter is that the underground economy has been increasing in recent years at a rate 2.5 times faster than the measured economy—all of it uncounted in our income statistics!

Another major understatement of income growth in America stems from the tremendous increase in recent years of federally disbursed "noncash" benefits, which are not counted in the Census statistics, either the per capita or social unit ones. One estimate shows that the market value of such benefits has soared from $6 billion per year in 1965 to $99 billion per year in 1982, in constant 1982 dollars—an increase of 1,650 percent! The big-ticket items in this category are food stamps, Medicaid, Medicare and rent supplements.

In addition, growing numbers of middle-class Americans receive growing amounts of noncash (and therefore noncounted) income from their employers. Group health plans are the most significant of these, which these days may include dental, psychiatric, and optometric services.

The Census Bureau estimates that nine out of ten Americans receive some noncash benefit! By 1980, noncash transfers (government monies to poor and nonpoor, plus employer fringe benefits) probably amounted to about $200 billion! That was more than 9 percent of all personal income, compared to perhaps 4 percent for 1970. That missing extra 5 percent per year does not show up in income growth statistics because it is delivered in services not cash. But those services cost real money—and they are real income.

Beyond all that—and that is a lot to move beyond—was a distortion in the housing portion of the Consumer Price Index that has had the effect of diminishing census-measured personal and family income by about 6 percent over the last twelve years. One more log on the fire of income underestimation.

So then, almost everywhere we look, there are factors that mask and dilute real income growth, both family income and per capita income. Older families, younger families, smaller families, female-headed families, all pull down the social-unit statistics, with only the rise in two-earner families to compensate.

The underground economy, the rise in noncash income, and overstated inflation data act to depress not only the rise in family and household income, but per capita income as well.

This sounds like a statistical argument. It is not. Statistics reflect society. Our society is changing; we ride a surfboard atop a sociological tidal wave. Old people are living longer, Baby Boom babies are growing up, women are more independent, the birthrate plunges. We flout the tax men (and other authorities), our government disburses huge sums, workers take their raises in fringe benefits, inflation grows.

Our society is changing in deep ways. When it changes, statistics must reflect those structural changes. In the case of income, that job has not yet been fully accomplished. Real income growth is understated.

By how much is it understated? Hard to say.

A few tenths of a percent or so for the underground economy, another few tenths for changing family structure, yet a few more tenths for noncash income, a smidgen for the housing inflation miscalculation—*every year*, year in and year out, compounding itself inexorably—adds up to real money.

Remember: we are talking about *growth* rates, which only rise one, two or three percent per year. We are talking about how fast things are getting better. These are highly leveraged rates. If you add a few tenths of growth here and a half a percent there, the real growth rate goes way up.

We began this chapter by showing a 28 percent increase in per capita income from 1970 to 1983 using Bureau of Economic Analysis data. It seems clear (to this author at least) that that is not only a better number than family and household numbers, but in itself lower than the reality of the rise.

There is, by the way, plenty of additional statistical evidence confirming the idea of real income growth. Thus, real "disposable" income (after tax) is also up over time—confounding conservatives who like to say income is up but it's all taken by the government. Hourly compensation was up the least but it was up by almost 10 percent, and in any event, was distorted downward by the changed configuration of the labor force. Earnings by specific occupation were up. The number of households with annual incomes of more than $35,000 (measured in constant dollars) rose two and a half times faster than the nation's total household count. Moreover, what's happened, has happened across the board.

Writing in *American Demographics* magazine in December of 1983, economist Fabian Linden summed it up well: ". . . each year, except for intermittent recessions, millions of American households move from lower to middle-income brackets, and other millions move from the middle to the well-to-do brackets." Linden goes on to predict that the movement up the income scale will accelerate in the 1980s as the Baby Boom babies mature and move into those age brackets always associated with higher earnings.

All this creates a real problem. The basic media story of the last dozen or so years has been an unrelieved tattoo of stagflation, recession, unemployment, and foreign competition. Yet the material in chapter 20 shows real macroeconomic growth. The material in chapter 21 from the *Statistical Abstract* shows real growth in personal expenditures. The data presented here, I believe, show clearly that we have made substantial progress on the personal income front. Subsequent chapters—about housing, women, blacks, the elderly among other subjects—will further verify these trends.

Reader, beware!

Sooner or later you are going to have to make a choice: media—or data.

CHAPTER 23

Poor-mouthing

THE POLITICS OF POVERTY

A big real increase in income in recent years. Americans buying cars, going to the symphony, playing golf, traveling.

Fine. But what about poor people?

The troubled, tangled story of "fighting poverty" characterizes the bizarre manner in which we sometimes deal with statistical reality, social reality and social policy in the United States.

It is a story of activism, politics, media megabucks, and statistical sloppiness. It is a classic case history of our earlier thought: *good news is bad news.*

The poverty story, as a big, recent, American story, began in the early 1960s. John F. Kennedy had become President. Supposedly, he had "learned" about poverty while campaigning in the West Virginia primary in 1960. An important book about poverty, *The Other America* by Michael Harrington, was published in 1963. Harrington's book made the point that the poor were still very much with us—forty to fifty million of them, Harrington estimated. These poor, Harrington said, were harder to notice than in earlier times because the form of poverty had changed. People were not gaunt from hunger; they did not wear ragged clothes. They were, he said, the "invisible poor."

The idea of poverty as a national, unrecognized, scandal took a quantum jump when President Lyndon B. Johnson declared the "war on poverty" early in 1964. It was a feisty moment in Washington. The poverty warriors seemed to give birth to a new program every day: Headstart, VISTA, Community Action, Rat Control, Job Corps, Neighborhood Youth Corps, to name a few.

At about this time (1965), government statisticians agreed on a way to measure poverty, and the poverty statistics soon began to pour forth like a mighty stream.

There was a predicate behind all this poverty-pushing: poverty in America was a scandal, it needed discovering, it needed measuring, it needed a war, because nothing was being done about it in America.

That idea, while politically and tactically sound, was substantively plain wrong. That judgment is made with a bit of forelock-tugging and foot-shuffling. Your author was a speechwriter for LBJ. During that bubbling time of the midsixties, I often wrote speeches for the President about poverty.

The public LBJ position did not, to say the least, go out of its way to acknowledge earlier progress. The Johnson speeches did not make a point of noting that from 1950 to 1960 (mostly Republican years) the amount of social and welfare expenditures in the United States had more than doubled. Viewed in per capita, constant (1979) dollars, the amount went from $465 per person to $705 per person, a ten-year increase of 52 percent.*

Official poverty numbers for earlier years were not retrospectively calculated until somewhat later, but rest assured that if the numbers were available, the Johnson speeches would not have stressed the point that the "official" poverty rate dropped from 33 percent of the population to 18 percent during the time period 1949 to 1964. Of course, if you think about it now, such a decline is almost self-evident. After all, those were years of solid economic growth: more people in America were doing better than ever before, and a rising tide lifts many boats.

---

* In fairness to me, as author, if not speechwriter: in *This U.S.A.* (which I wrote in collaboration with Richard Scammon and which was published in 1965) we pointed out that while the problem of poverty was real, the popular estimates of its extent were grossly inflated. After reviewing the income data of the 1950s, we said: ". . . the rich are getting richer—and so are the poor."

Why didn't LBJ stress continuity of progress in fighting poverty?

As will be noted in several contexts later on, politics does not work that way. The possibility that LBJ would have said in a speech, "Well, it's true that there was much headway made in fighting poverty before I became President . . ." is about as unlikely as the idea that anyone of his speechwriters would have written that speech for him. LBJ had a crisis factory at work in the White House, and crisis factories produce crises, not balanced assessments of progress. The media, needless to say, reported on the activity of the crisis factory.

There is a legitimate rationale for such crisis-galvanizing. Even if poverty was coming down, even if America was spending more on social welfare programs, that didn't mean America was doing enough about it.

It was Lyndon Johnson's view that we ought to do more. And "more" is often only do-able when the public is aroused. (This idea, that bad news may help us, only *appears* to be contrary to the theme of this book. Johnson did not give up wrong news—he didn't say poverty was worse, only that there was too much of it, while neglecting to mention progress. This idea will be pursued later.)

In any event, in the Sixties, more was done. Consider what happened. Measured in constant (1979) per capita dollars, social and welfare spending in America went from $705 in 1960 to $1,329 in 1970—an increase during the decade of 89 percent. That compares to a 52 percent increase during the 1950s—a big difference, and moreover, growing from a higher base.

———

There was, to coin an acronym, ITROI—an Increase in the Rate of Increase.

The percentage of people in poverty declined in a striking way—almost halved. In 1960 the percentage in poverty was 22.2 percent. By 1970, it was down to 12.6 percent.

How was this good news of the Sixties treated? What did Americans learn of it?

In the midsixties, when race riots broke out in American cities it was repeated as an article of faith that they were caused by "deteriorating conditions of poor people in the ghetto." (The data showed exactly the opposite.)

As we moved on in the decade, it was said, "The war on poverty is being abandoned in favor of the war in Vietnam." (As a share of federal budget outlays, "defense" went down from 49 percent to 40 percent from 1960 to 1970, while the share for "human resources" went up from 28 percent to 39 percent. All this during the Vietnam War!)

Good news was bad news.

Looking at the rhetoric of the Sixties through an ideological prism, it should be noted that it was liberals who were making the case that conditions were deteriorating for poor people in the ghettos. It was liberals who said the war on poverty was being abandoned for the war in Vietnam.

Conservatives were saying other things, but none of them positive, either. They said of the effort to reduce poverty, "It will never work." They noted with glee and wonder that the federal government spent more per year to put a boy through Job Corps than it cost to put a boy through Harvard. They called a federal program to eliminate rats "a civil rats" program.

It was a time for big laughs.

No recognition for progress in the Fifties. Scorn for progress in the Sixties. Then the numbers began to change in several ways during the 1970s.

It was, recall, the advent of the era of DITROI. And it was, in more ways than you think, the beginning of the cashless economy: credit cards for the well-to-do, food stamps for the poor.

The decrease in the rate of increase affected not only the economy generally, but the shares that economy offered to poor people. Consider this progression in the broadest measurement we have to gauge the government commitment to the needy:

SOCIAL WELFARE EXPENDITURES
AS A PERCENT OF GNP

		Percentage Increase From Prior Share
1950	8.9%	
1960	10.5%	18%
1970	15.2%	45%
1980	18.7%	23%

Source: U.S. Social Security Administration.

Clearly, the pattern of change in the 1970s was different from the 1960s. The share of GNP for social welfare did not increase by almost half in a single decade as it did in the Sixties.

But spending kept going up substantially. In fact, because it started from a higher base, the actual number of dollars per capita (after discounting for inflation) went up more in the Seventies than in the Sixties! In 1970 a total of $1,354 per person was spent on social and welfare spending. In 1980, it was $2,140. The total amount in 1980 was $492 billion—more than the *total* GNP of the United Kingdom that year! Almost half a trillion dollars!

Here the story gets muddled. The money in the 1970s was being spent on social welfare expenditures all right. But was it helping poor people?

The muddle is compounded by the sometimes strange nature of the American statistical establishment. The poverty standard was created as a *cash* standard at a time when *cash* was the basic weapon of the poverty warrior. The sequence of poverty (cash only) numbers looks like this:

PERCENTAGE OF PEOPLE BELOW THE POVERTY LEVEL

1959	22.4%
1969	12.1%
1979	11.6%

Source: U.S. Bureau of the Census.

Liberals screamed. No progress! Nixon, Ford and Carter don't care about the poor!

But the no-progress view of poverty ignored one big fact: as the various poverty programs grew during the late 1960s and throughout the 1970s, most of the government help going to the poor people (almost 70 percent by 1980) was not in *cash* but in *services:*

Consider the food stamp program. It began in 1961 with a $13 million appropriation. By 1970 it was at $551 million—about half a billion dollars. In 1982, the amount of federal outlays for food stamps was $10.2 *billion*! Over 21 million persons were receiving food stamp aid. That involved one out of every eleven Americans!

But *not a penny* of the value of those food stamps was counted in the official calculation of "poverty" in America. Food stamps—although they can buy what money can buy—are not "cash." They are "in-kind" benefits.

Or consider Medicaid. Back in 1970 the total spending on Medicaid was $4.8 billion. By 1981 it had gone up to $30.4 billion. After inflation, the 1981 spending was almost three times the 1970 amount! Now, in its effect, Medicaid gives poor people a credit card to buy a critical service from the best vendors there are. Poor people with a Medicaid card can, and do, go to doctors and hospitals of their choice.

Now, if these medical services are bought, they cost a substantial amount of money. Yet, for all its value, not a penny of Medicaid services was counted as income to poor people. After all, Medicaid is said to be an "in-kind" payment, not a "cash" payment.

And so it goes. When it comes to computing poverty, not only are food stamps and Medicaid not counted, but neither are public housing subsidies. Those are the big noncash programs that aren't counted. Some smaller programs that aren't counted include legal services, day care, transportation services, counseling, energy assistance, educational programs, and the Earned Income Tax Credit, which provides tax reimbursement for the working poor.

The growth of "in-kind" transfers in just the big areas (food, medical, and housing) went, incredibly, from $5.8 billion per year back in 1965 to $98.5 billion per year in 1982—*in constant 1982 dollars!* Yet, federal statisticrats did not count that money in computing the amount of poverty.

Now, these service programs were typically initiated and expanded by liberals. Accordingly, one would think that liberals would say, "Statisticrat, please count those services in your poverty computations. Those are good programs. They are working. They are the equivalent of cash. Poverty is declining. Our liberal philosophy is paying dividends."

That is not what liberals said in the 1970s. What they did say was: "America has abandoned the poor. Poverty is not being reduced. Just look at the numbers."

It has been said of liberals that when setting up a firing squad they will form into a circle. Case proved. Liberal programs dismissed by liberals. New liberal political rallying cry: "We have failed, let us continue!"

The conservatives, abandoning earlier Neanderthal criticisms, dealt with the issue in two entirely contradictory ways.

First, they agreed with the liberals. Poverty wasn't coming down, right? We're spending a lot of money on it, right? It must be wasted money, right? It's going to poverty pimps and beltway bandits, the conservatives said. The generic political phrase for it was "throwing money down a rat hole," and, made more credible by liberals trumpeting failure, a profitable political phrase it was. In the broadest sense, it was one of the key phrases that legitimized—and helped elect—Ronald Reagan.

At the same time, other conservatives were saying something else: "Count it. Count all those in-kind services that are being given to the poor. Give a cash valuation to the food stamps, Medicaid, and housing subsidies."

One Congressional Budget Office study counted "in-kind" benefits in 1976. It showed the poverty rate not at the official rate of 11.8 percent, but at 6.4 percent, which is rather different. It became a very controversial study.

Liberals attacked it, but conservatives ran with the numbers. By the end of the decade, conservatives were saying poverty was licked. We won! End of the war! Hooray! (Of course, they added, it was only a Pyrrhic victory: poor people were made dependent on the Big Daddy welfare state and had their initiative stolen.)

Consider this rancid mixture of politics, ideology, and statistics.

Liberals said liberalism *wasn't* working, therefore spend more on it.

Conservatives said liberalism *was* working, therefore stop it—except when they said liberalism wasn't working, therefore stop it.

Such is the high level of discourse in our nation's capital.

Finally in 1980, the Senate Committee on Appropriations directed that a full-bodied study be conducted on the impact of "in-kind" services on the poverty data. The Census Bureau commissioned Dr. Timothy Smeeding of the University of Utah to direct the study. By 1982, the study—showing 1979 rates—was ready.

The Smeeding study calculated the effect of in-kind services on poverty in nine different ways. Using the Smeeding "market value" approach for food, housing, and all medical care, the 1979 poverty rate comes out to be not 11.1 percent but 6.4 percent.

Trace now the progress in poverty:

PERCENTAGE OF POPULATION
BELOW THE POVERTY LEVEL

	Official	*Counting Noncash Income*
1959	22.4%	—*
1969	12.1%	—*
1979	11.6%	6.4%

* Not calculated. But the government supplied very few noncash benefits in 1959 and 1969, so the actual poverty rate cannot have been very different from the official rate in those years.
Source: U.S. Bureau of Census—Technical Paper 50.

Or, very roughly: poverty was halved in one decade, then halved again in the next. That is a Super Number.

That good news was reported as bad news. The numbers were attacked again. For by the time the statistics came out, poverty was going up, a conservative President was vulnerable on the issue and the circumstances of the poverty debate had changed again: a double-dip recession began in 1980 and got worse in mid-1981.

The recession-induced increase in poverty—including (as is proper) noncash benefits—looked like this:

PERCENTAGE OF POPULATION
BELOW POVERTY LINE

1959	22.4%
1969	12.1%
1979	6.8%*
1980	7.9%*
1981	9.0%*
1982	10.0%*

* Includes non-cash benefits, which were negligible in 1959 and 1969.
Data from "Estimates of Poverty Including the Value of Non-Cash Benefits: 1979 to 1982" (Bureau of the Census). The study represents a continuation and institutionalization of the Smeeding study discussed earlier. Because of procedural changes the Smeeding 6.4 percent rate for 1979 converts to 6.8 percent above. Both the Smeeding work and the new Census series offer *nine* different ways of calculating poverty to include noncash benefits. All substantially reduce the cash-only "official" rate. The rates

This was a serious development, clearly losing ground that had been gained earlier. Were poverty to continue trending upward in this fashion, it might be worthy of a Negative Super Number.

But recessions, even twinned and deep ones like those in 1980 and 1981–82, don't last forever. As might be imagined, 1982 was followed by 1983. And 1983 turned out to be a full year of robust recovery. As this book goes to press, we have seen six more months of economic growth in 1984 and economic projections are upbeat at least through the end of the year.

After a lag time, such a vigorous economic recovery tends to make itself felt favorably on the poverty rates—primarily because unemployment rates come down.

The poverty data for 1983 are not yet available as this book goes to press, but it is not likely that they will be much different from the 1982 numbers. After all, while in 1982 unemployment went *up* from a relatively *low* base, in 1983 unemployment went *down* from a relatively *high* base—the *average* unemployment rate for the two years was about the same (9.7% vs. 9.6%.) But 1984 is a very different story: an unemployment rate dropping from an already diminished base—reproducing an average of 7.7% for the first six months, with a 7.1% rate in June, 1984.

Accordingly, I offer a trend before its time:

PERCENT OF POPULATION BELOW POVERTY LINE

1959	22.4%
1969	12.1%
1979	6.8%*
1982	10.0%*
1983	10 %* (guesstimate)
1984	8–9 %* (guesstimate)

* As earlier, including noncash income, market value basis.

shown above are the "market" valuations of food, housing and medical benefits, which account for about 90 percent—but not all—of the noncash benefits going to the poor. It is the method that reduces poverty most, and the one many economists think best reflects empirical reality. The medical component of the rate includes "institutional care," which causes some statistical problems and may properly be said to slightly overstate the amount of poverty reduction by about three-tenths of 1 percent.

So, after all is said and done, with a bad bump in the road, poverty in America will probably have gone down by almost two-thirds in a quarter of a century!

Super Number.

═══

Well, in the early 1980s something else was going on as well. It began in 1981, when Ronald Reagan sent his program to the Congress—and torn fur flew.

Reagan said it was time for an end to the decades of waste, fraud, and abuse, of bloated liberal giveaways, of pumping up the poverty purveyors. This would be done (he intimated) by his new budget, which featured "cuts." These proposed "cuts" made him very popular with conservatives, and with many middle-of-the-roaders, too.

Democrats responded by saying, in effect, ohmigod, that barbarian is cutting this and cutting that, cutting food stamps, cutting school lunches, cutting student loans, cutting welfare—he's savaging poor people, he's taking from the needy and giving to the greedy, and he's doing all that *by cutting the Safety Net*. The Democrats' opposition to the "cuts" made them very popular with many of their key constituents: poor people, students, blacks, the education establishment, the welfare establishment, government workers, and so on.

At about the time that "cuts" became Topic A, the economy went into an authentic recessionary nosedive. Unemployment went up, interest rates stayed high, an economic theory called "supply-side" was deemed to be "radical." Networks in rating wars competed with one another to show the tragedy close up. Food lines were standard evening television fare, learned psychologists expounded theories about the emasculating effects of unemployment, a few suicide stories spiced the cake. Then there appeared in the *Atlantic* magazine an interview with Reagan's director of the Office of Management and Budget, David Stockman.

Stockman's remarks generated a great controversy. He said— and/or it was said he said, although he said that what he said wasn't really what he meant when he said it—that Reagan's policy wasn't really supply-side, it was old-fashioned, conservative, trickle-down economics, snuck in by a Trojan horse, designed on the back of an envelope, validated by changing the computer program to make the printout fit the scenario, and besides, things were so chaotic no one really knew what was going on.

For this candid revelation of how the budget process usually works (conservatives try to sell conservative ideas, liberals try to sell liberal ideas, and both sides work it out on the back of an envelope first, by computer second) Stockman was "taken to the woodshed," not only by the President, but by most everyone else.

It was generally assumed in media land that the Stockman confession only validated the growing idea that trickle-down was destroying the Safety Net, and that the poor were the victims.

Well, Stockman said something else in that *Atlantic* article that was mentioned a few times and then forgotten. This:

> There was less there than met the eye. . . . Let's say that you and I walked outside and I waved a wand and said, I've just lowered the temperature from 110 to 78. Would you believe me? What this was, was a cut from an artificial Congressional Budget Office base.

Two budgets later, in 1983, the *New York Times* ran a glossary of budget terminology. It defined "cut" as follows: "a cut is often just a smaller increase."

It is true: what cut means in Washington is not what cut means in English.

The original (Fiscal Year 1982) proposed Reagan social welfare "cut" of $39 billion was only a *cut* from a projected *increase*. It actually increased the total amounts of social welfare spending. It was, to use a by now familiar phrase, a "decrease in the rate of increase." Moreover, as the legislative brokerage went on, Reagan didn't even get much of the DITROI that he had proposed.

Contrary to reports, and although there is plenty of room for genuine political debate about priorities, the Safety Net was not sundered.

Verification: First, for a working definition of the Safety Net, consider an aggregation of all the federal payments made to individuals for food, housing, medical care, welfare, Social Security, unemployment, and so forth. (These include both "cash" and "in-kind" payments.)

Consider two time frames next. One runs from 1970 to 1981, chosen to show the flow of the 1970s, concluding with the last year for which President Jimmy Carter had general control of the federal budget. The second runs from 1981 to 1985, chosen to show the impact of the Reagan years, beginning with the last Carter year as a base and running through the budget proposals for the latest available Reagan year.

What happened to the Safety Net? After discounting for inflation, this:

FEDERAL SPENDING ON SOCIAL SAFETY NET

1970	$155 billion
1981	$367 billion
1985	$403 billion

(Calculated in constant 1983 dollars.)
Source: Office of Management and Budget.

Well, clearly the net has expanded.* The growth, however, has recently been diminished sharply. During the first period (1970–81), spending on the Safety Net increased by a yearly average of 8.2 percent. During the second period, spending on the Safety Net increased by 2.4 percent per year. That's a big difference, particularly so if you recall that the growth rate must offset population growth of about 1 percent per year during the period.

There is a somewhat sharper difference between periods if we look at the Safety Net not in terms of a simple spending increase, but in terms of its share of the Gross National Product. Such a "share" mea-

---

* There is no universally accepted definition as to which programs constitute the Safety Net. It should be understood that many of the "payments to individuals" totaled here go to persons and households that are far from destitute. Unemployment insurance, for instance, often goes to people who, while in a tough spot at the time, are situated firmly in what we would call the "middle class." Just the same, it is not inappropriate to describe such payments as part of a Safety Net, for they do break economic falls, and in their absence many otherwise middle-class recipients would be badly off indeed.

For those who would prefer to define the Safety Net as only those programs which serve the already poor, as demonstrated by means tests, economist John Weicher of the American Enterprise Institute has provided the numbers in a book entitled *Maintaining the Safety Net*. From 1970 to 1980, federal expenditures on Low-Income Benefit Programs, in constant 1983 dollars, went from $26.1 billion to $60.3 billion. In 1983, expenditures went up to $66.8 billion. Within that total, some programs went up—Supplementary Security Income (SSI), Housing Assistance, Food and Nutrition Assistance, Medicaid—and some went down—AFDC, Low-income Energy Assistance, Earned Income Tax Credit. But none went down drastically, and the total was up.

In the Human Capital Services area, which provides secondary services—training programs, community centers, counseling and so forth—the changes were more severe. Total constant dollar spending went from $16.6 billion in 1970, to $27.8 billion in 1980, to $17.7 billion in 1983. This reflected primarily the Reagan administration's decision to scrap the controversial CETA program.

surement can give us a good answer to the question, "Is society lessening its commitment to the welfare state?"

The numbers go down a bit, and look like this:

SHARE OF THE GNP GOING TO
SAFETY NET EXPENDITURES

1970	6.8%
1981	11.5%
1985	11.3%

Source: Office of Management and Budget.

Four major points emerge from the various sets of numbers presented here.

- The Net has continued to grow in absolute terms
- Roughly speaking, the *growth* of the net has slowed way down
- The *share* of our wealth going to the Net has declined slightly
- The Net remains intact.

There are a gross of caveats to put up against these facts—enough surely to fuel the political debate for the rest of the decade.

Caveat: it can be legitimately argued whether the Safety Net held because of the policies of the Reagan administration, or in spite of them. Surely, Democratic political pressure made it more difficult for Reagan to cut social welfare spending. On the other hand, even the original Reagan budget proposals still maintained a real rise, albeit smaller than what ultimately emerged in the executive-legislative budget process.

Caveat: Within the broad rubric of the Safety Net, some programs were in fact actually cut in real dollars, while others went up. There are legitimate arguments about the balance of these changes, and the arguments are important because not all expenditures in the safety net go to the disadvantaged. Some—there is a dispute about how much—goes to the middle class.

Thus, it is noted, spending on food stamps, a program for the disadvantaged, has gone down in real dollars. True enough, it is countered, but the decrease has been minimal, there were in fact some real abuses in the program, and the cuts within the program affected not the truly needy but those at the marginal upper edge of the program.

Caveat: It is also noted that a great part of the Net is Social Security, that Social Security has absorbed most of the increases in the Net, and that Social Security is essentially a "middle-class" program. All that is essentially so, but if the calculation of the Net is made without Social Security, *it still rises* in real dollars—by 7 percent from 1981 to 1985.

And there is something else. It is rarely stressed that one big reason Social Security is largely a "middle-class" program is because of a strange reason: it works. When this author started writing books on demographics in the early 1960s, there was a simple way to locate poverty in America: look under the column marked "over 65." But today, tens of millions of middle-class elderly are middle class *because* growing Social Security payments make them middle class. Social Security is their middle-class Safety Net in the most literal way. (See chapter 26.)

Caveat: it is maintained that the Net only went up because built-in programs were triggered by the recession. Although the broadly defined Safety-Net spending actually went up somewhat, even if it is calculated without recessionary trigger programs, there is some general validity to the thrust of that observation. But then again, that is the purpose of the Net: to save people from a precipitous fall when times are tough. It did that.

Caveats aplenty: But when all is said and done one big fact: the Safety Net remains in place.

———

Consider now what has happened to poverty during four tumultuous decades of American life, and how these developments were treated.

In the 1950s, those allegedly do-nothing Eisenhower years, a great deal was indeed done: poverty went down, and spending on the poor went up. But the rallying cry of Sixties social-welfare activists was that America had been dead in the water during the Fifties. This view, of course, was picked up by the press.

In the 1960s, America went through a big boom. The poverty rate went down sharply. Massive social-welfare programs were put in place. All this is recognized today as part of the good old days when America really cared. At the time, however, it was trumpeted in the press and on television that the war on poverty was a victim of the war in Vietnam, that riots were caused by deteriorating conditions.

In the 1970s, as massive amounts of in-kind services were extended to the poor, legitimately reducing poverty, it was said by liberals that we were no longer making progress, and by conservatives that rip-off was the order of the day—booze bought with food stamps, welfare cheats driving Cadillacs. You could see it all on "Twenty-Twenty."

In the 1980s, when the system faced a huge twin recession, poverty went up (three percentage points in three years) and the Safety Net not only held, but was expanded somewhat. What we saw on television and read about in the press were pictures and prose about street people, bag ladies, suicides caused by economic desperation, and greedy conservative legislative strategies, all encouraging the idea that the Safety Net had been ripped apart.

Now, as America is in a recovery, and poverty contracts again, the election-year political imperatives call for one more denunciation of a heartless government.

There is a pattern here. Whatever is happening on the poverty front is reported as bad news, one way or the other, even when the news is good, as it typically has been. *Good news is bad news.*

There is a stunning aspect to this. Making poor people into middle-class people is at the root of the American experiment. Every shred of evidence we have points to the fact that in forty-odd years since World War II, more of this bootstrapping happened than ever before, amid some monumental strains.

There are several sets of legitimate questions to be asked about this very positive development.

The first set: why did it happen? Did it occur because the government played an ever bigger role? Did it occur because the private economy boomed? Did perhaps the increased government spending erode the pace of the economic boom, thereby indirectly slowing the rate at which poor people were progressing? Did the economy boom in part because the expanded social services provided a more educated, healthier, more secure labor force?

Good questions. Find long answers in someone else's book. My short answer: poor people are better off because of *both* economic growth and governmental activity. Economic growth is more important right now than a further growth in social services. But we need both.

The second set of legitimate questions: After all the governmental help—all the food stamps, welfare payments, rent supplements, and Medicaid—have we eroded the values of those who still remain poor in America, robbing them of the psychological tools to lift themselves further from difficult circumstances? Have we created a dependency class? Is the Net too high for its own good?

Good questions. They will be discussed later. (See Part III, "Values.")

The third set of questions: Did we rob Peter to pay Paul? More precisely, did we rob the Pentagon to pay for poverty? If we did, have we left ourselves prey to a condition worse than poverty—geopolitical weakness in an unstable world?

Good questions. While poverty spending soared as a fraction of GNP, defense spending shrank. At the same time Soviet military spending went way up. Are we vulnerable? See chapter 48.

What is important to note about each of these sets of good questions is this: all acknowledge the reality that far fewer people are poor in America today than before. That is a central fact of our time. It is denied or diluted regularly by politicians and activists making speeches—liberals and conservatives—each with vigor, each for opposite motives. Liberals say we're not spending enough. That, they feel, will make us feel guilty and make us spend more. Conservatives say the spending isn't doing any good. That, they feel, will make us spend less. All this—negative left and negative right—is trumpeted in our newspapers and on our television programs.

Is there something wrong with a society that won't recognize and report its central successes?

CHAPTER 24

Recession on the Nightly News

UNEMPLOYMENT

Unemployment is often a tragedy.

That must be said before everything else that follows here. A person willing to work who is unable to find work represents an economic tragedy, a sociological tragedy, and frequently a deep personal tragedy.

In December of 1982, at the trough of the recession, the official unemployment rate as calculated by the Bureau of Labor Statistics was 10.7 percent. That was, indeed, "The highest unemployment rate since the Great Depression," to use a phrase that has become familiar.

Are we perhaps dealing with a negative Super Number?

=====

The unemployment story properly became a big story during the big recession. Television news told us all about it. As the reporters talked, we were shown pictures of worn people in long unemployment lines. We saw soup lines; haggard faces waiting for free food. Often the camera would pan across the threadbare forms of "street people." We saw scenes of makeshift trailer parks outside of Houston, where desperate Americans informed us that even the Sunbelt had no jobs available. We saw the agony of a foreclosed mortgage—a family severed from its home. And there was Studs Terkel telling us it was the Great Depression all over again.

Particular attention was paid to auto and steel workers laid off for a long time, whose unemployment benefits had run out and whose jobs, we were told, would never be restored. Vigorous men in the prime of life talked on camera about an erosion of self-worth and human dignity, about how they could not look their wives and children in the eyes.

Tragedy, to be sure.

At this point questions arise. Tragedy for how long? Tragedy for how many? Tragedy how deep? Tragedy compared to what and when?

These are hard questions to ask against a televised backdrop of hungry people, foreclosed homes, and scarred psyches. But they are questions that should be asked. After all, if nothing else, how can a wise remedy be shaped if the physician is not prepared to measure the extent of the illness?

We proceed on two tracks. We look at the numbers. We look at the images.

First, we ask, is the tragedy of unemployment accurately measured by the official Bureau of Labor Statistics unemployment rate, replete with decimal point? It seems so precise, yet that figure is the subject of great contention. Behind the contention about how long, how many, how deep, compared-to-what-and-when, is an omnibus question: what is the "real" rate of unemployment?

There is, after all, a "real" rate of growth of the Gross National Product, that is, a rate corrected for inflation. Is it also necessary to correct the unemployment rate to give us a better picture of what's been happening?

And second, perhaps more important: is the reality of unemployment accurately reflected by what we see and feel when we watch television? Whatever the actual rate of unemployment—does the media depict it as it is?

=====

It is complicated. Unemployment hawks, typically conservatives, take note of a statistical paradox: there is a lot of official unemployment even when the economy bubbles along at "full" employment. Thus, in the good economic year of 1978, the official unemployment rate was 6.0 percent.

That six-or-so percent represents the so-called "frictional" rate of unemployment.* The "frictional" rate of unemployment, as it turns out, is an aspect less of unemployment than of how we *measure* unemployment. Our system of data-gathering is based on a telephone survey supplemented with personal interviews, that asks, at root, two key questions: "Are you out of work?" and "Are you looking for work?" If the respondent answers "Yes" to both questions, he or she is officially "unemployed."

It is, when you think about it, a weird system.

It means, for example, that it is virtually impossible to be "employed" without first being "unemployed." The brightest graduate of Harvard, actively being wooed by a dozen corporations, is "unemployed." He is "out of work" and also "looking for work." Similarly, the teenager looking for his *first* job is *automatically* unemployed. The high-tech engineer who has *quit* a job before obtaining a new one is counted as unemployed. The woman who has moved to another city with her husband, whose company has transferred him, and who has left one part-time job and starts looking for another, is unemployed. They are all "out of work" and "looking for work," and all are adding to the grand national total unemployment rate.

But wait a minute. That Harvard guy isn't really "unemployed" by any sensible use of the word. Why should that teenager be "unemployed"—everyone has to start sometime. That high-tech fellow wasn't fired—he quit. Why is he counted as "unemployed"?

And so, the hawks say, this system overstates what's going on. Let's judge unemployment the right way: forget about all those folks who aren't "really" unemployed, let's blow away that "frictional" rate and total just those folks who have *lost their jobs.*

---

* Conservative economists peg the frictional rate at 6–7 percent; liberal economists at 4–6 percent.

Always willing to please, the BLS has one statistical series that does just that: it measures only "job losers." In December of 1982, the worst month of the recession, while the "official" unemployment rate was 10.7 percent, the "job loser" rate was 6.4 percent. That's still a lot, but quite a difference from 10.7 percent—the difference at that time between 11.9 million and 7.1 million unemployed people in America.

Fair enough. But of course the unemployment doves, typically liberals, look at some other facets of the unemployment puzzle. They too want to come up with a "real" rate of unemployment.

And so they ask, quite properly, what about "discouraged" workers? There were an average of 1.3 million of them in that worst month. They were "out of work," all right, but they were not counted as officially unemployed because they were not "looking for work." The BLS survey reveals, however, that the *reason* these 1.3 million were not looking for work was because they believed that there was no work out there to be had—they were "discouraged." Doves say they should be counted as "unemployed"; after all, it's the terrible economic conditions that are keeping them from looking for work, and consequently, from working.

Moreover, ask the doves, what about part-time workers? There were about twenty-one million of them in America in 1983. About one-third of them, a little more than six million, were working part-time for "economic reasons"—typically because *they could not find full-time work.* Count them as unemployed, say the doves.

Once again, BLS obliges. In one series, it adds to the official number both the "discouraged" workers and the appropriate share of workers in the "part-time" economy. From those additions emerge yet another "real" unemployment rate: 15.3 percent in the fourth quarter of 1982, when the official rate was 10.5 percent. A lot higher.

In short, it is very complicated. Yet a "real" rate, if it can be fashioned, is very important.

Recall now our two tracks of investigation: data and images.

My own sense of the matter is that, on the data side, unemployment has been overstated for some reasons that will be seen in a moment, that the situation will improve, but that it is still a severe problem. I concede, however, that the data argument can go on interminably among people of good will and good sense, each team backed by serried phalanxes of solid numbers.

I offer, however, no such charity on the image side.

Is unemployment better or worse than what we have been led to believe by the nightly TV horrors? How does it stack up against homelessness, hunger, psychological debilitation, loss of unemployment benefits, long-term futility about jobs that structurally disappear beneath silent smokestacks?

My answer is: unemployment conditions, for all their tragedy, are substantially better than what we have been led to believe by the media. Consider now some additional data and ask yourself whether they relate to what *you* have seen on the screen.

The people they show us on television always seem to have been out of work for a year or two. But is unemployment in America long term? Not typically. The *median* duration at the depth of the recent recession was 10.1 weeks, about two-and-a-half months. The *average* duration was 18 weeks, about four months.

Now it is no fun to be unemployed for three or four months; in fact, it is downright nasty. But, I submit, that is a long way from the televised image of "long-term, structural" unemployment. It is a long way from the cliché "he'll never get that job back."

The median length of unemployment in the state with the worst unemployment in America in the worst year for unemployment since the Depression—that would be Michigan, the locus of the then-battered automobile industry—was 21.8 weeks in 1982. That's about five months.

Interestingly, in Michigan unemployment benefits are among the highest in America: up to $200 per week (untaxed). During the recession they were paid for up to 55 weeks, more than twice the length of either the median or average duration of unemployment. That's quite different from the television report that "the Jones family has run out of unemployment benefits." Typically, Americans don't even come close to running out of benefits before they find new work.

Remember all the TV clips of unemployed families where both husband and wife have lost their jobs? BLS data show that among married-couple families experiencing unemployment, about 80 percent had at least one family member working, most of them full-time. In such circumstances unemployment may be tragic, but it is not likely to cut a lifeline.

Another bit of televised misinformation concerned a sin of omission, not commission. There were countless hours devoted (properly) to rising unemployment during the recession. But there was almost no attention paid to the fact that the percentage of people *employed* was near a historic high. The data showed 57.6 percent of the total adult population at work in the worst month of the worst year of the worst recession, *a rate about the same as that for the boom decade of the 1960s.** (Much of the rise is due to the number of women who have entered the labor force.)

Finally, teenage unemployment. It is perhaps the most misunder-stood statistic in the federal arsenal, particularly so in regard to black teenagers, as will be noted in another chapter. The unemployment statistic for all teenagers in the recession year of 1982 was 23 percent. It sounds terrible and television surely made it look terrible: teenage hoods, slack-jawed, vacant eyes, out of work, bound to get into trouble.

The actual story is quite different. The unemployment rate is cal-culated as a function of "the labor force." The labor force, in turn, is comprised of people who are working, or who are out of work but want to work. But about half of American teenagers (48 percent in 1983) are none of the above. Typically, they are full-time students. Thus, they are not "in the labor force," and not counted in the per-centages.

Accordingly, the cited 23 percent unemployment rate is really only about half that when viewed against the total teenage population. (Moreover, in the strange world of unemployment counting, most of those officially "unemployed" teenagers are also full-time students looking for *part-time* work.)

Another way to phrase the reality of teenage unemployment would be like this: of every 100 American teenagers in 1982, only five were not full-time students and were looking for a full-time job. (And of those five, three-quarters had either voluntarily *quit* their last job or were looking for a *first* job.)

And just one other item running against the grain. For all the me-dia hullabaloo about the tragic plight of the Vietnam veterans, their unemployment rate is about the same as nonveterans in the same age brackets, and considerably lower than that of the population as a whole (5.4 percent versus 7.1 percent in June of 1984).

What is the purpose of this exercise?

It is not to diminish the despair of those who suffer. The suffering is real; there is more than enough of it to go around. The unemploy-ment rate did recently reach all time post-Depression highs. As this book is published, the rate is still unacceptably high, although de-clining.

* In June of 1984 the percentage of people *employed* stood at an all-time U.S. high—61 percent.

The point is this: the nature of the unemployment problem in America is not what we have been led to believe. Unemployment does not typically involve street people or bag ladies—and we confer no dignity on the deep psychological problems of bag ladies by suggesting that their plight is due to too many Japanese automobile imports. Nor does unemployment typically involve hunger, at least not by any standard usage of the word.*

These are the extreme cases, to be sure. But the rest of the portrayal of unemployment has been almost as bad.

Their jobs will never be regained. That may be literally accurate but misleading. The data show that unemployed workers *do* go back to work fairly soon. If they do not get their old jobs back, they get other jobs—sometimes better ones, often during a recession, worse ones—

---

* Concerning the homeless: The data are very sketchy. How do you take a census of people who have no addresses? The first systematic (and controversial) national survey of the homeless was released by the Department of Housing and Urban Development in May, 1984. It estimated the homeless numbered 250,000 to 350,000, substantially lower than what had been previously supposed. An argument about the study's validity rages.

What information exists suggests that most of the homeless are not homeless directly because of economic circumstances. A study of New York City shelter clients by the city's Human Resources Administration in 1982 showed that only 19 percent of the individuals in the shelter were indentifiably there because of economic difficulties. The great majority of the rest were there for serious psychiatric, alcohol or drug problems.

In the late 1970s there was a wave of "deinstitutionalization" of mental patients under the theory that they could be treated more humanely and efficiently through outpatient centers and halfway houses "in the community." Unfortunately, many of the liberated ended up in the streets. The number of outpatient centers for the mentally ill expanded greatly during the 1970s (more than doubling) but some critics maintain that penurious governments still didn't do enough. Of course, all this begs a difficult question: in a society that has lenient institutionalization regulations, what can be done for those *who will not consent* to be treated?

As for hunger: The also controversial Reagan-appointed Task Force on Food Assistance reported in 1984 that hunger in America is not a major national problem, that it is not growing, and that adequate assistance resources exist if those in need apply for them. One of the dilemmas the task force faced was deciding what, in present-day America, constitutes hunger.

In a 1983 paper, Senate Budget Committee economist J. William Hoagland pointed to an irony behind the public perception of rising hunger. "The growth in state, local, church and private charity food assistance programs has in fact been stimulated by federal food assistance policies designed to make available surplus agricultural commodities to those organizations. . . ."

but within a few months they are typically back on payroll. See Chapter 33.

The cheese lines. Beneath the (recently raised) net of unemployment insurance is the normal American Safety Net. As we've seen in the last chapter, it is hardly the worse for wear. The cheese is extra, a new "direct commodity distribution program" to help those in need, as well as dairy farmers.

Crime. The networks liked to quote people who told us that the high unemployment rate was driving people to crime. It apparently wasn't. The crime rate was going down. See chapter 40.

Foreclosed homes. At a postrecession peak in the first quarter of 1983, 5.8 percent of all mortgage holders were thirty days or more behind in their payments. Of that 5.8 percent who were delinquent, less than one in eight, about *seven-tenths of 1 percent* of all mortgage holders, faced foreclosure. (Versus rates in the 1970s of about 4.5 percent delinquent and .33 percent facing foreclosure.)

What about diminishment of self-worth and psychological trauma? Are they as typical as they have been portrayed? Are three or four months of unemployment (typical), with unemployment compensation (typical), with the likelihood of a second earner in the family (typical) likely to lead to deep trauma, shattered families, battered wives? In some instances, to be sure, but very surely not typically or anywhere close to typically. Television doesn't lie, it only selects those truths it seeks to dramatize. But the notion, sold to us by television, of ongoing psychological trauma is nowhere near the norm of the unemployment experience in America. The real situation is bad enough without distortion.

But why bother with all these qualifications about televised images? Won't overstatement help galvanize the society to deal with a real problem?

Not in this instance.

First, in the long run, we are better served by facts not fictions.

Second, there is a policy dimension. Images, as much as data and maybe more, form policy.

The numbers are neutral. Conservatives may use the numbers to say, "Unemployment is not as bad as you see on television; government need not do too much." That's one plausible strategy.

But liberals could use those neutral numbers differently. They could remind us that General McClellan didn't attack, and thus lost battles, because he thought the enemy was so powerful and his own resources so paltry.

If liberals were to say that this unemployment situation is only bad, not catastrophic, that the persons in real need could be identified, perhaps they could convince their legislative colleagues, and the public, that the resources needed to deal with it are less than monumental. It's not an insurmountable problem, they might say, so let's attack. That, too, is a plausible strategy.

The images from the TV screen however—starving street people, suicides in trailer parks—render both the conservative and the liberal tactic useless. The correct remedy for what we see on television (were we to fully believe it) is hundreds of billions of dollars of crash aid. That won't happen in a time of megadeficits.

So we are left with the (wrong) perception of a mean society doing nothing important about starving jobless people. Thanks, television.

And finally: Even with all the qualifications, even with all the video-voodoo, does all this unemployment data add up to a Negative Super Number?

In 1982, we did have double-digit unemployment for the first time since the Depression. That surely qualified then as a NSN. As the political rules of the road allow, Democrats were more than justified in hanging it on Republican mismanagement.

On the other hand, something has happened since 1982, and Republicans have some counter-ammunition. The recent sequence looks like this:

UNEMPLOYMENT RATES

1978	6.0%	Carter
1979	5.8%	"
1980	7.0%	"
1981	7.5%	Reagan
1982	9.5%	"
1983	9.5%	"
1984—June	7.1%	"

Verdict: A *temporary* Negative Super Number.

Prediction: Regardless of which party is in power unemployment will go lower in the long-run future. Believe it or not, because of fertility trends discussed earlier, we are probably heading into an era of labor shortages. You don't have high unemployment when you have labor shortages.

CHAPTER 25

Cameo: Gramps Tells It Like It Is

INCOME AND OLDER AMERICANS

Consider the background of the great politicomedia show called "the Social Security Crisis," a feature attraction in 1982 and 1983.

For years conservatives had been making political hay by saying—shrieking—that "Social Security was going broke." In the spring of 1981, President Reagan sent a message to the Congress that said Social Security benefits would have to be cut by $46 billion to prevent it from going down the tubes. Budget Director David Stockman later warned that unless the Congress acted, we would face "the biggest bankruptcy in history."

The Democrats responded in kind, saying, in effect, "Ronald Reagan wants to take away your Social Security!"

A former Secretary of Commerce, Peter Peterson, wrote an important article noting that Social Security was nothing more than a "human chain letter game"—worse, it was "an unfunded liability."

As the political year of 1982 unfolded, or unraveled, television reporters went out into the field to see what senior citizens thought about Social Security going broke, about Ronald Reagan taking away their Social Security, about being part of a human chain letter, a veritable Ponzi scheme rip-off.

The senior citizens were apparently not pleased. The elderly folks that the networks put in our living rooms said, roughly:

I don't know how I'll be able to make it when they take away my Social Security!

It's my money; I put it in the system all these years. And now they're going to swindle me out of my money.

My wife and I can't get by now. We don't have enough to eat.

Let us assume, probably correctly, that each frightened and indignant elderly person we saw on television was stating nothing but the whole truth as he or she saw it. After all, the President said Social Security would go bust, the Democrats said nasty people were out to starve the elderly. The media fanned the flames; there surely are old and truly desperate people in poverty in America available for interviews. Beyond that, for many elderly people the golden years can be tough ones even with adequate income—fading health, adjustment to idleness.

But data-watchers are a beady-eyed lot. They look at facts and push aside emotionalism and sensationalism. They compare current facts to earlier facts. They assess statistical probabilities and, when pushed to it, political probabilities.

Let us suppose that during the Social Security feature presentation a network correspondent stumbled upon an elderly, flinty, data-watcher. A crew miked him, and trained a camera on him. The correspondent began an interview: "How about it? Social Security is going bust, they're taking your benefits away. Are you scared, angry, broke?"

"Well, no, not really," Data Watcher might well have answered. "Actually, the Missus and I are doing pretty well. I've been looking at the numbers, and I've been looking at how my friends are living. Not bad. You know, income for the elderly has been going up much faster than for any other group in America."

"How's that again?"

"That's right, son. Our income and the income of our friends has not only gone way up compared to others, but gone up much faster than the rate of inflation."

"But what about Social Security? It's going bankrupt; Reagan's going to cut it; it's a pyramid game; old people are up against the wall; doesn't that scare you?"

"Son, you're a bright fellow. Since when did the press start believing politicians? Do you know that in addition to our income from private savings and private pension, the Missus and I get a Social Security check every month for about $1,200—and my wife never worked. I have friends whose wives worked, and those couples get over $1,700 per month. I paid into Social Security for forty *years,* but I got back everything I ever put into the system within twenty *months* after I retired.

"Now, son, we're not rich. I stopped work in 1979, I never earned more than $18,000 a year—but I'm at top scale. Of course, not everyone's at top scale. But the *average* couple retired at age sixty-five gets about $750 per month. That's over $9,000 per year, but it's worth more than that because it's tax-free. And remember that most elderly folks own their house, free and clear of mortgages."

"But, Gramps, what about those cuts in benefits?"

"Those cuts aren't cuts; they're a decrease in the rate of increase."

"Now look here, you haven't answered all my questions. It's all a house of cards; it's an unfunded liability. All the other old people I've talked to say they're afraid."

"Young man, don't believe politicians or old people. Of course it's an unfunded liability. That makes it a chain letter game, it's true. Young people pay for old people. But you know, Social Security is so big that if it were a *funded* liability, it would have to own everything in America and part of Europe. But, young fellow, let me tell you something. I've been around a little longer than you, and I've figured something out: all life is a chain letter game."

"It is?" The correspondent signals his cameraman to come in for a tight shot.

"Yes, sir, it is. It works like this: I pass my genes along to my children, right? They pass their genes and my genes along to my grandchildren, right? That's the essence of life; genetics is a one-way chain letter game."

The reporter looks at him blankly.

"And economics is also a chain letter game, but it's a two-way chain letter game. I gave my money to my children to raise them right. They give their money to raise their children. Now, in primitive societies, they also have to give money, or food, back to their parents in their old age. A chain of money up and down."

"What does that have to do with Social Security?"

"Now just hold on a minute. People don't like to be a burden on their kids. So we try to save for retirement. Americans have been doing more of that recently. But we never seem to have enough saved up."

"Right. Things are terrible."

"Wrong, young pup. In advanced countries we've come up with a little trick. We don't like to take money from our grown kids. We don't want to be a burden. They don't like giving us money, either. We all get angry at each other if we do it that way. So we all sign a political contract to deal with what anthropologists would call 'the inter-generational transfer of wealth.' The young people *give* money to the government. I *get* money from the government. That way, we can both get mad at the government and keep on loving each other."

"But is that safe?"

"A political contract like that may be the safest thing there is, safer than any funded liability you can think of. I can imagine an insurance company going belly-up. Or big corporations. If they fail, private pension plans can go down with them. And I can even imagine the government not bailing them out. I can imagine every form of economic crisis, including runaway inflation. *But I can't imagine an elected government in a rich country not paying off the people who elect it. Can you?*"

"Well, uh, no."

"Son, we elect that government up there. There were 25 million people over age sixty-five in 1980. Most of them are eligible for Social Security. There were another 22 million between fifty-five and sixty-four. Most of them will soon be eligible for Social Security. And we vote. We are much more likely to vote than are younger people. So who's going to cut off our water?"

"Isn't that unfair to young people?"

"Only if it gets way out of balance. Hell, the money is going to *their* parents. What are they going to do, treat us like Eskimoes used to treat old folks? Put us on an ice block, float us out to sea, and let us starve to death? They can pay it to us directly or pay it to us indirectly. That's the human contract; it's a chain letter. We pay for them as children, they pay for us later. The earners pay for the nonearners. The young pay for the aged. They don't do that just in pensions, though. They do it for the police force. And the highway system. And for the defense of the country. We call that civilization."

"But what if it gets out of balance?"

"Then you rejigger the balance. The politicians get upset when they have to do it. They argue a lot over comparative nickels. Those nickels may add up to hundreds of billions of dollars—but it's nickels compared to the economy as a whole. And then they cut a deal."

"Who gets hurt in that deal?"

Data Watcher pauses for a moment, stroking his chin. "Good question, young fellow. Your questions are getting better. Maybe no one gets hurt, son. You know, one reason the system got out of balance was that us older folks are living longer. That throws both the short-term and the long-term actuarial equations out of whack. But say—it's not bad news that we're living longer—it's good news. It's good news for me now, it'll be good news for my son when he's my age. So to pay for that good news in the short run, we raise taxes a bit, cut the increase in benefits a trifle. Cheap at twice the price."

"What about the long run, sir?"

"The biggest part of the long-run problem is that my children aren't having enough children. They're eroding the pyramid's base, straining the human chain letter."

"How does that work?"

"Birth dearth. Baby bust. They're not having enough babies to pump enough money into the system thirty years from now. So they won't get as much out as they put in."

"Isn't that bad? How will they support themselves in their old age?"

"I don't think it's going to be a big problem as some people say. My kids can save more. I had four children when I came back from the war. They cost me a lot of money. Hard for me to save for retirement. But my kids are only having one or two kids. They should be able to put away more on their own, and won't need quite as much from the government. Or else they should go and have an extra one-third of a child. That would solve most of the long-term problem. And I'd like more grandchildren anyway. You know, if we have to raise Social Security taxes, maybe we ought to raise them only for those who have fewer than two children. They're the ones who aren't keeping the chain letter going."

"I see."

"I hope so. The senior citizens aren't bad off. Social Security is going to be fine. No one even talks much about the benefits we get from the Medicare part of Social Security. Or the rise in private pension plans. You know, my young friend, I'll tell you a secret: we've never had it so good."

"Sir, how would you like to go on 'Nightline'?"

CHAPTER 26

They Never Had
It So Good

THE ELDERLY

Ronald Reagan and Tip O'Neill and the rest of the politicians were all exaggerating. Social Security won't go broke. The benefit cuts were minimal.

And Gramps was right on a more general matter. This author, in this book, has generally stayed away from the easily ridiculed statement, "You never had it so good," even in those cases where the evidence pointed precisely to that conclusion. But not here. I state it brazenly: despite all the real problems that exist, the elderly in America never had it so good.

Let us work the case bottom-up, beginning with poverty. We come quickly to another Super Number. Data from three census years and an update:

PERCENTAGE OF ELDERLY (AGE 65 AND OVER) IN POVERTY (OFFICIAL CASH-ONLY DEFINITION)

1959	35.2%
1969	25.3%
1979	15.2%
1982	14.6%

Source: U.S. Bureau of the Census.

So in a single generation, the percentage of the elderly in official poverty was reduced by about two-thirds. That rate of reduction was much faster than it was for the population as a whole. Back in 1959, when 35 percent of the elderly were in poverty, the rate for the population as a whole was 21 percent. In 1982, the two rates of official poverty were about the same: 15 percent for the aged, 15 percent for all persons.

But it goes well beyond that. The "in-kind" benefits that have soared in recent years have gone disproportionately to the elderly. If these benefits, weighted as they are toward medical care, are "cashed out" by the Census Bureau's "market-value" formula, the incidence of poverty again goes down much more sharply for the aged than for the public as a whole. The full Super Number looks like this:

ELDERLY IN POVERTY

	Official	*Including Noncash Benefits*
1959	35.2%	—
1969	25.3%	—
1979	15.2%	5.0%*
1980	15.7%	4.7%*
1981	15.3%	4.2%*
1982	14.6%	4.1%*

Source: U.S. Bureau of the Census.

* Calculated on the "market value" concept, discussed in chapter 23. Because some economists believe that, because of the cost of hospital care, the value of medical benefits may be overstated among the elderly in this series, the Census Bureau publishes a subvariant market series that calculates the market value of all benefits *except* institutional medical care. That series is the one used here. Counting institutional care, the 1982 rate falls to 3.5 percent. The other methods of valuing noncash income produce an elderly poverty rate of 9.3 percent and 9.6 percent respectively—still a substantial decrease from cash-only levels. And 1983 and 1984 rates are expected to be still lower.

Why has poverty gone down so far, so fast, for the elderly in America?

There are some answers that involve government help designed for *all the disadvantaged*—whether old or not. There are answers that deal with government programs specifically targeted for the *elderly poor*. There are answers that involve government programs for *all the elderly*, poor and nonpoor. And there are answers, important ones, that have *nothing to do with government*.

Among the government programs for *all the disadvantaged,* the Medicaid program has been of particular value to the elderly poor. Medicaid expenditures for the elderly poor went up from about $1.8 billion in 1970 to about $13.1 billion in 1982. If those numbers are corrected for the medical inflation rate, the real increase still amounts to 170 percent in a decade. And of course the elderly in need also qualify for other general programs, such as food stamps, energy assistance, and rent supplements.

Of the government programs aimed directly at the *elderly poor,* the most important is called "SSI." The acronym stands for "Supplementary Security Income." (We are very good at sexy titles in this country.)

SSI is a federal welfare program for elderly, blind, and disabled Americans. It arrived almost without notice in 1974. The program has had the effect of destigmatizing a quiet transfer of funds to a group of Americans who need the money, and to whom most other Americans do not begrudge it.

Any couple age sixty-five or over whose total income is less than $472 per month is automatically entitled to SSI payments that will put them up to that level.*

A poor, elderly, American couple is thus guaranteed a cash income of about $5,664 per year. Now that is not a lot. It is, however, almost (not quite) at the official line (for a two-person family) where poverty ends (which was $5,836 per year when last calculated—in 1982).

Furthermore, the actual income for most recipients exceeds the guaranteed minimum floor, because applicants are not required to count as income state or local welfare payments and certain irregular cash payments. Beyond that, recipients remain eligible for in-kind benefits such as food stamps and Medicaid. Unlike some other welfare programs, SSI elderly recipients may retain their resources: home, automobile, some life insurance, and so on. Counting in-kind benefits typically available, the income of an SSI recipient would easily exceed the poverty threshold.

But all these "means-tested" programs that help the elderly poor are only the small tip of a very big economic iceberg.

Ironically, these days much of that icebergian help to the elderly poor is composed of *"middle-class programs."* Most Social Security payments and most Medicare payments go to people well above the poverty line. This fact, as noted earlier, is sometimes used to show that America has turned heartless, no longer interested in helping the poor.

---

* As of January, 1984. Payments are indexed to cost of living changes.

That is mostly wrong. One big reason that so many of the Social Security recipients are now "middle class" is precisely because Social Security has helped push them up into those brackets.

After all, something happened to turn a 35 percent elderly poverty rate in 1959 to an effective poverty rate of 4 percent just a quarter of a century later in 1982.

What happened was a massive, unprecedented transfer and redistribution of wealth, going on during a period of generally rising prosperity. It affected just about every senior citizen in America. As recently as 1950, only 20 percent of elderly Americans received Social Security. Today, Social Security and Medicare payments go to 90 percent of elderly Americans. SSI and Medicaid catch almost all of the rest.

Consider the mind-blowing Social Security numbers. Back in 1960, not so long ago as the chronological crow flies, the money flowing to Social Security beneficiaries amounted to $12 billion per year. A decade later (1970) that figure had soared to $33 billion. And in 1984, expenditures should amount to $185 billion!

Now, that is well over a fifteenfold increase in a single generation, but that is vastly overstating what happened. Corrected for inflation, the increase is only 460 percent. Only?

Those are the big numbers, for the society as a whole. But what about the amount of real money to a typical couple?

The *after-inflation* average monthly payment per couple went from $415 in 1960 to $508 in 1970 and to $738 in January 1984. That is a real increase of 78 percent.

Just from 1970 to 1984 (the purview of this book), Social Security payments went up by 45 percent. At the same time, real after-inflation income for the population as a whole in America went up by only 28 percent. Quite a difference: 45 percent versus 28 percent. That is one reason why experts not running for office say the elderly have done better than the rest of society in recent years.

All these increases, of course, helped raise millions of American elderly from poverty. Today we describe many of these once poor people with different words. They are called "middle class." And for most of these people the entire amount of the horrific "cut" of the 1983 Social Security compromise amounted to *a one-time, six-month delay in the posting of their 3.5 percent cost-of-living increase for 1983.*

A related reason for the boost of the elderly out of poverty is Medicare. It too is regarded as a "middle-class" program because it helps people not be poor.

There has been great political consternation about "National Health

Insurance" in recent years. It is said, by proponents, that America needs it.

Perhaps so. But we should note that, basically, the elderly already have it. Every elderly American eligible for Social Security is entitled to a Medicare card. (The few elderly poor who are not qualified for Social Security are covered by Medicaid.) As part of the Medicare program, one is entitled to hospital care, nursing services, and home health care. For a small additional fee (of $14.60 per month) Medicare Supplementary Medical Insurance ("Part B") provides physicians' services, psychiatric care, limited dental coverage, and home health care expenses. (In many states Medicaid additionally provides for hearing aids, eyeglasses, and prescription drugs.)

Increasingly, Americans have been using those entitlements. For example, from 1970 to 1981 the number of Medicare *claims* soared from 47 million to 163 million, about a 250 percent increase while the number of elderly was going up by 31 percent.

The medical care programs are used, and it would take a dazzling argument to suggest anything other than the idea that their advent and expansion played a great role in the extension of adult life expectancy described in chapter 5.

Well, now we are hearing about the crisis of Medicare. Conservatives say it's going broke. Liberals say benefits will be savaged. As with Social Security, both are wrong. There will have to be compromises, but the program will survive and the benefit cuts will be minimal. The costs to the economy will remain very large, but remember, it will go to our parents.

So far we have concentrated on how *government-related* activities have helped the elderly. There has also been a huge and growing gain on the *private* side. Private pension plans are growing remarkably.

Here is a Super Number in the making:

PERCENTAGE OF FAMILY UNITS AGED 65–69 ELIGIBLE FOR PRIVATE PENSION BENEFITS

1967	22%
1982	45%
1995 (projected)	66% (!)

Source: Towers, Perrin, Foster and Crosby for the Presidential Commission on Social Security, 1982.

The assets of the private pension plans amounted to $181 billion in 1967 and climbed to $788 billion in 1982. The projection for 1995 is $3 trillion dollars.

The number of plans in effect (serving one employer or a group) went from 13,000 back in 1950 to 150,000 in 1967—and to 760,000 in 1982! The projection for 1995 is *one million pension plans*.

In addition, about twenty million Americans have started Individual Retirement Accounts (IRAs) since their advent in 1975.

Now, getting older is difficult at best. But data watchers are people who ask: compared to what? Compared to when?

By those criteria, we find an elderly community that is healthier than ever, wealthier than ever before in relation to younger people, largely removed from real or official poverty, and politically more powerful than ever. There is only one way to characterize that situation: they never had it so good.

CHAPTER 27

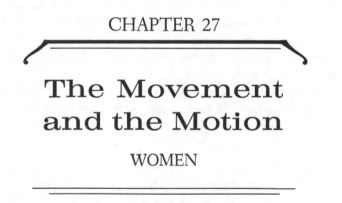

The Movement and the Motion

WOMEN

Roll back the clock to the mid-1960s and remember the most important and responsible things that "the women's liberation movement" (as it was then called) said women wanted and needed:

First, a role in the labor force; no more housewifery.

Second, not only a job, not just phone operators, nurses, secretaries— but a chance at *higher level jobs,* jobs of the sort men had.

Third, that meant access to *education*—real education, a college education.

Fourth, all that, of course, required *independence.* Women must be able to "control their own bodies," must not be regarded as mere appendages to men in a married state ("chattel," as some of the farthest-out feminists used to say). Independence, according to many in the women's movement at that time, meant it was all right to have a child or two, but a whole bunch of them could too easily mean a life of perpetual drudgery without the personal fulfillment of a career. Independence also meant that it was all right, perhaps even advisable in many cases, for women to live in an unmarried state. Another aspect of independence concerned politics: women had to get involved in elective politics in order to shape their own destiny in their own best interests.

Fifth, equality, most specifically equal pay for equal work. All this social, occupational, educational, and political independence should yield economic independence and equality.

There are long and involved arguments about whether the "women's movement" has been for good or for ill, whether it has reflected change or engendered change, whether it represented most women or just a few activists. Forget about those arguments for just a moment and consider that with the possible exception of the fifth item—there is a vigorous debate about income—the most important aspects of the "women's agenda" are either in place, or in the process of being solidly established with a demographic and political speed that is truly remarkable. Super Numbers abound.

Here is one: most married women are, for the first time in American history, at work in the measurable, money economy. The data:

PERCENT OF MARRIED WOMEN IN THE LABOR FORCE

1940	17%
1950	25%
1960	32%
1970	41%
1979	49%
1980	51%
1981	52%
1982	53%

Source: U.S. Bureau of the Census.

That is a *tripling* in four decades, which is a lot of change.

The change is apparent among all women, and most dramatic among married women who have children *under six years old.* Incredibly, during the period from 1960 to 1982, the percentage of married women who have preschool children and who are in the labor force has gone up from 19 percent to almost 50 percent!

It is useful to stress that number because it reveals the across-the-board nature of the march of women into the labor force. Today, clearly, the working woman is omnipresent in every demographic pigeonhole. That item from the agenda happened.

The idea, of course, was not just a job, but a good job. Consider first a few raw numbers to get a flavor of what has happened to women in the labor force, and how quickly it has happened. The data that follow compare the situation in 1970 with that of 1980, just one stagflationary, recessionary, retrograde, nonprogressive, spavined decade:

Put this in your memory. There were 38,000 female computer programmers then, and 99,000 now. That is an increase of 259 percent.

So sue me. America, as we know, has been overrun with lawyers. Women have contributed to the overrunning: there were 13,000 women "lawyers and judges" then, and 74,000 now. That is an increase of 556 percent.

Pray for us. There were 6,000 female clergy then, and 16,000 now.

Here's a headline. There were 61,000 female editors and reporters then, and 103,000 now.

Come in for a tight shot. There were 1,400 female radio and television announcers then, and 8,600 now. (Most of them, like their male counterparts, purveying bad news.)

Put this on your slide rule. There were 21,000 women engineers then, and 65,000 now. In addition, the number of female "engineering and science technicians" went from 93,000 to 219,000.

X-ray picture. There were 45,000 female physicians and dentists then, and 76,000 now.

A degree of change. There were 142,000 female professors then, and 233,000 now. The number of women "school administrators" went from 55,000 to 148,000.

All these numbers concern so-called "professional, technical, managerial and administrative" jobs that have been long regarded not only as the "best" jobs in America but also as typically "male" jobs. Perry Mason, Dr. Kildare, the reporters in "Front Page," the minister in the pulpit—all men. As the numbers show, these days the best jobs are no longer reserved for men.

The move is not only into white-collar jobs. Women are also rapidly gaining many well-paid blue-collar jobs.

Nail this one down. 12,000 carpenters then, 20,000 now.

Hard to brush off. 14,000 women housepainters then, 24,000 now.

Rivet your attention. 34,000 welders then, 46,000 now.

Finally, it is worth looking at certain sorts of mostly-government jobs that were typically "male only":

Stop or I'll shoot. There were 11,000 female police officers back then, 25,000 now.

Put this one out. 2,000 firefighters then, 4,000 now.

Don't trash the garbage person. 1,000 then, 2,000 now.

Punch this ticket. 69,000 bus drivers then, 177,000 now.

All in the course of a single decade, and the rate of change can be presumed to have accelerated in the years since 1980. The numbers are impressive, but of course they are only raw numbers. They are not aggregates of large occupational categories. They do not take into account the fact that the labor force was growing in any event. They do not compare the percentage of women in a given job to the percentage of men in the same sort of job.

But the aggregates are also quite impressive. There were 3.8 million women in those "best" professional, technical, managerial and administrative jobs back in 1960. By 1970, one decade later, that number had grown to 5.6 million. The most recent figure, from 1982, shows a total of 10.9 million. That's not quite a tripling in a single generation, but close to it. It's worth Super Number status: women are working at better jobs.

It is also true that some of the job categories mentioned were growing wildly with or without the added female component—computer programmers, for example. But even as that sector went through explosive growth, the female component grew substantially. Of all computer programmers in 1970 just 23 percent were women. By 1980, that figure was 31 percent and climbing.

The raw numbers do not show how small a percentage women still comprise in certain fields, despite recent growth. Women still make up only 18 percent of all "radio and television announcers." But in 1970 they comprised only 6 percent of the pool. Females make up only 15 percent of "lawyers and judges," but in 1970 they were only 5 percent of the total.

These data mask what is perhaps the most critical aspect of the female occupational picture: *the percentage of likely new entrants into a given occupation.*

Thus: it is not terribly damning to say that 85 percent of all lawyers and judges are still men, if it is also true, as it is, that 44 percent of all students studying law now are women. The latter measure shows the real change. After all, no one is recommending that we fire fifty-year-old male lawyers so that women can take their places. How many fifty-year-old women will go to law school? How many would accumulate twenty-five years of experience overnight? Intelligent feminism looks to equal opportunity to reshape the labor force over a period of time, as more egalitarian generations replace older ones. That reshaping is going on with remarkable speed.*

A dramatic change in educational patterns has made much of this occupational upgrading possible:

---

* As this is written, the issue of "equal pay for comparable worth" is wending its way through the courts. It has become a major concern for some feminists who maintain that women face economic discrimination even under conditions of equal pay for the same job, because women are typically employed in occupations at the lower end of the pay scale. Women are more likely to be nurses, less likely to be electricians. The advocates of "comparable worth" say a nurse is as valuable as an electrician any day, and should be paid about as much, *even if the free economic market doesn't normally reward nurses as highly as electricians.* Prediction: by the time it is judicially resolved, "comparable worth" will be much less of an issue than it is now. By then—whenever that is—even more women will be holding jobs that were once seen as the almost exclusive province of men. After all, will a female electrician fight hard to raise the wage of a male nurse?

COLLEGE ENROLLMENT
BY SEX 1960–1981

	% Male	% Female
1960	66%	34%
1970	59%	41%
1981	50%	50%

Source: U.S. Bureau of the Census.

Parity. Super Number.

Only a generation ago two-thirds of the Americans enrolled in college were men. Today, it's an even 50/50 split, which is just the way it's supposed to be in a nonsexist society.

This new situation can help us visualize the future. After all, if women make up only one-third of a college graduating class, it is logical to assume that no matter how unsexist a world they face, they will not likely occupy any more than one-third of those good jobs that require a college diploma in the years to come. But now that educational credentials are about equal, one more obstacle is out of the way.

The increasing education of women is not limited simply to the statistical concept of "enrolled in college," just shown. The changes are even starker in graduate schools. As recently as 1970, only 32 percent of the full-time graduate students in America were women. By 1982 that percentage had gone to 50 percent.

Moreover, 56 percent of all the enrollees in *adult* education programs are women.

＝＝

Independence.

There are arguments that "women's independence" is good for women or bad for women, good for society as a whole or bad for society as a whole. In the next section of this book—about values—some of those arguments will be explored. But there is not much argument about whether independence has been achieved and/or is being achieved. It has, and/or is.

The dictionary defines "independence" this way: "1. . . . freedom from the influence, control, or determinations of another or others. 2. an income sufficient for a livelihood."

Some of the demographic ways of measuring "freedom from the influence of others" concern marriage, fertility, and divorce. After all, life outside the married state, life with fewer children, surely cuts down the "influence of others" upon a woman.

Women are marrying later than they used to. In 1950, the median age of marriage for an American woman was 20.3 years. In 1981, it was 22.3 years. That sounds like a mere 10 percent increase over a span of three decades, but recall that few females marry before their tenth birthday or even their fifteenth birthday. If one were to pick, say, age eighteen as a plausible time when serious marrying can really begin in our sort of society, then a median marriage age of twenty means that young women are waiting two years before marrying. When that figure rises to age twenty-two (as it has) that means that young women are waiting four years to get married. That is not a 10 percent increase, but a 100 percent increase, and it plays itself out in important ways.

It means, for example, that as recently as 1970—just a decade ago— only 18 percent of women aged twenty-four were single (never married). By 1981, that percentage had more than doubled, to 37 percent. More independence, for a longer time.

Not only are women marrying later, but many more marriages are breaking up. The rate of divorces granted per 1,000 married women went from nine in 1960 to twenty-three in 1980. That is close to a tripling in one generation!

These are annual data about a specific event: divorce. These specific events accumulate from year to year. A person divorced in one year is typically still divorced in the next. When you add up all the people who are divorced at a given moment, you end up with a Super Number that looks like this:

NUMBER OF DIVORCED PERSONS

1940	1.4 million
1950	2.1 million
1960	2.9 million
1970	4.3 million
1982	11.5 million

Source: U.S. Bureau of the Census.

There is the future to consider. Current demographic estimates show that about *half* of the marriages entered into during the early 1970s will ultimately end in divorce.

In short, lots more divorce. Going back to our earlier definition of independence as "freedom from the influence, control or determination of . . . others," the rise of divorce seems to qualify. (Whether this is a positive or negative development, recall, we leave for discussion later in this book.)

Another increase in independence (judged by that dictionary definition) has come about via the sharp decline in fertility in recent years. This has been discussed at length earlier. Recall only the key numbers. Back in the late 1950s the annual "total fertility rate" reached 3.7 children per woman. Twenty years later, in the late 1970s, that rate had been halved to 1.8 children per woman.

Rounding the numbers (because it is difficult to diaper .8 of a child), the difference is between caring for four children and caring for two. Fewer years with diapers, fewer years with preschool children, lower total tuition bills—all add up to a pretty good operational definition of greater independence.

Or consider the startling rise in the number of abortions. There were 745,000 legal abortions in 1973. By 1980 the number had more than doubled, to 1.55 million.

Or consider the abortion ratio, that is, the number of abortions per 1,000 live births. For whites, the number was 175 back in 1972. By 1980, it was up to 428. For blacks it went from 223 to 645!

The catchphrase of the "prochoice" movement is that women should have "the right to control their own bodies." Leaving aside, for the moment, the morality of abortions, there is not much argument that a woman who has the ability to terminate a pregnancy has more "independence" than one who does not.

These trends toward independence—later marriage, more divorce, fewer children, legal abortion—tend to set in motion still other trends that further reinforce the notion of independence, and further fulfill the original feminist goals mentioned at the outset of this chapter.

Consider some facts about the changing nature of households in America. From 1970 to 1983, the number of family households increased by 19 percent, and the number of nonfamily households—mostly "singles," living independently—increased by 89 percent!

There is another household form that has grown sharply in recent years. A long time ago it used to be called "living in sin," it was fairly rare, and the Census Bureau didn't pay a great deal of attention to it. Today it is a sufficiently familiar phenomenon to have been enshrined by a census acronym: POSSLQ, pronounced "poss-ul-que." It stands for "Persons of Opposite Sex Sharing Living Quarters." That may not sound very romantic to you, but it did to the poet laureate of CBS, Charles Osgood, who wrote:

> There's nothing that I wouldn't do
> If you would be my POSSLQ.
> You live with me, and I with you,
> And you will be my POSSLQ.
> I'll be your friend and so much more;
> That's what a POSSLQ is for.

Osgood does not speak with forked data. There were 523,000 unmarried couples living together in 1970, and 1,891,000 by 1983. (Other millions once were POSSLQs but no longer are.) The studies on the subject indicate that by the late 1970s about one-quarter of young adults had cohabitated prior to marriage.

Insofar as POSSLQueing may be considered a form of "trial marriage," it may be easily regarded as a gain in independence for both women and men. After all, it is easier to split from a POSSLQ partner than to start lengthy chats with a divorce lawyer. For good or for ill, more independence.

And there is political independence. The numbers speak for themselves.

NUMBER OF WOMEN HOLDING ELECTIVE OFFICE

	1971	*1983*	*% Increase*
Congress	15	24	60%
State Legislatures	344	991	188%

Source: National Information Bank of Women in Public Office.

Female independence takes many forms. If one talks about young women living alone, or about POSSLQs, it can all sound rather exhilarating and liberating. There they are: women in the legislature, stewardesses by the pool at the highrise, young career women dining at good restaurants, climbing the ladder to success. There they are: women who used to be called "gay divorcees," back when divorce was unusual and gay meant gay.

But there is another side to independence. It's not just swingles and stews and career women who are more independent these days. It's mothers, too.

The number of female-headed households with one or more children under eighteen more than tripled from 1960 to 1982—from 1.9 million to 5.9 million! As recently as 1970 only 11 percent of American children under eighteen years lived with "mother only." By 1982 that percentage had climbed to 20 percent. That 20 percent amounted to more than twelve million children.

That is the other face of independence. Before examining its ramifications, which are many and often severe, it should be stressed that being a female head of a family is not a condition of life that is typically imposed on females. A woman is not forced to marry or to bear a child. A divorce or a separation can come about in one of three ways: a woman's decision, a man's decision, or a joint decision. Survey research by University of Pennsylvania Professor Frank Furstenberg indicates that in about 60 percent of the cases of marital separation women said the decision was "mostly their choice," and that in another 20 percent of the cases the decision was a joint one.

Now, that figure should be viewed cautiously. In many of those cases, for example, the husband may have made conditions so intolerable for the wife that she was left with little choice. Just the same, it is apparent that for many divorced and separated mothers, there was considerable approval of the marital break, and willingness to risk disruption for compensating benefits.

Families headed by females as a result of birth out of wedlock rather than dissolution of marriage are an even clearer case of voluntary action. We are talking, after all, about a period of time when both contraception and abortion have become easily available—in fact, with an ease never before present in American society.

Female-headed families, then, are most often the product of a series of lifestyle choices. We should assume that the women involved are acting in their own perceived best interests, after weighing the pros and cons. Of course, the children involved have no "choice," but typically their interests are also part of the parent's calculus.

Just the same, the decision to create a single-parent family can have painful aspects: children without an on-site father, a parent without an on-site helper, the breaking or bruising or straining of bonds with in-laws or friends, and so on.

The most obvious problem concerns *income*: if the major breadwinner is no longer on the scene (as is typical), where will the bread come from to provide properly for mother and child (or children)?

It can be a very serious situation, often heart-rending. There is a role here to be played by both the government and the courts—for instance, in providing adequate welfare payments when appropriate, and in enforcing child support payments.

I stress the basic lack of coercion in the forming of female-headed families because of a trendy phrase now climbing the charts of pop sociodemographics: "the feminization of poverty." It is said that poverty has been "feminized." The implication is that somebody out there, probably sexists, rigged the deck and did something to some women to make them poor. After all, when you "-ize" something you often impose something. Thus, we "tenderize," "terrorize," "homogenize" and "modernize."

That is a bum rap. A one-parent family (typically female-headed) has always been a major correlative of poverty. If, for a variety of reasons (most of them a matter of choice), the number of female-headed families goes up, then obviously the number of people in such families living temporarily beneath the official poverty line will increase as well. (As it has: from 1960 to 1980 the number of persons in poor female-headed families climbed from 10.7 million to 14.6 million.)

But that is occurring only because the at-risk population has increased sharply. (As it has: from 1960 to 1980 the number of persons in female-headed families—poor or not poor—soared from 20 million to 42 million.) Accordingly, the *rate* of poverty in female-headed families is generally declining. Here are the decade-to-decade rates and some recession-affected later data:

PERCENT OF PERSONS IN FEMALE-HEADED FAMILIES IN POVERTY

1960	50%
1970	38%
1980	19%*
1981	23%
1982	25%

Source: U.S. Bureau of the Census.

* Includes non-cash income. The cash only figures for 1980–82 were 37%, 39% and 41%. It is assumed that the 1983–84 recovery will pull down all poverty rates. See chapter 23, especially p. 155.

What has happened?

More so than before it seems that poverty in America has become a condition triggered by free choices.

The involuntary forms of poverty have been diminished: poverty from old age, from unemployment, from low wages (as we have seen earlier), from racial discrimination (as we shall see shortly). Much of the poverty we have these days is a side effect of massive but often voluntary life-style changes—sundered marriages and illegitimate childbearing. Female-headed poverty now accounts for 50 percent of all poverty. That this has yielded economic despair for some of our most vulnerable citizens—women and children—should be clear to all. Equally clear should be the fact that the situation has not come about due to a harsh society "-izing" anyone. Bum rap.

There is something else to be said about poverty that comes about from changing family structure. It is more easily remedied than the other kind.

The remedy is usually called marriage. It not only works, and works well, it is a remedy in wide usage. Indeed, marriage or remarriage is the rule, not the exception. Three out of four women who get divorced ultimately remarry. A 1983 Urban Institute study shows that among younger women with children the remarriage rate is even higher: 90 percent of the children of divorced mothers eventually live with two parents again.

And, as will be discussed in chapter 31, most unmarried mothers also ultimately marry—83 percent by age twenty-four.

When poor women heading families do marry, or remarry, they typically leave the poverty class, despite all the talk about "the culture of poverty" and "intergenerational welfare." More than half of the families receiving Aid to Families with Dependent Children (AFDC) have been on welfare for fewer than three years. A massive study of the poverty population conducted at the University of Michigan shows that from 1969 to 1978 only 2.6 percent of the population was "persistently poor" (at least eight out of the ten years).

Finally, this: even if poverty among female-headed families is at its root mostly a result of choices made by people trying to improve their condition as they sense it, even if women heading families are less likely to be in poverty than in earlier days, even if the amount of poverty may be less than it seems because of noncash benefits, even if most such poverty ends as a result of marriage—all this does not mean that female-headed-family poverty is not a serious problem for the women and children involved. Of course it is.

There are liberal solutions and conservative ones, governmental solutions and nongovernmental ones. No solution will be wisely crafted if it is based on a faulty premise. One of the faulty premises in the debate these days is the idea that female-headed-family poverty has increased because a harsh male-dominated society has landed one more punch on females. That's not what happened.

Of course, most women—about 85 percent even in recession-battered 1982—are not in poverty.

Typically, women are making more money than ever before. This is so because they are more likely than before to be in the labor force, more likely to be holding better jobs, and more likely to be better educated, all as noted in this chapter, and because all Americans are likely to be making more money, as noted earlier in chapter 22.

A big issue, however, remains: are women paid fairly? A woman can be making more than she used to, while still making much less money than a man does for similar work. If such a large differential exists, and there is no closing of the gap over time, it would at least in part negate the idea that we are moving toward "equal pay for equal work."

It is not a simple question. There is some elementary data—too elementary in this author's judgment—that back up the case for *unequal* pay.

Thus, one can look at 1982 income data and find that adult females earned only 50 percent of what men earned. An immediate objection arises. That's not a fair comparison: women are more likely to work part-time than men are.

All right. If we close the aperture of the lens a little bit and look at adults, men and women, who hold *full-time year-round jobs*, we come up with this well-publicized series of data:

MEDIAN INCOME OF YEAR-ROUND FULL-TIME WORKERS

	Men	*Women*	*Ratio Women to Men*
1970	$9,184	$5,440	.59
1975	13,144	7,719	.59
1980	19,173	11,591	.60
1981	20,690	12,460	.60
1982	21,660	13,660	.63

Source: Bureau of Labor Statistics.

So only a little progress, very recently, and we must wait to see if it is a one-year glitch.

I mention that this series of data is well-publicized because "Fifty-Nine Percent" became a sort of rallying cry for the women's movement in recent years, alleged to be clear proof of "unfairness."

But hold on. Aren't there still other correctives that ought to be added into this very difficult and controversial equation?

For example, how about job experience? (Women, as we've noted, have typically entered the labor force more recently than men.) Shouldn't that be factored in?

How about education? (Women, as we've noted, came to educational parity with men only recently, but there is no parity for middle-aged and elderly women.)

How about job mix? (These days women are becoming attorneys and doctors. But that was not so in earlier times.) Shouldn't that be factored in?

What about job preference? (Suppose, for a variety of reasons, women are more likely to *want* to be teachers than are men, and that teaching is not a particularly high-paid profession?)

What about job continuity? (Women, typically in order to raise a family, are more likely to leave and then reenter the work force.)

And that's just the easily quantifiable stuff. Consider the really tricky stuff: suppose you were an executive, male or female, and entirely nonsexist. Suppose your success depended on how well your department did in the future. Suppose you had a choice between promoting to an important job that involved traveling a smart, ambitious, well-qualified, thirty-year-old woman who had just gotten married and planned to have two children in the next few years, or promoting to the same job an equally smart, well-qualified ambitious, thirty-year-old man who did not plan to leave the labor force in a year or so. Whom would you give the promotion to? If you answer "man"—which is what is most likely to happen in the real world regardless of the law—won't such sex-based promotions ultimately show themselves in comparative income data? Even though they are not inherently sexist, only inherently realistic?

It is only after all those sorts of corrections are made that we should ask: Is it fair? And is it getting any better? It is after those corrections are made that we should ask the key question: will that thirty-year-old female have an even shot at the promotion even if she *doesn't* plan to leave the labor force? That question might well measure real income comparability, and real fairness, between the sexes.

Trouble is (of course) that all the data for fully corrected comparisons over time are not available. But what corrections are available tell an interesting story, with an interesting pattern. Here are the data for 1982:

MEDIAN FEMALE EARNINGS AS A PERCENTAGE OF MALE EARNINGS

All workers	50%
Year-round, full-time workers	63%
Year-round, full time workers of recent entry to the labor force and same age group, 18–24	80%
Year-round, full-time workers 18–24, with four years of college	83%
Year-round, full-time workers, 18–24, with four years of college and same occupation	88%

Summarizing the literature and the data, Dr. June O'Neill of the Urban Institutes reports that up to 90 percent of the differential between male and female wages can be explained by factors unrelated to sexual discrimination.

The pattern is both fairly clear and consistent with what some commonsense observations tell us about our society. One observation—apparent to all with eyes to see—is this: *an earnings gap clearly exists, and some of it is probably related to sex discrimination.* In some fields, for some sorts of jobs, it is not as easy for a woman to get ahead, or to get the same reward as a man would—even if she is equally qualified.

A second observation, equally apparent, is that there is less income discrimination than the popular arguments suggest, less than there used to be, and that there will probably be still less in the future.

In most fields, in most jobs, women are receiving closer-to-equal-pay for closer-to-equal-work.

Some reflections:

The changes in condition seen among women in America in recent years are as stark and sharp as any seen in this book. Women are much more likely to be working, to be better educated, to be working at a better job, to be better paid, to be more independent.

It can be argued—it is argued all the time by conservatives—that these changes have in many ways been harmful. At the heart of the case that neofeminism has been harmful is the idea that all those hearth-and-home women were sort of tricked into working, going to college, having small families, getting divorced. The tricksters, in this conservative view, were feminists, aided and abetted in their efforts at brainwashing by Liberal Media. It is said that it was society that suffered from this big trick: values eroded. This effect on society will be explored later in this volume.

For now, let it be noted that a historical appraisal of the data would not seem to back up the idea that American women were brainwashed. Rather, it would appear that the changes that have come about represent a true mass movement, not integrally linked to any particular brand of women's political activism:

- The age of marriage was rising before the public advent of "women's liberation" in the mid-1960s,
- Fertility rates were sinking sharply before the publication of Betty Friedan's *Feminine Mystique*,
- American women were moving into the labor force well before the renascence of feminism in the 1960s.
- American women were moving on to college in unprecedented numbers before the women's movement cried "sexism,"
- Women already in the labor force—better educated, staying single longer, having fewer children—were already moving into better jobs before the advent of quotas or affirmative action.

Because of more education, more experience, more independence, and smaller families, it is likely that these trends would have intensified with or without the advent of the "women's movement." At the same time, it is also likely that activist women's politics may have further accelerated some already accelerating trends. By how much is speculation.

It was, in short, a mass movement of unbrainwashed, untricked women all over America deciding that they wanted to live differently from their mothers. Tens of millions of Americans apparently knew what they wanted, and got what they wanted. When people know what they want, and get what they want by dint of hard work in a free society, conservatives are supposed to applaud their enterprise and moxie.

Of course, they usually don't. They fret nostalgically about hearth and home. They worry, properly, about politicizing the economy under pressure from feminist activists. But they take little note of real progress.

In this instance, surprisingly, part of their myopia is shared by media myopics. If our man from Mars in chapter 18 had wandered into one of the television networks, what would he have learned about what has happened to "women" during this last dozen years?

That Jimmy Carter fired his women's advisor (Midge Costanza); that Ronald Reagan didn't appoint enough women to high jobs and undermined the effort of a woman described as a "munchkin" to singlehandedly revise the federal legal code (which turned out not to need much revision); that the president of the National Organization for Women said women hadn't made any income progress, and the Equal Rights Amendment was sabotaged by sexist politicians; that the women's movement swore eternal political revenge on those who didn't support ERA; that the gender gap was the political wave that would wash aside all in its path.

Ho hum. They got the wrong story again. Where was the big story, in all its many varieties, that women were indeed getting what they wanted? You might have learned that from the commercials showing a young woman reading the *Wall Street Journal,* but not on the news. The story we got from journalists was all Movement and no motion.

CHAPTER 28

Cameo: Tape Excerpt

ERA OF LIMITS?

Note: Carbon dating indicates that the audio-tape fragment in question comes from the Mid-American Era, probably in the mid-1970s. It is believed that the oft-used word "Ohpeck" refers to a cartel of small nations that produced an energy source called "oil." Archeologists believe that the tape fragment was recorded in the evening in

the central room of the dwelling of an American writer named Cleeshay during a Mid-American Era ritual called "cocktail."

The understandable parts of the excerpt are reproduced here:

Deep male voice: ". . . the era of abundance is over."

Soft male voice: "It's the end of the era of cheap fuel. That's what
does it."

Deep male voice: "Prices of energy are going to keep going up.
We're running out of oil. Ohpeck will keep raising prices."

First female voice: "What it really means is that the American
dream is over. It was built on cheap energy."

Second female voice: "The American dream was a single family
home in the suburbs. The single-family home ethic . . ."

Deep male voice: ". . . is finished. Young people will never be
able to support a suburban house anymore. Ohpeck made the cost of
energy too high to air-condition a single-family house. . . ."

Second female voice: ". . . or to afford two cars. That's what's
needed to live in the suburbs—two cars. To commute, to shop. . . ."

Soft male voice: "We need conservation and smaller cars. Carter
said the 'Moral Equivalent Of War' was needed. That's how to fight
Ohpeck."

First female voile: "Yes, 'M.E.O.W.' We need something. Mass
transportation is one thing we're going to need. People won't be able
to drive their own cars to work."

Deep male voice: "And smaller houses. Attached houses. Apartments. In the city."

Soft male voice: "Young people won't do as well as their parents.
The public opinion polls show it. There's a malaise. They'll never
get their own house. Interest rates are going up. That's because
Ohpeck caused inflation. Young people can't afford a house at those
rates."

First female voice: "Well, maybe it's for the best. It's the jolt we
needed to realize that we've been living beyond our means."

Second female voice: "All those tacky houses in the 'burbs. There
never was much quality of life out there: beltway, gas stations,
McDonald's. Good riddance."

Deep male voice: "It's an era of limits. That's what Jerry Br— . . ."

Note: The tape fragment ends at this point. "Mass transportation"
referred to bus and rail modes of human mobility. "Carter" was President of the U.S. from early 1977 to early 1981. The reference to
Jerry Br— is not yet understood.

CHAPTER 29

Split-Level Super Numbers

HOUSING

Beware of archeological evidence.

We have two Super Numbers from the decennial census for future archeologists. The first is the number of housing units built in the 1970s and in earlier decades:

NUMBER OF NEW HOUSING UNITS BUILT (IN MILLIONS)	
1900–09	3.6
10–19	3.6
20–29	7.0
30–39	2.7
40–49	7.6
50–59	16.0
60–69	16.3
70–79	21.6

Source: U.S. Bureau of the Census.

To put those 21.6 million *new* housing units built in the Seventies in perspective, it should be noted that the number is greater than the entire *existing* housing stock in France, or England, or Mexico.

That large number, of course, is in part due to the fact that America was more populous than in earlier decades. More people need, and build, more houses. But the 1970s *rate* of new construction was also very high—26 percent of the total housing stock standing in 1980 was constructed during the 1970s. That ratio of new-to-old housing was the highest in sixty years. That doesn't sound much like the end of the era of abundance.

Just about everything else that happened on the housing front also contradicted the popular wisdom.

Thus, despite the much touted energy crisis and despite the chatter at Claude's, the preponderance of the new housing in the Seventies was built in the suburbs or the country (48 percent in suburbs, 38 percent in country).

Thus, most of the new housing built in the Seventies were single family homes (64 percent).

Thus, public opinion polls show that most Americans still want to live in a single-family house. A recent poll in Minnesota showed that three-fourths of the people lived in single family homes—and 63 percent of those who didn't, expected to do so sometime in the future.

Thus, in the decade of the energy crisis, the number of dwellings in America with air conditioning doubled: from 24 million to 48 million over the decade. Ohpeck anyone?

Thus, although gasoline prices more than tripled during the decade, census data show that the percentage of Americans using public transportation to get to work sharply declined. In 1970 the rate was 9 percent. By the end of the decade, 1980, it was down to 6 percent. The number of automobiles soared, as did the number of families with two and three cars, as shown in chapter 21. (Cars, however, did get smaller and more fuel-efficient.)

If all that isn't enough to cause prognosticators to prognosticate their own demise, consider that while "small is beautiful" was the watchword of a decade, the amount of living space per person went up by 18 percent. That is a lot. In fact, it is an increase equal to the *combined* increase of the three prior decades. The standard measurement for "overcrowding" in the United States is "more than 1.01 persons per room." Back in 1970, the percentage of Americans living in such overcrowded conditions was 7.0 percent. By the end of the decade that figure was 4.5 percent.

Not exactly a picture of the American dream becoming an American nightmare. There were more houses, more in suburbia, more with air conditioning, more space per person, and so on.

Still, the popular concept of the American dream involved more than just a house in the suburbs. It involved *owning* that house, and being able to own it at an age young enough to bring up children in it.

By those standards, the dream has never been more real. Here is our second housing Super Number:

PERCENT OF HOUSEHOLDS LIVING IN
OWNER-OCCUPIED DWELLING*

1940	44%
1950	55%
1960	62%
1970	63%
1980	65%

Source: U.S. Bureau of the Census.
* The percentage of American *individuals* living in an owner-occupied
   dwelling is 69 percent. (Family households are more likely than single
   households to own their own residence.)

The apparently small rise in the rate of total home ownership
masks a very significant rise in the percentage of *young people* who
own their own home. That is, to say the least, a far cry from the popular conception of young-husband-young-wife-interviewed-in-video-clip-
golly-we've-saved-and-saved-but-we-just-can't-seem-to-ever-afford-a-
house-of-our-own-it's-not-fair.

MARRIED COUPLES UNDER 35 WHO
OWN THEIR OWN HOMES

1950	38%
1970	49%
1980	62%

Source: U.S. Bureau of the Census.

Now there are reasons behind all these housing numbers; they
didn't just happen. The biggest reason is obvious: more wealth.
Young couples need wealth to buy a house. Many factors have contributed to creating this new wealth. Young people generally are making more money than they used to. Young people are marrying later,
which gives them more of a chance to save up for a down payment.
Once married, it is more likely these days that both husband and
wife will be wage earners.

But it wasn't all just a result of better-to-do young married couples. Additional wealth was the critical second-order factor behind another aspect of the housing boom, the soaring number of one-person households. Seven million such single households were formed in the Seventies. Typically these singles were either:

- maturing Baby Boom babies, now young adults and living alone, or
- divorced people, more of them than ever before, or
- elderly people, more of them than ever before.

With so many more single-person households it's no wonder that the total number of new housing units—owned or rented—went up so sharply.

Quite so. But what is the common denominator among young singles, divorced singles, elderly singles?

Wealth.

Young people typically used to live with their parents after finishing school, prior to marriage. But these days they earn more money and get a place of their own.

One reason the rate of divorce is up is because it is *affordable*. A working wife, or the wife of a well-paid husband, often has the money these days to establish a separate household, even if it may mean tight times for a while.

And the aged? In earlier times, an elderly widow or widower might well have considered moving in with the family of a son or daughter. These days, with higher pay-outs from private and public pension plans, more of the elderly opt to live alone.

The social aspect of these changes will be considered in the part of this volume devoted to "Values." There is a great argument now about whether these changes are generally beneficial or harmful. But for good or for ill, they are surely made possible only by greater wealth. (And it is the central point in this part of this book to demonstrate that we have more wealth.)

So far, we have generally dealt only with a time period that ended when the 1980 census was taken on April 1, 1980.

But what has happened since then? After all, we went through two recessions. Once again it was said that the American dream had self-destructed. Again it was noted that young people couldn't afford a home. The problem this time was not that oil was scarce. This time it was money that was scarce.

Interest rates soared to an all-time high. FHA mortgages reached a peak of 18.55 percent in September of 1981. The cost of carrying a mortgage of $75,000 at 18 percent interest is $1,130 per month; at 10 percent interest it is only $658 per month.

New housing starts plummeted. In "normal" years starts average about 1.7 to 1.8 million per year. But there were only 1.3 million starts in 1980; that sank to 1.1 million in 1981, and then down to 1.0 million in 1982. The 12-month period from July 1981 to June 1982 saw only about 900,000 starts, a disastrously low level.

But recessions do end, even the deepest one since the Great Depression. Interest rates do come down, even from highest ever rates. Builders—broke, battered, and busted—do gently dip their toes into a new real estate market. And what toe-dipping builders found was: buyers. Lots of buyers.

By the end of 1982, annualized housing starts had gone up from the midyear low of 900,000 to 1.3 million. The rate for all of 1983 was 1.7 million. The first five months of 1984 proceeded at an annual rate of about 1.9 million.

———

In the rest of the 1980s the housing situation should get even better before it gets worse. This is so not primarily because of the remarkable resiliency of the American economy, which is in fact both remarkable and resilient.

There will be a housing boom in the 1980s because of aging babies. Recall from our earlier exercises that 80 million babies were born in the United States between 1945 and 1965, a tidal wave of infants. Like most of the rest of us, every twelve months these babies have been getting one year older.

The peak year of the Baby Boom was 1957. In that year, 4.3 million Americans were born.* This volume is being published in 1984, when the peak-year-1957-Baby-Boom-babies will be twenty-seven years old, continuing to swell the ranks of young married couples. Moreover, those ranks will stay fat for quite a while. (The baby born in 1965 won't be thirty until 1995.)

What this means is clear: additional family formation. That means there are only two possibilities for the 1980s. Possibility one: those young married adults, with a child or two, often college-trained and in two-earner family units, will move in with their parents, or double up in some other way. Possibility two: there will be a housing boom.

Now one can predict a housing boom without predicting what

---

* Born, by the way, into a recession (1957–58), which was sandwiched rather neatly between two other recessions (1953–54 and 1960–61).

kind of a housing boom. It could be a housing boom in cities, rural areas, or suburbs; it could take the form of big sales of free-standing single-family homes, of attached single-family row houses, of apartments in either a garden or high-rise configuration, of mobile homes; it could be a boom of big units or small units, full ownership, condominiums, cooperatives, or rentals. It could be a boom that sputters periodically as interest rates and the economy do funny things. But those eighty million young adults have to live somewhere. That means a housing boom.

There is a larger implication to this demographic situation. All those babies born from 1945–65 will not only set up their digs in the 1980s. They will buy drapes and rugs for their dwellings. They will buy cars to put in their garages, and sparkplugs to put in their cars. They will buy vacation trips to the Grand Canyon. They will buy electric popcorn poppers. And cameras and VCRs. And orthodontic care for their children. They'd better buy books.

They will have plenty of money to pay for all this and more. They are typically well educated. They are typically in two-earner families. They typically have few children drawing on their income.

And so, just as the Baby Boom shaped the nature of the 1950s, another boom, an economic boom directly related to the earlier demographic boom, will shape the 1980s.

Welcome to the years of the Adult Boom.

CHAPTER 30

War Games

EDUCATION

In the spring of 1983, the National Commission on Excellence in Education issued its long-awaited report. Perhaps because it was put out at a time when the defense budget was being vigorously debated, the wordsmith who drafted the report dipped deep into the well of military metaphor. The report is entitled, "A Nation At Risk." Its preamble states, "We have . . . been committing an act of unthinking unilateral educational disarmament."

Escalation ensues: "If an unfriendly foreign power had attempted to impose on America the mediocre educational performance that exists today, we might well have viewed it as an act of war."

Remember the Maine!

Going nautical for a moment, the report pinpoints the problem: "The educational foundations of our society are presently being eroded by a rising tide of mediocrity that threatens our very future as a Nation and a people."

Remember Mediocrity!

Have we really disarmed ourselves? Are our educational howitzers silenced? Are classroom cluster bombs destroying our children? Will Japanese and Russian mathematicians ride surfboards on our rising tide of mediocrity, making us a second-class power doomed never to close the Excellence Gap?

———

The argument can be, and should be, divided into two parts: quantity and quality.

If one looks at American education through the prism of *quantity*, the commission's report can be described as nothing more than plain foolishness. Moreover, it should be noted that in the educational field at least, many measurements of quantity imply great qualitative progress as well. If the number of women engineers went up three-fold between 1970 and 1980 (as it did), that should not be dismissed as a mere quantitative quirk.

Let us take a quick march from nursery school to graduate school and beyond to gain a flavor of what has gone on in recent years in this nation of ours that is allegedly losing an educational war.

First, consider preprimary school enrollment. It is generally believed that it is sound educational practice to start children in nursery school and/or kindergarten. Back in 1970, just a little more than a third—38 percent—of American children aged 3–5 were so enrolled. By 1982 that figure had climbed sharply to 52 percent.

Now that is a quantitative measure, it is true: a 37 percent jump in just a dozen years. But this sharp quantitative jump means that more children are being exposed to the good things that stem from such early education: socialization, discipline, language arts, arithmetic skills, and so on. Significantly, the rate of increase has been sharpest for those who need it most. Today the in-school rate for black children from female-headed households is equal to the rate of the total population, after having started from a much lower base.

The quantitative aspects of education in the elementary and junior high grades have remained about constant in recent decades. Such education, of course, is compulsory, and up through ages fourteen and fifteen, the in-school rate remains about where it has been—at 98 percent.

What happens after that, however, is remarkable. In brief: the high school dropout rate, once the most publicized horror story in American education, has been dropping like a stone. Consider this dazzling sequence of numbers:

PERCENT OF ALL PERSONS AGED 25–29 NOT HIGH SCHOOL GRADUATE

1940	62%
1950	50%
1960	39%
1970	25%
1982	14%

Source: U.S. Bureau of the Census.

Super Number—and not exactly the portrait of a nation that has lost interest in education.

The tale of what happens in college is not dissimilar, although with a novel twist. There are several ways of measuring it. The first is the percentage of the young population that actually *graduates* from college:

PERCENT OF ALL PERSONS AGED 25–29 WITH FOUR YEARS OR MORE OF COLLEGE COMPLETED

1940	6%
1950	8%
1960	11%
1970	16%
1982	22%

Source: U.S. Bureau of the Census.

That record, while quite impressive in its rate of growth, still leaves the impression that only (roughly) one in five Americans get to college. But that vastly understates what's happening. What about those who complete, say, one or two or three years of college, or who go to a two-year college?

To get a still broader look at the college situation, we look again at age twenty-five to twenty-nine for "median years of school completed."

MEDIAN SCHOOL YEARS COMPLETED, AGE 25–29

1940	10.3 years
1950	12.0 "
1960	12.3 "
1970	12.6 "
1982	12.8 "

Source: U.S. Bureau of the Census.

A big jump in the Forties, steady progress since then. A median year ranking of 12.8 years means that the *typical* American young person (almost) completes his or her freshman year of college. Or, stated another way, *well more than half of our youngsters go to college!*

There is yet another aspect of college education that should be considered. Until now we have been talking, quite properly, about *rate:* what *percentage* of a given population is in school or has already completed school at a given level.

As opposed to rates, absolute numbers can be misleading because they fluctuate so sharply depending on the fertility rates of an earlier era. If you have a Baby Boom, then eighteen years later you are going to have a college enrollment boom.

Still, when the numbers are as stark as these, they deserve consideration:

COLLEGE ENROLLMENT

1940	1.5 million
1950	2.7 million
1960	3.2 million
1970	7.1 million
1980	11.6 million
1981	12.1 million
1982	12.3 million

Source: U.S. Bureau of the Census.

Absolute number Super Number!

It is important. One of the big harum-scarum arguments of the Excellence folks concerns how those remarkable Russians, those jovial Japanese, those engaging Englishmen, fearsome Frenchmen, great Germans are pumping out so many high-tech hot shots, that they're going to run us ragged, beat us silly, and take away all our money, and it will serve us right.

It is important because even if the *rate* at which American students opted to study engineering were down (which it's not), that would still not necessarily mean we were producing *fewer* engineers. For the record, we are producing many more: 80,005 bachelor degrees in engineering were conferred in 1982, compared with 44,479 in 1970. That is an increase of 80 percent in twelve years of "unthinking unilateral educational disarmament."

Those engineering degrees are mostly at the bachelor's degree level. What about graduate degrees?

In 1970, American universities conferred 209,000 master's degrees. In 1982, that figure was 296,000 an increase of 42 percent. That doesn't sound like an educational disaster.

In 1970, American universities conferred 30,000 doctoral degrees. In 1982, that figure had grown to 33,000. True, that increase of only 10 percent is substantially less than the increase of the total enrolled college population during that period. There is a demographic reason behind this. As the Baby Boom babies have begun to pass out of the universities, there is less relative demand for additional college professors (which is what many Ph.D.s are aiming for). Even so, it is an increase, not a decrease.

There is another factor to consider: "adult education." In the dozen years from 1969 to 1981 the number of people taking part-time classes, job training, correspondence courses, or studying in community organizations went up from 13 million to 21 million!

So much for more or less formal and accredited education in America. That leaves out only some very high quality but unaccredited programs run by little companies like IBM, AT&T, and GM. In those little internal schools, employees study things such as lasers, metallurgy, and computer design, sometimes at postdoctoral levels. Experts believe there has been vast growth in such educational enterprises, but almost no way to keep track of them, because the companies involved typically offer no degrees and publish few statistics.

(Why no degrees? One of several reasons offered: If AT&T gives a degree in lasers, it is too easy for IBM to steal away AT&T's man. After all, Scientist Jones from AT&T can knock on IBM's door and say, "I've got a postdoc in optical fibers; would you like to hire me?" If he's hired, then AT&T has lost a huge corporate investment in Jones. If, however, Jones has no new degree, only new knowledge, his skills may be somewhat less marketable. He can say he's been doing some in-house learning, but after all, how can one measure that?)

If a tree falls in a forest and no one is around to hear it, has it made a sound? In this instance, yes. The fellow who has just completed the equivalent of a postdoctoral degree in fiber optics at AT&T is not likely to be hit with a technological first strike by foreigners.

And so it goes. It is hard to find a quantitative datum that looks gloomy.

We have heard that budget cutting has hurt pupil-teacher ratios, eroding the quality of education in America. But data from the U.S. Center for Educational Statistics say otherwise. Pupil-teacher ratios for public and private schools at elementary and secondary levels have not only gone down, but have gone down substantially in recent years. In public schools, for example, there was one teacher for every 20 secondary school students in 1970. By 1980, the number was 17, a 15 percent decline.

It has been said that teacher qualifications have been declining. One can argue about what teachers really learn when they get advanced training (and we will be talking quality in a moment). But there is little doubt that teachers are getting more training:

PERCENTAGE OF CLASSROOM TEACHERS
WITH MASTER'S DEGREES

	Elementary Schools	Secondary Schools
1970	21%	37%
1983	45%	48%

Source: National Education Association.

It's been said that we are not spending enough money on education. Yet in 1970 we spent, on all levels, public and private, a total of $70 billion. By 1983 that figure had gone up to $215 billion. After inflation, that is 20 percent more money (for 3 percent fewer students).

It is said that the American education establishment is not responsive. That is said because when the establishment does respond there is no longer a story worth talking about. There was a doctor shortage, for example. Big scandal. Not enough medical schools. Only 5,612 M.D.s conferred in 1950, only 7,032 in 1960, only 8,314 in 1970. Yet, by 1980, the number of M.D.s conferred was up to 14,902. No more doctor crisis. New story: a doctor glut. ("Dr. Glut, I have this funny pain . . .")

We are told that aid to students is on hard times. Back in 1970 federal aid to students amounted to $3.4 billion (in 1983 dollars), serving 2 million students. In 1983 the comparable numbers were $11.4 billion going to 7.9 million students, a vast increase.*

So what's all the fuss about?

It is said that American education is suffering from an erosion of quality.

Well, maybe. But someone ought to tell that to the extra millions of tots who are getting a head start in nursery schools and kindergartens. Or tell it to the many extra millions of teenagers who do not drop out of high school. (Perhaps they are taking more driver's ed and less Latin than before, but a high school degree, even with some

---

* There was a small, well-publicized cut from 1981 to 1983. The 1981 data show $11.9 billion for 8.4 million students. Most of the students cut from aid were from higher-income families, as income eligibility limits were placed on some of the programs for the first time.

nonacademic courses, prepares one for life better than just two years of high school does. After all, you can't get a bus driver job without a high school diploma.) Someone ought to tell that to the millions of American women who now attend college at the same rate as men, compared to only half that rate twenty years ago. And someone ought to tell the additional 90,000 young Americans (compared to 1970) who *each year* acquire master's and doctoral degrees that their years of bone-crushing study are merely quantitative, and that they are mere intellectual flotsam on a rising tide of mediocrity.

There's quality in all that quantity.

Let us consider the quality-erosion case straight on. There is some truth to it, and a good deal of silliness as well.

Most of the foreign comparisons are plain bunk. This is so for one elementary reason: compared to foreign countries, a much larger proportion of young people in the U.S. go on to a more advanced level of education.

We have noted earlier that more than half of U.S. students go on to college. But in Japan, only 26 percent of high school graduates proceed to college. The rates in most of the European countries (East and West) run in the range of 7–15 percent.

Naturally enough, these massive differences throw off most tests that seek to make comparisons. Consider what happens if one tests in the upper high school years. In America that means testing both our bright and our not-so-bright youngsters. But in foreign countries most of the not-so-bright young people have already been pushed out of school, many of them into menial jobs.

Such comparisons are plainly preposterous. The proper comparisons should be between identical cohorts: say, their top 10 percent compared to our top 10 percent. Interestingly enough, when such comparisons are made, American students do about as well as foreign students in every field except foreign languages. (Of course, the way the world works these days, it's much more important for a Dutch student to know English than for an American student to know Dutch.)

Just as our success in bringing so many students into the educational system brings down our ratings in comparison with other nations, so too do our recent successes make comparisons with *ourselves* look bad.

Consider, for example, the Scholastic Aptitude Test "crisis." From 1970 to 1981 average SAT scores went from 460 to 424 on the verbal section, and from 488 to 466 on the math test.

Now, a part of that "crisis" is an American success story. Think about it: The very bright still take the SATs, so do the fairly bright, and now, because more students go on to college, so do many of the not-so-bright. Is it any wonder, then, that average SAT test scores have come down over time?

There have been a number of studies examining the real versus statistical declines in SAT scores. While the magnitudes differ, all agree that some significant portion of the decline is attributable to the changing universe of who takes the tests.*

It should be noted that insofar as there was a real decline in test scores—and there was some—it has apparently ended. Math and verbal scores went up slightly in 1982 and held steady in 1983.

In summary: a moderate decline, statistically somewhat distorted by egalitarian success, and now ended. Is such the stuff of educational disaster?

Some of the other criticisms of American education make much more sense. A few are of truly major proportions.

The argument about curriculum is an appropriate one. There has indeed been a decline in the time devoted to the "hard" subjects: English, mathematics, government, language, the sciences. There has been, at the same time, an increase in softer, often nonacademic subjects. Driver education is popular, so are sex education, home economics, "bachelor living."

This seems to be a quite legitimate area for reform. The Excellence in Education Commission's recommendations are valid: more English, math, science, social studies, foreign language, and a dash of computer science.

While there has been a growing amount of silliness in nonacademic high school courses, some of the classes make a good deal of sense and deserve to remain in the plan of study. If driver ed reduces automobile fatalities, why not keep it? If bachelor living and home economics teach how to handle a checkbook and a cookbook, keep them. If Sex-ed reduces out-of-wedlock births, keep it. These sorts of courses are legitimate, if not academic. After all, who wants to live in a country where pregnant teenagers—overdrawn at the bank, unable to cook even a simple soufflé—crack up the car?

Actually, the commission wisely does not come out for a *reduction*

---

* A major 1977 study by the test's makers, the Educational Testing Service of the College Board, concluded that about a third of the decline in average scores was attributable to the expanded universe of test-takers.

in such courses. It quite properly talks about *increasing* academic course requirements, as well as homework time (which has fallen), the length of the school day, and the length of the school year. The commission also asks for higher teacher standards, merit pay and higher pay for teachers, achievement testing, higher college entrance standards, all of which seems to make sense.

One truly serious problem in American schools concerns the rise of violence and the erosion of discipline. Most of the evidence is anecdotal—the child who spends his lunch money to pay for "protection," the schoolteacher raped by a student.

There are some hard data, all bad. Recent studies (1982) indicate that from 14–25 percent of students in secondary schools sometimes fear for their safety. Teachers sometimes feel threatened as well. A 1982 survey indicates that 25 percent of teachers across the country are concerned about physical attack once or twice a semester. Only one-half of 1 percent of teachers are actually attacked in a typical month, but that amounts to over 5,000 teachers nationwide. Way too many. It is a sad state of affairs, tempered somewhat by recent government data indicating that the incidence of violence and criminality has levelled off in recent years after climbing in the 1960s and early 1970s.

Again, the commission's report makes a sensible recommendation: get tough. In practice, says the commission, that means "considering alternative classrooms, programs and schools" to deal with continually disruptive students.

═══

What happened? What happened in the last couple of decades for there to be—at the same time—more money for education yet a lowering of standards, more teachers yet less discipline, fewer dropouts yet lower SAT scores, greater rates of college attendance yet more "Mickey Mouse" courses—and a well-meaning blue-ribbon citizen panel that talked about a "rising tide of mediocrity" and "unilateral educational disarmament"?

I will spare the reader one more long psychohistorical hysterical analysis of "What Happened In The Sixties." Suffice it to say that something did happen, and it wasn't minor-league stuff. It was a high-grade American-style eruption that comes along only once in a while.

In education, this eruption involved huge new sums of money, allegedly innovative teaching methods, social-policy imperatives, such as busing and the elimination of the track system, the rewriting of textbooks to conform to the political agenda of one group or another (feminists, blacks, historical revisionists), and vigorous public reaction to all of the preceding.

Eruptions, even if essentially beneficial, do not immediately lead to coherent policy. The well-meaning desire to keep more youngsters in the educational system can lead to lower standards. The well-meaning desire for racial equity can lead to the destruction of appropriate student placement along academic lines. The well-meaning desire for sex education, driver education, bachelor-living courses can take time away from more academic course work.

Well-meaning social volcanoes ultimately calm down. That is happening now. The obvious trick is to keep the good and discard the bad. Although the Excellence Commission smoothly refuses to acknowledge the vast progress we have made in recent years, its recommendations clearly follow the standard keep-the-good-change-the-bad philosophy that is appropriate in sweeping up after a volcano. Their excellencies obviously do not argue that America should go back to high dropout rates, low preschool enrollment rates, lower college attendance levels.

Still, the Sixties left their mark. In retrospect it seems clear, to this author at least, that the academic community lost its nerve during the hothouse years. Students, puffed up with their own importance ("We're the brightest, best-educated, most concerned young people in American history"), demanded "relevance" in their schoolwork.

Activists demanded everything from revisionist courses in American history to elimination of parietal rules. Some such "nonnegotiable" demands made a good deal of sense, others were bizarre.

Many faculty members, who were paid to educate students on the theory that they knew more than the students—collapsed. Instead they would learn from the students—that self-anointed brightest, most concerned generation in all American history. Academic requirements soon eroded.

This general attitude, as it related to textbooks, discipline, dress codes, teacher standards, curriculum filtered down throughout the education system. Some of the results, as the commission reports, were harmful.

But what is often ignored was the almost immediate response to academic spinelessness.

The "back-to-basics" movement formed quickly. Some right-wing groups quickly got into the act, made their point—and often overreacted. (It is one thing to demand a full political spectrum of books in a school library, but another to purge liberal works.)

Soon a broad consensus formed that went wall-to-wall, from conservative to liberal. If the academics were folding, the parents were not. Parents elect politicians. A politician's spine is typically exactly as stiff as that of the constituents who elect him.

By the late 1970s, state legislatures began establishing (in some cases reestablishing) minimum competency tests in their high schools. By the early 1980s, the legislatures in thirty-six states had so acted. North Carolina's statute, to take one good example, has worked well. It went into effect with the high school class of 1980. When first administered to that class as juniors, one out of six students failed. Those who flunked were given three more chances to pass the test before graduation. They were offered heavy tutoring. Each time the exam was taken, half of those who had previously failed passed. By graduation time, only 2 percent of the class was denied a diploma.

Teacher certification provides another good example of the turnaround. By 1981, a dozen states had begun to tighten certification and accreditation standards, despite much opposition by the National Education Association, an organization that takes wildly liberal positions while representing middle-of-the-road teachers.

There remains a shortage of math and science teachers. But teachers' colleges in a number of states have come up with programs to increase their output. New federal funds are becoming available to local school districts and the National Science Foundation to improve science and mathematics education. At a higher level, corporations that depend on colleges for scientists and engineers have set up endowments to support specific university faculties and programs.

New high schools for especially bright youngsters are being set up. Often modeled on the Bronx High School of Science, New York City's superschool, such institutions are now in place in North Carolina, Houston, Philadelphia, Washington, D.C., Boston, and elsewhere. By 1983, more than three-fifths of the secondary schools in America had microcomputers in their classrooms.

And teacher salaries, which had dipped somewhat in the 1970s, are climbing again in the 1980s, up by 6.3 percent in 1983.

So the postvolcanic, Hegelian sorting-out proceeds. We keep the good; we rectify at least some of the bad. The result, I suspect, will be better than anything we ever had. Despite the difficulties, we probably are already better off now than earlier. An ancient admonition: keep your eye on the bagel, not on the hole.

Bagelwise and Hegelwise, consider the upshot of all the turbulence in American education. Consider it particularly in relation to the pointed thrust of the Excellence Commission report, which asserts that we're not keeping up with foreign competition.

I offer first into evidence the scores of cute television news items about twenty-three-year-old American whiz kids who have already made their first million doing hi-tech hijinks with computer games or computer programs. Where did all these little American geniuses learn such skills? In Japan? In Russia? On Mars? No. The rich little urchins picked it all up in the U.S., apparently avoiding the pitfalls of our horrific low-tech, no-tech schools. After all, those millionaires are not dropouts.*

Anecdotal evidence? Yes. But is there a better way to gauge the real worth of our schools by an international standard?

Perhaps. Consider students who leave their countries to study elsewhere. They can, typically, choose to go to school almost anywhere in the world. They can study engineering in Japan. They can study mathematics in the Soviet Union. They can study the humanities in England or France. Or of course they can study in the United States, where supposedly we are falling behind in the hi-tech race, our students and teachers are barely literate, we have "unilaterally disarmed" ourselves, and so on.

Here's what we've seen recently:

FOREIGN STUDENT ENROLLMENT
IN U.S. INSTITUTIONS OF HIGHER EDUCATION

1970	135,000
1975	155,000
1976	179,000
1977	203,000
1978	237,000
1979	264,000
1980	286,000
1981	312,000
1982	326,000

Source: Institute of International Education.

---

* It was reported in the *Wall Street Journal* that a computer software show in New Orleans in early 1984 announced it would bar people under age sixteen from the floor—except if "the individual is the president or other executive officer of the exhibiting company." The alert reader will note that such examples contradict a central point of this book: that our news media concentrate on bad news. That is so, but not in relation to "human interest." Teenage hi-tech millionaires are news, even if the next item on the program deals with the failure of American education.

Somebody loves us. Is there a reason for this? Consider the views of some Japanese educators, quoted in the *Christian Science Monitor* in 1983:

> The Japanese education system . . . turns out uniform quality manpower . . . [but the system] does not sufficiently develop the individual in ways that lead to scientific or technical breakthroughs, where the U.S. retains a lead.
>
> —Tadashi Sasaki
> *Chairman, Japanese*
> *Committee for Economic*
> *Development*

> Japan has a much shorter history in science than the United States. Graduates in new fields of science and technology still are a smaller proportion of the population than in the U.S.
>
> —Kazuhiro Fuchi
> *Computer Scientist*

> Japan's industrial competitive power will be very strong in the 1980s. But in the 1990s? The potential power of U.S. science and technology is tremendous, partly because of the U.S. educational system, partly because of science research funds poured into American space and military endeavors.
>
> —Nobuyuki Fukuda
> *President*
> *Tsukuba University*

And then at the other end of the educational spectrum, it would be unforgivable not to include this excerpt from a 1983 *Washington Post* news story:

WHY WON'T PRE-SCHOOLS LET CHILDREN BE KIDS

> Many pre-schools are using workbooks and ditto sheets that were published specifically with older children in mind. They are testing 3-year olds for "readiness," offering French and Spanish lessons for children who can barely ask for a glass of water in English, providing hands-on computer programs in basic math skills and issuing three-page reports that evaluate a 3-year old's contribution to group discussion, ability to identify a rhombus, separate shades of color and shake hands with "appropriate greeting."

Can *you* identify a rhombus? Is it possible we are educating a nation of grinds? Should that be the subject of a crisis-oriented presidential commission?

=====

Now that you mention it, there is a small question to be asked about presidential commissions that sheds some light on a larger question we are dealing with in this volume.

The question is this: is there ever likely to be a well-publicized and accepted presidential commission that concludes by saying, "Things are going pretty well" or, "Things aren't so bad"?

When such reports come along, they are usually ignored. Occasionally they are attacked (homeless and hunger come to mind). But the presidential commissions that we hear most about almost invariably are the ones that tell us that we're running out of resources, or that we're poisoning ourselves, or that our health-care system is scandalous, or that we are sitting on a racial tinderbox, or that our government spending is largely "waste, fraud and abuse."

The National Commission on Excellence in Education was in such a tradition, and it was received traditionally.

There are always plenty of vested interests around to endorse and trumpet the dark view of a commission dedicated to bad news. That's how it worked out with the work of their educational excellencies. For liberals, a domestic crisis like education always means more government spending. For President Reagan and other conservatives the commission's report was proof positive of the failure of American liberalism in one important field of human endeavor. The teachers liked the commission's call for higher teacher salaries. School boards liked it because it could be used to push the teachers to the wall. And of course the press had a field day with it. The press surely had no reason to ask about the doubling of preschool enrollment, the decline of the dropout rate, the increase in rates of college enrollment, all those foreign students, the lower pupil-teacher ratios, the increasing number of engineers and scientists and so on and on.

So much for presidential commissions. That leaves only a final question that is at the heart of this book, and indeed, already asked here once before: who has a vested interest in noting success?

CHAPTER 31

A Rising Tide

BLACKS

The reader may be excused if at this point he or she asks for a breather from so much unexpected good news:

A suburban housing boom sparked by young buyers, rather than the much advertised derailing of the American dream. More people getting more education, contrary to the impression that budget cuts have short-circuited American advancement. Old people doing so much better, despite the grimness on the nightly news. Women moving steadily up the ladder of socioeconomic status.

So much positive news—and all at the same time. In searching for some logic behind such simultaneous advances, one comes to an ancient thought: "a rising tide lifts all boats."

An idea so obvious, so graphic, so powerful, so persuasive can only be challenged by a towering intellect. Herbert Stein, my colleague at the American Enterprise Institute, is such, or has such, and he has issued just such a challenge. "A rising tide," Stein has noted, "does not lift the boats that are under water."

Indeed it is just that idea that has formed the basis for one of the major arguments of our time. A potent case has been made that one of the great problems of contemporary America concerns such sunken boats. There may be progress, it is said, but so many people are being left behind. A permanent "underclass" remains, we are told.

To many, the condition of blacks in America has become a model for such a sad state of affairs. It is being said that much of the black community in America, or at least some of it, represents just such a boat under water. It is said, with merit, that the recent recessions, have battered blacks particularly hard. At best, it is said, things are getting no better. Such, then, is our target for inquiry: is the boat for blacks sunk, sinking, splitting apart, rising for some but sunk for many others?

To begin, there is, first, a central fact known to all: *blacks are still well behind whites in America.* But behind that fact are some stunning successes, and some catching-up that is so startling as to have been unimaginable twenty or ten years ago. And yet, there are also some apparent stark failures that pervade the black community, diluting much of the progress—and some of these apparent failures are not simply a result of recent recessions or a political climate less than fully attuned to black problems.

Can this set of trends and apparent countertrends be made whole? We begin with the success stories. They are substantial and straightforward. They include: suburbia, attitudes, education, and fertility.

It has been generally held that "suburbia" is the locale of the American success story. That's where folks move to raise kids in a nice house with a "rec" room and some green around it, where schools are better, where crime is less of a problem. But it has been a scar on the American body demographic that, until recently, suburbs were (accurately) described as "a white noose" around our cities.

No more. The white noose is becoming a polka dot scarf.

A Super Number from decennial censuses:

NUMBER OF BLACKS IN SUBURBS	
1950	1.7 million
1960	2.5 "
1970	3.6 "
1980	6.2 "

Source: U.S. Bureau of the Census.

Some of that increase, of course, is due to the simple fact that there are more blacks in America today than there were yesterday. But that is not the whole story, or even most of it. From 1970 to 1980 the number of whites living in the "burbs" went up by 28 percent. During the same period, the number of blacks went up by 72 percent!

There is another way to see what is happening:

PERCENTAGE OF ALL BLACKS
LIVING IN SUBURBS

1959	12%
1960	13%
1970	16%
1980	23%

Source: U.S. Bureau of the Census.

Now, that 23 percent figure is still well behind the white rate (48 percent), but growing much more quickly. Black movement to the suburbs progressed substantially faster in the late Seventies than in the early Seventies, and demographers believe that the trend is accelerating.

Another indicator of improving black residence patterns can be seen by looking at home ownership rates. Many of these homes are in suburbs. The numbers look like this:

PERCENTAGE OF BLACKS OWNING A HOME

1940	23%
1950	35%
1960	38%
1970	42%
1980	44%

Source: U.S. Bureau of the Census.

Now that is almost a doubling in a forty-year period. Home ownership is surely one of the key aspects of American economic and social well-being. Such a rise is surely a major index of black progress.*

Now, it would not be correct to assume that a move by a black family to a suburb represents an arrival in Valhalla.

---

* White home ownership rates are also up; see chapter 29. But starting from a lower base, black rates have gone up faster. In 1940, the black homeownership rate was 52 percent of the white rates. By 1980, it was 64 percent.

To visualize all those six million suburban blacks as residing in four-bedroom split level houses with two-car garages, grilling steaks at barbecues in spacious backyards, wearing aprons with silly imprinted slogans like "Kiss the Cook," drinking beer and chatting easily with smiling white neighbors would not be quite right.

Life is not like that for everyone in the suburbs. There are poor people there, as the well as well-to-do. There are people living in small, by now rundown garden apartments. There is crime in the suburbs. There are plenty of suburbs where a white exodus takes place when blacks move in.

Still, one task of social science is to ask "compared to what?"—and by that standard the suburban trends stack up as solidly positive. Consistent with public perception, the data show clearly that a black family moving from a central city to a suburb is more likely to have more living space, more likely to have its children in better schools, and less likely to encounter violent crime.

Moreover, such a prototypical black family is more likely than its central-city counterpart to live in integrated surroundings. Census demographers Larry Long and Daphne Spain estimate that 70 percent of the blacks who have moved to the suburbs go to neighborhoods that are predominantly white.

Other census experts knock down the idea that this migration is simply "spillover" from the black inner-city ring. Much of the movement—an increasing amount—is to outer suburbs.

====

To suggest that black-white tension does not exist in suburbia (or in America) would be preposterous. But it would be equally preposterous to suggest that things haven't been improving.

Consider some attitudinal straws in the wind concerning race:

As recently as 1963, a Louis Harris poll showed that only 47 percent of white Americans would be upset "only a little" or "not at all" if "blacks moved into this neighborhood." By 1978, Harris showed that the percentage of white Americans holding that essentially nonracist view had climbed to 70 percent. That still leaves a lot of whites with big problems about residential integration, but such a change over only fifteen years is quite substantial.

In a sense, that change is all the more remarkable against the backdrop of changing circumstances. James Joyce noted that there was no anti-Semitism in Dublin because there were so few Jews. Well, until very recently, there were very few blacks in suburban locales to be concerned about.

One might have expected that as blacks became home owners, moved to suburbs in big numbers, competed successfully with whites for neighborhood space and good jobs (as we shall see in a moment), the irritability/discrimination quotient might well have gone up. It has not. It has gone down.

Significantly, this softening of racial attitudes is found in just about every other measurable aspect of white attitudes toward blacks.

- In 1972, the percentage of whites who said they "would vote for a qualified black for President" was 74 percent. A decade later, in 1982, the percentage had climbed to 86 percent.
- In 1956, only 51 percent of whites said, "White students and Negro students should go to the same school." By 1982, the figure was 91 percent. Quite a change. (National Opinion Research Center.)

Most critically, there is no measure on any public opinion question dealing with the whole constellation of black/white attitudes that shows anything but a steady *increase* in tolerance.

Now consider education. Here is a Super Number: *more than a million blacks are in college today.*

It is a legitimate Super Number. It should change the way we see our situation. Consider the progress over time:

BLACKS ENROLLED IN COLLEGE

1950*	114,000
1960	227,000
1970	522,000 (!)
1980	1,007,000 (!!)
1982	1,127,000 (!!!)

Source: U.S. Bureau of the Census.
* nonwhites

It is true, of course, that some of this geometric expansion of black enrollment in college is owing to demographics. There was a black Baby Boom as well as a white one. But what has happened on American college campuses goes far beyond that. From 1970 to 1981, the number of white students enrolled in college went up by 37 percent, and the number of black students enrolled in college went up by 117 percent.

These million-plus blacks in college today provide a tip-off about what has already happened in the black community, and what is likely to happen in the future.

Thus, it would be difficult to visualize a boom in black college enrollments without a prior increase in the rate of blacks who completed high school. There was such an increase. As recently as 1970 the black high school dropout rate was twice the white rate, 22 percent compared to 11 percent. By 1982 the black rate was down to 16 percent, while the white rate was unchanged at 11 percent.

There is yet another way to see what's been happening. The following set of data, concerning blacks in their late twenties, is as dramatic as any in this book. The numbers tell a story that would have been hard to imagine only a few decades ago:

MEDIAN YEARS OF SCHOOL COMPLETED, BY RACE, AGE 25–29

Year	White	Black
1950	12.0 yrs.	8.6 yrs.
1960	12.3 "	9.9 "
1970	12.6 "	12.2 "
1981	12.8 "	12.6 "
1982	12.9 "	12.7 "

Source: U.S. Bureau of the Census.

For at least a century it has been said, accurately, that blacks have been "catching up" to whites. It has been, and remains, a tortuous march. But note that these remarkable numbers present the beginnings of a dim outline of a very different image: "caught up."

Remember, the data deal exclusively with black and white young adults. The top line deals with people who were young in 1950—and the disparity between black and white was, roughly speaking, the difference between a white high school graduate (12 years schooling) and a black elementary school graduate (8.6 years schooling). That was only three decades ago; it was already the postwar world.

By 1960—Jack Kennedy, missile crisis, civil rights—the gap was still large: a white high school graduate (12.3 years) versus a black dropout (9.9 years).

By 1970 it was much closer. Pushing the data a bit, the differential is between a white with some college (12.6 years) and a black high school graduate (12.2 years).

And today we are talking about whites with some college (12.8 years) and blacks with some college (12.6 years).

We shall be returning to these numbers; they are critical. Consider their meaning. What have we heard about black youngsters? Answer: black teenage unemployment, black teenage crime, black teenage illegitimacy.

But what else can and should be said about black youngsters in this day and age? That they are typically going to college. That their educational experience is not very different (at least by this measure) from that of white youngsters.

This is heady stuff for us realists of an optimistic propensity. This is the future; these are *young* people we're talking about. Those million-plus black college students are still going to be around a half a century from now. With college training, isn't it logical to suggest they will be getting better jobs? And decent housing? And that they will be more involved in the political process? Isn't there a better chance for greater social stability as we move toward parity?

Now, in fact, it's not really that good. Parity in educational attainment may be statistically in sight—and surely that is not a statement that could ever have been made before—but in sight is not in hand. Blacks are more likely than whites to go to junior colleges rather than four-year colleges, more likely to go to public rather than private schools. Black test scores and grades are lower than white. These factors are not to be gainsaid, although even in these areas there is evidence that closure, if not parity, is taking place.

On balance, and without question, young blacks are going farther up the educational ladder than ever before.

======

We move on, staying for just a while longer on the sunny side of the street.

Question: if blacks are doing so much better educationally, is that progress—following the classic American model—being translated into better jobs?

Answer: Yes.

Sometime during the late 1970s, unnoticed and unheralded, a statistical milestone was passed. More blacks were working in white-collar jobs than in blue-collar jobs.

The two most prestigious, most remunerative occupational categories in the Bureau of Labor Statistics nomenclature are "professional, and technical," and "managerial, and administrative." Census and BLS data show that from 1970 to 1982 the proportion of blacks in the best jobs went up faster than for whites: 25 percent for whites, 65 percent for blacks.

In 1970, there were 802,000 blacks in those highest occupational brackets. By 1982 there were 1,533,000. That is an increase of 91 percent in just a dozen years.

Of course, this is no random development. When you start doubling and doubling again the numbers of black *young* people in college, pretty soon they will get out of college and go to work. Soon, the number of blacks in the "best" jobs starts doubling too. The data confirm this: it is indeed *young* blacks who are disproportionately in those jobs.

These grand numbers deal with macro categories that are quite abstract: "professional," "managerial" and so on. What is happening can be made clearer if we tighten the focus a bit. Here are comparisons of blacks working at specific occupations in 1970 and 1982:

BLACKS EMPLOYED IN CERTAIN OCCUPATIONS, 1970, 1982

	1970	1982
Accountants	17,000	60,000
Computer Specialists	9,000	41,000
Engineers	13,000	38,000
Lawyers, Judges	3,000	18,000
Life, Physical Scientists	7,000	11,000
Physicians, Dentists	10,000	21,000
Nurses, Dieticians, Therapists	71,000	153,000
Clergy	13,000	14,000
Social Scientists	3,000	18,000
Writers, Artists, Entertainers	27,000	62,000
Public Administrators	13,000	31,000
School Administrators	14,000	48,000

Source: U.S. Bureau of the Census and Bureau of Labor Statistics.

Truly major increases, in less than a ten-year period. Black lawyers suing black doctors for malpractice, black accountants adding it all up, black writers and social scientists explaining what it means—but only a few more black clergy to offer succor!

While numbers of these magnitudes are more than just the tip, they are still only the top of the iceberg. Blacks in those "best" jobs constitute 17 percent of employed blacks in America. The comparable white rate is 29 percent. There is progress, but not parity.

But how is the rest of the iceberg faring?

Quite well. The "white-collar" category includes not only the top-of-the-line jobs just listed, but sales and clerical workers as well. Some of these vocations are not very well paid—retail salespeople, book-keepers. But some of them can be quite well paying—for example, insurance agents, stock and bond salesmen. Blacks have been moving into the rest of the white-collar jobs in numbers disproportionate to whites.

The rate of blacks in blue-collar work has correspondingly declined, but all the loss has been in unskilled, semiskilled, and farm categories, while the numbers and rates of skilled workers (such as electricians, plumbers, and machinists) has gone up.

Contrary to white patterns, the rate of blacks in "service" jobs has not gone up. However, this trend is a clue to a salutory situation: the number and rate of blacks, predominantly women, categorized as "cleaners and servants" has gone way down. There were 569,000 in 1970, and only 207,000 in 1982!

Here is how the overall picture was described by two University of Michigan economists, Glenn Loury and Jerome Culp, in 1979: "Minority workers entering the labor force have nearly achieved parity with their non-minority counterparts, both in skills and in earnings. Corporate and government practices toward minority workers, students and citizens have undergone radical change . . . An emerging elite, professional class of minority workers has developed whose members are, in many instances, better rewarded than their non-minority counterparts. As time goes on and older cohorts are replaced by younger ones, we may expect to see a lasting reversal of the historical patterns of racial economic inequality."

———

A lower birthrate is usually regarded as an indicator of economic advancement. Here is what has happened recently:

BLACK BIRTHRATE
PER 1,000 WOMEN 15–44 YEARS OLD

1950	137*
1955	155*
1960	154
1965	133
1970	115
1975	88
1980	88

Source: U.S. National Center for Health Statistics.
* Black and other nonwhite.

That is a stunning decrease. Because of the high incidence of out-of-wedlock births, this development is complicated and will be discussed again in a few moments. For now, however, let it be regarded as another positive sign.

Moreover, on the subject of births, let this be noted: while both the white and black infant mortality rates have come way down in recent years, and while the black rate remains higher, the actual reduction of black infant deaths was about twice that of whites.

Sunny trends: College graduates doubling and doubling again, professionals and managers doubling, suburbanites doubling, families smaller, more tolerant attitudes—and cleaning ladies halving.

Something is going on. Other signs:

In the dozen years from 1970 to 1982, the number of black military officers doubled (to about 16,000) while total U.S. officer strength went down by 110,000.

In eight years, from 1969 to 1977, the number of black-owned businesses in America went from 163,000 to 231,000. The 1977 figure is the last census number available. But a survey of the top hundred black businesses by *Black Enterprise* magazine shows total sales climbed from $1.1 billion to $2.2 billion from 1972–1982 (in constant 1982 dollars).

And it was on the political scene where the progress was perhaps most dramatic. From 1970 to 1983, the number of black congressmen doubled from 10 to 21. The number of mayors went up 523 percent, from 48 to 251 (including Detroit, Los Angeles, Chicago, Philadelphia, Washington, Atlanta, New Orleans). The number of state legislators went from 169 to 379. All "other" elected legislators climbed from 1,242 to 4,955, an increase of 400 percent in just a dozen years—all this before Reverend Jesse Jackson announced that he would open up the political system to blacks.

Something is indeed going on, and it is good.

The big question, however, is whether something else is going on at the same time that is not so good.

=====

The list of what is said to be not good for blacks includes: unemployment, teenage unemployment, crime, income, family decomposition.

These are neither small nor tangential areas of the human condition. One can prattle on about blacks living in suburbs, getting almost as much education as whites, moving into better occupations—all in the context of a less racist society. But such gains would be subject to dilution if blacks were not making more money, or were suffering massive unemployment, or were in growing danger from criminals and/or committing more crimes or were living in circumstances where family life is eroding. Indeed, there is some truth to some of that; and indeed, some dilution of our earlier sunnier report. Such negative conditions, to the extent that they exist, also buttress the previously mentioned notion of the "underclass."

To begin, before digging into specifics, let me offer some capsule judgments:

- *Black Unemployment*: Not good under usual circumstances. Dreadful in a deep recession such as we have recently had.

- *Black Teenage Unemployment*: Exaggerated. Not as important as we have been told.

- *Black Crime*: Very bad, but probably not getting any worse, and perhaps getting somewhat better.

- *Black Income*: Actually pretty good, getting better, though jolted by recession.

- *Black Family Decomposition*: By standard value systems and standard measurements, getting worse. Again, however, there are some important caveats worth pondering.

UNEMPLOYMENT

There is a simple and ugly formula to describe black unemployment in America in recent years: *it is twice the white rate*. This constitutes a Negative Super Number.

The rate varies a little from time to time. Black unemployment was 1.8 times as large as the white rate in 1975. It was up as high as 2.3 times the white rate in 1978. In the tough recession year of 1982, it was exactly 2.0 times the white rate, about what it was a decade ago, and two decades ago, and three decades ago—always about twice as high during good times and bad, during booms and recessions. In 1983, it was up again—to 2.3 times the white rate.

Ratios are interesting but they mask a critical point: when times get tough in America generally, they get extra tough in black America.

The last full nonrecessionary year was 1979. In that year, 5.1 percent of the white labor force was unemployed. That is roughly considered "full" employment, as described in chapter 24. In the same year, the black rate was 11.4 percent—a deep, recessionary rate.

Now 1982, unlike 1979, was not a nonrecessionary year. It was the pits. The white unemployment rate in December of 1982, at the very pit of the pit, was 9.6 percent—very bad. The black rate was 20.9 percent—a disaster, worthy of a Double Negative Super Number.

The ratio of black to white unemployment was no worse in the bad year of 1982 than in the good year of 1979. (A ratio of 2.2 to one.) But if black unemployment goes from roughly 10 percent to 20 percent while white unemployment goes from 5 percent to 10 percent—the amount of *actual increase* has been twice as much for blacks as for whites.

There were, roughly, one million *additional* black unemployed, comparing 1979 to 1982. An unemployment rate of 21 percent smacks of an earlier American circumstance: the Great Depression, when the total American unemployment rate reached 25 percent in 1933.

Conditions improved somewhat in 1983 and 1984. Black unemployment dipped from 21 percent in December of 1982 to 15.0 percent in June of 1984, as the economy generally picked up. But that rate is still tragic.

It is a bad situation, fully deserving all the public attention it has received.

TEENAGE BLACK UNEMPLOYMENT

The same cannot be said of the black *teenage* unemployment rate.

As noted in chapter 24, there is probably no American statistic that is more misused than "teenage unemployment," and this is particularly so as applied to blacks because the rates are higher than for whites. Headlines scream: "Black Youth Unemployment Climbs to 50 percent." We are told, or it is implied, that these teenagers are condemned to a culture of poverty, that they will never enter the mainstream economy, that they have abandoned hope, that they are pushed into a life of crime, dope, or welfare.

As described earlier, much of this is poppycock. To sense what is happening, think deep thoughts about teenage unemployment.

The first thing we know about it is that it involves teenagers. What do we know about teenagers and the teen years—for blacks and whites?

We know that teenagers, many of them, are in school. We know that teenagers, most of them, live at home. We know that teenagers, most of them, are not heads of households, not responsible for the primary welfare of others.

We know that teenagers, many of them, are on the move. They are finishing school, they are going into the military, they are looking for work, they are starting work, they are switching jobs, they are quitting jobs, they are having romances, some of them are having babies, some of them are getting married.

We know something else about teenagers, white and black: they are in the last stages of a serious, long-term discombobulating disease called childhood. Teenagers are typically not very responsible, not very organized. They carouse, drink, and fight at rates far above those for adults.

We know one other big fact about the teen years: they end.

All this, as we shall see, distorts the statistical system that attempts—with little success—to measure all teenage unemployment, and, for our purposes now, black teenage unemployment.

Let us refigure, this time considering race, our calculations made in chapter 24 regarding teenage unemployment. Consider one hundred black teenagers.* You may begin—for statistical purposes—by forgetting about sixty-five of them. They are "not in the labor force."

Why not? Most—about three-quarters—are in school, going to classes, going to afternoon basketball practice, horsing around after school, hopefully doing some homework. Some of the young females, married and unmarried, are at home tending young children. These

---

* Based on January 1984 Bureau of Labor Statistics data.

fully occupied young people, students and mothers, are "working" full-time in every real sense. But they are not counted as either employed or as "in the labor force" only because they do not have "a job" and, for good reason, for they *are not looking for one*.

So, the base from which "teenage black unemployment" is calculated includes only about a third of all teenage blacks.

Of the thirty-five black teenagers who are in the labor force, eighteen are "at work."

That leaves, of the original hundred, seventeen who are "out of work," that is "unemployed." Now, many of those seventeen are also in school full-time—about seven. In other words, those seven, counted as "unemployed," *have* a full time occupation (student) and are *also* looking for a paying job, typically part-time.

That leaves ten teenage blacks out of a hundred who fit the bill for what "teenage unemployment" typically means to most people who hear about it on television: that is, young people not in school full-time, looking for work and unable to find it.

Who are these ten? Well, some of them are surely the ones we hear so much about: ill-educated, crime-prone, in the culture of poverty and so on. But most of them are just young kids looking for a job, quite possibly a first job. Remember (chapter 24) that under the American system of counting unemployment, as soon as anyone decides to look for a *first* job, he or she is automatically "unemployed."

Interestingly, once you remove full-time students from the mix (which is proper), the rate of teenage unemployment—for black and white—is comparable to that for adults.

Even if one should (foolishly) accept the teenage unemployment numbers as popularly presented, there is something important to be said about these numbers: just as the teen years end, so do teenage unemployment rates. For example, black unemployment by age looked like this in early 1984:

BLACK UNEMPLOYMENT BY AGE, JUNE, 1984

Age	Rate
16–19	34%
20–24	25%
25–34	16%
35–44	10%
45–54	8%
55–64	6%

Source: U.S. Bureau of Labor Statistics.

As a black (or white, for that matter) teenager gets older, he or she is less likely to be unemployed. Why? No surprise here. He or she becomes a young adult and begins to settle down.

Despite the alarums that unemployed black teens will never get into the workforce and will live their lives in a cycle of welfare dependency, the statistics show otherwise. That (roughly) 50 percent unemployment rate for black teens becomes a 30 percent rate, then a 20 percent rate, then a 10 percent rate, as the young people get older. The same process, at different levels, goes on for whites as well. Such data do not typically describe a "sunk boat."

CRIME

Crime in America is a damn serious problem. And crime in America is disproportionately a matter of race, both on the criminal side and on the victim side.

Blacks comprise about 12 percent of the population of America—and commit 47 percent of the violent crimes, according to arrest records.

Blacks are almost twice as likely as whites to be *victims* of a serious violent crime.

In 1981, about 9,000 blacks were killed in America, victims of homicide, compared to 11,000 for the entire rest of the population, despite the fact that blacks comprise only about one of every nine Americans.

So: blacks are disproportionately likely to be mugged, raped, robbed, assaulted, and murdered—and are disproportionately likely to be muggers, rapists, robbers, assaulters, and murderers.*

It is a dreadful situation—literally full of dread. Blacks are more likely than whites to live in dangerous neighborhoods, fearing for their lives and property.

We ask here a simple question, while acknowledging a nasty circumstance: *Is black crime in America getting better or worse?*

We know something about *total* crime rates. Since 1980, by one measure at least, violent crime is down by about 10 percent in the U.S.

The trend is of sufficiently recent vintage that it is difficult to determine whether this decline is occurring more or less rapidly in the black community. One may hope that the black criminality rate, per-

* Most violent crime is *intra*racial, not *inter*racial: in 1980, fully 83 percent of crimes against blacks were committed by blacks; the white-on-white rate was 75 percent.

haps influenced by a disproportionate recent gain in education, will indeed fall more quickly than the white rate. That remains to be seen. For the moment it is still a dreadful situation.

INCOME

What about income? There has been much talk about how blacks are not doing well.

It is complicated. Blacks do make substantially less money than whites. Having noted that, we note too that the income picture for blacks is substantially better than it was, and has improved relative to whites as well. And having noted that, we further note that the recessions hit blacks hard.

Consider first 1970 to 1980. As with whites, the most quoted data has been the most negative series available: "median family income" Using those figures, the data for blacks from 1970 to 1980 looked quite gloomy. Black family income, in constant 1980 dollars, actually declined about 4 percent, from $13,325 to $12,764. The ratio of black median family income to white dipped from .61 in 1970 to .58 in 1980.

As might be expected, these numbers engendered much pessimism. It's Reconstruction all over again!

It is because of such talk that the topic of income is put in the "possible bad news" section of this chapter, rather than in the earlier "good news" section—where, on balance, it probably belongs.

There is, in fact, a convincing explanation for the disappointing family income numbers and ratios. The circumstances that made the black family income data seem bad actually concerned family structure and what whites were doing much more than it concerned black income.

Recall from chapter 27 that rates of women in the labor force went up sharply during the 1970s. The rates went up most sharply for white women. (Black women, poorer, were already likely to be in the labor force.) This increased the proportion of high-earning white two-earner families. This development inflated the "white" side of the black-white proportions.

There was yet another external factor that accounted for the slight decrease in the actual dollar amount that black families earned from 1970 to 1980. It was caused mostly by the sharp rise in female-headed black families. This increase in "family decomposition," which will be discussed in a moment, has the economic effect of lessening the number of black families with two earners, and of increasing the number of black families with one woman earner or no earner at all (typically poorer families).

So changing *white occupational* demographics (more two-earner families) and changing *black demographics* (more single-parent families) starkly changed the mix of the families whose incomes were being compared. These changes—*demographic* changes, not *income* changes—worked against blacks when it came to averaging the income data.

But what about income seen as income, unmuddled by changing demographics?

Two census economists, Gordon Green and Edward Welniak, have directed their attention to that question.* They asked: what would those doleful black-white family income proportions have looked like if the demographics hadn't changed?

Their answer is of vital importance. The official numbers, recall, showed real black family income from 1970 to 1980 both going down, and going down as a percentage of white income—from $13,325 to $12,674, and from 61 percent to 58 percent. But if you "freeze" the demographics—that is, observe what would have happened had not demographic structure changed among both whites and blacks—a very different result appears. Median black family income goes *up* from $13,325 to $14,830, and goes up as a function of white income from 58 percent to 66 percent!

Income is up. Families of a given type were making more in 1980 than were their counterparts in 1970.

This picture is confirmed if we look at the per capita income numbers stressed in chapter 22. We use those data here for the same reason as earlier: to screen out changing demography. We seek to compare apples to apples over a period of time, and are less interested in comparing apples and lizards.

From 1970 to 1980, white per capita income as measured by the Census Bureau in constant dollars went up by 16 percent. Starting from a lower base, black per capita income went up faster—21 percent.

That was the picture up to 1980. From 1980 to 1982, during two recessions which, as described earlier, hit blacks harder than whites, black per capita income declined more sharply than white: down 4.7

---

* "Changing Family Composition and Income Differential," August 1982, Bureau of the Census.

percent versus down 1.2 percent. Still, for the entire 1970–82 period, per capita black income was up a trifle more than white: 15.4 percent *vs.* 14.3 percent. Projections for the 1980 to 1984 period by former Federal Reserve Board Governor Andrew Brimmer show a sharper aggregate income gain for blacks than for the population as a whole— 19 percent higher, or, after discounting for faster population growth, 15 percent higher.

On balance, we see then a picture that is familiar: blacks well behind whites, but catching up, bumped by recession, resuming a climb. That pattern—low base, higher rate of increase—has been common to most of the black/white comparisons presented in this chapter: educational attainment, occupation, suburban residence, elected officials, military officers, and now income as well.

Indeed, it would be most unlikely, probably impossible, for many of those positive developments to have taken place in the black community unless income had also gone up. You don't move to the suburbs because you're making less money. You don't make less money when you get a better job. You don't make less money, if you go on to college. If you're catching up in jobs and in the suburbs, it stands to reason you're catching up in income. And so the data show.*

FAMILY

But what of the changing structure of the black family in America?

It is becoming increasingly female-headed. This change has been a major one; it has dominated the public discourse. Few, if any, would argue that it is a change for the better.

The attempt here will be simple. First, to briefly lay out the facts— many of them quite stark and gloomy, but some of them more complex and perhaps less sad. Second, to ask some questions about the situation. Only questions; I have no answers. Third, to relate the black family situation to the popular ideas of a growing and permanent black underclass. And fourth, to let this situation bring us to a further examination of the notion espoused earlier in this chapter—that conditions in America are improving not only for Americans in general, but for blacks in particular.

* There is particularly heartening confirming evidence concerning income patterns for *young* blacks. Another study by Gordon Green of the Census Bureau shows that in 1970 the average hourly wage of black males just entering the work force was 80 percent of the average white wage. By 1980, that ratio was up to 88 percent.

We begin with another Negative Super Number.

PERCENTAGE OF BLACK FAMILIES WITH CHILDREN UNDER 18 HEADED BY A WOMAN WITH NO SPOUSE PRESENT ("FEMALE-HEADED FAMILIES")

1960	21%
1970	31% (!)
1980	47% (!!)
1981	47%
1982	46%
1983	48%

Source: U.S. Bureau of the Census.

More than a doubling in a single generation!

The great majority of these female-headed families are those created from three sources: divorces, separations, and births out of wedlock.

There has been an increase for blacks in each of these sources in recent years. Of these, the increase has been the sharpest—and most worrisome—among families resulting from births to unmarried mothers:

BIRTHS TO UNMARRIED WOMEN AS A PERCENTAGE OF ALL BIRTHS, BY RACE

	1970	*1980*
White	6%	11%
Black	38%	55%

Source: U.S. National Center for Health Statistics.

More than half of all black babies born these days are born out of wedlock!

The numbers for blacks who are divorced or separated are also way up:

CURRENTLY DIVORCED OR SEPARATED PERSONS
PER 1000 EVER-MARRIED PERSONS

	White	Black
1970	59	195
1980	114	329
1983	129	347

Source: U.S. Bureau of the Census.

It is time now to ask some important questions: does all this add up? To what? Do these harsh facts fit in with other things we know? Are the facts perhaps not quite as bad as they seem?

On the surface, of course, the situation seems grim—pure and simple. More than half the black babies born today are out of wedlock. Almost half of black families with young children are female-headed.

But hold on. Do the trends of female-headedness correlate with other trends?

Think about young blacks. We have learned they are not dropping out of high school. More go on to college than ever before. More go on to good jobs than ever before. More live in suburban surroundings than ever before.

There is an apparent disconnection. We do not normally associate teenage mothers of out of wedlock babies with trends showing advanced educational attainment, good jobs, suburban residence, and so on.

One theory is at hand to reconcile these apparently contradictory trends: the permanent underclass. Sunken boats. It is said that *some* blacks are moving ahead, but others, the underclassniks, aren't. The underclass theory would say that those young blacks graduating from high school, moving on to college, getting good jobs, living in the suburbs are only one part of the picture. The other part concerns young girls mired forever in a tangle of welfare, poverty, and premature motherhood, a group, probably growing, for whom conditions are getting worse and worse. There is indeed some evidence to back this idea of polarization in the black community. There is more income inequality among blacks than among whites, and the disparity within the black community is growing.

But still, something is wrong with that as a total theory. The magnitudes on both sides are simply too large.

Remember that 55 percent of black births are out of wedlock. These numbers are up; the underclass must be growing.

But remember also that 80 percent of black females graduate from high school. A million black youngsters are in college today; millions more have already had some college; millions more are on the way. Thus, the underclass should be shrinking. Apparent contradiction.

But could it be that some of the same young people are on both sides of the equation? That some of those upwardly mobile young people are having children out of wedlock and are still (generally, over a period of time) upwardly mobile?

Shouldn't we then perhaps wonder whether something else is going on behind those apparently horrendous rates of illegitimacy and families headed by females?

Such an exercise might begin with the observation that in the past decade, more so than at any other time in American life, an out-of-wedlock birth is an act of free choice. (See chapter 27.)

Contraceptive services are available under Medicaid. Abortion was made legal by the Supreme Court in 1973. Abortion is not paid for by federal Medicaid but many states, including many of the most populous ones, provide payments for abortions as an add-on service. It is offered in many private charity clinics, and in any event, is an inexpensive procedure. Data show that the number of black abortions tripled from 1972 to 1980 and the abortion rate for blacks is well over twice as high as for whites. Illegitimacy, in short, is not typically an *imposed* condition. (As Roger Wilkins has noted, "The Reagan Administration did a lot of bad things, but it didn't make the babies.")

Female-headed families also stem from divorce and separation. As described in chapter 27, those conditions, too, are most often the result of changing social values and life-style choices.

If illegitimacy and female-headed families are increasingly freely chosen states, we may ask this: why are they increasing in the black community?

Normally when people act voluntarily, we assume they do so *in order to improve their condition*. What happens if one looks at the increase in black female-headed families from such a vantage point?

One answer concerns the welfare system in America. For many years conservatives have said that the welfare system—typically applicable only when there was no "man in the house"—encourages the formation of female-headed families, via illegitimacy or divorce or separation. That view has by now achieved much wider acceptance. In May of 1978, in Detroit, Senator Edward M. Kennedy, no conservative he, addressed the National Association for the Advancement of

Colored People. After describing and denouncing social and economic conditions for blacks in a way that bears little resemblance to the facts and views sketched out in this chapter, Kennedy discussed welfare and illegitimacy, as follows:

> . . . we say to this child—wait, there is a way, one way you can be somebody to someone. We will give you an apartment, and furniture to fill it. We will give you a TV set and a telephone. We will give you clothing, and cheap food, and free medical care, and some spending money besides. And in return, you only have to do one thing: just go out and have a baby. And faced with such an offer, it is no surprise that hundreds of thousands have been caught in the trap that our welfare system has become. . . .

That is one piece of the puzzle. We seem, in at least some instances, to be rewarding young black women who opt to have a child out of wedlock. It is plausible to assume that they believed they were *improving* their circumstances, even if we, in our wisdom, believe they have made a choice that may condemn them to a dead-end life of poverty and welfare.

Is it possible they know something that we don't?

They might know, for example, from firsthand observation, that not every young black woman who bears a child out of wedlock is trapped for the rest of her life. Far from it.

Most young women, black and white, who have out-of-wedlock children do indeed get married. A study by researchers at the Urban Institute shows this clearly. Of black women who bear an out-of-wedlock child, 74 percent marry by the time they are twenty-four.

An out-of-wedlock child does not preclude a later intact family. It does not automatically condemn a mother or child to a life forever snarled in a tangle of social pathology. Chances are it is a temporary condition.

What else is going on behind the scenes? We know that this largely voluntary act of out-of-wedlock parenting is increasing not only among blacks but among whites. As the data on p. 237 show, blacks have a much higher rate of illegitimacy than whites, but the white *rate of growth* is greater than the black. (From 1970 to 1980, a white increase of 93 percent, a black increase of 47 percent.) It is passing strange, isn't it, that the talk about the growth of white illegitimacy concerns a "change in values," while the talk about black illegitimacy concerns "the perpetuation of a cycle of welfare and poverty"? Is it possible that some of what's true for whites is also true for blacks? A value change rather than a permanent underclass?

And what about the divorce-separation component of the "broken family"? That surely is not solely a black phenomenon. We hear a drumbeat of statistics about how one in three marriages or one in two marriages in America will end in divorce. When we consider that as a white experience, we again hear about "changing values": well, it's said, divorce is a function of affluence, and after all, maybe it's better for all concerned if an unhealthy marriage is sundered. Liberal feminists, in particular, make this argument.*

Is it possible that some of what's true for whites is also true for blacks? That more money in the black community—private and public—has provided blacks with more family options than before, just as it has for whites? That most black women who are divorced, remarry, just as is the case with white women?

And while we're on the question of differential sociology (that *is* the subject we're on), what about the Swedes? The rate of illegitimacy in Sweden is about 40 percent, about three and a half times the U.S. white rate. No one seems to think it means a self-perpetuating tangle of pathology among white Swedes. Why does it automatically mean that among black Americans?

Nor, by the way, is America being flooded by a tidal wave of black babies born out of wedlock. Notwithstanding everything else mentioned here, let it be understood that the "illegitimate birthrate" among blacks has actually declined in recent years:

BIRTHS PER 1,000 UNMARRIED BLACK WOMEN

Year	Births
1960	98
1970	96
1980	83
1981	81

Source: U.S. National Center for Health Statistics.

This is a complicated statistical situation, but important to note. As mentioned earlier in this volume, fertility rates in America have gone way down in recent years, and blacks were very much a part of the decline. As part of this, the black illegitimate birthrate also fell—from 96 out-of-wedlock black babies per 1,000 unmarried women in 1970

* So does the author, as will be noted later.

to 81 in 1981, as the table shows. It is only because the black *marital* birthrate has gone down even faster that the *proportion* of births that are illegitimate has gone up.

What is going on here?

As promised, I will not try to answer that question. I will not because, in large measure, I do not know the answer.

I ask the question only because it has been somewhat too simply brushed to the minus side of the ledger. It is not a simple question, and the valid answers ought to be color-blind ones. If the feminization of the family among whites is seen as a not-all-bad cultural phenomenon that induces an economic penalty, perhaps a similar but much more prevalent tendency among blacks ought to be viewed the same way.

I repeat. It is not a happy development. It rates a Negative Super Number. But there is more to it than meets the eye.

=====

Scorecard. On the positive side: blacks are doing much better in education, occupation, residence, politics. Home ownership rates are up. There are more black businesses. The black birthrate is down. There is more tolerance.

On the perceived negative side: Income is better than perceived. Teenage unemployment is overstated. Adult unemployment is very serious among blacks and was exacerbated by a deep recession. It is worthy of a Negative Super Number. Crime is extremely serious. The disproportionate amount of black female-headed families is, quite simply, mystifying. It doesn't seem to correlate with other major positive trends among young blacks; it is judged on standards not applied to others. It is, nonetheless, a serious and unfortunate situation—another Negative Super Number.

Reasonable people, obviously, may differ on how to balance these trends.

I see it this way: these past dozen years have not been an easy time in American life. We have experienced inflation, recession, stagflation, changes in values, and changes in demographic structure. I believe, as this book seeks to demonstrate, that Americans have made progress during this difficult time. I believe, as this chapter seeks to demonstrate, that black Americans—despite some negative developments—have been very much a part of that progress. The gap is closing.

UNDERCLASS

Progress does not automatically preclude the idea that some blacks are destined to remain in a "permanent underclass." Progress, theoretically, could come in a split version: as mentioned at the beginning of this chapter: "a rising tide does not lift sunken boats."

But I am somewhat dubious about the permanent underclass proposition, be it applied to blacks or to others in our society.

First: there is *always* a segment that remains behind when any group makes progress. There are poor Jewish Americans and poor Italian Americans and tens of millions of poor WASPs, all pinpointed and pigeonholed in the 1980 census.

The important questions about the underclass are whether the proportion of people in that condition is being whittled down, and whether people have a decent chance to escape. That has happened among Americans as a whole (chapter 23), and there is every indication that it has happened among blacks as well:

Fewer. The black high school dropout rate has declined. Black per capita income has gone up. Blacks are beginning to move from central cities to suburbs. Blacks are going from worse to better jobs. The poverty rate is down from 1970 (when in-kind income is counted.)* Poor blacks are *less* poor than their earlier counterparts were because of in-kind income. The great majority of black female-headed families sooner or later move into an "intact" family state.

Escape. The landmark study of the Institute of Social Research at the University of Michigan cited earlier in this book shows that relatively few Americans are consistently poor. Poverty is a revolving door. That is true for blacks as well as whites. Eleven percent of the black population remained "persistently poor" during the 1969–79 time frame of the Michigan study—much higher than the white rate, but lower by far than any single-year black rate.

---

* While the black poverty rate remains higher than the white rate, the inclusion of in-kind income brings the black rate down more quickly than the white rate:

PERCENT OF BLACKS IN POVERTY
COUNTING NON-CASH INCOME

1970	33.5%
1982	21.5%

On balance: the permanent underclass as measured economically, is both shrinking and not very permanent. There is a rising tide lifting many boats—including some that once appeared to be sunk. There has been progress for blacks.*

* And for others as well. A book of this sort obviously cannot provide measures for each and every racial, ethnic, national, or religious group in America.

But things don't typically happen in a vacuum, unrelated to the rest of the universe. In a nation where GNP is growing, where the Safety Net has expanded, where real income has gone up, where more people are educated, where life expectancy has gone up, most people—and most groups—are doing better. After blacks, Hispanics are the largest group often referred to as plagued by the underclass problems. Be it noted that since 1973, when the Census Bureau began measuring data separately for Hispanics, their per capita income has increased much more rapidly than for any other major group in America. It is not terribly hard to understand why when one realizes that from 1973 to 1982 the number of Hispanic workers in the top "professional" and "managerial" white-collar categories went from 406,000 to 775,000—a 91 percent increase!

CHAPTER 32

Cameo: Claude's Mother

COMMERCIAL INNOVATION

Tapping away at his word processor, hard at work on an article about American business, Claude Cleeshay finished his sentence.

He turned to his new desk phone, and without lifting the receiver, punched a button. The machine automatically dialed twenty-two numbers in five seconds: twelve numbers of his MCI code, the three numbers of an area code, the seven digits of his mother's phone. A fiber optic line carried the call most of the way from Washington, D.C., to the cellular radiophone in his mother's car, situated at that moment in a shopping mall in Stamford, Connecticut.

"Mother," said Claude, as he paced about his study, his voice picked up by the sensitive microphone on his desk console telephone, "how are you?"

"Fine, Claude. I was just doing some Christmas shopping. I bought three video games for Ellie's kids, and a software package for little Robert. That little rascal told me he wanted me to get him his own laser disk player. Really, Claude! I can't spend $500 for a Christmas present. Maybe next year the price will be down. You remember what happened to ballpoint pens. They used to cost $10, but now . . ."

"Mother, that sounds fine. But how are you feeling?"

A froggy voice says, "All monitored systems are functioning normally."*

"Mother, is that you?"

"No, Claude, I just turned the key in the car and it spoke to me. I'm just pulling out of the parking lot."

"Fine, Mother. But how are you feeling?"

"I'm feeling fine. How are you feeling, Claude?"

"Mother, how is your eye? You've only been out of the hospital for two weeks."

"Oh, Claude, stop fussing. Cataracts are simple these days. The surgeon uses lasers."

"I know, Mother, I know. Just checking. Have a nice day."

"Goodbye, Claude," said his mother, putting her car into automatic cruise gear.

Wearily, Claude turned back to his word processor, tried to pick up his train of thought, pushed the split-screen button to check his notes. Green luminescent letters appeared on the screen: "STRESS FACT THAT AMERICA AND AMERICAN BUSINESS HAVE LOST THE URGE TO INNOVATE."

* That audio recording plays in a 1984 Chrysler when things are working right. The statement could be the title of this book.

CHAPTER 33

Where There's Smoke, There's Smoke

BUSINESS

Were Claude's article on American business to follow the standard bad news outline, it would, after denouncing our lack of innovation, proceed along roughly the following course:

- Because we haven't innovated, we are "deindustrializing,"
- Contributing to that process are foreign powers who do innovate, and who are taking over our markets,
- Foremost among these countries is Japan, which works wonderfully because it has an "industrial policy,"
- We therefore need an "industrial policy,"
- Because that would overhaul the shortsighted practices of American business, which include too many mergers, lack of long-term planning, and too little creative risk-taking.

In this chapter, lest Claude go astray, some facts and a few ideas are offered that call that standard story into question.

Is it possible that the content of Claude's everyday world of lasers, fiber optics, word processors, new phone systems, cruise controls, personal computers, video disk players, and automobiles that talk—all relatively recent innovations that were developed in America—are merely aberrations in an otherwise retrograde process of American technological erosion?

It is possible. So let us proceed beyond specific innovations to broader measurements. Consider, as one way of toting up research and innovation, the Nobel Prize awards in the sciences—chemistry, physics, and physiology/medicine. Notice how poorly U.S. citizens have fared:

NOBEL SCIENCE PRIZES

Time Period	% To U.S. Citizens
1901–44	17%
1945–59	51%
1960–69	49%
1970–79	55%
1980–83	68%

In 1983, Americans won *all* the science prizes!

Now, that is not a statistical picture of a nation that has turned on its heel and walked out of the laboratory. Of course, the sample is small, and it's a lagging indicator—prizes are awarded for work done earlier. Like lasers and word processors, it is possible that Nobels ring no bells as indicators of overall scientific health.

Neither, probably, do these excerpts from an article in the *Wall Street Journal* of October 21, 1983, by staff reporter Diane L. Coutu:

> When the Max Planck Society, West Germany's leading scientific research institute, needed a divisional director recently, it mounted a world-wide talent hunt. . . . they eventually focused on a West German scientist temporarily working in the U.S. . . . "We made him an offer he couldn't turn down," says Robert Gerwin, the society's spokesman. . . . "He turned us down. He told us that only America provides the right 'atmosphere' for doing good scientific research."
>
> . . . (G)overnments all across the Continent are fretting that Europe is lagging [the U.S.] badly in the scientific race. They fear that Europe's future economic growth will be hobbled. . . .
>
> Arno Penzias, vice president of research at American Telephone & Telegraph's Bell Laboratories, says, "I don't want to say that Europeans do research purely for fun and the Japanese purely for profit, with Americans in the middle achieving the perfect balance, but there you have it."
>
> Mr. [Frank] Press [president] of the [U.S.] National Academy of

Sciences adds, ". . . England has Oxford and Cambridge, but we have 50 of these things. It's our source of great talent, and you won't find it in Japan, Germany, France, or even England to the extent that we have it here."

Let us widen our focus and go beyond news clips.

Consider the number of scientists and engineers in the U.S. who are employed in "research and development." Back in 1970, there were 547,000 Americans so engaged, according to the National Science Foundation. By 1983, after a decade in which it was said that the U.S. was bowing out, or being pushed out, of the research race, the number went up to 743,000. That is a gain of 36 percent.

It was said during the 1970s that American research was being starved, specifically because defense-related research was pushing out healthier private research. What actually happened was the opposite. In constant dollars: from 1970 to 1983 research and development for the military went up by 13 percent, from $20.7 billion to $23.4 billion. At the same time, R and D in the private sector went up 74 percent, from $26.9 billion to $46.7 billion.

Nor, by the way, do we compare poorly to other nations. In 1982, we spent 2.5 percent of our GNP on R and D. That is about the percentage spent in 1981 by the Germans (2.68 percent) and rather more than the wondrous Japanese (2.36 percent) or the French (1.97 percent). The nation that ranked highest in the R and D sweepstakes was the Soviet Union (3.47 percent), but one must wonder how productive those Soviet investments are if they still feel constrained to steal research and technology from other nations.

In any event, research is a classic example of the beneficial effects of an economy of scale. Although the American *percentage* of GNP for R and D is in the general range of other nations, we are (still) far ahead in *absolute* amounts spent for research, because our GNP is so much larger (about double the Soviets' GNP, for example).

What's going on? If, among other things, America keeps winning Nobels, increases its number of researchers, increases the amounts of research spending, and outspends (by far) any other nation in R and D, then why do we keep hearing so much about how we're losing our edge?

There is an axiom that helps describe the situation: "Where there's smoke, there's smoke."

"DE-INDUSTRIALIZATION"

Here is how the smoke/smoke proposition works.

There are, to be sure, areas of industrial activity where American business has fallen behind, in part because of flagging innovation and apparent laziness on the R and D front. Automobiles come to mind first. The Japanese learned how to build fine small cars, how to produce them inexpensively, and how to market them effectively in the U.S. The public consensus in America for at least a decade now is that Japanese small cars are better than American ones. To some extent, of course, all this was a result of superior Japanese R and D.

Because automobile manufacturing has been such a fabled and integral part of the American industrial landscape for so long, any news about it, particularly bad news, becomes big news. And so, when Japanese imports climbed from 6 percent of the American car market in 1965 all the way up to 28 percent in 1982, the media machine began blowing smoke. Add in a couple of recessions that brought total automobile sales down from 11.4 million units in 1973 to 8.0 million in 1982. Puff, puff goes the media smoke machine: decline in the auto industry reveals decline in U.S. innovation, research and development.

Similar stories accumulate. The steel industry, another American classic, is savaged by declining auto sales, by recession, by new substitutes for steel, and—most publicized—by foreign competition, often producing steel more cheaply in mills that, we are told, are more-modern-than-America's. Our television sets show us the blast furnaces that once lit up the evening sky of Ohio's Mahoning Valley—dimming, dimming, and out.

Not dissimilar stories are told about clothing manufacturers, television-set production, cameras, motorcycles, and so on.

Smoke here, say the media; smoke there, say the media. Where there's smoke, they say, there's fire. One big result of the fire, we are told, is "de-industrialization." We are losing our manufacturing base.

But are we really? Is there really fire where there's smoke? Smudge pots in the fields don't mean fire; cigar smoke doesn't mean fire; automobile exhaust fumes don't mean fire.

Is it possible that smoke in autos, steel, cameras, and clothing doesn't mean fire in American industry? Consider the *manufacturing* sector. That's the sector, we've been told, where a beast called "de-industrialization" lurks.

It is true that from 1970 to 1981 manufacturing jobs in the motor vehicle industries went down. But the decline was not great: from 797,000 to 784,000, according to the Bureau of Labor Statistics. Then, during the big recession year of 1982, a dive down to 705,000. But in the recovery year of 1983 motor vehicle employment went back up to 845,000 (November data). Is it possible that much of what was seen as "de-industrialization" was a much less exotic phenomenon called "recession?"

Some sectors surely lost jobs, even after economic recovery. Consider the years 1970 and 1983. Employment in the manufacture of "radio and television receiving equipment" went down from 133,000 to 92,000. The number of jobs in the "blast furnace and basic steel products" category dropped sharply from 627,000 to 343,000. Textile mill jobs went from 976,000 to 764,000. The number of people employed in apparel manufacturing dropped from 1,365,000 to 1,199,000.

Major drops. Clearly, if these magnitudes were replicated across the entire industrial structure, it could be a serious situation, perhaps actually a "de-industrialization." One might then observe the wisps of economic smoke and posit fire.

But emphatically, that's not what was happening. During this same period, manufacturing jobs involved in producing (innovative) "office and computing machines" went up by 78 percent (from 283,000 to 503,000). The number of jobs involved in the manufacture of (innovative) "medical instruments and supplies" almost doubled, up 96 percent from 83,000 to 163,000. Innovation in communications and electronics increased manufacturing jobs in these two sectors from 865,000 to 1,225,000. Innovation helped boost jobs in the manufacture of "guided missiles, space vehicles, parts" from 11,000 to 147,000.

When you add it all up it looks this way: in 1970, there were 19.37 million manufacturing jobs in America. Thirteen years later, in 1983, there were 19.27 million such jobs—just about the same. Some de-industrialization! Moreover, this constant-sized work force increased its total production by about 30 percent—from about $500 billion in 1970 to about $650 billion in 1983 (constant 1983 dollars).

What happened is not terribly complicated or new. As shown, many "smokestack" industries and "old-line" manufacturing industries did indeed get hurt in varying degrees. But these manufacturing job losses have been picked up in other manufacturing sectors, often in what are popularly called "high-tech" industries. A word processor, for example, is a high-tech product, but it is also a product that is put together in a factory. This evolution from smokestack to "high-tech" in-dustries, from old-fashioned to new-fashioned, is sometimes seen as a sinister process. There are dislocations; people lose jobs; politicians seek to protect them. Fair enough.

But this volume is not about political compassion. It is about a na-tional reckoning. In that pursuit, let it be noted that the trend from old-fashioned to new-fashioned and from smokestack to high tech is at least as old as the Industrial Revolution. Such evolution is both a harsh and a healthy process in a free economy. Automobiles were the high tech that took jobs from buggy makers. Steel was the high tech that took jobs from wood mill workers and iron casters. Power looms and sewing machines were high tech in their day. Tractors and other agricultural high tech played a big role in increasing agricultural pro-duction—and in pushing lots of farmers off small farms where the horsepower was provided by horses, not tractors. A lot of people in America ended up working neither on farms nor in factories, but in offices. As we shall see shortly, that is still happening. After all, manu-facturing jobs are only staying even in a growing economy. There's real growth someplace.

The television newscaster extends sympathy to the out-of-work steel worker. The voice-over says, "his job may be gone for good." Possibly so. But recall that the father of the newscaster worked in radio, not television. His grandfather may have worked on big weekly magazines like *Collier's* or *The Saturday Evening Post.* An earlier ancestor was a medieval scribe. They all lost their jobs, and they didn't get them back, either.

They got other jobs; so did their sons and daughters. There was per-sonal travail involved, but a good deal of economic health as well, at least as seen over a long sweep of time.

Six months from now, or a year from now—or two—the prototypi-cal steel worker, speaking in broad statistical terms, will either regain his job or get another fairly good one, quite possibly in a white-collar field. Speaking unstatistically, there will be some individual steel work-ers who will be hurt. Some elderly ones may not be reemployed. Some will end up with jobs earning less than $22.21 per hour that was the standard wage-and-benefit package negotiated by the United Steel Workers. It is a harsh process.

But more harsh still would be a situation where no change took place in American industry. That would indeed lead to foreign take-over of our markets and real de-industrialization.

IMPORTS

The changing employment situation is, of course, not just a function of job-shuffling innovation in America. There is a foreign dimension as well—a politically explosive dimension.

Cars are the most obvious example. First Beetles from Germany, then a dazzling array of Datsuns and Toyotas undercut American automobile manufacturers. There are similar stories to be told about steel, apparel, cameras, radios, plastics, and even souvenirs that say, "My Dad was in Tarpon Springs, Florida, and all I got was this lousy Tee-Shirt," which has a label in it that says, "Made in Taiwan."

Question: Is all this good or bad for America?

As we shall see, it is geo-politically advantageous and we ought to applaud it. It is economically good, and we ought to applaud it. There are abuses in the system, and we ought to yell about them.

After World War II America encouraged international trade in order to help create a prosperous, peaceful, commercially coequal community of nations. Our primary goal was geopolitical stability, not just additional American prosperity. Every time you see a Japanese car, or an Italian pair of shoes, or German industrial equipment, or fashion knock-offs from Taiwan, you are seeing the fruits of a monumentally successful American postwar policy. Even if that policy has cost us some jobs, which is doubtful, and very difficult to measure one way or the other, it has been worth it. Would we really want a world with a rich America and a poor and snarling Europe and Japan?

JAPAN

The only legitimate case against the global market is that what has happened has, from the U.S. view, succeeded *too well*. Such a case has indeed been made recently regarding the Japanese.

Those Japanese have the answer, many businessmen like to tell us. That's why we're losing jobs to them. Business, labor, and government cooperate, we are told. Unions don't hassle business. The government doesn't hassle business. The Japanese pick sunrise and sunset industries. The workers never get laid off. They sing the corporate anthem in the morning. The Japanese, we are told, have adopted American quality control and do it better than we do it. They rip off all our new technology and produce it faster and cheaper than we do. Is it any wonder that their cars, cameras, and VCRs are wonderful?

They do things right over there, we are told by our corporate Japan-worshipers. They will be the next superpower!

Well, the Japanese have indeed been very successful economically in recent years. But in various ways, this has helped many Americans. If their small cars are both better and cheaper than ours, Americans who buy them are getting a good deal. That's what Adam Smith's "comparative advantage" was all about (and why import quotas are a bad idea).

Smith aside, the Japan-worshipers ignore some facts. A 1983 study conducted by the Japan Productivity Center—a Japanese-government supported organization—found that American labor productivity per worker is 1.54 times that of Japan. One reason Japan has a less efficient economy than ours is that they are highly protectionist. The Japanese housewife with a yen for steak pays about $11 a pound for it—because the government protects the Japanese beef grower from American beef imports. That rips off the Japanese housewife and the American farmer. No fair!

In the long run, though, protectionism doesn't help. The Japanese standard of living, although it has grown rapidly, is still below that of the U.S. The best way to demonstrate this is by comparing the number of hours a typical Japanese worker and a typical American worker must labor in order to afford a particular item. A 1982 study by the Union Bank of Switzerland defined a "marketbasket" of basic goods and services commonly bought by a family of three, and calculated that the average worker in Tokyo would have to work 530 hours to pay for such necessities, while the average worker in New York would only have to put in 268 hours, and in Los Angeles only 196 hours!

There is one other thought worth pondering about the Japanese economic miracle. They're doing some of it on our nickel. The U.S. spends almost 7 percent of its GNP on defense. The Japanese spend about 1 percent. We protect them. Superpower indeed!

Question: how dazzling would the dazzling Japanese economy be if—all those years— it had had a military budget 600 percent larger than what it actually had? How much would the cost of a Toyota go up if Japanese taxes on the workers and the corporations that produced the vehicle had to carry that 600 percent increase? It's said the Japanese can't raise defense spending because voters won't support such increases out of fear of resurgent militarism. OK. Let them just write out a check to America for the proportional difference in our defense budgets. That's only fair, and it would reduce our deficit.

On balance, does the Japanese model have something to offer us?

Do we really need—or want—American workers singing the American Can corporate anthem each morning? Do we really need— or want—round-heeled labor unions? Or round-heeled government regulators? Or protectionism?

We have done rather well with our open and adversarial way. Even if there were a marginal economic gain in going over to Japanese-style economic and labor regimentation, which is doubtful, it is not in the American style. It would surely yield cultural and political turbulence of high order.

So how good are the Japanese? Probably not as good as we've been told, but pretty damn good anyway. It's their system, for their culture. It seems to work well for them.* It may have a few lessons for us— but only a few.

THE OTHER 80 PERCENT

Left by the wayside so far in our discussion of American enterprise is a rather critical fact: about 80 percent of American jobs are not now in the manufacturing sector. And the most encouraging portrait of American business is to be drawn precisely from the nonmanufac-turing sector.†

From 1970 to 1981—a period that encompassed four recessions— here is what happened in that part of American business outside the manufacturing realm:

---

* There is some evidence of dissatisfaction with the Japanese system even among the Japanese. In 1982, the Gallup organization polled simultaneously in America, in most of the European countries, and in Japan. In America, says the Gallup megapoll, 50 percent of the respondents have confidence in "major companies," in Japan, only 25 percent do—dead last among the nations polled. In America, says Gallup, 80 percent of us are proud to be Americans. In Japan, it's 30 percent—next to last in the rankings. In America, 84 percent of the respondents take "a great deal of pride" in their work—in Japan, only 37 percent do. It gets worse. On a "satisfaction with life" scale, the Japanese are last again. Hispanics and blacks in America are twice as likely as your typical Japanese to be "very happy." The data are controversial, but there is recent University of Indiana survey research data that backs it up.

† Manufacturing *never* represented the majority of jobs in the U.S. Not even close. In 1920, 39 percent of U.S. workers were so employed. By 1960 it was 31 percent, in 1970 it was 27 percent, and in 1983 just 21 percent. As noted earlier, there has not been a decline in the *number* of manufacturing jobs in recent years. It is the *share* they represent in the labor force that has gone down.

There was an 82 percent increase in the number of jobs in the *mining* sector, mostly in the "oil and gas extraction" sub-category. This increase in jobs represented, in large measure, the vigorous and proper market response to a critical situation: the OPEC caper. (See chapter 15.)

The number of *construction* jobs went up by about 650,000 between 1970 and 1981. As noted in an earlier section, many of these jobs built the housing needed by a generation of Americans who came of age in the 1970s. In addition, because the locale of work in America moved toward offices, a vast new inventory of commercial office buildings was suddenly needed. Anyone who thinks that America stopped growing in recent years ought to look at "before" and "after" photographs of downtown Houston, Dallas, Los Angeles, and Washington, all in the Sunbelt; or New York City, Philadelphia, and Boston, all very much not in the Sunbelt.

There was an increase of a quarter of a million jobs in the *communications* subset of the "transportation and public utilities" sector. The people in these jobs helped reduce the cost of long distance phone calling by about 50 percent since 1970.

There was, from 1970–81, a monumental jump of 5.5 million new jobs in the *wholesale and retail trade* sector, most of them in the sub-category of "eating and drinking places." This number highlights the advent and incredible growth of fast-food chains, which have changed America—a change for the better, in this author's judgment. The food is generally inexpensive and wholesome. The establishments are clean, convenient, available—and omnipresent. Moreover, in an era when the number of American teenagers looking for employment has exploded, it is the fast-food emporia that typically provide the jobs.

More than 1.5 million new jobs were added in the *finance, insurance, and real estate* sector. A well-to-do America with a growing population of young adults setting up households needs a small army of real estate professionals to buy houses, mobile homes, and condominiums, and to rent apartments. A rich nation with ever greater numbers of well-to-do people needs other well-to-do people to invest their funds in pension plans, IRAs, Keogh plans, money market funds, and the like; it needs a vigorous insurance sector that allows people to roll dice creatively with the future, knowing that they are protected from a bad roll.

And there was a gain of more than 7 million jobs in *services*. The numbers are simply incredible: in 1970 there were 11.5 million Americans so categorized, and eleven years later, in 1981, there were 18.6 million!

Much has been said about this new army of service workers. They have been welcomed as the heralds of a "postindustrial" society, and shunned as the advance guards of an "underdeveloping" society that needs "reindustrialization."

But everyone agrees that service workers provide services. That is what happens in a wealthy society. People produce enough so that they can afford to pay other people to perform tasks for them. These service workers, in turn, earn enough to purchase both goods and services.

Some service workers are found near the bottom of the occupational spectrum and are relatively poor. The chambermaid in the hotel is a service worker. But some service workers are very rich. John Riggins, the Washington Redskins' fullback, earns about $750,000 per year. He is a service worker. The IBM employee in a three-piece suit, with an attaché case filled with cute little tools, who fixed the word processor on which this book was transcribed from second draft to third draft, is a service worker. The surgeon is a service worker, so are mechanics and architects.

All these occupations have increased sharply in the last decade. Many of the workers are either self-employed or working for small enterprises. These workers, these enterprises, fill "felt needs"—an exercise instructor, a rock group, a hairdresser, a gardener, an income tax advisor. They reveal a business structure that probes into every crevice of human desire to see if there is a way to fulfill a need, and turn a buck. These occupations, recall, have not grown up at the *expense* of the more obviously productive sorts of jobs: manufacturing, mining, construction. Those fields have generally held their own, or grown at a moderate pace.

Now what on earth is wrong with that?

FAILING THE FAILURE TEST

As an outgrowth of the late great recession, the case was made that American business is failing. Business failures, it was said, indicated economic failure. An overconcentration on acquisitions and mergers showed a different kind of spiritual failure. A depressed stock market showed failure. And the cause of so much failure was, said many liberals, bad management on the part of businessmen or, said many conservatives, the result of dumb government meddling. Let us investigate.

Business failures? Well, yes, there was an increase in the number and rate of businesses failing during the twin recessions of 1980–82. That is not surprising during a recession. The number of failures in the last fully healthy year, 1979, was 7,600. In 1982, a full year of bottom-dropping recession, the total of failures went way up to 24,300.

But look at a five-year span, not a bad idea with these sorts of numbers. From 1961 to 1965, for example, there was an average of 14,849 business failures per year. From 1978 to 1982, including the whopper of 1982, there was an average of 14,800 business failures—slightly fewer, and against a much larger base. (Nor was the liability of the failed firms any larger than in earlier years, when expressed in constant dollars.)

That only scratches the surface. Almost unnoticed during the great fail-wail was a very curious fact: the number of new incorporations was at an all-time high! In the same tough recession year of 1982, for example, there were 567,000 new incorporations, about twice as many as the average number only a decade earlier—and almost 25 times the number of business failures in the same year. A part of this change is due to considerations of tax law, but only a part.

Obviously, there are many more businesses in America today than there were even a few years ago, and the number keeps going up much faster than business failures. Evidence from our best source— income tax returns filed—indicates that there were 12 million businesses in America in 1970, and 16.8 million ten years later in 1980— a 40 percent increase.

Most of these businesses are small businesses (84 percent of the 1980 total are partnerships or proprietorships). The small-business sector is one of the most dynamic within our economy. Of the roughly 10 million jobs created between 1977 and 1981, three-quarters of them were created by firms with under 500 employees.

URGE TO MERGE

Mergers! Acquisitions! Conglomerates! Rapine! Plunder!

In the late 1970s and early 1980s, in the wake of several highly publicized and dramatic corporate mergers the case was made that merger mania had taken over the corporate world, and that the urge to take over rather than produce was motivating American captains of industry.

Interesting thought. Trouble is, the numbers work the other way. Here are the data concerning the number of mergers and acquisitions:

MERGERS AND ACQUISITIONS

	Number	Billions of 1983 Dollars Paid
1968	4,462	$122.7
1969	6,107	64.2
1970	5,152	41.9
1971	4,608	30.9
1972	4,801	39.6
1973	4,040	37.3
1974	2,861	25.2
1975	2,297	21.8
1976	2,276	34.9
1977	2,224	35.9
1978	2,106	52.1
1979	2,128	59.4
1980	1,889	53.3
1981	2,395	90.2
1982	2,346	55.4
1983	2,533	73.1

Source: W. T. Grimm and Co., *Mergerstats* (annual).

There have been fewer, not more, acquisitions and mergers in recent years, and in real dollars the amounts involved are fluctuating in the same general range, certainly if applied to today's far larger economy.

What about the argument that corporation acquisitions are in themselves a bad thing? We hear a great deal about "hostile" takeovers. Corporate plunderers, so goes the argument, complain about the lack of capital, but then spend billions to grab another corporation, equally venal, whose executives care not a whit about stockholders or nation, only about their own golden parachutes, which are nothing more than personal payoffs for selling out.

The diverted funds argument is mostly hokum. The money stays in the system. Company A uses capital and borrowed bank funds to buy the shares of Company B. When the takeover is completed, Company B's shareholders get Company A's money. What do they do with it?

Put the money right back into banks. The next client at the bank window is Company C, which borrows money to build a new rolling mill. All the transactions have been on paper only. Capital was not, except for a short-term loop, diverted from productive use.

The only real slippage was incidental and psychic. The competing specialty law firms of Sturm and Drang, working for Company A, and Pelf and Pilfer, working for Company B, have pocketed a few million dollars. Probably more important, for months the upper management of Companies A and B were thinking more about tender offers than about how to produce better products. Still, these are typically huge corporations; the few million in legal fees is coffee money, and 99 percent of the executives are still going about their business.

As for the golden parachutes, they are indeed a scandal, albeit legal. Corporate management cannot be expected to represent corporate or stockholder interests fairly in deals in which they feather their own nests. On the subject of legal scandal: it ain't right for corporate fat cats in a *publicly protected industry* (like autos) to take huge pay and options raises while asking labor to cool its demands.

A word about *most* corporate acquisitions—the "nonhostile" ones. They often provide an infusion of capital, management, talent and synergistic marketing capability. The result is often a healthier, more efficient business.

STOCK MARKET

It has been said that an indication of the ultimate failure of American business was revealed by the sad condition of the stock market. That was an interesting argument before August 1982, when the value of stocks on the New York Stock Exchange had plunged, in real terms, by 23 percent over the previous nine years.

But from August of 1982 to January of 1984, the real value of the NYSE stocks climbed by 36 percent.

MANAGING POORLY

With so many specific charges leveled at the poor, old, pitiful business community (lack of research and innovation, too many mergers and acquisitions, inability to respond to import competition), and with so many apparent symptoms of disaster (business failures, a deteriorating stock market, an economy big on fast food and weak on steel), it is no wonder that there has sprung up a unified field theory to explain why American business has laid an egg.

In brief, the theory says: *American managers don't manage well.*

The argument goes this way: business schools have been pumping out beady-eyed MBAs whose God is the hand-held calculator, interested only in short-term profit on the balance sheet and damn the long-term implications for corporations or society, afraid to invest capital long-term in America's future, afraid to spend money on research and development. Our businesses, it is said, are run by modern day bottom-lining, noncompetitive, corporate buccaneers whose pirate ship is named "Discounted Cash Flow."

It is a serious charge, one that goes to the very essence of capitalist theory. Adam Smith saw an "invisible hand" that guided entrepreneurial activity simultaneously toward two goals: individual enrichment and—because entrepreneurs made money by satisfying society's needs—the betterment of the society as a whole. The new theory sees a different dynamic: the invisible hand is rifling the cash register.

We begin with some facts. Richard R. Wert, dean of the Amos Tuck School of Business Administration at Dartmouth College, and Dennis E. Logue, a professor at the same institution, have attacked the idea that American business hasn't been investing enough. The growth of capital spending in America, they note, has not really declined very much. It was growing at a rate of 3.9 percent per year from 1947–72 and dipped only to 3.6 percent during the allegedly investment-short years of 1972–80. (That's growth in both periods, not decline.) Moreover, in the manufacturing sector alone, just the area where underinvestment has allegedly hurt us most (cars, steel, appliances, and so on), the rate of growth in capital spending has soared in recent years. From 1947 to 1972 it was 2.4 percent per year. And from 1972 to 1980 it was 6.9 percent. Underinvestment?*

We have seen data earlier showing that research and innovation are a long way from dead in the U.S. High tech and pharmaceuticals are only two examples from a long list showing that Adam Smith's invisible hand still operates: juvenile geniuses and drug company moguls seek creative enrichment and mankind is the cobeneficiary.

But what about quality? Competition? Risk?

Unlike business investment and research, those aspects of our busi-

---

* There was a slowdown during the recession of 1981–82; now there is a pickup again.

ness condition are hard to measure by statistics. So I offer some impressions gathered over the years.

Listen to the way the McDonald's folks talk about how they buy their beef or grade their potatoes. They are not seeking quality because they are nice guys who simply want to be sweet to consumers. They are seeking quality because of Burger King and Burger Chef and Wendy's and the tens of millions of teenagers who rate fast-food joints the way *Guide Michelin* rates restaurants.

Both the McDonald's executives in Chicago and the individual McDonald's franchisers in the field know one thing: their businesses will not survive if people start saying their hamburgers don't taste good.

The fast-food chains are extremely competitive in many other ways. Talk to them about pricing. If Burger Chef lowers prices to 65 cents per burger, then McDonald's usually follows. If they don't, they lose customers and they know it. If the restrooms in one chain or one store are dirty, they lose customers.

Professor John Kenneth Galbraith believes that we operate increasingly in a world of "administered prices," where competition plays an ever smaller role, allowing industrial moguls regularly and unimaginatively to squeeze a safe stream of high profits from unwary customers. Such is not the sense one gets talking to the men who run the nation's food chains. These executives come from a world where housewives clip coupons worth a nickel and go from one chain store to another because the price of peanut butter is a penny or two less. When enough women cross the median strip to shop at a competitor's store, your store can go bust. It's a risky business. Compete? Those fellows will cut each other's hearts out!

There is competition and risk at the penny level and at high levels as well. The scholars who say American businessmen are afraid of risk have not heard oil men belittle other oil men for being chicken, because they would not invest a quarter of a *billion* dollars in a prospective oil field, which even the chicken-callers acknowledge is nothing better than a crap shoot, with the odds five or ten to one against.

The spectacular failures give the best sense of the risks involved. Some years ago geologic surveys showed that oil might be located offshore in the George's Bank area off of Massachusetts's coast. From 1979 to 1982, five oil companies put up $1.1 billion in drilling and leasing expenses, and found nothing.

But there are successes, too. From 1970 to 1982, American oil companies, big ones and many small ones, invested $400 billion in the pursuit of new oil and gas sources. Some of the investment was generally safe. But much of it was drilling into just one more crap shoot, with long odds.

Encouraging all this risk were—profits. Your friendly oil man rolled big dice because he knew that there were potential big profits—really *big* profits—around the next bend. Risk—and profit—still drive the system in a healthy way, and helped turn an energy crisis into an oil glut.

Competition? Of the top 25 companies in the year 1900 only two are on that list today: Dupont and Procter and Gamble (famed as candle-makers at the turn of the century.)

Plenty of risk, quality, and competition, even as the critics carp. Even businessmen often can't see the forest for the trees. Like the rest of our society, they have learned to declare that the sky is falling. Yet the managers end up managing pretty well.

A great caterwaul about overregulation erupted in the mid-1970s. Businessmen said that a wave of new federal regulations—and the self-righteous and antagonistic attitude behind the regulator's smile—made it very difficult and costly to conduct certain sorts of businesses.

A second complaint dealt with tax policy. It was said that it was becoming unwise and unprofitable, to invest.

Businessmen claimed it was tax policy and the costs of regulation, real and psychological, that led to less research, less investment, less competition. The high cost of regulation, it was said, was driving out the little guy. The drug folks came to Washington and complained that regulation was preventing them from developing new drugs. The high-tech folks came to Washington and said their industry was stag-nating because it could no longer attract venture capital to gin up new products.

Luckily, the lobbyists left some people back at the lab who didn't get the message. Soon new drugs and home computers and video games and every imaginable gimmick were on their way to market.

Regulations and tax policy may indeed have harassed American business. But such was the underlying strength of the system that it went right along its merry way, complaining, looking for loopholes, lobbying, complying with, and trying to dodge, a blizzard of regula-tions, but always producing, producing, producing.

Curiously, while all the (often legitimate) complaints about regu-lation were being aired, something else was happening: deregulation.

Airlines, trucks, buses, broadcasting, phone service, all found some comfortable regulatory havens shattered. At the bars and at the semi-nars the same businessmen who had denounced *regulation*, were now denouncing *deregulation* of their own industries. Many airline executives said dereg would hurt airlines and the public, American Telephone and Telegraph said dereg would hurt AT&T and harm the public. Television broadcasters said that deregulation would hurt the television industry and harm the public, and besides, why did we need more than three networks anyway?

As deregulation has progressed, the controversy about its value rages. But no serious analyst would deny that deregulation has considerably increased competition, this at a time when one big argument against the business community is that American business had forgotten how to compete.

All of a sudden there is Ma Bell competing with MCI and Sprint for long distance calls and with Radio Shack for crazy new phones that do everything but salute the flag. Trucking company executives who routinely used to schedule their trucks to go one way loaded and one way empty (their schedules set by regulations) suddenly found themselves competing with Mom and Pop operations that were able to work it out so their trucks could carry goods both ways. Big airlines flying routes long protected by a Civil Aeronautics Board umbrella suddenly found themselves in a Darwinian economic jungle. What was Air Florida doing in Toledo? How could anyone compete with the Eastern shuttle on the strength of a bagel in a basket (New York Air)? Braniff was an innovator—how could Braniff go under? Fly from New York to California for $99? And from New York to Kansas City for $160? What is a Peoples Express?

Competition reigns.

———

There may be a pattern in all this frenetic business activity. The pattern involves the lack of a clear pattern. Our business system, like the rest of our system, is more open than ever. Our systems respond, in the market and in the legislature, or die.

If you can't make a buck at smokestack industries, try oil or high tech. If that doesn't work, try fast food and nursing homes. If regulation is hurting the drug business, lobby against the regulations and simultaneously figure out ways to keep producing new drugs, or else foreign firms will produce all the new drugs. If tax policy is making it difficult to draw venture capital into the high-tech businesses, then lobby for changes (which was successfully accomplished). If some of the merger activity is turning out to be stultifying, then unmerge, spin off businesses to executives who will run them as entrepreneurs (a new trend).

Every trend has a countertrend. The stock market is underpriced? Not for long. Business failures are up? So are new business formations. What happens if you are not flexible enough? Not responsive enough, not lucky enough, not quick enough? You get in big trouble—witness the American automobile industry.

Making gas guzzlers when people wanted misers and then, curiously, making small cars when customers wanted big cars again, making expensive cars with expensive labor using outdated manufacturing equipment, treating labor cavalierly—doing all this while Japanese manufacturers were doing it the right way—hurt plenty. Profits plunging, losses growing, market share declining, workers out of work, political pressures mounting, Chrysler on the ropes, such were the fruits of unresponsiveness.

But the response to unresponsiveness has yielded a new round of responsiveness. American automobile manufacturers make better cars now, and treat workers better. Labor unions—an often unappreciated source of industrial stability—go to givebacks, when they have to. Regulators ease up. The sight of recession sharpens the mind. The business system in America is not working badly. It responds in one way or another.

In Washington, in New York, in universities and board rooms, in think tanks and at editorial meetings, the talk is of money supply, the velocity of M-1 and big deficits. Of course these things affect our economic health, but something else much more important is going on.

One gets the sense of an arcane conversation going on among learned economic experts standing at the edge of a superhighway. They don't agree on much except that they have all been wrong in the past and don't quite understand how the system works. While they are arguing about disintermediation rates, a huge eighteen-wheel trailer truck is barreling down the road, ready to blow them aside. That eighteen-wheeler is the American economy itself, the largest, most innovative, most prosperous economic machine in all history. Sometimes the vehicle sputters for a moment or two, a tire may be low, the steering linkages getting a little loose. But we fix it as we go along and it just keeps barreling along.

Economic theory has faltered. The economy is doing pretty well.

CHAPTER 34

The Rest of the World

INTERNATIONAL PROGRESS

While this book concentrates on America, it is relevant to note that a good part of its thesis can be universalized; much the same kind of good news/bad news case can be made about the rest of the world. It is not only the American condition that has improved. *The human condition has improved.*

I offer here only a once-over lightly. Consider first the poor nations of the so-called Third World. What do we hear about them? Unrelieved poverty, population explosion, hunger, illiteracy, ill health. But here are some data vignettes to lay alongside that picture, distilled from World Bank data for the "lowest income" nations. The nations involved include Bangladesh, China, Zaire, India and thirty others. Their populations total 2.2 billion, about half the world total.

- From 1960 to 1982—that's just one generation—life expectancy at birth in these lowest income nations went up from 42 years to 59 years!
- It's no wonder—during the same time the number of physicians per capita *doubled.*
- Health involves nutrition as well as doctors. From 1974 to 1980—in just six years—the daily per capita calorie supply in the poorest nations went up from 2036 to 2218, 97 percent of the "daily requirement."
- From 1960 to 1980, the number of literate adults in the LDCs went from 480 million to 1.2 billion. As a percentage of a growing LDC population, that amounts to a rise from 39 percent literate to 56 percent literate in a single generation. Things are changing.
- Nowhere is the change in the poorest countries more apparent than when measured by energy consumption. The use of energy resources to replace human drudgery, be it with a tractor or an electric light bulb, is the hallmark of the move from a

pre-modern to a modern society. In the last two decades, energy consumption per capita in the developing countries has gone up by 81 percent!

- Communications. People in the poorest countries—even peasants in remote areas—are beginning to find out what's going on in the world. The number of radios per capita in the developing world went up 266 percent in just the sixteen years from 1965 to 1981. Many of these radios are shortwave, which means that a peasant in a mud hut may be able to hear the Voice of America, the British Broadcasting Company and Radio Moscow. (Our news and their propaganda.)
- Real income has increased remarkably in the world's poorest countries. From 1960 to 1982, GNP per capita went up at a rate of 3.0 percent per year, despite a huge gain in population. Should that rate continue, real income per capita would double every 24 years—going up about sixteen-fold in a century.
- From the early 1960s to the early 1980s, the total fertility rate (TFR) in the low income countries dropped from 6.0 children per woman to 4.1 children per woman.
- Contributing to all of the above was official development aid from the rich nations. In constant 1980 dollars, development assistance donated by free industrial nations went from $18.2 billion in 1970, to $27.4 billion in 1983.

Now it is true that these sorts of data are very, very broad. They can be manipulated in a variety of ways to prove almost anything. Thus: most of the numbers deal with an entire generation, roughly 1960 to 1980, but, as in the U.S., progress was generally sharper and wider in the Sixties than in the Seventies. Thus: there were losers as well as winners in the mix. Thus: progress in the Seventies can be split between those nations that had oil and those that didn't, with the oil nations doing much better. Thus: the recent oil glut has tended to reverse matters. Thus: the recent global recession hurt almost everyone.

Still, the evidence is clear. In the poorest, most backward, least developed nations of the world—where the news we hear is almost always bad, where indeed many truly sorry conditions remain—the human condition has improved remarkably.

(We ignore in this quick analysis those nations the World Bank describes as "middle income." These include the real success stories that are often commented upon: South Korea, Venezuela, Ivory Coast, Brazil, etc.)

What about the rich nations? Because more precise data are available, we look now only at the last decade or so—from 1970 on. And we use data basically from those nations that make up the Organization for Economic Cooperation and Development (OECD). These include not only the U.S. and Western Europe, but Japan, Canada and the Antipodes.

These nations, like the U.S., have been roiled by recession and rattled by inflation. And even more than the U.S., most of the nations have been harshly buffeted by unemployment. The news on their television sets has also been glum. But here are some data:

- Per capita income, after discounting for inflation, went up over 23 percent from 1970 to 1981—about 2 percent per year.
- The number of cars per 1000 persons has gone from 364 in 1970 to 534 in 1980.
- The number of young people graduating from college went up by 70 percent in the last decade, while the college-age populalation went up only 5 percent. Not so bad for a maligned decade.

There is a final piece to the puzzle. We have statistically toe-dipped everywhere but in the Communist world—in UN parlance, the "East European Non-Market Economies." How have they fared?

Also well—despite all the stories of economic stagnation. Some data:

- Life expectancy at birth went up from 68 years in 1960 to 72 years in 1981.
- There was a physician for every 683 persons in 1960, and one for every 356 persons in 1980.
- The GNP per capita went from $4,974 in 1970 to $6,414 in 1982.
- The number of students going on to higher education went from 11 percent in 1960 to 20 percent in 1980.

As may be guessed, I am not in the business of shouting hosannas about the Communist nations. But facts are facts, and the facts are fairly clear: the Communist nations too have moved ahead in the economic realm—although, where comparisons are valid, they have generally moved forward at a slower rate than in the free world. (Their big problem isn't bread; it's liberty.)

All in all, plenty of progress in every area of the world. And if one wants to reaggregate and look at the whole world at once, here are a few statistical sidebars of the spavined Seventies:

Ringing in your ears: 7.5 phones in use per 100 world inhabitants in 1970—and 11.5 in 1980.

Auto convince you: 194 million cars in use in 1970—and 316 million ten years yater. A 63 percent increase while world population went up by 23 percent.

Flying high: The number of world airline passengers more than doubled during the decade, from 312 million to 645 million.

The green revolution: In constant dollars, GNP per capita went up from $2,299 in 1970 to $2,716 in 1982.

Shocking Electricity generated went up by 62 percent from 1970 to 1982.

A logical question arises: Is the author a little bit daft? After all, is it plausible that almost everywhere we look at home, and almost everywere we look abroad, there is progress? Is it possible the author is gilding a lily?

A logical answer arises: The logic of the situation tells us that just as it would be most unlikely for progress to occur in only one sector of our society, it would be unlikely to occur in only one sector of the world. Call it trickle-down, or bubble-up, or interdependence, the component parts of an economy are related. Sooner or later, we share the same new technologies, the same medicines, and often the same procedures. It's no wonder we're all doing so well. We are living at a moment when things are getting better.

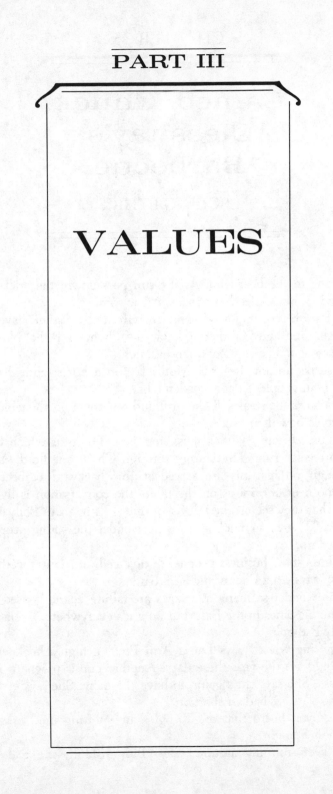

PART III

VALUES

CHAPTER 35

Cameo: Chuck Cleeshay's Barbecue

ERODING ETHICS

It is spring in the heartland. As the sun goes down, the crickets are chirping in Chuck Cleeshay's spacious backyard.

Chuck is an accountant. He and his wife, Polly Esther, have three grown children. His brother, Claude, left home for the Northeast many years ago. They are not often in touch.

The steaks are on the grill. Moths fry on a bug-sizzling hanging lantern. Four couples sit a wooden table.

Chuck takes the steaks off the grill and sets them on the table. The eight people bow their heads.

"Bless us, O Lord," Chuck says, "for these Thy gifts which we are about to receive from Thy bounty through Christ our Lord. Amen."

Although no martinis are served at this backyard barbecue, although no beer or wine is on the table, the conversation is lively.

"It's what they see on the television that does it," says Polly Esther Cleeshay. "There's so much sex, it's no wonder the young people are so charged up."

"All those show business people are divorced, or living together, or on drugs," says Chet Frett of the local bank.

"It's no wonder so many marriages are falling apart. It used to be just in the big cities in the East, but now it's everywhere. Even here," says Polly Esther.

"It's getting worse," says Laura Ann Frett, a high school teacher. "You should see the girls these days! Another one is pregnant in my civics class. She says she's going to have the baby. She says everyone else in the class has had an abortion."

"I guess you heard that the Klingles are splitting up?" asks Reverend Louis Straight.

"He's been running around," says Billy Kilduff, the real estate broker.

"Not only him," LaVerne Straight says, "but her too."

"How are the kids taking it?" asks Jane Kilduff.

"I'm not sure they'll know the difference," says LaVerne. "She works nights. He works days—I don't think the kids ever see their parents."

"It's no wonder the youngsters are going wild," says Chuck. "Drugs and drinking. Massage parlors. Rock 'n' roll. Pornography."

"We sure don't see them in church," says Reverend Straight.

"Someone told me that Klingle's boy is queer," says Chuck. "Can you imagine that?"

"I can imagine it," says Polly Esther. "It's what they see on television."

"It's what they learn in sex education class in high school," says Chuck. "They tell 'em queer is okay."

"They don't pray in school. It's no wonder the family is falling apart in America," says Reverend Straight, "just falling apart."

"And not only the family," says Chet Frett. "Just try to get people at the office to put in a full day's work! Forget it!"

"The work ethic is gone," says Jane. "Why should people work, if they can get it for free on welfare? It's the politicians; they don't have any discipline. They give away everything to anyone who has a vote. If they don't have the money, they just print it up."

"There's no responsibility anywhere," says LaVerne. "People buy everything on credit, then they go bankrupt and start all over."

"People just don't care about others anymore," says Billy. "They just care about themselves."

"That's what causes all the crime. They just do what they want," says Chet. "They rob and steal and rape. I see it on TV all the time."

"And cheat on their taxes," says Chuck Cleeshay. "I see it on their tax returns. You'd be surprised what I see."

"They care about themselves all right, but not about their country," says Billy. "You don't have that patriotism anymore."

"It's the television," says Polly Esther.

"And the schools," says LaVerne. "I see those textbooks. They say we're the bad guys, that we murdered the Indians. No wonder no one's patriotic anymore. No wonder the Russians are pushing us around all over the world."

"It's a shame," says Chuck. "We just don't have values in this country anymore."

=====

Some notes on some themes before we try to get specific about the murky realm of values, which does not lend itself easily to specifics:

The first big argument dealt with in this book—that the quality of life is eroding—is made most intensely and most persuasively on the liberal side of the spectrum. It's mostly liberals who say "the enemy is us," who warn of the carcinogen-of-the-month, who tell us that James Watt wanted to pave Yosemite, probably with dioxins.

The second big argument—that the economy is in a shambles—has been endorsed over recent years across the political and ideological spectrum. Carter said Ford screwed up the economy; Reagan says Carter screwed up the economy; the Democrats say Reagan screwed up the economy; big labor said we're in a depression; big business says the Japanese are invading. Labor says unemployment's a disaster; business says inflation's a disaster. Almost everyone seems to agree that deficits are going to get us. It's been a wall-to-wall coalition of gloom and alarm from far Right to far Left. One and all, as we have seen, have been at least exaggerating when not plain wrong.

As proof positive of the even-handedness of this volume, we now deal with an argument that seems to come mostly from the conservative side of the aisle. It is this: *our values are eroding*. This is happening, so goes the case, because our discipline has eroded on the personal level, and partly as a result, on the political level as well.

To be sure, some liberals are also in the values game. Liberals will denounce the stupor of television violence, condemn the crass materialism of plastic America, abhor militarism and jingoism. But just as the momentum for environmentalism came from liberals, it should be acknowledged that the public outcry over values has come from the heartland, not the coasts; from Reaganauts, not McGovernites; from fundamentalists, not modernists.

I make this point because of an irony with a point to it that tends to universalize my general thesis here. In one sense, conservative naysaying is somewhat hypocritical. Conservatives, unlike liberals, complain that we are drenched in bad news, soaked in negativism, a complaint the author obviously shares. But when it comes to values, conservatives have their own tidal waves of bad news, their own thunderstorms of negativism.

The point is this: almost everyone in the public arena in America makes a case that we're in big trouble. Bad news is pervasive. As we shall continue to note, that view is often wrong—wrong when it comes from conservatives, wrong when it comes from liberals.

═══

As with the allegedly eroding economic situation and the allegedly eroding quality of life, the charges about values and discipline are serious ones and not without at least some merit. After all, despite its public genesis on the conservative side of the culture, who among us—liberal or conservative, religious or irreligious—is not concerned (for example) about young people and drugs? Or violent crime? Or illegitimacy?

And so I ask in this part of the book these questions:

- Have our values changed?
- If they have, is that bad?
- If it's bad, is it getting better?

My answers are these:

- Less than you think.
- Better than you think.
- Correcting more quickly than you think.

=====

In large measure, what we have been talking about so far in this book deals with "conditions and behavior." It has been maintained, for example, that we are healthier, wealthier, better housed, more educated. It has been noted that people are moving to rural areas, that more immigrants are arriving. Conditions and behavior are changing.

Now, as we step into the dim area of values, it may be wise to pause for a moment to think about just what it is we will be talking about. Values, as used here, primarily concern "beliefs," as opposed to "conditions" or "behavior," although there is often an intermingling of all of the above, and we will touch on all three ideas.

It gets complicated. The key point to remember as we proceed is not to automatically confuse what *happens* with what we *believe*.

=====

The changes in values seem to break down into two general categories: private and public.

The *private* values—religion, family, sex—are dealt with sequentially in the chapters that follow.

The values that affect our *public* way of life must be dealt with in a somewhat more complex arrangement. There are two chapters (39 and 40) in this Values section that treat certain public issues—work and crime. But as the focus on public values expands, we will move into another section of the book—about politics—first dealing with domestic politics and then foreign policy, without losing interest in the values issue. Along the way, we will look at patriotism, confidence, tolerance. Stay tuned.

But in all of these areas, private, public, political, the basic three-step formulation usually seems to hold up. There's been less change than you think; it's been better than we've been led to believe; where it's gone overboard, it's self-corrected more quickly than might have been imagined.

======

These three ideas—less, better, quicker—do not seem to be co-equal. One looms somewhat larger than the others. My evidence comes mostly from many years of animated discussion with some unusual people.

It is my good fortune to be a Senior Fellow at the American Enterprise Institute (AEI), a leading think tank in Washington, D.C. At AEI, I am coeditor of a magazine called *Public Opinion*. Although we believe our magazine publishes distinguished articles of general interest, our claim to fame is "Opinion Roundup," a regular twenty-page center section that presents the distilled results of public-opinion polling in America and around the world.

Many of my colleagues in this endeavor are social scientists of the highest caliber. Social scientists can be ranked like yachts. My co-editor at *Public Opinion* is Seymour Martin Lipset, surely a world-class sociologist, most recently coauthor of *The Confidence Gap*, a study of American attitudes about institutions. (Lipset's coauthor is William Schneider, another AEI Fellow and a regular contributor to *Public Opinion*.) The consulting editor for the "Opinion Roundup" section is Everett Carll Ladd, who is also director of the Roper Center for Public Opinion Research, affiliated with the University of Connecticut, Yale University and Williams College. Our magazine also has a contract with the Roper Center, which is the most complete archive of survey research in the world. Social scientists at Roper work with us in preparing and distilling our selection of polling material.

The maestro of this effort is Managing Editor Karlyn H. Keene, who has herself written at length about what the polls mean. She was preceded in her post by David Gergen, who left a perfectly good job to become communications director for the Reagan White House.

Now, when "values" are at issue, it is not usually possible to use documentation as precise as the demographic and economic data we have seen so frequently in this book. Knowledge typically comes from a softer set of numbers—derived from public opinion polls. Public opinion data are more impressionistic. The numbers can say many different things to different people. "Statistical impressionism" is a bizarre phrase, but in many subject areas no serious student of survey research should claim much more capability for his trade.

Well, at *Public Opinion,* we have pursued statistical impressionism with a vengeance. We sift through mountainous piles of poll data, we consult with our authors in America and around the world. We banter back and forth, usually joined by our other editors. Victoria Sackett and Nicola Furlan. Impressions form. And over the years, one startling theme has surfaced over and over again in our conversations. It can be heard as a delicate flute solo—a single line on a graph—again with rich string accompaniment—stacks of charts—yet again as a piano melody—well-argued data-backed articles—and finally as a thundering full-bodied sociological symphony, with pounding drums, blaring trumpets, and crashing cymbals.

That shocking theme is: *continuity not change.*

The key concept in our triad of less-change/better-change/corrective change—is "less." *Less change in values than you think.*

What makes this notion startling is that it runs counter to almost everything that most Americans read about, hear about, or talk about, counter to what's on television, what's in the newspaper, what's in the classroom, what's supposed to be in the culture. People naturally enough think about change. In a media culture, like ours, that general concern is compounded exponentially.

And so, over the years—particularly over the last twenty or so—we have heard about change that has allegedly wrenched us from one era to another. After all, there were riots, Vietnam, the drug culture. There was what is always called "the trauma of Watergate." There was the generation gap, the sexual revolution, a crime wave, and women's liberation. There was the energy crisis and there was inflation. There was malaise. There was the greening of America, future shock, the "Me decade," the culture of narcissism, megatrends, the gender gap and "new ideas," courtesy of the 1984 campaign of Senator Gary Hart.

So much talk about change. And all that change, remember, followed tumultuous decades of depression and war.

It is, then, startling to talk to Theodore Caplow. Professor Caplow was head of a team of sociologists that spent several years in the late 1970s in Muncie, Indiana, the small midwestern American city that had been studied, as "Middletown," by sociologists Robert and Helen Lynd in the 1920s and the 1930s. Using the Lynds' 1920 data as a baseline, Caplow and his colleagues set out to measure the change that had taken place in the ensuing half century in a community that has come to be known as "typical." They worked in Muncie for six years, and have begun to produce a remarkable series of books.*

When it was all over, I interviewed Caplow on PBS and asked him about his general conclusions.

After noting some change, Caplow said this: "If Rip Van Winkle had fallen asleep in the late 1920s and had awakened in the early 1980s, he really wouldn't find things that different."

Now don't get me wrong: there are things that have changed in the values arena. Big things. We shall be discussing those changes. But it is the idea of continuity in a time of turmoil that keeps coming up when we statistical impressionists talk about the data in our ongoing bull sessions. It is that view that takes primacy (although not dominance) in the discussion of values that follows.

* The first of their published findings: *Middletown Families: Fifty Years of Change and Continuity* by Theodore Caplow, Howard M. Bahr, Bruce A. Chadwick, Reuben Hill, Margaret Holmes Williamson. Minneapolis: University of Minnesota Press, 1982.

CHAPTER 36

In God We Trust

RELIGION

Our general case is that the change in American private values has been less stark than portrayed.

That is not the case with religion. It's not that there has been only a slight erosion of religious values. There is hardly an objective standard that shows *any* recent erosion of religious life in America. In fact, a funny thing may have happened on the way to moral degeneration: in some ways religious activity got stronger.

A quick sketch of the facts:

Since the late 1960s the rate of Americans who attended church or synagogue "in the last seven days" has remained almost constant. That rate was 42 percent in 1969—and 40 percent in 1983. Moreover, the data show that another 16 percent had attended church or synagogue at least once within the past month, although not within the past week.

George Gallup, Jr., believes that this constancy in church attendance actually masks some upward change. People under thirty are typically less active in church than are their elders. In the Seventies, as the Baby Boom cohort became young adults, they tended to depress the national averages. In the Eighties, says Gallup, these young adults will move into middle age and church attendance should climb.

Other indices already show an increase in religious activity.

Gallup data show that during the four years from 1978 to 1981, the percentage of adults receiving religious education (Bible study, retreats, college courses, and so on) climbed from 17 percent to 26 percent. The sharpest percentage increase was among young adults. There has also been a significant increase in the rate of teenagers engaging in Bible study. (According to popular reports of teenage behavior, we might assume that such activity takes place in the early part of an evening that will later be devoted to dope, pornographic movies, and promiscuous sex.)

And consider college students: In 1975, 39 percent said that religion was very important in their lives. In 1983 that number was 50 percent. The 1983 Gallup survey also showed that the proportion of college youth who said that their religious commitment had become stronger since entering college was *twice* the percentage saying it had become weaker!

Some of the best-selling books in the last decade in America have been religious books. Gallup polls in 1982 found that 32 percent of Americans had watched religious programs on television during the prior seven days. Religious organizations get almost half the country's philanthropic contributions. Consistent with all of this, a plurality of Americans believe that religion has been gaining influence:

Question: At the present time, do you think religion as a whole is increasing its influence on American life or losing its influence?

	Increasing	Losing
1970	14%	75%
1983	44%	42%

Source: Gallup.

Numbers, numbers, numbers. But what about values? Do Americans still believe in God? After all, in theory at least, Americans could be going to church or feel religion is more influential because there has been new attention paid to the Social Gospel—Central American death squads, nuclear frigidity, and so on. That might tell us a lot about churches, but not much about deeper questions of religious belief among the people in the pews.

We have numbers about beliefs, too. A massive study by Gallup in 1982 found not only that most Americans continued to accept basic religious principles, but that they were also far more likely to do so than residents of other major developed nations:

Question: Which, if any, of the following do you believe in?

	Percentage "Yes"	
	"God"	*"Heaven"*
U.S.A.	95	84
Italy	84	41
Great Britain	76	57
West Germany	72	31
France	62	27
Japan	39	20

Source: Gallup, 1982 (European Value System Study Group).

* The figures for Ireland, not listed here as a "major" country, are about as high as the U.S.A. numbers. We are, by any global standard, a very religious people.

There is yet another way to see this. Within Protestantism, for example, the headlines have gone to mainline Protestant churches moving in public ways toward less traditional and less overtly religious values.

But the result of all this detraditionalizing has been quite dramatic. In the last five years church membership has remained about constant. But that covers up some significant internal movement within the religious world. Those churches that have been liberalizing, detraditionalizing, and politicizing have been losing members. And the more traditionalist churches, mostly fundamental and evangelical, which have retained the quaint belief that religion has more to do with God than with Central America, have been gaining.

This trend is also apparent within Judaism. As reform and conservative rabbis concentrated on Vietnam and arms control, it was the orthodox congregations that gained the most members.

One explanation for this trend has been "political conservatism." There is a belief, fostered by political activists of the Left and the Right, that religious fundamentalists in America are a massive and growing right-wing force. Liberals raise money and raise consciousness on this proposition. (Falwell is coming! Falwell is coming!) Conservatives use the same idea to flex their political muscles. (Vote our way or we're going to get you in November!)

The fact is, American evangelicals (for one example) are a pretty middle-of-the-road lot:

	Evangelicals*	All Voters
Favor death penalty	51%	52%
Favor government programs to deal with social problems	54%	53%

Source: Gallup, 1980.

* Evangelicals defined as respondents who satisfied three separate criteria: indicated they were "born again" or had had a "born again" experience, had "encouraged someone to believe in Jesus Christ," and believed "the Bible is the actual word of God and has to be taken literally word for word."

But here is one issue where there is sharp divergence:

	Evangelicals	All Voters
Favor *requiring* prayer in public school*	81%	54%

* This is a tougher statement than the normally phrased version which deals with *voluntary* prayer.

Source: Gallup, 1980.

These folks are not conservative. They are religious.

So are most Americans, at least as much so as ever before, and maybe more so. Continuity, not change.

CHAPTER 37

No Nuclear
Meltdown

FAMILY

In the realm of private values, nothing demonstrates our thesis and its tangents better than what has been heard in recent years about "the family."

The case of the foundering family should be familiar, if for no other reason than because so much of its demographic base has already been described here: more divorces, more working women, more singles, more unmarried couples, more illegitimacy. When all those factors are combined with a subject we haven't yet dealt with—an alleged increase in nonmarital sexual activity—then the case for familial dissolution becomes not only sociological but sexy.

And so we have been regaled in recent years by one story after another announcing the meltdown of the nuclear family. Indeed, it is this idea more than any other that has scared the pants off of traditionalists in America.

Much of this is hokum. Much of it is hokum because, as we shall see, the concept of a strong family should be measured mostly attitudinally, not demographically. Much of it is hokum because there has been a massive confusion between values and behavior. Much of it is hokum because our central values thesis—Less-Better-Correcting—holds up. Many of the changes in the American family have probably been salutary. Insofar as some of the harmful changes have indeed been harmful, they are now reversing. And much of it is hokum mostly because there has not been much of a change at all. Continuity, not change.

ATTITUDES

Family has been, is, and undoubtedly will remain the most important value in our lives.

The public opinion data provide a strange picture if one tries to back up the notion that family values are fracturing. In 1982 the General Social Survey of the National Opinion Research Center (NORC) asked respondents about the importance of "one's own family and children":

ASPECT OF LIFE:
OWN FAMILY AND CHILDREN, 1982

"Unimportant"	2%
"Somewhat important"	1%
"Important"	97%

Source: NORC, 1982.

Of course, that might be expected, but it is interesting to note that while only 3 percent of Americans ranked family as less than important to them, in the same poll 58 percent ranked "politics and public life" as less than important, and 26 percent ranked "religion and church" that way.

Family is important. In recent years, Yankelovich, Skelly and White have been asking whether a "happy family life" is the *most* important value. It's a good question. After all, we've lived through a time characterized as a "Me Decade," we have been bombarded by the glories of "self-actualization" and exhorted to "do your own thing"—hardly code phrases that would lead one to think that family values are regnant.

Yet, in 1981, about three-quarters of the respondents (77 percent) indicated that family life was indeed *most* important to them. By contrast only 13 percent of the respondents said that "opportunity to develop as an individual" was their most important value, only 7 percent said that a "fulfilling career" was most important, and in this money-grubbing land of ours, only 4 percent said "making a lot of money" was most important. Moreover, these proportions changed only slightly from 1973 to 1981, the years Yankelovich, Skelly and White was asking the questions.*

* Because strong family values were taken for granted by pollsters until relatively recently, there is little direct, continuous polling data going back many decades. Back in 1940, however, Gallup asked a similar sort of question: "If

So family life is "important." It is "most important." And as surveys tell us, it's also "satisfying." Polling in the early 1980s by the National Opinion Research Center showed that 87 percent of respondents derived a "very great deal" or a "great deal" of satisfaction from "family life"—the number-one ranking of all aspects of life brought up by the interviewers, which included "friendships," "health and physical condition," "nonworking activities/hobbies," and so on.

Family relationships are important, most important, satisfying, and "frequent" as well. NORC polls in 1982 and 1983 show that 53 percent of Americans "spend a social evening with relatives" at least "several times a month." This compares with 19 percent who, over the same time frame, "go to a bar or tavern."†

Important, most important, satisfying, frequent—and "happy," too. Recent NORC polling shows about two-thirds of married Americans reporting that they are "very happy with marriage," while roughly another 30 percent report they are "pretty happy." The actual "very happy" figures were all between 65 percent and 68 percent in each of eight polls taken from 1973 to 1982. Talk about continuity.

All that, and Americans want even more:

Question: Many people feel we are undergoing a period of rapid social change in this country today and that people's values are changing at the same time. Which of the following changes would you welcome, which would you reject and which would leave you indifferent?

---

you could be sure of only one of the following which would you choose—wealth, a happy home or an interesting job?" The happy home choice won out, but with only a 69 percent rating, lower than the modern levels. In any event, the recent data is so overwhelmingly positive that if there has been any decline since earlier times, it can only have been modest.

† Some historical perspective:
"It used to be thought that families living in modern cities had little contact with their relatives. This idea was suggested when people compared the apparent individualism of their own family lives with their fondly held, though often misguided, images of the "good old days." During the past two decades, there has been much careful research on kinship ties, and the general findings of these studies are (1) that kinship ties are extremely important in contemporary urban society and (2) that the existence of a vital all-embracing extended family of the 'good old days' was mostly a myth." *Middletown Families,* 1982, op. cit.

"More emphasis on traditional family ties"

Welcome	86%
Reject	2%
Indifferent	11%

"More acceptance of sexual freedom"

Welcome	23%
Reject	49%
Indifferent	28%

Source: Yankelovich, Skelly and White, 1982.

So: the family, as seen through the lens of national public opinion polls, is important, most important, satisfying, omnipresent, and people want more of it. What scholarship there is on the subject suggests clearly that none of this is new. It is old. It is as ever. It is continuity, not change. Bliss.

DEMOGRAPHICS

So the core value of family has survived, and with flying colors.

But those who make the case for the change in family tend to ignore these *attitudinal* data about values and concentrate instead on the idea that *demographic* and *behavioral* change really reveal changes in values. Is that valid?

The keystone of the sociodemographic case for family erosion goes something like this: "Aha! Statistics show that only 35 percent of American households are made up of what was once seen as a traditional family—husband, wife, and offspring." Therefore, it is implied, only 35 percent of us are traditional, while the other 65 percent of us are not. That's the trend, it is said: the traditional family is eroding, the wave of the future is singles, swingles, divorced people, female-headed households.

Sounds bad. But some of that formulation is just plain silly. It's only a snapshot in time. And some of it is not silly, but quite complex.

As we've seen, there *are* more nontraditional households than before, but that doesn't give a clear answer in itself. For example: Americans live longer these days. That means that typically they have more years of life left after their last child leaves home. That boosts the percentage of the population who do not live in a husband-wife-children mode. But are an eighty-year-old husband and wife really to be counted as "nontraditional" just because they've lived long enough to see all their children leave home?

Likewise, some households are counted "nontraditional" because they are composed of young married couples who haven't had a first child yet. But what could be more square than getting married before having a child? That's the traditional way of doing it, you know.

Is it "nontraditional" that young Americans are marrying about two years later than they used to a couple of decades ago? Comparatively, perhaps, but a woman getting married at twenty-two (the median age in 1980) doesn't sound like a very nontraditional life-style.

Is it really very "nontraditional" that young people these days earn much more money than their counterparts in earlier times and consequently can afford to live as singles before marrying, rather than boarding with parents?

Yet all these changes in life-style reduce at any given moment the percentage of Americans in the "traditional" family configuration, lending some statistical, but little human, credence to the idea of family erosion. For these people, marriage and family are still, or will be, the central facts of their lives.

So it is not quite so simple as the foundering-family folks have made it out to be. The focus must be made tighter to yield some coherence. For example, back in 1970 the percentage of children under eighteen who lived in a household with both parents was 89 percent. By 1982, that rate had diminished to 79 percent. That is, of course, an important change, and one that gives a better sense of how much one aspect the "nontraditional" family may really have grown in recent years, from about one in ten to about two in ten.

In short, the demographic case for the breakup of the traditional family is more complicated than usually understood. On balance, it seems somewhat less potent than the bad-news press clippings that have heralded the proposition.

Bolstering this idea, and getting behind much of the complexity is another thought. It yields some Super Numbers. Consider what seems to me to be the most relevant question about traditional family values: what percentage of Americans *EVER* enter into the traditional family model?

That, I think, is the right question.

For in its essence, the family is forever. It is the forming act of our lives. Once done it is typically irreversible. If ever done, it is dominant. Thus a man and a woman may start out as singles. They marry fairly late in life—in their thirties—and have, say, two children. That act of marriage-and-children will quite likely be the locus of most of the personal relationships of these four people for many decades, even if that original marriage should end in divorce. The mother is still a mother after a divorce. The father is still a father. The children still have parents. These are, typically, lifetime relationships, stemming from a traditional family, even if the divorced parents should remarry and perhaps raise a second traditional family, starting all over again.

Accordingly, if we are to look for evidence pro and con regarding the alleged erosion of the traditional families, we should be looking most carefully at whether there has been a lessening in the rate of people who opt to partake in its most long-lasting and permanent aspects: marriage and children. We need time exposures, not mere snapshots.

We can get a good sense of that with Census data. By their late thirties and early forties almost all women who will ever get married, have been married. By their late thirties and early forties almost all women who will ever have a child, have had a child. So if we observe women at that age we can see some history.

Here is a marriage Super Number:

WOMEN NEVER MARRIED
(BY AGE) 1982

Age	% Never Married
25–29	23.4%
30–34	11.6%
35–39	6.4% (!)
40–44	4.7% (!!)
65 and over	5.6%

Source: U.S. Census Bureau.

Look carefully at those exclamatory numbers. They tell us that roughly nineteen out of twenty women age thirty-five to forty-four have married.

Now, women aged thirty-five to forty-four in 1982 were born from 1938 to 1947. Most of them have lived as young adults through all or much of the Women's Liberation activity. They have likely entered the labor force (unlike their mothers at corresponding ages). They have read all the magazine articles about the death of the family. They have heard all the talk about independence described in chapter

27—and possibly have been influenced by some of it, as described in that chapter. But when all is said and done—they have married.

Now, of course, we don't know yet what will happen, maritally, to those women aged twenty-five to twenty-nine. Census demographer Arthur Norton suggests that their nonmarried rate will be 8–10 percent by the time they reach their late thirties and early forties, which would be a few points higher than the current cohorts. We shall see. Still, even at that estimate, at least nine out of ten American women will marry. In short: we marry. Marriages start families. We are a family-starting folk.

There is a similar Super Number concerning children:

PERCENT CHILDLESS AMONG EVER-MARRIED WOMEN, BY AGE, 1982

Age	% Childless
25–29	27.5%
30–34	15.4%
35–39	10.2%
40–44	7.6%
50–59	9.7%

The women age thirty-five to thirty-nine came to prime child-bearing age as fertility rates were plunging and family values were being publicly challenged. Still, 90 percent have already had children. That is not unimportant to our argument here. Recall that a pregnant woman is said to be "in a family way."

Now, some of the cards are still out: we don't exactly know what will happen to those twenty-five to twenty-nine-year-old women as they get older. Norton estimates that about 12 percent will never bear a child, a somewhat higher rate than in recent years. We'll see. But again, even if that is so, it means that more than seven out of eight women will become mothers, hardly the portrait of a nation going out of the family business. Coupling this data with earlier (chapter 11) material we see a pattern: women will have fewer children than in earlier years—but almost all of them will have children. Small families—but families.*

---

* The incidence of so-called "barren" women was much greater in earlier years. In 1950, fully 20 percent of the 40–44-year-old married women were without children, compared to the 7.6 percent rate today, or Norton's projection of 12 percent for the future.

A recent study of the Population Reference Bureau makes the point clearly:

> . . . there is no evidence of an embracement of childlessness. Substantial portions of Americans continue to value parenthood, believe that childbearing should accompany marriage, and feel social pressure to have children. Only a very small percentage view childlessness as an advantage, regard the decision not to have children as positive, believe that the ideal family is one without children, or expect to be childless by choice.†

America is still in a family way. Less change than you think.

BEHAVIOR

The fact that the core family values are secure and that the demographic change is less than assumed still does not entirely rebut the idea of starkly changing values. There have been major changes in behavior. Do these signal major changes in values?

Consider divorce.

Our stated formulation holds: despite major changes in behavior, less change in values has taken place than you might think, such value changes as there are may well have been for the better, those value changes that may have been harmful seem to be self-correcting.

As noted earlier (chapter 27) there has been a sharp increase in divorce in this country. Rates more than doubled from 1960 to 1980. Not only that, but Americans seem to approve:

Question: Is it right or wrong for a couple who can't get along to get a divorce?

	Right	Wrong
When children are involved	72%	28%
When no children are involved*	87%	13%

Source: NBC/AP, September 1979.
* 45 percent of all current divorces involve no child under 18.

† "The Changing American Family," *Population Bulletin,* vol. 38, no. 4 (October 1983).

But have our underlying values changed? Does an increase in the rate of divorce indicate a decrease in the value of marriage? Does it degrade the value of family?

There are reasons to think not. Divorce typically is temporary. People who get divorced tend to remarry: within five years of divorce, eight out of ten men remarry, and seven out of ten women remarry. That is not exactly a portrait of marriage as an institution on the ash heap of history. Scholars of the family believe that divorce generally represents dissatisfaction with a specific spouse, not with the institution of marriage.

And then there is the question of whether the higher divorce rates in America are "good." The immediate reaction, at least as usually heard in the public arena, is that more divorce is not good. Divorce is a "problem"; there are all those single-parent households, children without on-site fathers, female poverty, and so on.

But we must return again to a central idea mentioned in both the chapter about women and blacks: divorce is, essentially, a voluntary act certainly for one partner, often for both. For whatever pain it may cause—and that may be substantial—most people get divorced because they believe that a divorce will yield them, and their families, a better life than they had before. That life, typically, was one made at least somewhat miserable by a marriage turned sour.

Viewed from that perspective, we have moved ahead in recent years. In earlier times, an unhappy union may have been continued because there were not adequate financial resources, personal or governmental, to support two households. But higher incomes and a higher social safety net have changed much of that. Options once available only to well-to-do people are available to many more people today.

Who are you, who am I, who are the passionate moralists who decry a higher divorce rate to say that what man and woman have sundered should be put together?

Being in favor of a liberal divorce system, however, is not the same as saying that the current high divorce rate is wonderful, and by God, the higher the better. Americans don't believe that.

There are indications that for all the advantages that may come with a liberal divorce policy, there is also a point of diminishing returns, and that as a society we may have passed that point. Here is the roller-coaster trend:

Question: Should divorce be made *easier* to get?

	% *"Yes"*
1960	10%
1968	19%
1974	34%
1976	28%
1978	28%
1980	21%
1982	24%

Sources: Compiled by *Public Opinion* magazine from Gallup, 1960 and 1968. NORC 1974, 1976, 1978, 1982. Research and Forecasts for Connecticut Mutual Life Insurance Co., 1980.

Maybe, the public seems to be saying, we went a little too far, maybe the permissiveness of the early Seventies was too much.

That attitude seems to be translating into behavior patterns. In 1982 the number of divorces went down, by 3 percent, for the first time in twenty years. The drop continued in 1983, down to the lowest rate since 1977.

So divorce has not eroded the value of marriage, and it's probably begun diminishing. Less change, some of it for the better, and correction of what excess may exist.

CHAPTER 38

The Sexual Evolution

SEX AND PERMISSIVENESS

That divorce is no disaster, that our recorded opinions about family remain highly favorable, that demographic change in family structure reveals less real change than meets the eye still does not entirely do away with the argument about foundering family values.

A huge part of the argument concerns sex. It is a serious argument that goes well beyond who's in the sack with whom. Listen, then, to Clare Booth Luce, a woman of intelligence and experience, worth quoting here at some length because her views will lead us to some interesting places:

Is the New Morality Destroying America?

History . . . tells us that . . . whenever sex becomes, as we would say today, "value-free," the family structure is invariably weakened; crimes of all sorts increase . . . and then more or less rapidly all other social institutions begin to disintegrate, until finally the State itself collapses. Rome is perhaps the most famous example . . .

Today 50% of all marriages end in divorce, separation, or desertion. . . . The marriage rate and birthrate are falling. The numbers of one-parent families and one-child families is rising. More and more young people are living together without benefit of marriage. . . . Premarital and extra-marital sex no longer raises parental or conjugal eyebrows. The practice of "swinging," or group sex, which the ancients called "orgies," has come even to middle-class suburbia.

Despite the availability of contraceptives, there has been an enormous increase in illegitimate births, especially among 13–15 year-olds. The incidence of venereal diseases is increasing. Since the Supreme Court decision made abortion on demand legal, women have killed more than six million of their unborn, unwanted children. The rate of *reported* incest, child-molestation, rape, and child and wife abuse, is steadily mounting. . . . Run-away children, teen-age prostitution, youthful drug-addiction and alcoholism have become great, ugly, new phenomena.

The relief rolls are groaning with women who have been divorced or deserted, together with their children. The mental-homes and rest-homes are crowded with destitute or unwanted old mothers . . .

Homosexuality and Lesbianism are increasingly accepted as natural and alternative "life styles."

. . . In the last decade, hard-core film and print porn, which features perversion, sadism and masochism, has become a billion dollar business . . .

Now when we examine the "new" sexual morality, what do we discover? We discover that the new sexual morality comes perilously close to being the old universal sexual immorality, whose appearance has again and again portended the decline and fall of past civilizations. . . . The principle on which the new sexual morality is based is sexual selfishness, self-indulgence, and self-gratification. Its credo is I-I-I, Me-Me-Me, and to hell with what others call sex morals . . . (Clare Booth Luce, *The Human Life Review*, 1978)

Not exactly your everyday conservative portrait of America getting better every day in every way. Who said only liberals are nay-sayers?

Yet, Mrs. Luce raises most of the correct issues—from homosexuality and "swinging" to self-indulgence and selfishness. And through the prism of sexual behavior she comes to a powerful, more general theme that is a mainspring of conservative thought: *permissiveness leads to personal and national decay*.

What to make of this argument?

To begin, Mrs. Luce is loose with both some facts and some implications. Moreover, the cited extract is from 1978, and there have been some important changes since then. At the risk of some repetition, some of the facts are worth a very quick rundown.

Thus: the actual number of marriages is going up—to a record high in 1982. The marriage rate has not fallen; it is stable, about where it always has been. The birthrate is indeed low, but no longer falling. Americans have smaller families—but they have families, in fact, which are more likely to have *some* children than in some earlier times. America is still the most religious country in the developed world.

Thus: rest homes are crowded with old women, not because of male irresponsibility, but because women are living longer and outliving their husbands. It is possible that increased welfare has increased dependency, but it is certain that we instituted welfare programs to provide for women and children who were already in need and who were not being taken care of.

Thus: if modern "swinging" equates with ancient "orgies," then what's new? For that matter there is nothing new about runaway children, teenage prostitution, youthful alcoholism, incest, child molestation, rape, child and wife abuse. And while the reporting is much more prominent these days, *Middletown* authors maintain that there is little, if any, evidence that any of these distressing phenomena are any more prevalent today than in yesteryear. Drug addiction, surely a severe problem these days, was also common in the early years of the century. (The drug of choice was opium.) Read Tocqueville for a sense of epidemic alcoholism on the American frontier. The fact that human beings live in a world with some very ugly aspects—and always have—does not establish the case that our values are eroding.

Let us look at the rest of the Luce/conservative idea, concentrating on those facts and arguments that are more solidly rooted. The case generally boils down to two parts: greater sexual permissiveness, and the broader consequences of permissiveness.

What do we really know about sexual values and sexual behavior? The data are incomplete and hard to develop. Still, we have some things to work with.

To begin with the obvious: sex is more public these days, and more attention is paid to it. The sexual revolution has become big news: demonstrations for the easing and eliminating of campus parietal rules in the Sixties and Seventies, the emergence of homosexual politics, the advent of *Playboy, Penthouse,* and *Hustler,* the acceptance of urban "combat zones" of porno films and massage parlors, soap operas that deal regularly with incest, extramarital affairs, and lesbianism.

Not only is sex newsworthy these days, but the individual participants are far more open about their behavior than before. Unmarried teenage girls show up pregnant in high school, homosexuals march in Gay Pride parades.

But there is a big question behind all this going public: is sex only more open, or is there more of it?

When the sexual revolution began to hit the front pages, it was assumed that *behavior,* as well as *publicity about behavior,* had changed massively. Upon a sober second look, it seems as if there was probably somewhat less change than imagined.

In a simple formulation, the theory of a massive change in sexual behavior involves the ideas of a virgin past and a promiscuous present. Both sides of that formula are questionable.

Consider premarital sex.

If there ever was an America pure as the driven snow, it surely did not show up in census results. Current Population Surveys from 1952–1956 show that of young women marrying for the first time, 19 percent either had already borne a child or would give birth less than eight months after marriage. In the parlance of the time, this means that about one-fifth of America's pristine young ladies "got caught." That is not an insignificant proportion. One must ask, after all, another question: what percentage participated but did not get caught?

The studies of Alfred Kinsey showed that 36 percent of American women born between 1900 and 1920 had experienced premarital sexual intercourse by their twenty-fifth birthday. Some purity! Some snow!

The evidence of a less-than-pure America extends beyond mere data and well into what really counts: folklore and anecdote. Where did all those traveling salesmen stories come from? What was going on in all those folkloric backseats of all those cars? What was so scandalous about that scandalous decade of the Twenties?

Of course, folklore and the media may well have been exaggerating, then as now. But consider these comments by mothers cited by the Lynds in *Middletown,* published in 1929:

> It's girls' clothing; we can't keep our boys decent when girls dress that way.

> Girls are far more aggressive today. They call the boys up to try to make dates with them as they never would have when I was a girl.

> Last summer six girls organized a party and invited six boys and they never got home until three in the morning.

The fact that America was less than virginal then does not mean we are not more sexually active now. We are.

The conservatives are correct in saying that both behavior and attitudes have changed. But expert opinion generally seems to suggest that the amount of change has been less than popularly described.

One review of the data going back to 1940* says the ascendant trend in premarital sex "seems more gradual or evolutionary than revolutionary . . . while it may be true that attitudes and an openness to talk about sexual behavior have occurred . . . there is little evidence of any sudden massive change in adolescent sexual behavior in terms of pre-marital coitus."

A study† that seeks to quantify that evolution shows that in 1971, among unmarried teenage women (fifteen to nineteen) residing in metropolitan areas, 30 percent had experienced intercourse before marriage. By 1979, the rate was up substantially to 50 percent—with a corresponding 70 percent rate for male teenagers. Rates, however, are believed to be lower in rural areas, which would pull down any national average.

In any event, that almost half the young women in America have had sexual intercourse by age twenty is surely significant. There is, however, a major qualifier: research indicates that much premarital sex is reserved to one partner, whom the subject women expect to marry. Much of it, then, sounds more like love and sex than promiscuity.

The increase in more liberal premarital sexual *behavior* was apparently matched by a more liberal *attitude* toward it as well. Here is an example:

Question: If a man and a woman have sex relations before marriage, do you think it is always wrong, almost always wrong, wrong only sometimes, or not wrong at all?

Percentage Saying "Always Wrong" or "Almost Always Wrong"

1972	49%
1974	46%
1975	43%
1977	41%
1978	41%
1982	38%

Source: National Opinion Research Center.

* J. Diebold, Jr., and R. D. Young, "Empirical Studies of Adolescent Sexual Behavior," *Adolescence,* Spring 1979.
† M. Zelnick and J. Kantner, "Sexual Activity, Contraceptive Use and Pregnancy Among Metropolitan Area Teenagers 1971–1979," *Family Planning Perspectives,* Sept./Oct. 1980.

Surely a change, but, again one that seems less than revolutionary. About half the population thought premarital sex was wrong a decade ago—and about 40 percent still think so. Another way of stating these results is that, on balance, about 90 percent of the American opinion spectrum has not changed their mind about premarital sex in the last decade.

So, on balance: some real change in sexual behavior, but probably less than generally believed. Some change in sexual attitudes, but probably less than generally believed.

Finally, there are the most recent reports, with no full studies available for documentation, which seem to indicate something of a turnabout. In October of 1983, the *New York Times'* Richard D. Lyons surveyed the scene and reported:

> A marked decrease in casual or promiscuous sex has been occurring in the United States in the last several years, many experts believe.
>
> Psychiatrists, public health workers and law-enforcement officials say . . . that such a decrease has been taking place . . .
>
> 'A wind of conservatism is sweeping the country,' said Dr. June M. Reinisch, director of the Kinsey Institute for Research in Sex in Bloomington, Indiana.
>
> This . . . change in attitude has been observed in recent years among heterosexual men and women students at Ohio State University by Dr. Nancy Clatworthy, an associate professor of sociology there.
>
> Dr. Clatworthy, who conducts surveys of sexual activity every five years, said the percentage of women who said they had engaged in premarital sex rose markedly through the 1960s to 80 percent in 1975, then dropped off to 50 percent in 1980.

Or, in the words of psychologist Joyce Brothers, "People found instant sex as satisfying as a sneeze."

In short, to review a familiar theme: somewhat less change than generally believed, and some self-correction when excess was sensed.

Consider extramartial sex—adultery. Folklore takes us back at least to Hawthorne's *Scarlet Letter*. (Or, as the tune from *Music Man* goes, "I hope, I pray, for Hester to win just one more 'A' . . .")

Back in the 1950s Kinsey's research revealed that about half the married men and less than a quarter of the married women had participated in extramarital sex. Twenty years later (1972–73) sex researcher Morton Hunt reported only slightly different results: 48 percent of the men and 24 percent of the women had engaged in extramarital sex. Comparing his data with Kinsey's, Hunt wrote:*

> . . . our data in this area suggest that in the past generation there
> has been almost no measurable increase in the number of American
> husbands who ever have extramarital experience, and only a
> limited increase in the number of American wives who do so. These
> findings will seem surprising if not unbelievable to many persons. In
> the last decade . . . we have all been subjected to a barrage of
> propaganda to the effect that sexual exclusivity in marriage is
> obsolescent. An endless stream of books and articles and an endless
> parade of guests on TV talk shows have informed us that such
> exclusivity is archaic, or male-chauvinist, or unsuited to modern life,
> or unnecessary, or absurd, and that a number of alternatives are
> more workable, more sensible and more fun. Books advocating
> permissive marriage have outsold almost everything but diet
> books . . .

Academic and magazine surveys in the early 1980s tend to confirm and update Hunt's findings of unchanging male rates and only slightly increasing female rates.

Recent public opinion polls also bear out the view that extramarital sex is frowned upon. Back in 1973, when the National Opinion Research Center started polling on the question of extramarital sex, 85 percent of respondents felt that it was either "always wrong" or "almost always wrong." In 1982, the same question yielded an 86 percent response. Continuity.

Consider homosexuality. Lots of publicity, but apparently no change in behavior.

There has been much talk about high school sex-education classes that discuss homosexuality as an "alternate life-style." We have seen much on television news about homosexual marriage. Conservatives have gone into orbit about the legitimization and glorification of homosexuality in the popular culture: music, movies, the dance, television, and so on.

But the latest studies indicate that, depending on the definition used, about 5–10 percent of the adult population are practicing homosexuals. That is roughly the same incidence reported by Kinsey in the early 1950s.

* Morton Hunt, *Sexual Behavior in the 1970s,* 1974.

Nor has there been an attitudinal change. While all the homosexual hoopla was going on, NORC was in the field, asking whether "Sexual relations between two adults of the same sex . . . is always wrong, almost always wrong, wrong only sometimes or not wrong at all." In the 1973 poll 80 percent of the population chose wrong/almost always wrong. In 1982, the percentage was 78 percent, well within the margin of sampling error.

As with other data concerning sexual attitudes, there are no solid time lines available for earlier eras. But negative opinion at around 80 percent is high indeed, and could not have come down too much in any event.

Continuity. Core values and traditional behavior withstood a media wave.

=====

So much for some facts about behavior and some facts about attitudes. There has been some liberalization although not as much as we have been led to believe.

But, in all fairness, the conservative argument is not primarily about facts. A looser sexual code is morally wrong, many conservatives say. Further, they maintain, looser sexual standards are not just wrong in themselves, but wrong because of their consequences. More sexual freedom and more permissiveness yield a lack of personal responsibility, an erosion of family, and ultimately more cosmic woes. The effects of such permissiveness are harmful. Recall Mrs. Luce's reasons for the fall of the Roman Empire.

Well, there are no data to demonstrate that nonmarital sex is morally good—or morally bad. But something can be said about effects. In that sense, the second leg of our values tripod holds up: the effects of sexual permissiveness have not been anywhere near as bad as have been reported or predicted.

It was said, for example, that looser sexual standards would erode strong feelings about family, but as we have seen, that has not happened. It was said that divorce erodes the concept of marriage. But the very high rate of remarriage argues against that idea. It was said that looser nonmarital sexual morals would lead to more extramarital playing around, but we have seen that attitudes toward infidelity are overwhelmingly negative and that there have been only minimal changes in behavior.

It was said that a looser sexual code would yield promiscuous sexual behavior among young people. But premarital sexual behavior in many instances seems to yield not round-heeled promiscuity, but rather a form of serial monogamy. Coed dorms were supposed to yield sex orgies, but reports from campuses indicate that boys and girls who share the same dorms seem to regard each other as siblings than as playmates. One thing coed dorms have done is make it somewhat easier for young men and young women to meet under circumstances less strained than a college social—often described in earlier times as a "meat market." Where there was promiscuity, there seems now to be somewhat less of it: not as much sneezing.

We can pursue this argument about effects to other aspects of this section. Divorce, separation, single-parent families were supposed to yield children who are unhappy, lacking confidence, unable to function, and so on. There is little evidence that this has happened. Family experts tell us children are pretty resilient. And remember, the proper comparison is not between a happy intact family versus a sundered family. It is between a sundered family and an intact *unhappy* family. Which is worse?

Working mothers were supposed to yield "latch-key children" who lacked parental attention. But there is little evidence of damage done, and some data that suggest benefits for the children. A 1983 review of the research by the National Institute of Education found that children of working mothers did about as well in school as children whose mothers were at home.

A looser sexual code was said to lead to greater rates of venereal disease. Sadly, it probably has done that. But because of modern medicine, the effects of venereal disease are not nearly as serious as in earlier times, in fact, typically curable.

Another alleged effect of a looser sexual code: unwanted pregnancy. I dodge here the prochoice/prolife moral argument. If you believe abortion is murder, its legalization is surely sinful. If you do not, it should be noted that it surely reduces the number of unwanted pregnancies.

If the effects of more open, more permissive sexual behavior are less bad than announced, it is also appropriate to at least list some aspects that are perhaps beneficial. The POSSLQ phenomenon often takes the form of a "trial marriage" that can help presort successful unions from unsuccessful ones. Removing guilt from sexual activity allows for greater sexual pleasure. The availability of premarital sex diminishes the incidence of "marrying for sex," not the best factor upon which to base a marriage. Homosexuals are not better off if they are forced to deny who they are. Is a person who needs a pornographic fix better off if it is hard to obtain? Out-of-wedlock birth is a real problem, but even that, as noted in chapter 31, has another side to it.

Very well. The personal effects of permissiveness are probably less bad than conservatives believe. But aren't there limits to permissiveness?

Of course there are, but they are most effective when self-imposed. Such limits, moreover, are self-imposed more often than one thinks. That indeed is the third link of our values argument: excesses tend to self-correct.

This argument about family and sexual values is largely about young people. Society, properly, cares most about its young. They are the future. The original case against permissiveness was directed mostly at the notion that it would corrupt the young—in terms of sex, morals, family values, work, patriotism. It is against this backdrop that we ought to take a quick look at young people today.

They have not been corrupted.

There are two ways to see this: by ignoring the data, and by paying attention to the data.

Ignore the data. Go talk to some young people—maybe your own children. The ones I meet are mostly hard-working, well-motivated young men and women, certainly not the sex-crazed, drug-addicted, self-centered, indolent, unpatriotic youngsters who were supposed to be the fruits of a permissive time. To the contrary: they work hard. Perhaps the difficult economic times have made them face reality with a clearer eye than the young people of a decade or two ago. And how selfish and unpatriotic can young people be if armed forces enlistment rates soar, as they did, after two hundred marines were killed in one tragic day in Beirut in 1983?

Or pay attention to the data. As we survey the surveys at *Public Opinion,* it seems that something funny may be happening. Young people today are more conservative on a number of issues than their immediate elders. This is almost unheard of in the polling business.

Here is one example:

Question: Should a woman be able to obtain a legal abortion if she is married and doesn't want any more children?

	"Yes"
18–24-year-olds	43%
30–34-year-olds	51%

Source: NORC, 1980–83.

Not only are youth sometimes more conservative than their older siblings today, they are also more conservative than their counterparts of one decade ago on certain issues:

18–24-YEAR-OLDS IN FAVOR OF THE DEATH PENALTY FOR CONVICTED MURDERERS:	
1980–83	71%
1970–74	48%

18–24-YEAR-OLDS SAYING MARIJUANA SHOULD NOT BE LEGALIZED:	
1980–83	61%
1970–74	56%

18–24-YEAR-OLDS SAYING EXTRAMARITAL SEX IS ALWAYS WRONG/ALMOST ALWAYS WRONG:	
1980–83	84%
1970–74	74%

Source: NORC.

Old proverb: if it looks like self-correction, talks like self-correction, and responds to pollsters like self-correction, it probably has something to do with self-correction. That should tell social conservatives that our values aren't spinning pell-mell out of control.

Does that answer all the concerns about values that bedevil conservatives?

No. Permissiveness, conservatives note, also has a public component.

CHAPTER 39

Working Hard or Hardly Working?

THE WORK ETHIC

What's the problem with looser values?

Social-issue conservatives have a serious case to make. Mrs. Luce's excerpt gave a flavor of it. Boiled down to the bone, the logic and the extension of the argument goes something like this:

"Look, the problem isn't merely chastity or, homosexuality, or pornography. These are only distressing symptoms.

"The problem is discipline. It is responsibility. And a lack of discipline is contagious. A society that eschews discipline and glorifies instant self-gratification in personal matters like sex, runs a severe risk that such values will spread into public arenas.

"The values of instant gratification, permissiveness, irresponsibility—call it what you will—have already spread into the workplace. Blue-collar workers are more interested in deer-hunting than in making automobiles; absenteeism is rife; quality is shoddy. No discipline. We are left vulnerable to our international competitors, and we have been commercially savaged.

"Of course it goes beyond the work ethic. What is behind the crime wave if not the extension of permissiveness into the public arena? If one needn't be concerned about controlling sexual desires, why be concerned about material desires? Why not rob, steal, mug, and murder to get what one wants? No discipline.

"But the ripples spread even wider. From personal values to personal behavior to public activity—to political activity. What has bedeviled us politically in recent years? Inflation and deficits!—the political equivalent of quick gratification. Short of money? Print it up! Borrow it from your children! No discipline.

"And further ripples. What is the foreign policy of quick gratification? Reduce your defense spending; use the money for social programs. Ignore the present danger. Ignore the fact that an ideology that detests and destroys personal freedom is on the march. Defer the hard choices to the next generation, when the choices will be much harder, more dangerous. Defer the decision as to whether we will defend a system that honors the ideals of individualism, liberty, and indeed, personal gratification (in moderate amounts). Such are the final wages of personal irresponsibility!"

═══

To get a sense of the possible progression of values from private to public, we look at "work" in this chapter, and "crime" in the next. "Politics" follows as the topic of the next section of the book.

Regarding the work ethic: Does our theory of Less-Better-Correcting hold up? Has there been less change than we've been led to believe? Has some—much—of the change been for the better? Has some of the possibly damaging change yielded to self-correction?

Consider employment rates. In recent years, the percentage of adult Americans in the labor force has *climbed* to record high levels:

PERCENTAGE OF ADULTS IN LABOR FORCE

1940	53%
1950	59%
1960	59%
1970	60%
1980	64%
1984	65% (April)

Source: U.S. Bureau of Labor Statistics.

What a strange phenomenon in a nation whose work ethic is allegedly declining! Now, the major reason for this increase is the movement of women into the labor force. But women are people, are Americans—aren't they? And it's not just women. Despite all we hear about teenage unemployment (which is indeed at high levels), the "participation rate" among teenagers in the labor force has also reached an all-time high in the last few years.

What about unemployment, which has been high in recent years?

It surely doesn't bespeak an erosion of the work ethic. Statistically speaking, "unemployment" means "looking for work." The point here should be clear: a high rate of people "looking for work," combined with a high rate of people actually working (which we now have), is diametrically opposed to the idea of an erosion of the work ethic. People looking for work want to work.

Interesting story: even after the recent recessionary trauma, there is still some absenteeism in the auto plants. In the fall of 1983, I asked a foreman at General Motors' huge Lordstown, Ohio, plant why this was so. "All those guys are running a second business or a second job," he said. "They take sick leave here so they can work on their other stuff." That is not the portrait of a population without a work ethic.

It is often said that one big cause of the alleged decline in the work ethic stems from the fact that Americans don't like their work, find it boring, find it dehumanizing. Therefore, so goes the case, workers turn off and don't produce efficiently.

Not so. There is very little evidence to support the idea that Americans don't like their work:

PERCENT SATISFIED
WITH WORK

1963	86%
1965	82%
1966	86%
1969	87%
1971	81%
1972	85%
1978	87%
1982	85%

Source: Gallup.

Much satisfaction. Continuity, not change.

It's not all roses, however. Along with their satisfaction, Americans do see a problem that is at least tangentially related to satisfaction and the work ethic:

Question: Would you say Americans are taking more pride in
their work now than ten years ago, less pride or about
the same amount?

More pride	11%
Same amount of pride	25%
Less pride	64%

Source: NBC/AP, 1979.

Perhaps more distressing is a May 1981 *Los Angeles Times* poll that
shows 71 percent agreeing that "American workers are not turning out
as much work each day as they should." And it may well be getting
worse: an earlier (1973) Gallup survey on the same question had
shown 63 percent agreeing.

There are some mitigating aspects to this perceived decline. Americans say people take less pride in their work, but that's *other* Americans they're talking about, not themselves. A 1980 survey by Research
and Forecasts, Inc. asked Americans whether *they themselves* were
"doing a job well" and 93 percent said yes. Moreover, 73 percent said
they found their job interesting. A 1982 Gallup cross-national poll
showed that 84 percent of Americans take "a great pride" in their
work, compared to a 36 percent rate in European countries and only
37 percent in Japan, allegedly the great repository of the work ethic.

Americans also (still) believe in the work ethic because they believe
in success, and believe that work yields success:

Question: How important is success in your work?

Very important	63%
Somewhat important	33%
Somewhat unimportant	3%
Very unimportant	1%

Source: *Los Angeles Times*, 1981.

Question: Do you think it possible nowadays for someone in this
country to start out poor and become rich by working
hard?

Possible	69%
Not possible	29%

Source: CBS/NY *Times*, 1981.

These ideas are also very prevalent among young people. Fully 85 percent of high school seniors disagree with the statement that "people like me don't have much chance to be successful in life."* But they know that success is not automatic. Eighty-five percent of students also believe that "most adults have worked very hard to achieve their goals," and are willing to make similar efforts and sacrifices to accomplish their own life objectives.†

Perhaps one reason most Americans believe that upward mobility can still happen is because they have seen it in their own lives. In a unique set of surveys conducted from 1972 to 1980 the National Opinion Research Center asked Americans about their own occupations, about their father's occupation, and whether there had been an intergenerational change. Here are the results:

OCCUPATIONAL MOBILITY	
Upward	52%
No change	26%
Downward	22%

So then: Americans at work at greater rates than before, satisfied with their work, taking pride in their own work, believing that they will get ahead by dint of their efforts (and concerned that other people aren't putting out enough).

Continuity. Less change than you think.

Also operative are the other two pillars of our general thesis: self-correction if things get excessive and the idea that some of the changes may be for the better.

Self-correction. When the economy was booming, all the anecdotes came in about how lazy the work force had become. And indeed, there is some logic to that. If you know that you can easily get a good job if you leave the one you've got, you may well be inclined (in the words of an immortal ballad) to tell the boss to "take this job and shove it." Somewhat less pungently, in a hot economy, workers may indeed pay less attention to quality and may be more likely to plead sick and go fishing.

But when times turn tough, as they have since 1979, the anecdotes

* 1981, University of Michigan, Institute for Social Research.
† *The Mood of American Youth,* 1984, National Association of Secondary School Principals.

change. Now we hear (and we see on television) about workers who will take pay cuts to keep their jobs, about workers who pay extra attention to quality so that our cars will be as good as Japanese cars, and so on. Trade unions have reflected these attitudes. Always berated for selfishness (as opposed to the always eleemosynary spirit in the business community), unions have acted responsively and responsibly in the crunch of recession.

Next question: Is some erosion in the work ethic really a bad thing? Heresy! Contradiction!

Not at all. Part of the purpose of work in a modern industrial society is strictly utilitarian: people work hard in order to feed themselves and their families, to provide shelter and clothing.

And part of the purpose of working hard is to be able not to work so hard. The goal of increased productivity is to give people a higher standard of living. We have seen much evidence of just such a higher standard in this book. That standard also includes more vacation time, shorter work weeks, shorter working hours per day—that is, time to goof off, to go to a movie, to read a book, to go shopping, to be with the children, and so on.

Now one may say that decadence and irresponsibility are apparent when a factory worker has his mind on a fishing trip rather than on the proper installation of a muffler. It may be called a sign of softness when that same worker refuses to work overtime, even at time-and-a-half. Yet the whole idea of an affluent working class is that they be able to think about aspects of life other than mere subsistence. As the years roll on a new balance is struck: technology boosts our productivity, the resulting new wealth lets us relax a little bit more, slightly diminishing our work ethic. Our net material affluence then grows more slowly than it might under a go-go work ethic. On the other hand, people enjoy themselves more. In fact, when you think about it, perhaps a little of that has already happened. Who's to say it's bad?

Less change than you think. Correction when necessary. Some of the change is positive.

CHAPTER 40

Getting Tougher

CRIME

The explosion of crime in America probably represents the strongest support for the conservative case that eroding *private values* yields eroding *public values* yields eroding *public behavior*—and that we all suffer for it.

Conservatives say that as part of the permissiveness of the 1960s, we became "soft on crime." Accordingly, they maintain, it became more difficult to apprehend, arrest, convict, and incarcerate a criminal. Criminals have plenty of street smarts and knew exactly what was happening; they knew they could more likely succeed at criminality. And so, say conservatives, the new permissive private values encouraged the growth of crime.

What do we know about crime in America? What do we know about its connection to values? In brief, in relation to our three-step formulation:

Is crime better than you think? *No.*

Is there less crime than commonly believed? *We don't really know.*

Has there been a correction? *Probably.*

For sure, crime is not "better than you think." Crime in America involves old people being smacked around by young thugs, young girls raped and psychologically scarred for life, more than 20,000 murders a year—an average of one every twenty-five minutes—as well as theft, burglary, and robbery at very high levels.

The applicability of our second rule—"less"—is harder to assess.

Before trying to quantify the situation, there is one towering fact that must be mentioned at the outset: by any subjective or objective measurement, there is plenty of real crime in America. Too much, by far. By my lights, no matter how measured, the rate of criminality in the U.S. represents a Negative Super Number.

Acknowledging the rotten state of affairs, it is still appropriate to ask: how much?

Measuring crime is a complicated problem involving demographic trends, techniques of reporting, and public attitudes. The first cut at it reveals a steady increase until 1980. The incidence of "violent crimes known to the police" (the longest running FBI series available) climbed from 160 crimes per 100,000 inhabitants back in 1960 to 364 in 1970 and to 581 violent crimes in 1980. That is a twenty-year increase of 263 percent! The violent crimes tabulated are: murder, rape, robbery, and, the largest category, assault.

Property crime is about ten times more prevalent than violent crime, and has gone up nearly as fast. The FBI series shows 1,719 property crimes per 100,000 inhabitants in 1960. That figure went up to 3,621 in 1970 and 5,319 in 1980. That is a twenty-year increase of 209 percent! The crimes tabulated are burglary, larceny, and car theft.

There may be reason to doubt that the actual increase in crime in the 1970s was as sharp as the FBI numbers indicate. The operation of the FBI's crime-reporting system was improved dramatically in recent years. Some of what appears to have been an explosion of criminality may be in fact the result of improved efficiency by police departments in discovering and *recording* crimes.

Criminologists who hold that view point to the results of a National Crime Survey sponsored by the Bureau of Justice Statistics and actually taken by the Bureau of the Census.

The NCS is a survey count of "victims" themselves. Every six months 132,000 individuals are queried regarding their exposure to crime.

The results of the National Crime survey since 1973 do *not* show a tremendous crime wave during the 1970s. In fact, from 1973 to 1980 there was virtually no change in violent crime, and somewhat of a decline in property crime. The data seem to say: high crime in the Seventies, but not getting worse.

So: both sets of data show plenty of crime; there is an argument about whether it got worse in the 1970s. What about the third aspect of our formula—correction? Is a bad situation getting better? Is there a reversal?

The answer to that question—after many years of waiting—seems finally to be yes.

From an elevated level, crime has fallen slightly in the first three years of the 1980s. According to the increasingly inclusive FBI index, violent crime retreated modestly in 1981 from its 1980 high of 581 crimes per 100,000 population. A year later, 1982, the number fell by about 3.5 percent. In 1983, the rate was down by over 5 percent and accelerating downward in successive quarters. The index closed the year 1983 at about 525 violent crimes per 100,000 population, a decline of nearly 10 percent since 1980.

The same pattern was apparent in the realm of property crime. It topped out at 5,319 in 1980, dropped a little in 1981, dropped by more than 4 percent in 1982, and was down by another 7 percent in 1983, to a rate of about 4,725, which would be a cumulative drop of over 11 percent.

This pattern is confirmed by the victim's survey, in which every category of crime—violent and property—was lower in 1982 than in 1981, and much lower again in 1983. Nearly every category of crime is at its lowest level since the survey's inauguration in 1973.*

Why is crime declining?

There is, first, a big demographic reason. Criminality in America is age-sex specific. Crimes, particularly violent ones, are most typically committed by young males. In 1981, according to FBI data, males committed 81 percent of the serious crime in America. More than three out of five serious crimes were committed by persons under age twenty-five.

Because of the Birth-Dearth following the Baby Boom (see chapter 11), the pool of potential criminals has already begun to diminish, and will continue to go down:

NUMBER OF MEN AGE 18

1979	2,183,000 (peak year)
1980	2,153,000
1981	2,143,000
1982	2,129,000
1983	2,043,000 (projection)
1984	1,922,000 (projection)
1985	1,864,000 (projection)
1990	1,751,000 (projection)

Decrease 1979–1990: 20%*

Source: U.S. Bureau of the Census.

* These numbers have been clearly projectable for a long time. It was 15 years ago that Harvard Professor James Q. Wilson (author of "Thinking About Crime") said that he would like to be an adviser to whomever was elected president in 1980. It would be easy, Wilson noted, to tell that president to declare war on crime, wait a few years and declare victory. Wilson understood an elementary truth: fewer potential criminals yield fewer real criminals. And so it has happened.

* Who will be the first television correspondent to report that all those network stories that said the recession was driving crime rates up—were dead wrong?

But the beginning of a crime drop is probably not due just to demographics. Society has been responding. If soft public values triggered or abetted the crime wave, tougher public values then came to the fore and played an important role in curbing crime.

Consider what has happened since 1970.

Much more money is being spent to combat crime. In 1970, at all levels of government, $8.6 billion was spent. By 1979, the figure was $26 billion—an increase of 62 percent after discounting for inflation.

During the same time, the number of people employed in the criminal justice system (expressed in the equivalent of full-time positions) went from 775,000 to 1,178,000—a 52 percent increase.

Private anticrime spending is also very high. Americans spent $200 million in 1982 on burglar alarms alone. They made "personal security" a $4.7 billion business in 1982, a sales level rivaling that of the personal computer industry.

In the face of increased juvenile crime, statutes have been changed to allow prosecutors to try juveniles who have committed serious crimes as adults. More juveniles are going to trial.

There has been a substantial growth in the number of neighborhood associations dedicated to crime prevention and detection.

The death penalty was retrieved from unconstitutionality.

All this public toughening has had a payoff. The number of convictions and imprisonments has increased. These numbers show dramatically the ebb and flow of how we deal with criminality:

CONVICTED PERSONS RECEIVED BY PRISONS FROM STATE AND LOCAL COURTS

1960	89,000
1965	88,000
1970	79,000
1975	130,000
1980	142,000
1981	160,000
1982	177,000

Source: Bureau of Justice Statistics.

In the Sixties, incarcerations went down while crime went up! But that caused public outrage—remember all the law-and-order rhetoric?

After a lag time, rhetoric yields reality. Soon, public action synchronized with new, tougher public values. More people, about twice as many, were sent to prison per year than just a decade earlier.

These conviction rates are not small potatoes. They have helped lead to a major increase in the total prison population. In 1970, there were 196,000 persons in prison. By 1982 there were 412,000 persons in prison—more than double.*

These developments can reduce crime in two ways. There is a likely deterrent effect. Criminals, after all, have a pretty good sense of when crime does not pay, when it does, and when it might. As that risk-reward ratio changes, it may well convince some potential criminals to go into another line of work.

And perhaps most important, there are those extra people in prison— 216,000 additional ones since 1970. We know one thing for sure about them; they are not on the street committing new crimes. Consider what this means for property crimes. A chronic offender is believed to commit at least ten crimes per year and possibly many more. Obviously, with more criminals in jail now, this can lead to an important further reduction in crime rates in years to come.

In short, our public institutions responded. This didn't happen by accident. The institutions responded because public values got tougher. Nowhere is this seen more clearly than in the public opinion polls regarding the death penalty. Here is the Gallup time line beginning with 1966, the year in which capital punishment was least favored:

DEATH PENALTY FOR MURDER

	"Favor"
1966	42%
1969	51%
1971	49%
1972	57%
1976	65%
1978	62%
1981	66%
1982	72%

Source: Gallup.

---

* Causing another problem: crowded prisons. The cost of construction of new prisons is high, and states are struggling to cope. Prison *operations* also cost a great deal. Public spending on corrections went from $1.7 billion in 1970 to over $6 billion by the end of the decade.

And if there is any doubt that the consensus for toughness has remained firm, consider how American opinions have changed regarding how the courts treat criminals:

"COURTS HAVE BEEN TOO EASY ON CRIMINALS . . ."

	"Agree"
1967	49%
1970	64%
1973	65%
1975	69%
1977	74%
1978	77%
1982	81%

Source: Harris.

Curiously, this toughening-up process both bolsters and dilutes the conservative case about values. Conservatives deserve great credit for both recognizing and publicizing certain harsh facts about our condition. It was conservatives who first made crime a big political issue. They made their case that permissive private values were tumbling into the public arena—and they claimed we ended up with more crime because of it. They properly scorned the liberal notion that "there are no bad boys only bad societies." Their activities have galvanized much public change, as noted.

But there is a paradox here. Conservative success undercuts some of the conservative gloom-mongering. There are pessimistic conservatives who believe that a liberal, open society will end up with government so permissive and so promiscuous that it will not self-discipline, but will slide ever more quickly down a slippery slope.

That's not what happened. The public responded. Then governments—local, state, and federal, those controlled by Republicans and Democrats, by liberals and conservatives—also responded.

=====

Just as liberals will tell you in panic that the quality of life has eroded, so will conservatives tell you fearfully that our values have eroded. Neither liberals nor conservatives are quite correct in these notions. For free societies, free people, adjust to adverse conditions. That should not be big news to students of American history.

The Sixties-Seventies crime wave was not the first one we've had. There was an increase in criminality following the Civil War and an organized crime wave during Prohibition. (The rate of homicides in America in 1860 is believed to have been at least five times higher than in 1960.) Each time, the public and the governments involved took action, and over time crime rates went down.

It is probable that the modest decline in crime rates that has just begun will continue for a while. As we have seen, there are demographic reasons for this—smaller cohorts of young men—and attitudinal ones—the public is still deeply concerned and that engenders action.

Moreover, when one considers the media equation, it is unlikely that public concern will diminish soon. Alas, there is still plenty of crime around to report, and it is unlikely and almost impossible to report in a dramatic way that crime is decreasing. After all, a semiannual line of statistics can never counterbalance the images of violence that have become commonplace on television. What can you show? An unrobbed store? An unraped woman? An unmugged elderly person? An unmurdered man? An unbusted drug pusher?*

Easy prediction: the perception of high crime will continue no matter what actually happens to the rates. This should prolong the political conditions that helped produce the real decrease. Hooray for bad news!

=====

Media notwithstanding, we have described a process in this part of the book. Private values haven't changed as much as you think, but they have changed. The change has been toward more openness and more permissiveness. Some of that change has been for the better, at least in this author's judgment. When it's been for the worse, there has been some self-correction. Some of those new permissive private values have influenced public activity. When that has become excessive, there has also been a public correction.

* Drug use is down—another example of "reversal." The latest data from the U.S. National Institute on Drug Abuse (1982) show solid declines from the late 1970s in the rates of "current use" of marijuana, hallucinogens, cocaine, inhalants, heroin, and other drugs among youths (12–17) and young adults (18–25). From 1979 to 1982, for instance, current marijuana usage decreased by over 30 percent for youths, and over 20 percent for young adults. An annual Gallup survey showed a further dramatic drop in usage in 1983.

  Alcohol use is also down. NIDA reports that current use of alcohol has dropped dramatically since the late 1970s. From 1979 to 1982 current use by youths dropped from 37 percent to 27 percent, by young adults from 76 percent to 68 percent, and by adults from 61 percent to 57 percent.

Or, in words that might soothe troubled conservatives, people in free societies act moderately in what they deem their own best interests, private and public; when they find out that they may have gone too far, they change, privately and publicly. What's so dangerous about that?

Indeed, it is a healthy, ongoing process. On the public side, that healthy process can be described in one simple word: politics.

Yet no one seems to think our politics are healthy. We now investigate that.

PART IV

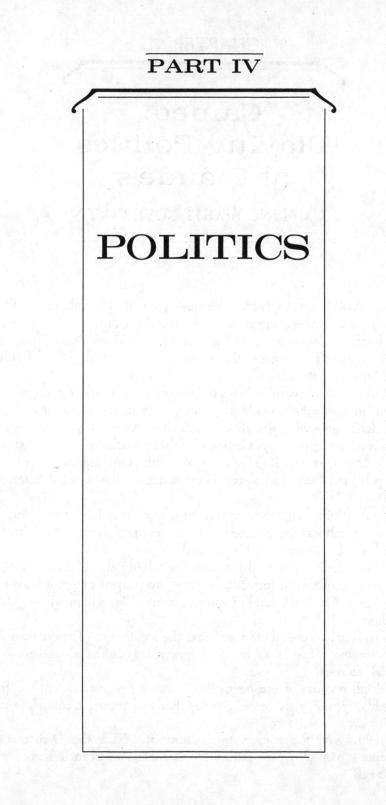

POLITICS

CHAPTER 41

Cameo:
Playing Politics
at Claude's

GRUMBLING ABOUT GOVERNMENT

The cocktail party at Claude Cleeshay's goes on. The columnists, the pundits, the bankers, the sociologists, the think-tankers, the anchorpeople, the businessmen, assemble and reassemble kaleidoscopically in small groups. The conversation rambles until—suddenly—a fertile topic bubbles to the surface.

"The problem is politics," says the anchorman, "that's why the economy is in a shambles, that's why the quality of life is eroding . . ."

"I don't agree with you about much, Mr. Anchorman, but I agree with you about that," says Claude's brother Chuck, in for a rare visit. "It's politics that does it. That's why our values are eroding—because our politicians are permissive. They dance to the tune of interest groups."

"You're right," says the anchorman. "The special interests control American politics. Big business, fat cats, political action committees, big labor. That's why the air is polluted."

"Those aren't the special interests I'm talking about," says Chuck, "it's because of special interests that the government makes it legal to kill fetuses. That's the kind of special interests I'm talking about, Mr. Anchorman."

"That's why people don't vote," says the sociologist. "They're turned off, alienated. They know the government is bought and paid for by special interests."

"It's all because of the new rules," says the political scientist. "In the old days the party bosses got together and picked a candidate in the back room. No more."

"Right," says the conservative columnist. "Now the Democratic nominee is picked by gays, radicalized teachers, American Indians, and feminists."

"Look at the presidents we've been getting," says the editorial writer. "They're terrible. That's the way it seems to us."

Claude has joined the group. "It's terrible," he says. "Where are the giants of yesteryear?"

"Right," says the lobbyist. "In the old days, there was leadership up in Congress too. Now every two-bit congressman has his own sub-committee and makes his own laws and has his own special interests."

"It's those staffs that are doing it," says the pundit from the conservative think tank. "The number of staff people in Congress has doubled in ten years. They run the Congress."

"And they're all liberal know-it-alls," says the businessman. "They're in bed with those special-interest groups."

"It's the courts," says the think tanker. "It's the imperial judiciary. Those liberal special-interest groups have lawyers who forum-shop until they find a liberal judge."

"It's the regulatory agencies," says the businessman. "They think they're God. They don't report to anyone. They run the country. And they listen to the liberal special interests, too. Consumerists drive us crazy. That's why we're so screwed up."

"It's the big-time Washington superlawyers that do it," says a liberal congressman, "they're everywhere, making millions representing special interests."

"And all those high-priced public relations people," says a young man from a liberal public-interest group, "they're the ones who make special interests so powerful by giving them so much attention in the media.

"You should talk," says a public relations man—"it's the public-interest groups—the *so-called* public-interest groups, that are really special interest groups and that get all the attention."

"It's conservative think tanks that set policy and really push special interests," says a liberal columnist.

"The government isn't responsive to the people," says the pundit from the liberal think tank. "The people want gun control and a nuclear freeze, but the conservative special interests give us the gun lobby and the military industrial complex."

"The problem is there's no leadership," says the middle-of-the-road columnist. "People get elected because they buy thirty-second spots on television."

"No leadership means no discipline in politics," says the anchorman.

"That's why we have inflation—no political discipline," says an economist from the conservative think tank. "If politicians were young women, they'd always be pregnant. They can't say no—to special interests or anyone else either. They spend and spend, but they won't tax and tax. They just print up the money."

"They can't say no to money, either," says Chuck Cleeshay, "they're all crooks."

"They take it legally," says the political scientist. "They give speeches to trade associations."

"Then they hit them up for campaign contributions," says the columnist.

"And then they pass laws for the same trade associations," says public-interest group activist. "It's all special interests."

"And what about Watergate?" says a voice.

"And Koreagate?" says another.

"Lancegate and Billygate," pipes up another.

A neoconservative defense intellectual has sidled up to the group. He is a very intense young man.

"You're all concentrating on trivia," he says. "It's worse than you think. Special interests may be destroying the world! When we satisfy special interests, we sacrifice freedom!"

The ice-cubes in the highball glasses lie still as the group turns to the defense intellectual, whose voice is rising as he goes on. "The Russians have gone through the largest peacetime military buildup in the history of the world," he says. "They've developed a blue-water navy to extend imperial power. They're knocking off countries all over the world, including in our backyard, Central America. And what are we doing about it?"

The previously voluble group has turned down the volube.

"I'll tell you what we've done," continues the defense intellectual. "Increased the budget for buses with wheelchairs! Increased the budget for farm subsidies! Always responding to special interests.

"And we niggle about it. Every nickel spent on defense is said to be more proof of a bloated military-industrial complex. Every time we look rationally at a situation where our interests or our values are threatened, the cry of 'another Vietnam' goes up.

"You know why? Because politicians are gutless and want to curry favor and want to hand out goodies to special interests—but don't want to face reality.

"Reagan was supposed to be better. Is he? Not much. Carter embargoed some wheat to the Soviets because of the invasion of Afghanistan, but Reagan—the big hawk—lifted the embargo. Why? Because of a special-interest group called 'farmers.' We didn't put Poland into default because of a special-interest group called 'bankers.' And we can never come up with a trade policy to squeeze the Soviets. A special-interest group called 'businessmen' wants to sell goods to them. You know what Reagan's slogan is? Crawl tall!

"It's politics that does it. Democracies are dooming themselves with decadent, permissive, undisciplined politics. The Soviets install new nuclear missiles pointed at Europe, and the Europeans respond by encouraging the Soviets to build a gas pipeline to make money off of the Europeans! Why? To save a few thousand jobs of people making the pipe for the pipeline! Decadence!"

There is a moment of silence—then the chatter begins afresh.

"Well, yes," says Claude Cleeshay, "but we buy the wrong weapons, and the military contractors get cost overruns from the Pentagon, and we buy goldplated white elephants. It cost nine hundred dollars for a screwdriver!"

"And when whistle-blowers blow the whistle, they're fired by gutless politicians," says the pundit from the liberal think tank.

"That's special interests, too. Big Defense," says the liberal columnist.

"It leads us into imperialism," says the liberal think-tanker. "The American people don't want war, don't want to spend more money on weapons, don't want to be butting in all over the world. But America does it anyway. The system isn't responsive. The special interests are doing us in."

═══

There is probably at least some truth to every charge made at Claude's. Yet I maintain that our political system is not only holding up, but flowering.

The basic complaints we hear these days obviously revolve around a single phrase: "special interests." There is a sense in the air that a tide of special interest, money and influence is washing over the system: political action committees, lobbyists, lawyers, think tanks, public-interest groups, fat cats, labor unions, feminists, environmentalists, right-to-lifers—to just begin a very long list. Conservatives say liberals are in bed with special interests. Liberals say conservatives are bought by special interests.

We are told that all this is bad.

It is not bad. It is good. It is good because it means that more people, in more ways, are participating in our democracy. We have had an explosion of participatory democracy.

That is very healthy as a political process. As we shall note, democracy gets better when more people play.

As we shall also note, this development is very sound as substance as well. Despite detours, the explosion of participatory democracy has shaped our politics and our policies in a healthy way in recent years and should go right on doing so.

Come along, then, to explore the new road map of American politics. See what didn't happen and what did. See why it's good process and good substance. See how it reveals that our values—in the crunch—may be holding up after all. See how parties and politicians will use the new situation to their advantage and ours.

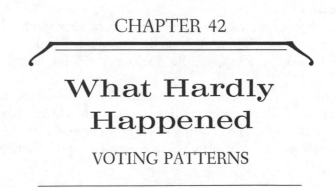

CHAPTER 42

What Hardly Happened

VOTING PATTERNS

We can begin this celebration of American politics by diluting, diminishing, and mostly doing away with the concern over low voter turnout. It's been a tragedy we've been told; it keeps going down; it's never been lower; it shows alienation; it means there's no mandate for this President or that President; it shows that people feel they don't make a difference.

To begin, there are the numbers.

Insofar as there has been a drop in voting participation, there is solid evidence to suggest that it was minimal, that it has probably ended, and that it has reversed. Besides, voting rates have been lower in the past.

National election statistics must be compared over four-year periods because there is a much bigger turnout when a President is up for election than in "off-years" when we elect only a Congress.

On the congressional side, here is a funny way of showing a decrease in voter participation:

VOTER PARTICIPATION

1974	44.7%
1978	45.9%
1982	48.5%

Source: U.S. Bureau of the Census.

Those are census data based on a postelection voter recollection survey taken two weeks after elections. Participation rates based on *actual voter counts* (as assembled by the Elections Research Center*) show a slight decrease in the early part of the Seventies but a substantial increase more recently:

VOTER PARTICIPATION

1974	35.9%
1978	34.9%
1982	38.1%

Source: Elections Research Center.

So: more voter participation on the congressional scene, not less.

The basic case for diminished voter turnout comes from the presidential side.

---

* The data for both series deal with participation as a function of the total voting age population. There are some statistical reasons that make the census survey more comprehensive than the ERC tabulation, and some reasons that make ERC more accurate than census. They cannot be properly compared with one another, but they show trends well when compared to their own time series, as is done here. In both instances, we show the data only from 1974 onward. Prior to 1974, persons aged eighteen to twenty were not permitted to vote in most states, making before-versus-after comparisons tricky, as will be discussed later.

Here is what the actual voter turnout data look like over time:

PERCENT OF THE VOTING AGE POPULATION WHO VOTED FOR PRESIDENT: 1920 TO 1980

Year	% Voting	Winning Candidate
1920	42.5	Harding
1924	43.8	Coolidge
1928	51.7	Hoover
1932	52.4	Roosevelt
1936	56.9	Roosevelt
1940	58.9	Roosevelt
1944	56.0	Roosevelt
1948	51.1	Truman
1952	61.6	Eisenhower
1956	59.3	Eisenhower
1960	62.8	Kennedy
1964	61.9	Johnson
1968	60.9	Nixon
1972	55.4	Nixon
1976	54.4	Carter
1980	52.6	Reagan

Source: U.S. Bureau of the Census.

Sort of a rollercoaster: low, higher, higher, lower.

You may play some games with the numbers if you wish. It has been maintained that Nixon, Carter, and particularly Reagan were almost illegitimate because turnout was so low in 1972, 1976, and 1980. Yet those turnouts, as can be seen above, were higher than the ones that first elected Franklin D. Roosevelt (1932) or elected Harry S. Truman (1948).

Games aside, there was a major drop in turnout starting in 1972. The five preceding elections averaged 61.3 percent, with very little election-to-election variance. The turnout for the next three elections, averaged 54 percent—way down. Why?

It is said it happened because of voter alienation, Vietnam and Watergate, and lack of trust in government. Perhaps; we shall discuss those ideas in a moment. But there were some demographic reasons for the drop that have nothing to do with alienation and are not particularly unhealthy.

The big drop in all voting participation rates occurred immediately after the enactment of the "eighteen-year-old vote" constitutional amendment in 1971, which immediately enfranchised eleven million young Americans.

That was a good amendment. If you're old enough to fight in the military, you should be able to vote. Trouble is, young Americans aged eighteen to twenty are about half as likely to vote as are middle-aged adults. Why is this so? Because young people are typically away in college, or they are in the army, or they have just relocated, or because they'd rather drink beer than vote, or because they'd rather chase girls (or boys, as the case may be) than vote—and so on.

This low rate of voter participation among newly enfranchised eighteen to twenty-year-old voters tended, of course, to pull down the total participation rate after 1972.

In addition, however, in the 1970s the whole voting population was getting younger, even without constitutional amendments. This came about (like almost everything else of interest in America in the 1970s) because the Baby Boom babies were beginning to reach young adulthood.

For the baby born in late 1947 (the first big year of the boom), 1972 was the first presidential year he or she could vote. In a great rush thereafter then, there were tens of millions of new young voters. In 1968 there were only 36 million potential voters under age thirty-five—while by 1980 there were 67 million! However, these people under age thirty-five still do a disproportionate amount of relocating, soldiering, drinking, chasing, and so on—and not voting. That, of course, diminishes total turnout. Here is a progression of voting behavior by age:

PERCENT VOTING, BY AGE

Age	% Voting
18–20	35.7%
21–24	43.1%
25–34	54.6%
35–44	64.4%
45–64	69.3%
65 and over	65.1%

Source: U.S. Bureau of the Census, 1980.

So there is a solid demographic reason for part of the decline in the overall voting participation rate: disproportionately high numbers of young voters in the total voter mix.

Good news: viewed demographically, it is likely that voter participation rates will be headed up in the years to come. The Baby Boomers are getting older each year. That tyke born in 1947 will be thirty-seven years old in 1984! That's about the age when voting participation rates start reaching their highest levels.

But the demographics are only part of the reason for the decline in the late Sixties and the Seventies. Experts estimate that somewhere between one-third and two-thirds of the decline was caused by the "younging" of the electorate just described.

What about the other part?

Voting participation rates did go down age-specifically as well. The reason generally given concerns the never-to-be-forgotten Trauma Twins: Vietnam and Watergate. It is said that Vietnam and Watergate—an allegedly unwinnable war and a thoroughly corrupted administration—caused extreme alienation from government, keeping people away from the voting booth.

Maybe. But it is an unproven theory at best, and there are several ideas kicking around that might lead one to believe it is unprovable because it is wrong.

Ask yourself: is it logical that when people get angry at their government they are *less* likely to vote? Whatever happened to the idea of throw-the-rascals-out? The only way the rascals can be out-thrown is by voting them out.

Well, the case is made that the present phenomenon is not outrage, which might engender heavy voting, but alienation, a "who cares" attitude. That, it is said, causes psephological somnambulism. Perhaps. But if you care to argue about it, the same set of circumstances and data could yield a conclusion that people don't bother to vote because they are at least mildly pleased with the system. If it ain't broke, don't fix it. (Anyway, survey research has shown that non-voters are no more cynical or alienated than people who do vote.)

Or consider 1976. America was well out of recession, inflation was low, the Trauma Twins were disappearing into the sunset, it was the bicentennial year, the tall ships were here, a number of reforms to make voter registration easier were already in effect, the public opinion polls showed a definite, measurable, substantial, optimistic bounce in the way Americans saw their nation—and on Election Day voter participation rates went down yet another notch.

Fact is, there is no solid all-inclusive theory that tells us why people vote at high or low levels. By some measures, American voter participation rates have always been somewhat lower than the other democracies (except for Switzerland). Yet cross-national public opinion data show that we are more optimistic, more patriotic, more likely to believe that we can shape our political destiny than are the citizens of other nations.*

In the U.S., participation rates have been relatively high at times (the Fifties up to the mid-Sixties) low at times (the Seventies and the Twenties) in the middle at times (the Depression Thirties). There have been major oscillations, and Rorschachlike interpretations. (Whose mandate was bigger: Kennedy with a big turnout and a slender win, or Reagan with a small turnout and a big win?)

There is another question: do low turnouts actually distort election results? Political scientist Raymond Wolfinger of the University of California at Berkeley has conducted research which suggests that if all the people who don't vote, did vote, the election results would be changed only slightly . . . an additional 1.5 percent for Jimmy Carter in 1980.

And finally, let us remember that whatever caused the decline and whatever it may mean, there is good evidence that it has turned around. We have noted this turnaround in congressional races earlier in this chapter. There is evidence that it has already happened in other sorts of elections as well. Writing in the *Washington Post* in early 1984, David Broder reported:

> In all but one of the twenty largest states—the exception was
> Pennsylvania—the vote in the most recent gubernatorial race ex-
> ceeded that of the previous contest. In more than half the states the
> increase exceeded 10%.

* Actually our turnout compared to other democracies may be better than generally stated. American turnout formulas are different. Election analyst Richard M. Scammon estimates that if U.S. voting turnout were computed by the same formula as that used for European countries, our averages would rise by eight to ten percentage points, a level that would exceed Switzerland's and closely approach those of Canada, Ireland, Japan, and the United Kingdom, putting the U.S. at about the middle of the democratic turnout spectrum.

Moreover, as the U.K. scholar Ivor Crewe notes in *Democracy at the Polls*, the United States, with its primary and general elections and its national, state, and local elections offers the average voter three or four times as many "voting opportunities" than do other democracies. Our turnout may be low, but we vote more often.

Additional evidence, particularly heartening, seems to be headed our way: the prospect of increased black participation. Black voting rates went up sharply between the congressional elections of 1978 and those of 1982 (a sharper increase than that recorded for whites). With the highly publicized anti-Reagan sentiment within the black community, with well-publicized black registration drives under way, there is reason to think that the 1984 turnout for blacks will be up, relative to 1980.

That will be good for democracy (it's better when more people participate). It will be good for blacks (increased numbers voting generally increases clout). Whether it turns out to be good for the 1984 nominee of the Democratic party is more complicated. If the bigger black vote is brought about in a contentious manner (and many observers believe that Reverend Jesse Jackson is nothing if not contentious), then the surge in black registration may bring out extra white voters—probably conservative and likely to vote Republican. But whatever the calculus of these alternative Newtonian actions, one thing seems fairly certain: rising turnout.

The same pattern is clear elsewhere in the electorate. On the mostly liberal side there are major voting registration initiatives being pursued by labor, women's groups, gays, and the nuclear freeze movement. This is being at least partly counteracted by conservative voter registration drives by fundamentalist religious groups of which the Moral Majority is only one. The president of the U.S. Chamber of Commerce, Richard Lesher, maintains that 25 percent of businessmen in America are not registered, and 40 percent do not vote. He pledges a massive drive to turn out this constituency that he says believes in "limited government."

Looking at the entire electorate, pollsters in both parties—Peter Hart for Walter Mondale, and Richard Wirthlin for Ronald Reagan—are predicting a substantial upturn in turnout for the presidential race in 1984 with yields likely to be close to the pre-1972 age adjusted rates.

In short: more voters. If there ever was a problem, it's probably over.

CHAPTER 43

What Did Happen

EXPANDING PARTICIPATION

So: one thing that did not happen in our recent politics was a major diminishment of American voter participation.

What did happen?

An explosion of participation in other aspects of American politics. This has principally taken the form of campaign contributions and interest group activity. In the argot: cash and clout and players.

Before we try to assay the merits and demerits of the cash-clout-players boom, we ought to try to measure it.

That is difficult. Some lobbyists register; some people lobby unofficially, yet legally. Campaign contributions of money are now wholly measurable, but "in-kind" contributions (for example, the value of the volunteers who man a phone bank on behalf of a labor union) are much more difficult to gauge. Most assuredly, there is no comprehensive way to do a total accounting that will measure the growth of public-interest groups, law firms, think tanks, public relations agencies, and so on.

Still, there are some things we know, and they are stunning.

Here are some Super Numbers:

DONATIONS TO CONGRESSIONAL CANDIDATES BY POLITICAL ACTION COMMITTEES

1972	$ 9 million
1974	$ 13 "
1976	$ 23 "
1978	$ 35 "
1980	$ 55 "
1982	$ 83 "
1984 (est.)	$120 "

Source: Citizens Research Foundation.

That is well more than a twelve-fold increase at a time when inflation roughly doubled and the number of members of Congress remained constant.

There was an even sharper rise in the number of political action committees:

NUMBER OF POLITICAL ACTION COMMITTEES

1972	113
1974	608
1976	992
1978	1,653
1980	2,551
1982	3,371
1984 (est).	4,000

Source: Federal Election Commission.

All the logical suspects are included in those numbers:

There are almost 1,500 corporate PACs. (Tenneco and Standard Oil of Indiana were the two biggest spenders in 1982, with about half a million dollars each.) There are almost 400 labor PACs. (The United Automobile Workers are the biggest spenders, at $2.2 million.)

There are about 750 "ideological" PACs. (Two conservative groups, the National Congressional Club and the National Conservative Political Action Committee are tops, with about $10 million each. PACs run by liberals Walter Mondale and Edward M. Kennedy each spent over $2 million.)

There are more than 600 PACs for "trade associations, membership groups, and health professionals." (The top five PACs in this category are realtors, doctors, a pro-gun group, builders, and environmentalists.) There are about 50 agricultural PACs (dominated by milk).

But the list goes well beyond the logical suspects. Among the new PACs are the HIP PAC (Hispanics in Politics), BAKE PAC (Independent Bakers Association), JUST PAC (Join Us to Stop Teddy), as well as BACK PAC, BLAC PAC, WHATAPAC, PEACE PAC and the SUN STUDS PAC.

And of course, it's not just PACs. Total spending for congressional elections went up almost fivefold from 1970 to 1982—from $72 million to $344 million—with an estimate of $425 million for 1984. The money comes mostly from individuals, not PACs. The cost of a typical U.S. Senate race went from $600,000 to $1.8 million during the years 1976 to 1982.

And those are just congressional races. Spending in the presidential races went from $91 million in 1968 to $275 million in 1980—with a 1984 spending estimate of $350 million.

That's still not all of it, not even close. The Citizens Research Foundation, which does outstanding analytical work in the field, prepares estimates for total political spending—federal, state, and local, for all candidates, as well as for ballot issues. Such spending totaled $300 million in 1968 and $1.2 billion in 1980. The estimate for 1984, according to CRF director Herbert Alexander, is $1.8 billion!

Politicking, quite simply, is well on its way to becoming a two-billion-dollar business!

But that's only *election* activity. Much of our booming participatory politics takes place after the confetti has settled. Cash buys clout indirectly as well as directly. More cash in the system increases the number of players.

Consider the number of lawyers practicing in Washington, D.C. Members of the D.C. Bar went up from 17,000 in 1973 to 32,000 in 1980. Those lawyers typically represent clients participating in the governmental process in one way or another. In 1980, a President was elected who was going to get government off our back, limit the power and activity of Washington. The number of lawyers in D.C. from 1980 to 1983 went up from 32,000 to 39,000, mostly during a recession.

The Greater Washington Research Center has made some other estimates: about 500 corporations had Washington offices in 1980—twice as many as had offices in the capital in 1970. The number of corporate employees in those Washington offices *tripled* during this time. These people may be assumed to be part of the participatory boom.

During the 1970s, the number of trade associations operating out of Washington went up at the astonishing rate of about one per week—from 1,200 to 1,700. Some were old groups relocating to the Capitol; many were new groups. During the recessionary years of 1980–83 the number of employees of trade associations went up from 40,000 to 50,000.

From 1970 to 1983 the number of registered congressional lobbyists grew from about 1,250 to 6,500. These were not just the corporate fat cats that had come to town to play politics. The twelve who reported spending the most money lobbying (in the final quarter of 1982) were, in order of monies spent:

TOP SPENDING LOBBYISTS

Common Cause	$442,537
Handgun Control, Inc.	356,443
American Petroleum Institute	222,413
Sierra Club	212,052
American Postal Workers Union	176,927
American Medical Association	163,717
Citizens' Committee for the Right to Keep and Bear Arms	159,532
U.S. League of Savings Association	157,803
AFL-CIO	153,119
Audio Recording Rights Coalition	132,636
American Farm Bureau Federation	121,031
National Rifle Association	116,788

Source: Records and Registrations Office, House Clerk.

That's a pretty good cross-section of America: business and labor, oil and environmentalism, progun and antigun, doctors and farmers.

Think tanks are a uniquely American phenomenon. There are currently about forty independent (nonuniversity, nongovernment, noncorporate) public policy research centers. There are sixteen in Washington, D.C. The three largest in Washington (The Brookings Institution, the American Enterprise Institute, the Heritage Foundation) have a combined budget of more than $30 million. AEI's budget went from $1 million to $10 million in a ten-year span.

By law, think tanks do not lobby, but they can be very influential. Brookings likes to think it invented the American welfare state; AEI thinks it invented deregulation. The Heritage Foundation thinks it invented Ronald Reagan.

Political scientists Kay Lehman Schlozman and John T. Tierney have investigated the growth of private organizations with offices in Washington.* They looked at a sample of those organizations mentioned in *The National Journal* over a four-year period (1977–80). These include civil rights groups, social welfare organizations, union-sponsored lobbies, think tanks, charitable, religious, and recreational groups, as well as corporations.

---

* Kay Lehman Schlozman and John T. Tierney, "More of the Same: Washington Pressure Group Activity in a Decade of Change," *Journal of Politics*, vol. 45, 1983.

The private organizations were queried about their political work-load. Fully 3 percent reported that their activity was diminishing. Another 9 percent reported that their workload was unchanged. And 88 percent said their political activity had increased.

Schlozman and Tierney report that the growth of private organizations in Washington was not evenly distributed across the board. They report that the number of corporate offices grew at a much slower rate than did public-interest groups, civil rights groups, and social welfare organizations.

Another study, by political scientist Jack L. Walker,* with a some-what different definition of interest groups, also shows a stark rise, particularly in "citizens" groups. They have doubled in number since 1960.

It's not just groups either. Surveys of the American National Election Study at the University of Michigan reveal that the proportion of Americans who had "ever written any public officials giving them your opinion," and had ever engaged in "writing a letter to the editor on a political subject" about doubled from 1964 to 1976.

Enough data. We have measured the participatory explosion in terms of cash, PACs, lawyers, lobbyists, letters and organizations. Everything is up—way up.

Cash and clout and players washing across the political landscape in recent years like a swarming green tidal wave.

Only one simple question remains: Is this good or bad for us?

---

* "The Origins and Maintenance of Interest Groups in America," *American Political Science Review,* vol. 77, 1983.

CHAPTER 44

Cameo:
The Case of the
Morose Member

THE VIEW FROM THE HOUSE

The case has been made that this explosion in political activity has been unhealthy.

To get the negative idea with its full flavor let's visit for a few busy moments with a typical Member of Congress, in his office. A bell has just rung twice, a light has flashed—fifteen minutes to a vote on the floor. But luckily for us, the Member has time to get a few things off his chest. He speaks:

"I'll tell you this, pal. The Congress used to be fun; now it's a hassle. It used to be exciting; now it's demeaning. It used to be a great honor; now people look at you as if you're swimming in an oversexed cesspool.

"Most of the problem comes from the special-interest groups. There used to be just a few.

"But now it's crazy. The feminists come to me and say I'm sexist. The gays say I'm insensitive. The right-to-lifers say I'm a baby-killer. The freezeniks say I'll blow up the world. The Jews are worried that I'm slipping on Israel. The blacks are worried that I'm slipping on civil rights. The Greeks think I'm soft on Turkey. The old people think I'm soft on Social Security. Every one of these groups has a Political Action Committee, or lobbyists, or public-interest organizations, or solid contacts with the media. They can bombard me with constituent mail. They play me like a drum. Do you think that's fun?"

There is a moment of embarrassed silence. It is not fun. The congressman continues.

"Of course the business guys are still up here looking for goodies. Except now they've got ten times as many guys working the Hill. They want tax breaks. They want to keep the unions in their place. They say they're for free enterprise and free trade. But it's a funny thing; they want to deregulate everyone's business but their own. The steel guys want to keep foreign steel out. The auto guys want to keep foreign cars out. Some free trade!

"The unions beat up on me and say I'm soft on Reagan. They want a few little things too. That cargo be moved in American ships, even if it's more expensive. That foreign cars be built by Americans. That imported goods stay out. That the government direct the economy. They've got PACs, too. Hundreds of them.

"And then there are environmentalists. They work with the unions on some things. They're all liberals. Hah! Except they differ sometimes on trivial issues like economic growth: the environmentalists think we have too much, the unions think we have too little.

"The consumerists are around: food prices are too high, they say. But the farm groups say American agriculture will go bust if prices don't go up.

"They all have PACs, lobbyists, lawyers, trade associations, grass-roots campaigns. There's ten times more pressure than before, twenty times more—who knows?

"I have to hear them all out. They're all big players these days; they have the big cards: money and votes.

"You know what it costs to run for a House seat these days, pal? The average is about a quarter of a million dollars. In a contested seat in a big city, or near one, it's a lot more. A lot of that's for television time, if you can afford it. And direct mail. And public-opinion polls. And phone banks—do you have any idea what it costs to equip and staff ten phone lines for the last six weeks of a campaign? About twenty grand!

"The special interests say all they want is 'access.' Well, maybe. Except if you give everyone access, when do you have time to be a legislator? How can you think intelligently about nuclear arms with a hundred freezniks in your outer office? Or about abortion when all those ladies with red roses are getting ready to mug you?

"Access? If you give them access and then don't vote their way, they still campaign against you. Hit lists! The environmentalists put you on a 'dirty dozen' list and campaign against you and call you a polluter. If you're against a big defense increase, NCPAC campaigns against you and says you're soft on the Commies. It's called 'negative campaigning' or 'independent expenditures.' What it is—is sleaze."

Our friendly Member seems to have it all out of his system. Two more bells ring in his office and another light brightens—ten minutes to a vote. The Member gets up as if to leave, and then turns again to his inquisitor:

"And the press. Talk about participation. Every two-bit paper has a

Washington bureau these days. The TV guys are everywhere. They're participating like never before. Those guys are impossible. Since Watergate, all they want is scandal. Wilbur Mills with a stripteaser. Wayne Hays with a secretary who couldn't type but could do other things. Sex scandals with pages—girls and boys! Dope and booze! Sometimes I think that the most famous women in American politics must be Elizabeth Ray, Paula Parkinson, Fanne Foxe, and Rita Jenrette!

"If they don't get you on sex or booze, they come after you about where you are. If you're in Washington, they say you're never home and you're out of touch with the voters. If you're at home with the voters, they say you're vacationing and not doing the job in Washington. If you go overseas to learn something about what you're voting on, they say you're on a junket.

"But mostly the press is after us about cash and clout. I'm not talking about criminality or bribery—not Koreagate or Abscam—but campaign contributions and special interests. They say we're on the take legally. And there is some truth to that.

"By the time the press has worked us over, the public thinks we're sex maniacs, drug fiends, goof-offs, and legal crooks. But what the press never seems to write about is that we live in two places at the same time, miss too much family life, work fourteen hours a day, six or seven days a week, at a wage much lower than we could make in private industry. You just try to keep up two residences and put three kids through college on $72,000 per year.

"I'll tell you, I don't like it anymore. It's not fun anymore. It's life in a nasty fishbowl. I may not run for reelection. Who needs it?"

The venom out, the Member is calm. Again, bells ring, a third light flashes—five minutes to vote. The Member begins his peroration:

"You know we've done a lot of it to ourselves. We have more congressional staff people than ever before—more committees, more responsibility—but we're less organized.

"In the old days the leadership ran things: the Speaker, the leadership, the committee chairmen. We had some unity. Party discipline could protect you from some of those special interests. You could always say, 'I'd like to go along, but . . .'

"No more. We've reformed the Congress. If a committee chairman is too tough, we bust him. It seems as if almost everyone has a subcommittee these days—there are 251 of them! Young guys who have served two terms are chairmen of subcommittees that affect huge industries! They don't give a damn what their committee chairman wants. They're building little empires. And who helps them build empires? Special-interest groups. PACs. Lobbyists. Trade associations. Government bureaucrats who undermine their own executive branch. Public-interest groups. Everyone. The Members are being raped—and they love it—on an individual level. But we don't govern well anymore."

The Member is halfway out the door, off to vote. He concludes:

"Been nice talking to you. Always good to hear your point of view. I'd like to talk some more when I come back, but I've got to meet with the fellows from SNACK PAC. You know, the Potato Chip and Snack Food Association. There's a big potato-chip factory in my district. Then I've got the gays and the missile people coming in. 'Bye now, pal."

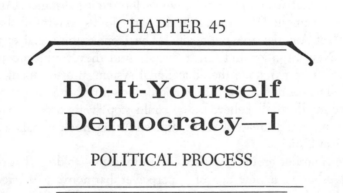

CHAPTER 45

Do-It-Yourself Democracy—I

POLITICAL PROCESS

While the Morose Member is off visiting with potato chips, let us step back from the hurly-burly of his political life and ask whether the cash-clout-player explosion has been helpful or harmful for the rest of us. After all, the Constitution was not written so that Members could have a fun job. In fact, the Constitution may just have been written to keep plenty of heat on Members. And that's what's happening these days.

Has the Participatory Explosion worked out well for America?

I believe so. There are two ways to look at it—as process (this chapter) and as substance (next chapter).

The psephologist Richard Scammon has noted that America has in the twentieth century contributed two particularly noteworthy advances to the idea of democracy. Both involve process: the primary election (in the early part of the century) and the public opinion poll (toward the middle of the century). Both gave more power to the people.

The primary broke the back of the political party by denying it the power of nomination, and bestowed a great gift to voters who believed they knew better than party apparatchiks about whom to choose to run for office. The public-opinion poll also gave voters more influence: when candidates in an election knew that their opponent knew how the voters felt, candidates dared not stray too far, too often, from those voter sentiments. There was still room for leadership on the basis of principle (that's often good politics) but less leeway for candidate arrogance.

These days, process is particularly important in our democracy. There are several reasons for this.

First, if we've learned anything about government in recent decades it is that we don't know a whole lot about substance. An army of experts came to Washington in the early 1960s convinced that they could "get America moving again." The Democratic social engineers of the New Frontier and Great Society said they could end poverty and racism, reinvigorate the educational system, provide medical care for all. The economists said they could "fine-tune" the economy. The defense intellectuals believed they could stop "wars of national liberation" and could create a stable and enduring nuclear balance with the Soviet Union.

Later, another group of experts—Republicans—told us that détente would usher in a new age of superpower harmony. Most recently, economists from the supply-side told us taxes could be cut and revenues increased, that inflation would be halted without recession.

It all didn't quite work out as planned. Much progressive domestic activity did indeed take place. But no one associated with the development of those programs would deny that in many instances there were unintended side effects that were harsh. Examples: did increases in welfare payments help trigger the sharp increase in illegitimate births? Did social welfare spending outrun its taxing supply lines, setting off big deficits? On the international side: counterinsurgency warfare didn't work out in Vietnam, we didn't end the nuclear arms race, and détente vanished under Soviet tank treads in Afghanistan.

So, beware of experts. Fact is, we human beings still don't know a great deal about how the world works. To some large measure, social science turned out to be a God that failed. Economists these days don't claim to understand much except that there is a lot they don't understand. Activists who believe in big government keep on trying, but are much humbler people, and don't believe in it as much as they once did.

When political promises and programs don't work out so well, it's said that skepticism increases and voters "turn off." Alienation allegedly rises. A nation, still basically healthy, can become more dispirited than it ought to be.

It is against this less than terrific backdrop of the *substance* of democratic governance that we should consider advances in the *process* of democratic governance.

For the process of democracy is terrific. It serves as an antidote for disillusion. The activity itself is of the essence. When people participate in politics—directly or indirectly—they believe they can shape their own destiny. When people believe they can shape their destiny politically, they calm down. They do not riot or try to overthrow the government. They do not sulk. They feel less alienated. When asked by pollsters, they will agree with the statement, "I live in the best country in the world." They go about their day's work with vigor and spirit. That spirit can, in fact, change their destiny for the better. Process yields progress. Process becomes substance.

So, let us now note the addition of· a third American streamer to the bonnet of democratic process. Let us call it, alternatively, "participatory democracy" or "dollar democracy" or "cash and clout and players." Whatever you call it means (as we have seen) that more of us are involved in the game, directly and indirectly. More power to the people. More power to more people.

What does all the money buy? What does all the participation get for the participants?

Influence. How? For whom?

Cash can buy clout directly, by helping an ally win an election.

And more importantly, cash can gain influence indirectly, by supporting causes and the players who argue causes publicly. Thus, cash supports lobbyists—from the National Rifle Association to Common Cause—to inform and persuade legislators. Cash supports think tanks and public-interest groups to "change the climate of ideas." Cash supports battalions of public relations operatives—to hustle the press—on behalf of everyone from defense contractors to feminist organizations. Cash supports people to develop mailing lists to whom long letters with short words will be sent—all this to raise still more money to gain still more clout.

Cash-yields-players-yields-clout by supporting activists, who contact voters, who then contact their legislators and squeeze them until the Members of Congress say "Congress isn't fun anymore." The participatory process yields clout by supporting demonstrators who march in front of the White House and get on the evening news. Participation yields clout through meetings that get covered on the evening news and in newspapers.

Who gains from all this? Special interests, to be sure. But how special are they? Often, they are not so special—their base can be quite broad.

When environmentalists raise money from direct mail, foundations, and philanthropists, they set up little rabbit warrens near Dupont Circle in Washington, D.C., underpay their idealistic help, and represent people interested in preserving and enhancing the natural environment of America. They lobby, promote, investigate. Then, when a "proenvironment" President (like Jimmy Carter) comes into office, the people in the rabbit warrens accept four or fivefold increases in pay and go to work at the Council on Environmental Quality or the Environmental Protection Agency or the Department of the Interior, where they pursue much of the same agenda they pursued as environmental activists outside government. In or out, they generally represent millions of Americans—perhaps tens of millions—who are concerned about the environment.

For whom else is the money buying influence?

When executives at the Big Biz Corporation shake the tin cup and raise money for a corporate Political Action Committee, who's giving? Who's getting? How much? Who's benefiting?

By law, contributions to a PAC can come only from individuals—not corporations. The donations involved are not large, at least not by earlier political standards. The law provides that even the fattest of felines cannot contribute more than $5,000 to a PAC. In 1982, fully 87 percent of the monies raised by corporate PACs came from contributions of less than $500. In any event, no individual can now contribute more than $1,000 to a candidate for a federal election (twice that if a primary election is involved). A contributor cannot give more than $25,000 per year as a total for all federal campaigns. Double that for a married couple. The amounts have not been adjusted for inflation since 1974, while the Consumer Price Index went up by 105 percent from 1974 to early 1984.

Who's getting? Typically, of course, the PAC will donate to legislators believed to be supportive of the well-being of the Big Biz Corporation and of the business community generally. No PAC can give more than $5,000 to a candidate, or twice that if the candidate runs in both a primary and general election. The average corporate PAC donation to a candidate was about $600 in 1980.

Who benefits? Well, surely the people who donated to the PAC. But those people are not typically fat cats or zillionaire robber barons who own a huge business. They are usually salaried middle-level managers of the corporation. Some of the contributors are well-salaried indeed, some not so well-salaried. But as managers, they may be assumed to represent the interest of the corporation. These days, there are about 42 million shareholders in American corporations—an all-time high, and about 18 percent of the adult population. There may be even more shareholders than there are environmentalists. If one counts in the 55 million Americans who belong to pension plans backed by investments in American corporations, then those people and their families outnumber environmentalists, and, in fact, comprise a majority of Americans. (Many of them, of course, are also environmentalists.)

When, in the course of events, a "probusiness" President (like Ronald Reagan) comes into office, some of these corporate types invariably will be found moving into government ranks—perhaps serving in EPA, CEQ, or the Department of Interior, replacing some of the activist environmentalists. When they do, as in the case of environmentalists, they will often tilt toward policies they have espoused on the outside—in this case, "probusiness" policies that they would describe as "proeconomic growth" and very much in the interest of those tens of millions of American shareholders.

Well, it may be asked, what about working men and women, not the upper-crust shareholders and elitist environmentalists? Well, it might be answered, the labor unions are not exactly political slouches. Not only were the unions the first big players in PACs, but in addition to money, they are able to offer major "in-kind" services to candidates. These include phone banks, mailing lists, door-to-door canvassers, and word-of-mouth from the shop steward to the union members—in short, the stuff of which politics is made. Because most union labor is affiliated with a central organization (the AFL-CIO), a single, powerful central endorsement is possible in both primary and general elections. (That capability is lacking in the more atomized business community.) In the mid-1970s the Committee on Political Education (COPE) of the AFL-CIO began modernizing its efforts. Under the guidance of COPE director Alexander Barkan, one of American politics' most remarkable men, labor developed computerized lists totaling upward of ten million union members. Labor represents plenty of people and has plenty of clout.

What can be said of environmentalists, business, and labor, can also be said of feminists, doctors, the elderly, gays, Jews, farmers, blacks, Eastern Europeans, right-to-lifers, potato-chip manufacturers, and so on. They represent plenty of people. The mix of techniques used by these advocacy groups varies. Business may use more money and less "in-kind" services. Feminists need less money to successfully get their message to the mass media and, as a result, to the voters. Liberals used the think tank first (the Brookings Institution); in recent years the conservatives have probably used it more actively. Liberals have used the "public-interest" groups to much greater effect than conservatives, who were late in getting started.

I would maintain that all this frenetic activity, representing tens of millions of Americans who were less represented in the cash-clout-player equation of earlier times, yields something very important: a less alienated population.

I offer as my case in point direct mail.

Political theorists sometimes regard it as a tawdry practice, the pits of politics. It is junk mail, it is said. Worse, it is computerized junk mail.

Hundreds of millions of pieces of computerized political junk mail are sent out each year. It is said that this junk mail undermines all that is noble about democratic politics; it is said that the messages are simplistic and demagogic. It is said that direct mail is a tool that helps make single-issue politics possible and that single-issue politics are fractionalizing and atomizing voters into smaller and smaller groups, each with petty interests, often not in the national interest, often peddling negativism, even "negative advertising."

But think a moment. What are these purveyors of single-issue, computer-produced junk mail actually doing? They are selling us political dreams.

Open the envelope and inside—why, inside is a dream! Do you think that abortion is murder and ought to be outlawed? Send in $15 to make it happen. Do you think that the folks who are against abortion are assailing civil liberties and want to put Ronald Reagan in your bedroom? Send in $15 to stop it.

Do you think the nuclear arms race is madness? Send $15 to halt it. Do you think it's madness to let the Soviets be stronger than the U.S.? Send $15.

Interestingly, it was the "progressive" forces that first used direct mail effectively to finance "single issues": to stop the war, to cleanse the environment, to halt racism, to assail sexism, to promote consumerism, to enshrine Ralph Nader, and to make a common cause to purify government.

It took the folks on the right a while to catch up. But these days the postman's bag is also full of (often strident) conservative mail. Proprayer, prodefense, anti-SALT, antibaby-killing, antiunion, antiimmorality, antitaking our guns away, antibig spenders—the dreams are all carefully arrayed by ZIP codes. Save America from mushy-headed liberalism, the letters beg.

But the dreams of one mailing list stimulate the dreams of another. In the first years of the Reagan administration, the environmentalist mailings hit the jackpot by noting that Interior Secretary James Watt would pluck the last leaf from the last tree if the recipient didn't respond.

It is quite clear that in political terms these tactics are successful, both on the Right and the Left. Much of the money raised is wasted in the cost of raising the money. But what's left is used with great political leverage. A campaign contribution provides leverage, as we've heard from the Morose Member. A "negative campaign" fund has enormous leverage when it strikes a resonant and credible chord (but can backfire when it doesn't). The political leverage of small megaphone organizations in our nation's capital is sometimes awesome to behold. From the point of view of the $15 contributor, direct mail works. It helps friends and harms adversaries. It promotes causes the contributor believes in and harms the causes the contributor abhors.

But is direct mail—and all the new politics-playing—good for *America*?

We shall come to a fuller answer of that question in the next chapter. For now, let us note that it is surely good for *Americans*. The theory behind direct mail is that the dreams that are for sale for $15— dreams about power—can come true. Send in your check, says the copywriter, and you will change the world. And in a way that civics books never contemplated, the world is indeed often changed by the respondents.

So every mailing is a potential antialienation instrument. So too are all the other augmented forms of political activity we have been describing here: phone banks, lobbying, public relations, campaign contributions, and so on.

It is "participatory democracy" with a vengeance. That phrase was much revered by the Left in the late 1960s and early 1970s. Power to the people, they said. We need a New Politics, they said. Let's drive the monied fat cats from the temple of politics, they said. If only the people would come out and play politics, they said, then the war would end, the environment would be cleansed, women would be freed from bondage, and we would not nominate presidents like Lyndon Johnson and Hubert Humphrey in smoke-filled rooms, but presidents like George McGovern in open primary elections.

Well. Participatory democracy arrived. In fact it did play a major role in halting the war in Vietnam, and in igniting both the women's movement and the environmental movement. We now select our president outside smoke-filled rooms, in a well-ventilated season of primary elections, with a surprise every day.

But a funny thing happened on the way to the participatory McGovernite state. It wasn't only the Left that played politics. Voters who thought they had a right to keep their guns played politics. Voters who thought that liberals were rewriting their textbooks in ways that were objectionable played politics.

The fat cats were driven from the temple all right. W. Clement Stone* could no longer give Richard Nixon $2.8 million as he did for the 1968 general election. And philanthropist Stewart Mott could no longer give $400,000, as he did in 1972 to George McGovern's campaign.

After the Watergate election reforms, individuals could contribute only relatively small sums. This development tended to bring in tens of millions of dollars, contributed by hundreds of thousands of new donors. Their monies often went to PACs or other participatory organizations which directly and indirectly represented tens of millions of voters who had been proportionately underrepresented before the money storm hit.

In the bad old days it was fat cats, certain businesses like oil and milk, the unions, and certain cause groups such as civil rights that sat at the table when the cards of politics were dealt. These days more people are participating, Left and Right, rich and not-so-rich. That's very good.

Or, as Michael Malbin, editor of a recently published volume on campaign financing† says, "Almost any political scientist looking at the new system knows that whatever its problems, it is far better than what went on before."

====

The growth of dollar democracy has been a big story in recent American life. But once again, the press got the wrong story. Media

---

* W. Clement Stone—alone—donated more money to *one* politician than any PAC gave to *all* politicians in 1982.

† *Money and Politics in the United States—Financing Elections in the 1980s,* edited by Michael J. Malbin (Chatham House, 1984).

alchemy turned good news into bad news. When you think about it, it is the kind of story that would be almost impossible for a modern television journalist to get right.

Just try to imagine your favorite correspondent standing in front of the Capitol, hair blowing in the wind, saying, "The Federal Elections Commission revealed today that corporate and labor union PAC campaign contributions soared to an all-time high, indirectly representing tens of millions of American shareholders in the political process. In addition, contributions from ideological Political Action Committees also climbed to an all-time high. Particularly high sums were donated by environmental, prochoice, prolife, progun and antigun groups. This means the likelihood of more negative campaigning this fall, by both Right and Left, expressing with vigor the strong views of additional millions of Americans, reducing voter alienation, thereby strengthening America. Back to you, Dan."

That is not quite the way it has been played. Instead, we have heard a steady stream of "inside baseball" stories about how this congressman and that senator are supported by this or that big business seeking to gain tax breaks, to pollute the air, to make products less safe, to harm the consumer. We hear again and again about Members of Congress who vote like robots in support of policies espoused by their campaign patrons.

Now that is perfectly legitimate coverage. One of the big positive changes brought about by dollar democracy is that campaign contributors are now essentially public, which was not true in earlier times. Accordingly, it is the job of the press to find and publicize the fact that candidate A is raking it in from Big Oil and candidate B is getting big bucks from the Dirty Air PAC.

But concentration on such stories reveals a grievous flaw in the nature of our media system. This chapter is about the political process and the fact is that the media do a dreadful job of covering process of any kind.

The modern media system covers *events* with dash, style, accuracy—and sometimes even in depth. A plane crashes and the cameras are there in minutes; we see the grieving relatives; later we often find out the cause of the crash. Or a war: Bang! Shells land on Khe Sanh. Bang! Shell lands in Beirut. Bang! Dead bodies in El Salvador.

Events.

Process is much more difficult, particularly for television. We have noted this earlier: Death-by-Tylenol gets more coverage than all the drug advances of a decade. (Event over process.)

There seem to be four potential ways to cover a process story. It can be covered as good news or bad news. Subdivided, the good news or the bad news can be seen through a liberal or a conservative prism. Our press typically covers only one-fourth of a process story: the bad news, liberal style.

The dollar democracy story is a case in point. The liberal/bad news prism picks up the big rise in nasty corporate PAC money, and that story is played with gusto and an infinite variety of angles.

Hardly touched is what would be the countervailing *conservative/* bad news aspect. Thus, there is no story on national television about the migration to Washington of an army of environmentalists, feminists, freezeniks, and consumerists, all aiming to jump our politicians as much as any corporate PAC ever could.

And more important by far, the good news aspect of the entire process is ignored entirely. We have had a stunning increase in participation by both liberals and conservatives in our politics. That is a profoundly positive development. Hooray! More cash. Huzzah! More players. Yippee! More clout. Americans, more than ever, are practicing self-determination.

Try tuning in that story some evening.

CHAPTER 46

Do-It-Yourself Democracy—II

IDEAS AND ISSUES

Participation is good for Americans: it is the logical remedy for alienation, it helps people feel that they affect their destiny, it serves as a safety valve for political passions. But that is not enough. An expansion of participation could soothe the savage breast, but also yield a policy disaster. And so we talk in this chapter about substance, not process.

We ask: how are we doing? Has participatory democracy taken us to dark places?

I argue here that in a quite remarkable way our new politics have taken us to sunlit uplands, albeit over a bumpy road. Participatory democracy has helped to open up our lives, helped reinvigorate our business climate, helped improve the quality of life, helped toughen our resolve in a dangerous world. It has kept us (I think) away from extremism.

Democracy works. More democracy works even better.

There is a potential danger that hangs over the idea of more participatory democracy. Conservatives fear the process responds too quickly to voter passions, yielding permissiveness and runaway big government. Liberals fear that the money in the system rewards greed while the passion it plays to is jingoism.

Is it, perhaps, too much of a good thing? After all, viewed in an isolated way, participatory democracy offers no coherent plan of government, no discipline, no national direction, only the haggling and pressures of the political souk. It gets people playing all right, which is good. But is it so democratic, so free-form, that it could lead us willy-nilly down a primrose path?

That is one reason why conservatives worried so deeply about eroding values in the 1970s. More license, a softer social code, more regulation, more bureaucracy, more government spending, more inflation, less defense spending, all seemed to be in part the result of the unleashed passions and potency of participatory democracy. Liberals—as the conservatives saw it—seemed to dominate the process. Antiwar, antinuke, feminist, minority, gay, environmental participants dominated our television screens. Under cover of the media barrage, other liberal participants exploited the softened terrain: activist lawyers, new phalanxes of liberal congressional staffers, public-interest groups that lobbied shell-shocked legislators.

It was going overboard, conservatives said.

But by the early 1980s it was the liberals' turn to worry. The new participants seemed suddenly to form a conservative tide: the hit-listers were targeting liberals running for the Senate, the campaign money was rolling in to conservatives and Republicans, the corporate PACs were everywhere. Under this protective cover, said liberals, Ronald Reagan was destroying the Safety Net, polluting the environment, and destroying the possibility for arms control.

It was going overboard, liberals said.

There was a danger, sensed on both sides of the political equation: for all its merits as a process, the new participatory democracy could swing us from one policy extreme to another. A ship without a rudder will not last long in a storm.

Not to worry. We now have some history to go by. It is quite apparent that the ship has a rudder. The limousine of the participatory state has a steering wheel and brakes. It takes us where we want to go and where we ought to be going. It has taken the best of the Left, the best of the Right, and left us with the thriving politics of the contentious Center.

═══

Consider liberalism.

After decades of glory, it seemed to many observers that by the late 1960s and the early 1970s American liberalism—fueled by hyperactivist participationists—had taken a wrong turn. The decent impulses were still there, but often carried to extremes and sometimes subverted.

A liberalism that had once championed vigorous economic growth was seen suddenly to champion a low-growth environmental ethic that often seemed to scorn economic growth. A liberalism that had championed the idea of merit and denounced quotas turned around and endorsed quotas in all but name. A liberalism that had prided itself on a vigorous internationalist posture to combat totalitarianism of both Right and Left was perceived to have turned toward a policy of neoisolationism that featured political bidding to see who could cut the defense budget the most. All this was energized by new-style political participators: environmentalists, civil rights activists, antiwar demonstrators.

There was more, real and symbolic: a consumer consciousness that was seen to go from legitimate concern for product safety to a posture of antibusiness harassment, a feminism that became strident, an attitude about crime that was perceived to be more concerned with rights of criminals than rights of the victims. Again: movements fueled by participatory activists.

Looming above and beyond all this were hundreds of programs dealing with welfare, health, education, transportation, housing— some very good, some not as good, but with one common feature: neither governments nor taxpayers were willing to raise enough money to pay for them. The ensuing deficits were believed to be the trigger of a virulent inflation.

To some greater or lesser degree all these developments were blamed on the participatory explosion. Activists combed the halls of Congress. Every far-out idea, every well-meaning new program developed a big constituency and fresh armies of participants.

Perhaps the scariest part of the picture was that these developments took place under relatively moderate men in the executive branch:

Nixon, Ford, Carter. Accordingly, it was believed that the rise of the ever-leftward, ever-farther-out welfare state could never be halted, would never even plateau, never be made responsible, until and unless disaster struck. The special interests, the single-issue interests, could reach their voters, inflame them, and use them as bludgeons on legislators. It was sensed that the electoral sum of all the special interests added up to more than 50 percent of the voters. The special interests were in control. Accordingly, it was believed, there was no way to restrain runaway participatory liberalism.

There was no solace elsewhere. Europe was the model, it was said. There the welfare state grew inexorably, even when it brought economic blight along with it—as in "the English Disease."

Problem. There were surely good impulses in this participatory spasm: environmental reform, women's rights, consumer protection. There were bright and vigorous people coming into the process. And there were grievous excesses as well.

Question: how would a perfect political system operating in a country with perfectly wise voters respond to such a situation?

Answer: Curb the excesses. Keep what's good. Keep the new players playing. Search for a healthy counteragenda to throw out the excesses. Foster it by harnessing it, too, to the new participatory process.

That's about what happened. As the 1970s wore on, the conservatives also began to play cash-clout-players, often aping their liberal counterparts, and occasionally coming up with new twists. Business groups began to organize: more lobbyists, more public relations people, more corporate advertising, and of course a sophisticated utilization of the Political Action Committee. The conservative ideological groups intensified their efforts and found the necessary real and symbolic issues. The Panama Canal "giveaway" was one; property tax reform was another; opposition to the Equal Rights Amendment a third. Savaged by Watergate, the Republican party, always the better organized of the major parties, intensified its efforts at candidate recruitment, campaign finance, polling, and advertising.

Most important, all this activity was taking place in a country that was changing its mind about some very important ideas. Liberal participatory activists may have energized their special interest voters, may have incited the media, may have scared hell out of congressmen, but all the turmoil did not permanently convince the American people about large parts of the liberal agenda. Quite to the contrary. Too much tumult worked against those who were engendering the tumult. Moreover, there were events in the saddle that not only worked against the new and exaggerated liberal ideas, but in many instances seemed to demonstrate that liberal ideas were making some difficult things a lot worse.

Thus: the Soviets were building up their military strength through the 1970s. There was an argument about how fast and how much, but little contention about the general drift of the military balance and the appropriate response. Here is an attitudinal Super Number:

THINK GOVERNMENT IS SPENDING TOO *LITTLE* ON NATIONAL DEFENSE

1969	8%
1971	11%
1973	13%
1976	22%
1981	51%

Source: Gallup.

Most aspects of public opinion don't change rapidly. The magnitude and velocity of this change is almost unmatched in the annals of American survey research. It is particularly noteworthy because it occurred against the backdrop of an activist clamor that defense expenditures should be cut because America was not the global gendarme.

Further, by the early 1970s, inflation had become the "most important issue," cited by the public in Gallup's polling—and it remained in first place for a decade.

PERCENT SAYING "INFLATION" IS "MOST IMPORTANT ISSUE"

1964	4%
1972	27% (first year in first place)
1975	57%
1980	74%
1981	52%
1982	18%
1983	11%

Source: Gallup.

The specter of a runaway inflationary spiral has always been a hole-card ace for conservative politicians, just as the fear of unemployment has been a trump for liberals. The inflationary take-off in the late Seventies, no matter how much Jimmy Carter said it was all the doing of OPEC sheiks, was a liberal's nightmare.

Moreover, Americans were becoming disenchanted with "big government," in part blaming it for inflation. Now, as it turned out, the "big government" issue was not a simple one, as will be shown later. People don't want big government but they want the services provided by big government. Still, the issue is at least a rhetorical bonus for conservatives:

Question: In your opinion, which of the following will be the biggest threat to the country in the future—big business, big labor, or big government?

"Big Government"	
1959	14%
1967	49%
1968	46%
1977	39%
1979	43%
1981	46%
1983	51%

Source: Gallup.

The perception of rising government-induced inflation was a particularly big conservative bonus because, unlike the Soviet arms buildup, the issue was not seen to be caused externally. All those liberal activists, the public sensed, wanted even more big government.

There were many such liberal attitudes that came under ever sharper challenge at about this time. As we have seen earlier, as criminality increased there was a growing view that toughness was required. As recessionary clouds formed in the late Seventies, there was less talk of environmentalist slow growth and more talk about how to spur the economy back to vigorous growth. The latter-day agenda of the civil rights movement—busing, quotas—remained extremely unpopular. Conservatives, of course, encouraged and took the advantage in the turning of the tide of ideas.

But it is very important to know that they were only able to do it selectively. For while rejecting some of the liberal agenda, the public bought some of it—the best parts. Conservatives could be against busing and quotas but would be punished if they were seen to be against civil rights (nor did most of them want to be). Environmentalism became a motherhood issue; it could be (properly) picked at near its edges on the grounds of stunting economic growth, but no one ran for office on a platform of dirty air and dirty water—unless he was interested in losing big. Similarly, a candidate could oppose ERA, but would suffer if the public thought he was against the right of women for equal opportunity. The best remained.

So: this new-fangled, participatory, special-interest democracy self corrects just like the old-fangled democracy does. When it goes too far, it's a loser. This meant that by the late 1970s we heard Republicans noting, announcing, or bellowing (as individual styles directed) that if you wanted to vote for the special-interest party—the party of welfare mothers, union bosses, peaceniks, soft-on-crime professors, big spending bureaucrats, black activists, harsh feminists, antigrowth environmentalists—why, then, by all means vote Democratic. On the other hand, if you were interested in voting for the party that had *America's* best interests at heart—not special interests—why, then, vote for your friendly Republican.*

It was on such grounds that Republicans started winning many elections that they used to lose. Most notable was Ronald Reagan's victory in 1980, heralding, it was said, "a new era."

Why did it happen?

It was said then—and still said now—that Reagan won simply because people didn't like Carter. It is also true that a bicycle moves because its wheels turn. But why do the wheels turn? Why did Americans come to dislike Jimmy Carter?

Political popularity is not akin to being "well liked" by your friends and neighbors. Almost invariably when voters agree with a candidate, when they think he is successful in moving toward goals with which they agree, then they "like" the candidate. Remarkable traits of character will be discovered to back up their view: a candidate will be seen as wise, warm, and witty, it will be remembered that he was born in a log cabin. Is there any doubt that Jimmy Carter would have been better *liked* in 1980 if the inflation rate had been low, the economy

---

* So powerful was this theme that even liberal Democrats used it on other liberal Democrats, to wit Gary Hart's antispecial interest, union-bashing attacks against Walter Mondale in early 1984.

had been booming, gasoline had been thirty cents a gallon, and the Ayatollah had not been *Time*'s man of the year?

Jimmy Carter became unpopular because he became the symbol of so many things that American voters had come to dislike. There was a great and sad irony to this: Carter had run and won and was popular during the 1976 primaries when he was the middle-of-the-road candidate who was "anti-Washington." He was relatively unassailable when he was a candidate who could not plausibly be linked to all those special-interest groups of welfarists, feminists, peaceniks, busers, and so on.

But by 1980, by accident or design, by ignorance, foolishness, or inadvertence, Carter had come to be identified with all those issues and causes that so many Americans didn't cotton to. *That* feeling was *then* personalized; people said *then* they didn't like Carter. And in a *liberal* suburb of Washington, D.C., high school students took glee in wearing buttons that directed, "Send the Wimp Home!"

And all the interest groups in America, with all their lobbyists and all their public-interest groups, couldn't give much help to the candidate (Carter) who opposed their nemesis (Reagan). *The interest groups had become a large part of Carter's problem. As it turned out, the political sum was a lot smaller than a total of all the political parts.*

So: the ongoing nightmare that haunted conservatives turned out to be only a passing bad dream. A bigger welfare state, domestic everleftward liberalism, more neoisolationism were not inexorably determined by the continued growth of left-of-center participatory advocacy. That process was corrected through counterparticipation by activists and common sense by voters.

Inexorability is not a word in the vocabulary of democracy.

＝＝

Consider conservatism.

By 1981, another potential danger about participatory democracy was observed: that the Right, the conservatives, and the business community had learned to play cash-and-clout-and-players, special-interest dollar democracy so well, so potently, that they would shut out the rest of America. The "new era" was viewed by some pundits as one that would guarantee continuing political ascendancy for conservatism and for Republicans. Inexorability was said to have moved from Left to Right.

That didn't happen either.

Reagan started out well. A chastened band of Democrats was heading back to the center. A new era consensus formed during the early

Reagan period. Although the press concentrated on magnifying small differences, there was a rather remarkable agreement, across party and ideological lines, endorsing the basic lines of the Reagan program: an increase in the defense budget, a diminishment in the rate of growth of domestic programs, a closer scrutiny of regulatory excess.

But just as the Democratic Left learned in the Seventies, so the Republican Right learned in the Early Eighties: if you try to go too far in the new world of participatory politics, you get slapped down.

A combination of tough events, cheap shots, intense press scrutiny, monumental stupidity, and ideological rigidity—the standard fare of American politics—combined to bring about a sense that the Reaganauts and their activist backers had left the reservation.

There was a big recession. Was it Reagan's "fault?" Was it really caused by his "supply-side economics," allegedly "radical" in nature? No matter. The calculus of American politics dictates that the opposition blames the incumbent for a recession, that the media megaphone the charge, that the public buys some of it.

There were cheap shots. Ronald Reagan does not really want to blow up the world; he does not want to pull the nuclear trigger. But a few phrases out of context were trumpeted far and wide: "demonstration shots," "limited nuclear wars," and so forth.

There were more than the usual number of standard scandals, semi-scandals, nonscandals made to sound like scandals: the case of the pilfered briefing book (Debategate), the mysterious $1,000 in the safe of the National Security advisor, the deputy National Security advisor who had made much too much money too quickly on the stock market, the feminist aide who discovered after three years that Ronald Reagan was not a feminist.

But it was more than just a difficult economic moment and the normal cheap shots of politics. Pushed by activists of the Right, encouraged at times by the President's own far-out views, the Reagan team drifted near the outer edge of their mandate and sometimes outside of it. The opposition and the media made the most of it.

Americans wanted tax cuts all right, but when the perception formed (bolstered by at least some reality) that the Reagan cuts were tilted toward "the rich" and for "businessmen," the Reaganauts were harmed.

Americans did not want busing and quotas, but neither did they want a president to endorse tax exemptions for segregated schools.

Americans wanted a crackdown on welfare chiselers, but not on poor people. They wanted more military spending but not if it meant cutting college tuition help for their own kids.

Americans did not want to be weak or to give in to the Soviets, but they did not like the idea that the President might be dawdling on nuclear arms control talks.

Americans did not like environmental zaniness on the Left. Stopping a dam to save a snail darter only made common sense an endangered species. But James Watt, Reagan's man at the Department of Interior, was perceived to be a screwball from the opposite end of the spectrum. Meanwhile, at the Environmental Protection Agency, other Reaganauts were perceived to be just a bit too cavalier about pollution and toxic wastes.

The President had no one to blame but himself for the great Social Security flap. In May of 1981, he rather blithely sent a message to the Senate proposing cuts and caps in the system. After all, he seemed to say, I was elected to roll back big government. The Senate—with a majority of Republicans—quickly told the President exactly what he could do with his proposal, by a vote of 96–0. Needless to say, Democrats were prepared to exploit the issue in the 1982 congressional elections. Television spots showed a Republican scissors going snip, snip, snip, mutilating a Social Security card—a dramatization artfully presented courtesy of the Democratic National Committee.

Reagan and many of his conservative cheerleaders, his participatory platoons, his special-interest shock troops, had misread the American public. They felt, correctly, that Americans were disaffected by big government. But while Americans don't like big government, they don't want to do away with the services provided by big government. This gives conservatives some running room to shape policies, but nowhere near a free hand. A perceived shoot-from-the-hip cutback in Social Security benefits was not within these guidelines.

Well, between perceptions of tax cuts for the well-to-do, scorn for the environment, a blasé view of Social Security, tax help for segregationists, a cavalier regard for nuclear arms control, the Reaganauts—like their Democratic predecessors—became viewed as the tools of "special interests." Their special interests were not welfare mothers, unions, minorities, or gays. Their special interests, their activist participators, were perceived as "fat cats," "right-wingers," "the military-industrial complex"—all squeezing the little guy.

Democrats described much of this as "the fairness issue." It is an issue that throws fear into the hearts of Republicans. For at its root, it is the issue that elected Democrats to high office for fifty years. Just as Republicans had successfully attacked Democratic hyperliberalism, so Democrats attacked Republican hyperconservatism, with some real success.

=====

And then what happened?

Ronald Reagan did not become President of the United States because he is unskilled in political wiles. That is not the way the game works.

And Democrats are not the majority party because they stay out of touch with voters.

Think of how Reagan reacted. As he saw the trouble that right-wing activist positions were causing him, Reagan presented his views in a more moderate way. It was Reagan who decided *not* to "let Reagan be Reagan." Soon it was heard that "the pragmatists" were winning the battles in the White House—beating the "Reaganauts." For a while it seemed as if no man in American history had worked harder to establish and maintain the Safety Net than that great social democrat Ronald Reagan. No one cared more about arms control. Things at the EPA changed: Administrator Anne Burford suffered from ring-around-the collar and was replaced by squeaky clean William Ruckelshaus. James Watt went home, crippled.

As in the earlier case with liberals, the conservative's excesses were purged. But, again as in the liberal instance, many of the sound impulses stayed on, and were at least partially implemented: stronger defense, less regulation, more reliance on the free market, less growth of government programs.

Much the same moderating process has gone on in the Democratic party. One need not be a political genius to understand that no-growth, soft-on-defense, and big-spending are non-starters these days. Today Democrats denounce deficits, endorse industrial policies designed to foster growth, and come out for moderate defense increases.

Summing up: what happened on both sides of the spectrum? Democrats used special interests to their great benefit—and then got into trouble with them. Republicans used special interests to their great benefit—and then got into trouble with them. Excesses on both sides were purged from without and from within. The fights go on. Good impulses and active people on both sides were brought into the system. Both sides now compete for the high ground of the center. Such a long-range view does not jibe with the common broad characterizations of our recent Presidents as liars, crooks, bumpkins and dolts, or of our Members of Congress as venal hustlers.

When all the dust settles, we end up about where we ought to be, with the best from both camps: both parties pursuing economic growth, maintaining a moderately high Safety Net, endorsing environmental progress, calling for strong defense, prepared to negotiate arms reductions.

Of course, up close and in the trenches, our politics are as gamy as ever. Preposterous charges fly this way and that. Periodically, the hyper-participators surface again and flex their muscles. The going-too-far process begins afresh. But when all is said and done, centrism reigns in the vigorously contentious participatory state.

CHAPTER 47

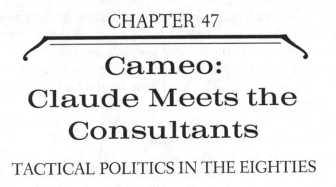

Cameo: Claude Meets the Consultants

TACTICAL POLITICS IN THE EIGHTIES

Off to the side of Claude's living room two political consultants, one a Democrat, one a Republican, are talking shop—about the future. Claude has ambled over.

"You had a golden chance," says the Democrat to the Republican, "and you blew it. You could have had the Eighties all wrapped up in a nice red ribbon. Reagan could have had it all—the Congress, the Presidency, the Courts, the Statehouse—everything but the Mayors. Now it's up for grabs."

"That's right," says Claude, "it's anyone's ball game."

"We got a little unlucky," says the Republican. "Almost 11 percent unemployment in 1982, right at election time."

"It wasn't just bad luck," says the Democrat. "When Reagan came in, in 1981, he was able to make the case that the Republicans were finally the party of the little guy in America. That really scared us. That's our bread and butter."

"I know," says the Republican.

"Reagan was taking factory workers from us," says the Democrat. "And ethnics. And Jews. And inner city peripherals. For a little while, almost as many Americans said they were Republicans as Democrats.

My God, it looked as if we wouldn't be the majority party forever."

"I remember it well," says the Republican. "It was a nice moment."

"It was a political earthquake," says Claude.

"But you Republicans blew it," says the Democrat. "Tax cuts for rich people—unbelievable!"

"Democrats on the Hill put a lot of that into the bill."

"I know that. You know that. But it's a Republican albatross. Make the rich richer. We'll use that for the rest of the decade. And Social Security!"

"That's a big surprise," says the Republican.

"And all those rich people in limousines for the inauguration—new White House china at a couple of hundred grand during a recession. You blew it. You're not the party of the little guy anymore. You're for fat cat special interests. You're the country club party again. You gave us back the fairness issue. That's our issue for the Eighties. Thanks."

"You're welcome."

"You're just lucky you didn't lose even more seats in the 1982 Congress. We should have really creamed you."

"You should have, you could have," says the Republican. "We let our special interest tigers get out of hand. Let Reagan be Reagan, they say. They want Reagan to be New Right. They lose us votes."

"I said thanks," says the Democrat.

"But you know why we didn't get stomped in 1982 and why we're not going to get stomped any time soon?"

"I'm listening."

"Because you guys haven't fully learned your lesson. You think you're going to make points by beating up on Reagan for wanting to cut domestic spending? You're not. Even Democrats want to cut domestic spending. You think you're going to make points because Reagan wants to raise defense spending? You're not. Even Democrats want to raise defense spending. You think you're going to make points by condemning America in Grenada? No way. You think most Democrats like the idea that there's a gay caucus in the Democratic National Committee? And thanks for Jesse Jackson. He's worth a few million votes for Republicans."

"What are you, a racist?"

"No way," says the Republican. "Jackson hurts you because he comes across as a radical, not because he's black. So, thanks."

"You're welcome," says the Democrat.

"You let all your special interest tigers out of the cage again during the 1984 primaries. The process dragged on so long that Mondale got pulled lefter and lefter."

"I know," says the Democrat. "The tigers are very hard to control. They help us, then they kill us. Voter-eating tigers."

"They give us our issues for the Eighties," says the Republican. "The Democrat party is still the party of elitist special interests: limousine liberals in favor of busing, feminists against family, gays against values—and big labor bosses, they're always worth a shot. The Democrat party is still the party of peaceniks and freezeniks who think America ought to stand in the corner."

"Ic," says the Democrat.

"Excuse me?" says the Republican.

"Ic," says the Democrat. "You forgot who you were talking to. It's not the Democrat party. It's the Democra*tic* party."

"Sorry."

"But what you forget is that we're learning," says the Democrat. "Our tigers are not nearly as bad as they used to be. We're for 4 percent real growth in defense. That's not bad. Even our anti-business tigers aren't anti-business anymore. Everyone's for growth. We're even against deficits. We're middle of the roaders. That's our counter-strategy."

"That's funny," says the Republican, "that's our counter-strategy too. We're for women. We're for Hispanics. We're for the safety net. We're learning. Our special interest tigers are better behaved too."

"If you're both heading for the center, then you'll be carbon copies," says Claude.

"Hell no," says the Democrat. "We're the party of the little guy. We can do what has to be done because people know we'll do it fairly."

"We're not the same," says the Republican. "The Democrats are being taken over by exotic interest groups."

"I don't get it," says Claude. "Do these participators help you or harm you in the Eighties?"

"Both," says the Democrat, "help and harm."

"Same with us," says the Republican. "They help if you can control them. When they go ape, they harm you."

"Aha," says Claude. "You both have to remember what John F. Kennedy said in his inaugural address: Those who seek power by riding the back of the tiger end up inside."

"Something like that, Claude. Something like that."

CHAPTER 48

Permissive
Patriotism
Saving the World

EPILOGUE TO VALUES AND POLITICS

There is a point where values and politics converge at a serious place. A single idea has been tracked through the last two parts of this volume. If one word had to sum up that idea, it would probably be "discipline."

In the values section we examined the conservative charge that our personal discipline had broken down: that our families were falling apart; that our sexual behavior had become wanton; that the influence of religion was diminishing.

We looked next at whether the alleged erosion of discipline in the personal realm had made itself felt in more public ways: was the alleged decline of the work ethic related to a new lack of discipline? And the crime wave?

We tracked the values argument further. We looked at our politics, where new, less-disciplined forms of behavior were apparent. Gone— or diminished—was the constraining role of the political party and the congressional leader. Suddenly, everyone was freelancing, on the Left and on the Right, each demanding justice for his or her own cause, often a parochial one. It may have been the political equivalent of the economic free market, but seen up close there were times when the process seemed to resemble nothing so much as a political temper tantrum—which is a long, long way from discipline.

Judgments were reached about values and politics but they were not as clear-cut as in our earlier sections. It wasn't quite like saying life expectancy went up, or old people never had it so good.

Well, yes, it was maintained here, our values had become more permissive, but not as permissive as you may have thought, and besides some of the new permissiveness was good and, anyway, the part that wasn't so good was changing. Well, yes, the cash-clout-players explosion had led to some excess, first on the Left, then on the Right, but, after all, the process self-corrected and we were in generally sound political shape.

It is time to deal briefly with a third and final aspect of the discipline question, closely related to the first two. Again, there will be less than definitive answers, much less, but again, what's here will be somewhat—only somewhat—optimistic.

The ultimate test of liberal values and free politics is survival.

There is an argument, going back to the case of ancient Rome, about whether freedom is so undisciplined that it self-destructs. Because America has come to be both the exemplar and the guarantor of freedom in the modern world, this has become essentially an argument about America.

The idea that freedom impales itself on the sword of permissiveness was the ultimate fear of our actors in Chuck Cleeshay's backyard. It is what Aleksandr Solzhenitsyn has warned us against. It is what has concerned conservatives, neoconservatives, attuned moderates, and some liberals too. It is what has scared hell out of the smaller free nations of the world. It is, in fact, the central argument of our time.

Our lack of discipline—so the argument goes—is reflected not only in private values, not only in public values in regard to work or crime or too much spending, but on the international side as well. Inevitably—that was the big word, inevitably—a licentious, decadent, permissive, undisciplined American society would not make the tough decisions to do what Americans are here to do. And what we are here to do is defend the fragile flower of liberty on this planet at this time.

The resolution of this argument—which is a continuing and unresolved argument—will be the ultimate test of my proposition here. Thus, one can maintain (as I do in this book) that America is a remarkably successful society, that our quality of life is improving, that our economy remains robust, that our values are stronger than you think, and so on. But if at the same time it turned out that this same America had shirked its primal duty, or smoothly redefined it out of existence, there would be little to crow about.

I confess, the thought haunts me. It is not impossible that it will come to pass in our time. Solzhenitsyn's angry remonstrations may be valid; permissiveness and flaccidity may drag us down.

Yet I doubt it. My sense is—it is only a sense, with some evidence attached to it—that America's values and politics, though changed, remain more than strong enough to do what must be done. I believe we remain a healthy and moral society. What has happened in the last half dozen or so years has demonstrated to me that the scenario of geopolitical gloom is, first, surely not inevitable, and second, probably plain wrong.

The post-Vietnam world was frightening to many—and with cause. There was a continuation and an acceleration of a huge Soviet military buildup. A new Soviet navy roamed the seas. Soon there was evidence that the Soviets were prepared to use their new tools of power projection—directly and via surrogates—on the Horn of Africa, in Yemen, in Angola, and then in Afghanistan and Central America.

In the late 1960s and 1970s, one team of American politicians said what we needed was to "reorder priorities," that is, to spend more on social welfare and less on defense. Backed by a wave of participating Democrats, that was one campaign promise that was kept, and doubled. Thus, back in 1960, in a nice balanced way, roughly 10 percent of GNP went for defense and 10 percent for social welfare. By 1980, defense had been halved to about 5 percent—and social welfare had about doubled to 20 percent!

Such a reordering is nice, and socially useful, but it is a long way from a disciplined reaction to a new reality. To many (including this author), it did not seem that a relative halving of the defense budget was the way to respond to the military buildup of a nuclear, potentially expansionist, adversary superpower that wished us ill and sought to diminish liberty in the world.

An intellectual cottage industry called "the lessons of Vietnam" had sprung up, and the lessons included ones such as "America is not the world's policeman," "it was an immoral war," "wars of national liberation are the tide of history," that the Vietnam War was "unwinnable" for America because we were fighting against the tide, that the American people had accordingly turned their backs on the war in Vietnam, that the real problems were North-South not East-West (Russia didn't matter; poverty did).

A second team of politicians and intellectuals—these on the Right—rejected the substance of those lessons, fought back, but after surveying the damage many of them wondered loudly whether "America had lost its nerve." This was not exactly a message of confidence from a superpower locked in a long twilight struggle as the watchman on the walls of freedom (to use some of John Kennedy's words).

Intellectuals Left and intellectuals Right seem to agree only that America couldn't or wouldn't or shouldn't hack it.

But there was—hallelujah!—a Safety Net beneath the cerebraliza-
tion. For despite all the turmoil, the bedrock of American values, of
American discipline, of America's sense of destiny had not disap-
peared. After all the talk of decadence, flaccidity, dissolution, and permissiveness, after all the hoopla about neoisolationism, the end of
American exceptionalism, and the diminishment of patriotism, after
all the talk of lack of nerve, Americans opted for strength, and by no
means ruled out the idea of being the principal actor on the world's
stage.

Consider: Vietnam was surely a tragedy and a disaster. Yet all
through the despair of the war, the polls show that a majority of
American people supported the policy of the President—Kennedy,
Johnson, Nixon, Ford. In a fairly clear test, Americans decided there
would be no President McGovern. Interestingly, despite the much
publicized activity on some campuses, the survey research data show
that young people during the Vietnam period were more hawkish
than their elders.

After the Vietnam War, both the veterans and the public supported
the men who served there, despite the media myth that Viet vets were
scorned. A monumental 1980 study by Louis Harris Associates, with
many complex findings in it, concludes, "The public rates its feelings
toward Vietnam-era veterans as very warm, and overwhelmingly believes that these veterans deserve respect for their service."

When asked to rank their feelings for Vietnam veterans and others
on a scale of one (very cool) to ten (very warm), the public responded as follows:

FEELING THERMOMETER

Veterans who served in Vietnam	9.8
Veterans who served in WWII or Korea	9.6
Doctors	7.9
Our military leaders	6.3
Television news reporters and editors	6.1
People who demonstrated against the war	5.0
Draft evaders	3.3

Source: Harris, 1979.

And those feelings were present both while the war was being fought and at the end of the decade.

		Agree Strongly	Disagree Strongly
Vietnam veterans deserve respect for having served their country in the Armed Forces.	1979	83%	—
	1971	80%	1%
The real heroes of the Vietnam war are those who refused induction and faced the consequences, not those who served in the Armed Forces.	1979	4%	54%
	1971	4%	68%

Source: Harris.

The national respect for our fighting men is reciprocal:

VIETNAM ERA VETERAN'S ATTITUDES

	Agree	Disagree
Looking back, I am glad I served my country.	90%	8%

Source: Harris, 1979.

Vietnam was a tragedy, and the American people know that. But it hasn't led to withdrawal symptoms or guilt complexes:

Question: Do you think the United States has a special role to play in the world?	
U.S. has a special role to play in the world	81%
U.S. pretty much like other countries	14%

Source: Roper, 1981.

Question:	Earlier on in American history, many people around the world thought the United States was the very best place in the world to live. Do you think it still is, or not?	
	Still is	90%
	Is not	8%

Source: Roper, 1981.

It was not only Americans who were not anti-American. Non-Americans weren't anti-American either. Around the world, despite much televised Yankee-Go-Home demonstration, support for the U.S. remains strong.

The United States Information Agency has, in a rather low-key way, been commissioning survey research from leading West European pollsters for more than a quarter of a century. The data are not publicly released until a year after they are received. The data are fascinating. After all the Yankee-baiting in the European media, despite portentous headlines about Europe heading for neutralism, it turns out that the image of America sounds like an old copy of *McGuffey's Reader*. These are the descriptives that Europeans typically linked to life in the United States:

- provide chances for people to get ahead
- provide equal justice under law
- adequate standard of living
- guarantee individual political rights
- religious freedom
- artistic diversity
- respect human rights of citizens

These were the top characteristics Europeans associated with U.S. foreign policy:

- helping poorer countries develop
- fostering human rights in other countries
- willing to negotiate most disputes
- trustworthy in negotiations
- wants agreements in reducing nuclear arms
- tries to dominate others economically (No one's perfect.)

Now, these Europeans do not see the whole world as rosy. For the record, here is how Europeans saw the Soviet foreign policy:

- uses military force to attain goals
- uses terrorism to weaken other governments
- seeks world domination
- supports subversion abroad
- increases risk of war

In 1982, Gallup did transnational surveys that showed clearly where Americans stood in regard to national pride:

Question: How proud are you to be a . . . (e.g., an American, Italian, Spaniard, etc.)?

Percent Saying "Very Proud"

United States	80%
Ireland	66%
Great Britain	55%
Spain	49%
Italy	41%
All Europe average	38%
France	33%
Japan	30%
West Germany	21%

Source: Gallup for the European Value System Study, 1982.

Americans are willing to back up that patriotic pride with more than just flag-waving:

Question:	Of course, we all hope that there will not be another war, but if it were to come to that, would you be willing to fight for your country?

"Yes"	
United States	71%
Great Britain	62%
Spain	53%
Ireland	49%
All Europe average	43%
France	42%
West Germany	35%
Italy	28%
Japan	22%

Source: Gallup for the European Value System Study (1982).

So Americans have not lost their nerve, or their sense of mission, or their patriotism, or their pride.

===

Sooner or later in a democracy, attitudes influence policy. And so, to borrow a formulation from the economic vocabulary, we witnessed a voter-led geopolitical recovery.

Consider what has happened almost imperceptibly in the last five years. Things began to change. The Soviets probably overplayed their hand when they marched into Afghanistan. The perceived humiliation of America in Iran served as geopolitical smelling salts that played a role in snapping us to attention. And politicians began to listen to their betters—voters.

President Carter began asking for increases in defense budgets and pushed the European allies to do the same. The European allies asked us to deploy missiles in Europe as a political signal.

Defense spending went up. Ronald Reagan did not create that trend, but he certainly rode it. And whatever else one may say about Reagan, he did deliver higher defense spending. (Today, liberal Democrats routinely call for 4 percent increases.)

The U.S. was challenged in Central America and responded with some characteristic political flailing about, but responded nonetheless. El Salvador is a still-standing domino. As this is written it is Nicaragua that is fighting rebels, an unaccustomed situation for a Marxist state.

Grenada was frosting on the cake; the slogan there was "Cuban Go Home."

It's not just Latin America. In Angola, the pro-Western insurgents of Jonas Savimbi seem to be pushing the Cuban-backed Marxists back to the ocean. In Afghanistan, the predicted easy Soviet win may have turned into a Soviet quagmire. Rather suddenly, across the Third World, no one seems to be looking seriously at the Soviet economic model. The less-developed countries already know how to be poor and inefficient.

In Eastern Europe, Poland and other nations are simmering. NATO, on the other hand, has not only survived its seasonally pre-dicted demise, but scored a victory on missile deployment. The leaders of the four big countries are solidly anti-Soviet: Thatcher, Kohl, Mit-terrand and Craxi. The French intellectual community now scorns Communism.

In Japan, the government has begun, finally, a semi-serious military program.

Vignettes:

- Prime Minister Thatcher attacks the Falklands, incurs heavy losses, and her poll rating soars.
- Several hundred Marines are killed in a terrorist raid in Leba-non—and the enlistment rate goes up in America.
- American troops invade Grenada. The public applauds, and would like to find another island to knock off.

All that is a long way from decadence, and international with-drawal.

Of course the geopolitical power patterns change, and even on a clear day they are hard to read. There is no Dow Jones Power Aver-age.

There are times when one must wonder. American performance in Lebanon was a sorry spectacle, as will be discussed in the next section. The defense consensus has unraveled to some extent, although it is a complicated attitudinal picture.* In well-publicized leaks the military establishment itself periodically shies away from American assertive-

---

* Compared to 1981, the polls show fewer Americans favoring "more defense spending." But they have generally gravitated toward a position of spending "the same" rather than "less." And, of course, "the same" these days is "more" than it was. Clear?

ness, pleading lack of support from "public opinion" (dabbling in a field where even experts don't know what's going on).

The Democratic party—the majority party—remains split on certain key issues of national resolve. Central America may well prove to be the testing ground of U.S. fortitude in this decade. In the spring of 1984, two Democratic liberals campaigned neck and neck for their party's presidential nomination. One (Gary Hart) favored a unilateral pullout of American forces from Central America, comparing the situation to Vietnam, demagogically predicting that "hundreds of thousands of young American lives" would be lost if we didn't withdraw. The other candidate (Walter Mondale) said first that we must use our power moderately and cautiously—noting that "guilt is not a foreign policy," and endorsing a U.S. role on the Central American isthmus. Then he too began waffling on the issue. The Congress, meanwhile, appropriates the money for our involvement, but often in a mean-spirited manner that tends to undercut the effort.

It is not always a clear picture, and not always a happy one.

Yet, we and our allies stumble forward, as democracies do, two steps forward and one back. Our chore is often made more difficult by the media, as will soon be noted. But the basic strength of democratic nations is with their voters. They do not want military adventure, nor imperialism, nor high defense costs. But even more intensely, they do not want submission. They know the score. After much to-ing and fro-ing, they ultimately give political bonuses to leaders who know the score. That makes fortitude politically profitable. That means, contrary to common belief, that a President can negotiate tough arms control from a position of strength and voter support. Our voters are the Archimedean lever that can move the world.

And so, it seems to me, that this very remarkable collection of free, prosperous, Western industrial nations will survive on this planet for a while longer, and so too will liberty.

═══

In the end, how does it all add up?

Looking at the political data, at the earlier values data, at the international data, I offer a thought: Americans in these last dozen or so years have set course on a unique national voyage. Americans want to be both tough and tender, stable and sybaritic. We are a nation of permissive patriots. We want it all.

In the 1970s, the critics of Left and Right saw the sybaritic, the permissive, and the tender and noted stark change. Good, said one side, we are shedding our hangups, and our imperialism. Bad, said the other side, we can't do it anymore, we've gone soft.

The media picked up these themes and, like the ideologues of both sides, ignored the underlying continuity, stability, toughness, and patriotism in the American fabric.

The so-called "post-Vietnam mentality" bounced back and forth: media to leadership, leadership echoing the media, media quoting the leadership, and public buying a little from both, more echoes and more echoes—leading to a serious situation.

It wasn't that America had lost its nerve, it was that too many people in high places were told it had, believed it, and began acting as if we had. A self-fullfilling prophecy was, for a while, self-fulfilling. It was a close call, until the voters began to straighten things out.

Self-fulfillment of bad news: that's a worrisome situation, which deserves—finally—frontal examination.

PART V

MEDIA

CHAPTER 49

The Bad News Bias

NEGATIVISM IN THE MEDIA

Of course it would be nice to begin here with one more stunning American success story. It is available. As noted at the very beginning of this volume, the American press corps is quite remarkable. Our television operations are technologically marvelous, advanced to a point that would have been unimaginable only a few years ago. We cover astronauts in space, we see wars as they happen, we see news twenty-four hours a day, we get read-outs of voter sentiment on election day. Our print journalists are no less proficient in their own way. Investigative reporters are into everything, as well they should be.

Media people these days are much better educated than in earlier days. There is very little evidence of corruption. There is plenty of raw, physical courage in the press corps. News budgets are up substantially from earlier years, correspondents girdle the globe, whatever that means. Good news indeed; after all, a free and vigorous press is the bulwark of our liberty.*

Hats off!

But there is a problem. If you believe much of what has been written here, the press is frequently getting and giving the wrong story of our time. They overdose us on bad news. It is time for our own investigative journalism—about journalism.

Consider, to begin, a very special substance: Distilled Essence of Media.

I define DEM thusly: the collective residue of a given story after all the pro-ing and con-ing, after all the caveating and countercaveating, after all the offbeat stories that do in fact give "the other side." The

---

* A reminder of how fortunate we are: The authoritative human rights group, Freedom House, regards both broadcast and print media to be free in only about one-quarter of the nations of the world.

DEM, in short, is what reverberates in a viewer's or reader's mind after the print and video folks pack up and move on to the next story.

Some examples: The DEM of the CIA story in the early 1970s was that the American intelligence agency had turned into a rogue elephant that went berserk, toppling governments, assassinating heads of state, using poison-dart guns and sometimes even itching powder.

One aspect of the DEM after the 1980 elections was that the Reverend Jerry Falwell and the National Conservative Political Action Committee (NCPAC) had become a new and major right-wing political force in America, and that such a force would sweep aside everything in its way.

The DEM in politics in early 1982 was that the nuclear freeze movement had become a new and major political force, and that it would sweep aside everything in its way.

The DEM in politics a little later was that the gender gap and feminist politics had become a new and major political force that would sweep aside everything in its way. (On the liberal side, such stories always seem to announce that the "old anti-Vietnam coalition has been re-ignited." Other candidates for re-ignition in recent years have included anti-nuclear power and anti-aid to El Salvador.)

The DEM of another story was that the social Safety Net had been shredded.

There may have been occasional dissenting views aired or written about these stories, but the DEM was clear—and, in my judgment, dead wrong in each instance. No surprise. After all, as we have seen, the Distilled Essence of Media was wrong regarding most of the big stories of the past dozen years:

While the quality of life was improving, the DEM told us (over and over again, in a thousand separate stories) that it was getting worse.

While the economy was progressing over a rough patch of ground—with more income per capita, more and better housing, more cars, 25 million new jobs, a higher rate of people going on to college, more Social Security—the DEM informed us that our condition was getting worse (with a thousand stories about hunger, homelessness, students without government loans, workers with jobs lost forever).

While American values remained generally stable, patriotic and progressive, the DEM was that everything was going haywire.

While our politics were entering what I regard as a new, robust, and fertile phase, the DEM concerned petty corruption, the evil of money, and slick political gamesmanship.

While the Less Developed Countries have begun to emerge into the modern world, the DEM was all about poverty, hunger, corruption, and coups, which in the LDCs are surely not news—at least not in the sense that they are something "new."

While the richest, freest, probably most powerful alliance of nations in the history of the world (that's what NATO is) has remained in fairly solid accord over the course of forty years, the media have concentrated only on the minuscule fissures.

And so it goes. Something strange is happening. This highly proficient, far-flung, incorruptible, technologically marvelous media system of ours usually gets its facts right. Our reporters are consummate professionals. There are indeed carcinogenic chemicals; there were recessions and cheese lines; there was a counterculture; there are some powerful right-wing politics; there is plenty of political cash making plenty of political waves. We are told all about those stories.

But the problem of media in the modern world is not that they don't get their stories right. They too often miss the right stories.

There is a pattern to what they get and what they don't get. They cover bad news. They don't cover good news very well or very often. We can recall here our earlier formulation: (1) Bad news is big news, (2) Good news is no news, (3) Good news is bad news. In short: there is a Bad News Bias.

Why? One big reason is that the most important and fascinating spectacle of our time is a process, not an event or an anecdote.

The modern media are spectacular at covering events and anecdotes: wars, elections, political scandals, welfare rip-offs, riots, budget cuts, the publication of last month's unemployment rate, space shots, a man surviving on an artificial heart, harmful chemicals discovered in the water supply, six dead people who took Extra-Strength Tylenol, a peace march. Events and anecdotes that make news are mostly—not entirely, but mostly—bad news. "60 Minutes" doesn't often do stories about people who really need food stamps and get them, and use them, legally.

If modern media cover events and anecdotes well, it is also true that they have great difficulty in covering the big stories about process—particularly stories about *the process of progress*. This was mentioned in passing regarding political participation. A good news process story—participatory democracy in action—was generally ignored.

One may argue about that one. But it goes much further. There were plenty of stories of blacks in urban riots (event). But where were the stories about a million young blacks going to college and other millions moving to the suburbs (process)? In the long run which is more important? There were plenty of stories about Illinois not ratify-ing the E.R.A. Amendment (event). But where were the stories about many millions of women moving into good jobs (process)? There were a few stories about the creation of the social Safety Net (event). There were plenty of stories about the perceived political shredding of the Net (event). There were almost no stories about tens of millions of Americans, over several decades, taking advantage of the Safety Net via Medicare, more Social Security, Medicaid—a process. Journalists often argue that their job is to report what's new and unusual. Yet that process is new, is unusual—and unreported.

Is Billygate more important than life expectancy? (Event *vs* process.)

Of course, the charge I make is not a plenary one. The increase in incomes is reported; the development of new drugs is mentioned. But, remember, we are talking about Distilled Essence of Media—the net result of the coverage. By that criterion, we are not well informed about the changing and progressive nature of our civilization. The press is not doing its job well. There is a Bad News Bias.

If you do not believe this intuitively after having watched last night's evening news, fear not, there are data.

Professor Michael Robinson of George Washington University and research assistants Maura Clancey and Lisa Grand examined every feature that appeared on network nightly news dealing with public policy issues during the first three months of 1983. There were 157 such features aired.

Here are the results of their content analysis:

17	Positive features
14	Neutral features
126	Negative features

An earlier study by Robinson (*Over the Wire and on TV*, with coauthor Margaret Sheehan) shows that television news is two-and-a-half times more negative than wire service news. As we shall note later, the TV news is more important.

A study by Holmes Brown of the Institute of Applied Economics compared economic data and their media treatment during the second half of 1983, a time of sharp economic improvement. His findings:

- 95% of the statistical economic reports were *positive*
- 85% of the in-depth or interpretive stories about the economy on network television were *negative*

A classic example reported by Brown: on November 4, 1983, ABC News reported a 0.4 percent monthly drop in unemployment as follows: "the news is not as good as it sounds . . . with so many factory workers unemployed, political pressure for an industrial policy will continue to grow." (Network executives contested Brown's study.)

Or consider one specific subject: nuclear power. Content analyses by the Batelle Institute and the Media Institute have shown that major media coverage of the nuclear story in the 1970s was both antagonistic and negative. The "experts" most often quoted were anti-nuclear: Ralph Nader and spokesmen for the Union of Concerned Scientists. In all, opponents of nuclear power received twice the coverage that supporters received. Yet a study by Professors Robert Lichter and Stanley Rothman shows that the vast majority of scientists support nuclear power, and that the greater their scientific expertise, the more likely they are to be supportive.

And the public knows what it is getting:

Television pays too much attention to bad news

True	64%

Newspapers pay too much attention to bad news

True	71%

Source: Yankelovich, Skelly and White, for the Public Agenda Foundation, 1980.

A later poll, taken by two of the alleged culprits:

Question: Do you think TV news concentrates too much on bad news and not enough on good news?

Yes	73%
No	22%

Source: ABC News/the *Washington Post.*

Why can't our journalists properly cover the process of progress? Why are they so negative? Several causes within the structure of modern journalism come to mind:

First, there is a *commercial negative tilt*—and there is not much argument about it. Bad news is exciting: scandal, war, murder. It is almost always available if you look for it. It sells papers; it increases television ratings. Moreover, this negative tilt reinforces itself. There is a finite amount of time or space for news ("the news hole"). If you run a lot of negative news there is less time and space for positive news.

Second, there is a *left-of-center tilt* in the news-gathering establishment, most apparent among the most influential journalists at the networks and leading newspapers. There are some pro forma arguments about this within the press community (to be detailed later) but when the hour is late and the glasses low, I have not discovered a whole lot of serious disagreement about it.

There is solid attitudinal data to back up the left-tilt notion. A study done by Professors S. Robert Lichter and Stanley Rothman found that 54 percent of leading journalists describe themselves as liberals, while only 19 percent place themselves as conservatives. (The comparable figures for the population at large are about 25 percent liberal and 35 percent conservative.) The percentage of such leading journalists voting for George McGovern in 1972 was 81 percent, compared to 39 percent of all voters. The Lichter-Rothman surveys, moreover, show members of the media elite as uniformly more liberal than the public on a wide range of economic, social, and foreign policy issues.*

Why is the liberal mentality less attuned to the reportage of the process of progress? Liberals are surely not against progress in itself. They not only believe in it, but in many ways believe in it more deeply than do conservatives. But liberals tend to believe that progress is necessary because these days the human condition is in sad shape. They believe that accentuating the negative will let the others see the problems and this, in a free society, will engender further progress. There happens to be a good deal of political validity to such a wolf-crying strategy, but it is surely not conducive to a mind-set that seeks out the story of the process of progress.

("Mind-set" is a key word in this discussion. As Austin Ranney correctly points out, a person can be liberal and still deal with the news fairly. I argue here that liberal-tilting is not typically a conscious decision. We all see reality through a filter. It is in the nature of the

---

* Should a "liberal" tilt be in conflict with "negative" tilt, it is "negative" that invariably wins out. The liberal press corps that voted heavily for McGovern in 1972 savaged him over the Eagleton situation. Our journalists have been likened to piranha fish: "If it bleeds, kill it."

modern liberal mentality to see reality as a set of severe problems, subject to solution through aroused concern, often through the instrumentality of government. The liberal bias is not conspiratorial. They're only telling the truth as they see it.)*

Third, there is an *adversarial* tilt to the media. Journalists are, almost by definition, *antistatus quo*. So are liberals. For both, the "establishment" is a prime source of our problems. Being antiestablishment links up with liberalism, but also with negativism. Accordingly, a story about a corrupt, dissembling, and heartless establishment seems to touch all the bases of the modern journalistic, liberal mind. It is not an accident that so much of our news is focused upon just such stories.

Fourth, *self-righteousness*. Since the birth of the Trauma Twins, Vietnam and Watergate, many journalists—typically younger ones— have come to believe that only their vigilant eyes can keep the nation from international adventurism, political skullduggery, and corporate corruption. Since Woodward and Bernstein saved America from Nixon, we have seen some young men and women who in an earlier era might have sought to save souls one by one in the ministry see the wisdom of trying to do it wholesale via the media. Such young journalists are no more self-righteous than the old-time run-of-the-mill preachers but no less so either. Self-righteous people don't typically go around pointing out how well things are going. They reflexively view the actions of others with alarm.

Commercially negative. Left-of-center. Adversarial. Self-righteous. Such are the components of the Bad News Bias.

It would be wrong to assume that such characteristics can be applied across-the-board to the entire journalistic establishment. As the solid work by Stephen Hess of the Brookings Institution has pointed out, there is a tendency to confuse the characteristics of the entire news community with those of the elite publications and the national networks. Hess notes that much of the news in America comes straight off the wires of the Associated Press and United Press International— and is pretty straightforward stuff. Then there is the specialized press— trade magazines, professional publications—which, as noted in the first section of this volume, typically do get the right stories. As Hess points out, there are 1,700 daily newspapers in America, let alone hundreds of radio and television stations, most of which are owned by

---

* A 1982 Lichter-Rothman study documented this with tests asking journalists to summarize neutral news stories and to interpret the action taking place in ambiguous photographs. It was found that interpretations reflected the subjects' political values.

people who are not negative, liberal, or adversarial. It would be naïve to suggest that the attitudes of owners do not sometimes influence the editorial view of their papers or stations.

Indeed, as noted, the Lichter-Rothman research on liberalism in journalism was a study of journalists who worked at the most influential media outlets: the newsmagazines, networks, and newspapers like the *Washington Post, Wall Street Journal* and *New York Times*.

But those elite media have enormous influence. They are where our leaders get their news, and what they respond to. Network television is in every living room across the land, the newsmagazines are in millions of mailboxes, the news services of the *Post* and *Times* are carried in hundreds of independent papers. The media elite have, above all else, an agenda-setting function. When they fan a -Gate story into flames, *everyone* must cover it, including AP and UPI.

In any event, some of the component parts of the Bad News Bias are not necessarily harmful when viewed singly.

Thus, the case can be made that a liberal tilt may even be mildly desirable. After all, other institutions in our society tilt to the Right: business, for example. Moreover, the Left tilt within journalism is probably somewhat less than it used to be. Many of the leading syndicated columnists in America these days swing from the conservative side of the plate: George Will, William Buckley, Evans and Novak, James J. Kilpatrick, William Safire. This is a relatively new development, at least in such proportions.

And the media establishment is not rigid-Left or always-Left by any means. The DEM of the 1980 election coverage (particularly on the analytical print side) included the notion that conservatives and Republicans had "the new ideas" while the Democrats and liberals believed in the tired policies of "a warmed over New Deal."* During the 1982 coverage of the English elections, the international press corps, as well as English journalists of the Left, flogged the hapless Labour Party nearly to death for its move toward "extremism." The journalistic Left in France has recently had much fun punching out Socialist Prime Minister Mitterrand.

There is also something to be said for drum-beat adversarialism. It may indeed play a role in undermining our belief in our institutions— particularly government (as will be discussed in a moment). But the standard defense of adversarial journalism is also correct: it keeps those bastards on their toes, and there is something to be said for that.

* Although, curiously, it was also said that Reagan was the nostalgia candidate from an earlier age.

There is even a good defense for negativism. There is plenty of bad news in the world and we ought to know about it; that is the role of the press.*

Put all together, these elements form the journalistic superstructure of the Bad News Bias. This bias both feeds and is fed by other parts of society. Politicians know that bad news attracts the attention of the television camera. So a liberal politician will hold hearings about starving children and a conservative politician will hold hearings about welfare scams. Men of letters, sociologists, political scientists, environmentalists, right-wing preachers, feminists and antifeminists know the same formula: if you want to get on the air, say something is terrible.

Periodically, the networks try to reform, try to give us good news, but their idea of good news is often fluff and not substance; in any event, tomorrow usually brings us a lead story about Congressmen taking drugs.

In any event, whatever its merits and demerits, it seems clear that the system as it now operates is set up to gather bad news and pump it out in a myriad of ways. There is a Bad New Bias.

And there is, then, a big question: is the Bad News Bias bad for us?

* I don't have much use for self-righteous smugness, nor do most senior journalists, many of whom acknowledge the problem among some of their younger colleagues.

CHAPTER 50

Ever Thus?

HISTORICAL PERSPECTIVE

Well, it is asked, even if there is a Bad News Bias—so what? After all, it's said—ever thus.

Wrong. The media system today is substantially different in degree and kind from anything we have seen before.

It's not that there wasn't plenty of bad news before, or that there wasn't plenty of complaining about it. American presidents since the time of George Washington have bemoaned the fact that the press only talked about gloom and doom. Abraham Lincoln didn't much like the negativism of Horace Greeley, editor of the *New York Tribune*. Why, Lincoln wondered, could Greeley not "restrain himself, and wait a little"—for positive policy results. And who would you guess said this: "I am so accustomed to having everything reported erroneously that I have almost come to the point of believing nothing that I see in the newspapers." Woodrow Wilson.

It was Arthur Krock of the *New York Times* who said that the administration of Franklin D. Roosevelt used "more ruthlessness, intelligence, and subtlety in trying to suppress legitimate unfavorable comment than any I know."

Of course the negativism of the press over the years did not just deal with the presidency. Consider the turn-of-the-century "muckrakers." They wrote of scandal, poverty, corporate rip-off, unfairness, disparity of wealth. Many of the muckrakers—Lincoln Steffens, Upton Sinclair, Ida Tarbell, to name just three—were journalists. Many of their exposés appeared first as newspaper articles before being expanded to book length. They were idolized and imitated by young journalists of the day.

Surely, much of what they said was valid. It did engender a wave of needed reform. Yet, just as surely, it was negativist in the fullest sense of the word. After all, by the turn of the century, the United States was already the most prosperous, economically fairest, healthiest country in the world. But the muckrakers saw only the muck. The Bad News Bias.

Ever thus?

No. The big change, of course, is television. Theodore H. White has written that the advent of television rivals the advent of the printing press in human history. It's big time stuff.

Remember, there were no television sets in America until the late 1940s. The census of 1950 showed only five million households with sets, all black and white. By 1970 there were sixty million. In 1980 there were seventy-nine million households with sets, mostly color sets. By 1983, there were an average of 1.8 sets in each of eighty-two million American households. For better or for worse we now have wristwatch television and video cassette recorders lest we possibly miss any bad news.

Much of the data about television have become part of our national consciousness: the television set in the typical household is turned on for between six and seven hours per day. By the time the average young American graduates from high school, that young American has spent more time in front of a television screen than in school.

Most Americans get most of their news from television—and the share of Americans who rely on television for news has been growing:

Question: I'd like to ask you where you usually get most of your news about what's going on in the world today? (more than one answer is permitted)

Source of Most News	1964	1972	1978	1982	Change 64–82
Television	58%	64%	67%	65%	+ 7%
Newspapers	56%	50%	49%	44%	−12%

Source: Roper Organization. Other choices included "radio," "magazines" and "other people," all at substantially lower levels.

Moreover, according to Roper, by two to one Americans say that in the event of conflicting reports, they would believe what they saw on television rather than what they read in their newspaper.

All this is new to the post-World War II world. But something in the system is much newer than that. In only the last few years the amount of public affairs programming on television has exploded.

Consider: as recently as 1961 there were nineteen hours per week of national public-affairs programming on the three networks. By 1982 that number exactly doubled, to thirty-eight hours per week! That doesn't count PBS, cable television, or local television news, all of which have also expanded their public affairs programming and have picked up a share of network audiences.

The magnitudes involved are stunning: On an average evening about 35 million people watch network television news. Another 12 million watch the network morning news and feature programs. In addition, news feature programs like CBS's "60 Minutes" and ABC's "20/20" command huge audiences. The average "60 Minutes" audience ran to 33 million people in 1983; it is one of the top-rated programs in television.*

* Source: Nielsen Television Index. I do not mention here the entertainment aspect of television. But that, too, is dominated by a negative view of the

Of course it is more than numbers about audiences and hours. Television presents news in a wholly different manner.

Compared to print journalism, television is more graphic and more poignant by orders of magnitude. When the Associated Press says "eight Salvadorans were murdered by right-wing death squads," that is one thing. When NBC puts the bloody, riddled cadavers in your living room and shows you the grieving widows and orphans, that is something else again.

Television also beats out print in another way: it can force attention to be paid to subjects often ignored by readers of a newspaper. Every newspaper editor knows, for example, that foreign policy news simply does not interest many readers. The same is true of national politics, unless an election is nearing or if a particularly important story is bubbling. Many newspaper readers, accordingly, will pick up their papers, glance at headlines about foreign policy and national politics, and quickly flip to the local news, sports pages, the weather, the stock market, Ann Landers.

That's not the way it works on television. Once you let the anchorman into your living room, and he then shows dead marines in Lebanon and their grieving mothers at home—you watch. If he shows you a presidential candidate (two years before an election) making a fool of himself, you watch. If he has tape from the FBI showing congressmen taking bribes from phony Arab sheiks—you watch. If he tells you hexo-drexo-bexo is poisoning the water supply—you watch. If he serves up junk-food journalism about the latest "-Gate" scandal—you watch. While there is some channel switching going on, some mindless in-one-ear-and-out-the-other viewing, it is much harder to flip the pages to get to the sports section. *The man is talking to you in your living room.* Accordingly, television can change the agenda of public concern in ways that newspapers cannot.

U.S.A. Several studies by the Media Institute show that the portrayal of businessmen, law enforcement officers, politicians, and other members of "the establishment" is typically one of venality, foolishness, criminality, or greed. Sample: the majority of characters who portray big businessmen on prime-time television episodes are depicted as criminals. A nonquantitative but incisive view of this situation is offered by Benjamin Stein in *The View from Sunset Boulevard*. And it is not just establishment figures who suffer. In 1983, Rev. Jesse Jackson complained that, "We [minorities] are not projected to be judges, journalists, physicists or thinkers. We are projected as less intelligent than we are, less patriotic than we are and more violent than we are."

In fact, some observers of the journalistic scene believe that the most important role now played by the *print media* concerns their ability to get *television* news executives to pay attention to a given story. Television is still fairly new in the news business. Television news producers are nervous about their own news judgments, and they often don't fully trust the judgments of their own reporters. Very often the *Post* and the *Times* propose—the networks dispose.

All those hours, all those viewers, all that impact, all that agenda-setting ability yields political power.

In every corner of the free world, politicians and planners ask, "How will it play?" They know their actions are both directed and constrained by press coverage, principally television, as never before. The media analyst Michael Robinson has written that in America, "the networks act as the shadow cabinet."

And all those hours, all that dramatic potency, all that agenda-setting, also yield another kind of power. Those television sets in our living room paint the portrait of our civilization. They suggest what we ought to think about ourselves. They could paint a portrait of an energetic people dealing, often successfully, with real problems. Or they can paint a detailed portrait of corruption, rip-off, sleaziness, heartlessness, hazard, mindlessness, stupidity, and rancor. They mostly do the latter, with an intensity and immediacy not available to newspapers or radio.

It was not ever thus.

CHAPTER 51

Is the Bad News
Bad for Us?

POSSIBLE IMPLICATIONS

Suppose there is a bad news bias. Suppose, as I have suggested, it is different in degree and kind.

It may be asked: so what? After all, even if there is a more pervasive, more potent Bad News Bias, we've survived and prospered in so many ways. If you don't believe that, just read this book: we still have strong and patriotic values, feisty politics, an improving quality to our lives, a strong economy. What's the problem?

Well, we are a strong society. But it is still altogether proper to ask this: has our strong society been harmed in some ways by the nature of our media system? And further, even more important: is it possible that we will be hurt—perhaps more severely—in the future?

Recall our early image of the modern press: Typhoid Mary.

Mary, you will recall, was a waitress. Back in 1919, she went about her business, innocently serving her customers crullers and coffee. As it turned out she also served up a little typhoid bacillus with those healthy breakfasts. Some of her customers—days later—got very, very sick with typhoid fever. *Something happened to the customers after exposure.*

We have had a video news explosion in recent years. More news, more dramatically presented, most of it bad news. *Has something happened to us because of the exposure? Is something likely to happen to us because of this exposure?* How are we to judge this?

An informed population, we have all believed almost reflexively, is the bulwark of democracy. Theoretically, a still more informed population is better yet. We do get plenty of straight news. But suppose that so much of the information we are getting—the Distilled Essence of Media on a hundred topics—is wrong, or wrong-headed, or skewed, or misleading? What then? After all, Mary also served nourishing food along with a little bacillus.

Suppose we are repeatedly told of scandal, violence, economic disaster, pollution, licentiousness, and so on, and not really told of the health and vigor of our society. Suppose this bombardment of bad news is increasing in intensity. Suppose, further, that there may be a cumulative effect to the Bad News Bias; a year of bad news may have a small effect, but a decade of it more of an effect, and a generation— still more.

If that is what is happening, even in a healthy society, has it hurt us—will it hurt us? Is bad news—incorrect bad news, that is—bad for us?

Well, of course, we don't know, any of us. There are some things that have already happened that may be plausibly linked to the bad-news bacillus. But data about the future are in short supply, and speculation has often yielded famous stupidity. Still, it is important now that we try. There is a lot at stake, as we shall see.

If we do not *know* the future, there are, however, some things about it that seem logical and reasonable, if not necessarily provable. I do not suggest here that we are in for a siege of media-induced typhoid.

There are lesser contagious diseases that can be quite uncomfortable.
Let us make a list of what the Bad News Bias could plausibly yield.

ECONOMICS

It has been said in recent years that America suffers from a low rate
of business investment. This lower investment rate, it is said, has
diminished our ability to compete and it slows economic growth. This
view, as noted earlier, has probably been exaggerated. Still, there has
been some problem with investment capital.

Well, what is an "investment" anyway?

It is a bet on the nature of the future. The investor—an individual
or a corporation—says to him or her or itself: things will be pretty
good in the future; if I invest a dollar now, I'll get a lot more back
later.

Sometimes the decision regarding investment is obvious and positive: a corporation with a fat order book, already using its facilities
three shifts a day, will likely build the new plant under consideration.
Sometimes the decision regarding investment is obvious and negative:
one does not invest in a new plant when the plant you have is already
modern, when it is working at only 60 percent of capacity and no one
wants to buy what you're selling.

But economics is about life at the margin. What will the investor
do when the decision is borderline?

If the investor believes—if it has perhaps been banged into his head
by a Bad News Bias—that the present is dreadful, that the past was
dreadful, what then? Will he be likely, at the margin, to bet on a prosperous and stable future? Only when pushed. And his lack-of-a-bet, or
his less-of-a-bet, is, of course, self-fulfilling. Less investment means a
less prosperous future. We may properly speculate that in some way,
to some indeterminate extent, the Bad News Bias has already done its
work.

Or consider interest rates. It is said our economy suffers from high
interest rates. The prime rate was 8 percent in 1970 and as high as
21 percent in 1980. The "real" interest rate (discounted for inflation)
used to be about 2 percent—nowadays it is about 7 percent.

Now, interest rates also are a bet related to the potential risks of the
uncertain future. Of course, as with investment capital, many factors

go into the setting of interest rates. But if a lender believes that he is living in an era where progress is the norm and we cope with our problems, and we are likely to continue to cope with our problems, he may not demand and will not get a "high" real interest rate. In the give and take of the money markets he may well settle for a "medium" interest rate.

But suppose the lender believes that, above and beyond high deficits, the political system is out of control, that poverty is growing, that seething blacks are ready to riot (as investment banker Felix Rohatyn predicted in 1982), that American industry cannot compete, that American schools turn out dolts, and so on. Such a lender would be a dolt himself if he did not demand a "high" rate of interest, or put his money in gold. So wrong bad news can be one factor in raising interest rates. That hurts the economy, for it's hard to keep an economy growing when the cost of money is high. There is an aspect of self-fulfilling prophecy here: incorrect bad news yields real bad news.

Talking about rates that are bets on the future—what about the birthrate and its economic effect? Isn't having a child the ultimate bet? If a young couple believes that America is prospering, that we are a healthy folk, that the world is somewhat stable—why then, they will not likely hesitate to do what young couples have done since time immemorial: have a few babies.

But suppose that some young couples (doped on daily fixes of bad news) believe the regnant Distilled Essence of Media: that the environment is degraded, that there are ever more hungry people in the world, that we're running out of space, that nuclear madness will probably destroy us all, that young people will never be able to afford a house, that they won't be able to afford to send their children to college, that our best days are behind us. Can such a couple be blamed for saying it's wrong to bring a child (or, more precisely, a second or third child) into that kind of a world? Is all this one factor behind our very low birthrate (see chapter 11)?

Will such a low birthrate harm us in the future? It surely will, if it really stays with us. As detailed in chapter 11, we know that in the future America will face a series of big social welfare problems (Social Security, Medicare, and so on) if the birthrate stays as low as it is now, and that those problems can become crises should the rate go any lower. There simply won't be very many young people and middle-aged people to pay the taxes to support the elderly. Taxes on the employed will be very high—or benefits very low.

Insofar as low fertility is related to the belief in bad news—bad news that is wrong and wrong-headed—then bad news can create a very difficult situation.

POLITICS

Speculations about the possible total cost of the Bad News Bias go far beyond economics.

Consider politics.

Political commentator David Broder has described a process he calls "the breaking of the President," wherein an innately hostile press corps ultimately savages the sitting President, regardless of who he is or what ideology he may represent.

I think Broder's phrase is accurate. It happens all the time. The press may give the Chief Executive a honeymoon for a while, but soon the long knives come out and the "breaking" process begins: a scandal somewhere in the administration, a policy feud between the secretary of state and the national security advisor (the real man bites dog story would be if they were not feuding) a story that the President has lost control of his White House staff, another scandal, a story that the President has "put his prestige on the line" on a big bill and lost, a story that the Congress no longer fears the President, big headlines about small drops in approval ratings in public-opinion polls, a feature about whether the President really knows what's going on, a new "-Gate" scandal where the President is urged to "lance the boil" (or boil a Lance), a story that what's really happening is "a battle for the mind of the President" (what's left of it, poor fellow), mock surprise that the approval ratings have gone even lower (I wonder why—after all, the dumb, out-of-touch klutz is doing the best he can), and so on. It has happened, in one form or another, to Johnson, Nixon, Ford, Carter, and Reagan.* It's not an accidental occurrence.

What happens is that hundreds of the best journalists in America are training their lenses on the President. Whenever he says something silly, or does something silly, or has appointed a person who does or says something silly, or is alleged by a third party who heard it from a second party to have said or done something silly, there is a story. Whenever there is venality—of any type, in any part of the executive

* The Robinson-Clancey-Grand study discussed earlier shows that television feature stories about Reagan in the first three months of 1983 ran 14–1 negative! This was at a time when many people in the press corps were muttering that Reagan was being handled with kid gloves.

branch—there are press watchdogs digging it out. Reader: imagine your own life under such continued professional scrutiny. How would you stack up? Do all your associates and competitors like you? Do you ever say things you don't really mean? Are any of your associates doing something that might not look so good on page one?

What's true for presidents and officials of the executive branch, is also true for politicians generally. Our journalists delight in portraying working pols as sneaky, dissembling, oversexed, loutish, sometimes crooked folks.

Now, this process is not new. We have seen that Washington, Lincoln, and Wilson felt put upon by the press. In fact, our press today is less scurrilous than in earlier years. The "yellow journalism" of the late 1800s was no tea party. What is new in the process is the impact of television and the amount of television coverage devoted to these sorts of things.

It is one thing to read a paragraph about an alleged political misdeed or miscue in Horace Greeley's old *New York Herald.* And it is something quite different to see, in your own living room, a horde of television cameramen doing a "stakeout" in the front yard of a cabinet officer who said, "cripple," a national security advisor who accepted a gift of a wristwatch, a budget director who made bad loans before he was budget director, a staff aide accused of doing cocaine, another of prescribing Quaaludes, a presidential brother who drinks too much and talks too much. When the quarry is cornered, we see him dodging reporters, going to his car, looking and sounding like the grinch who stole the welfare check. On a normal night that's what 35 million Americans see when they watch the evening news. If "60 Minutes" decides to throw additional logs onto the media fire, that's thirty-three million more viewers, all watching the camera come in for a tight shot on the victim's shifting eyes just as Mike Wallace goes in for the kill.

And what about "Abscam"? Old Horace Greeley was not able to watch a politician accepting cash dollars from a fake Arab sheik, all reenacted in his living room.

Well, let us not feel sorry for presidents. They have interesting jobs and walk to the office. Presidential appointees drive around in big cars with chauffeurs. Nor ought we pity our legislators: as Senator Robert Dole has noted, it's indoor work with no heavy lifting.

But is this process good for America? Does it engender what the political scientists call "political discontinuity"? Does it erode our confidence in our form of government?

As this book is published in 1984, we will have had six presidents in a twenty-one-year span. The 1970s saw increased turnover in both House and Senate. In his book *Channels of Power* the distinguished political scientist Austin Ranney has written: "(television) . . . has altered the culture significantly by intensifying ordinary Americans' traditional low opinion of politics and politicians, by exacerbating the decline in their trust and confidence in their government and its institutions. . . ." Commenting on the subject of presidential elections, Michael Robinson has written, "We should not lose sight of the fact that since the age of television—since 1960—there has been a near linear drop in public affection for the two major party nominees as expressed in national surveys."

Far be it from me to condemn the ancient democratic ritual of throwing the rascals out, or threatening to. It is surely a healthy option. But if the pace is accelerated, if the one major reason for the acceleration is that the media have convinced the electorate that they are being governed by a bunch of jerks and crooks, then that does not serve us well.

It is, to say the least, difficult to govern in a democracy when those governed are alienated from the governors. Moreover, much of that wonderful antialienation tonic that bubbles up from our vigorous system of participatory democracy (see chapter 43) can be dissipated by the angry red eye of television showing one more political rip-off. Legitimacy and consensus, the foundations of democracy, can erode. As mentioned at the outset of this chapter, there are paradoxes here, but not contradictions. Yes, I say, our polity is healthy; yes, I say, it is threatened by video nastiness and trivialization.

POLY-EC

Let us combine Topic A of this discourse—economics and the media—with Topic B—politics and the media—under a third rubric: "political economy and the media."

The major domestic dilemma in the democratic world today concerns the tension among several ideas that are at the core of the capitalist welfare state:

- the desire to provide a "Safety Net" for less fortunate citizens, which depends upon
- the willingness of the public to pay for the costs of such services

- which can be maintained only if there is ongoing financial discipline
- which keeps an economy strong enough to continue to provide such services.

Consider how the Bad News Bias makes each and all of these tasks much more difficult to accomplish.

First, we are told that things are much worse than they are: more poverty, blacks doing worse, poor education, rotten housing. All that we've done hasn't really worked well—but the remedy is clear: more spending by government.

Second, we get the overblown story that the social welfare system is being ripped off by arrogant welfare queens and poverty pimps. No wonder; after all, we are also told that the system is administered by government bureaucrats who are a bunch of incompetent fools.

Accordingly, John and Jane Taxpayer say to themselves, "I get it, I should pay more money for poor people, so it can be turned over by bumblers to swindlers."

Third, is it any surprise that there is a "taxpayer revolt," or that tax cheating is increasing? Why would anyone want to pay for that mess? Is it any wonder, accordingly, that the difference between what legislators believe we need for services and the amount they are able to raise (that is, the deficit) soars sky-high?

That deficit, of course, reduces the ability of the economy to function smoothly—making it ever more difficult to finance the services we need, yielding (so it is said) an intensified cycle of inflation and recession. More and deeper recessions mean still more dollars for social welfare.

A cycle of self-fulfilling bad news.

But suppose, just suppose, the Distilled Essence of Media about the welfare state was not one of squalor, rip-off and bureaucracy. Suppose the DEM—while still covering the real plight of the poor, while covering the real waste-fraud-and-abuse, while covering the real mindlessness and inflexibility of some bureaucratic guidelines—managed to present a broader picture, somewhat closer to the truth. Suppose it were understood—hazily, perhaps, but understood nonetheless—that poor people have made enormous progress in this country in recent years, that waste-fraud-and-abuse are a relatively minor part of the picture, that while some regulations and guidelines are silly most of them address problems that are not simple ones and do not lend themselves to easy answers. Suppose it were understood, after all is said and done, that the welfare state has been helping poor people to help themselves. That is what's been happening, you know.

If more of the public felt that way about things, wouldn't it be:

- easier to cut some spending (on the theory that things aren't nearly as bad as you think) and
- easier to raise revenues (on the theory that the programs are useful)
- thereby lowering the deficits (by closing the gap between spending and receipts)
- thereby lowering interest rates, improving economic growth, raising GNP, raising tax revenues, raising the amount of monies available for both people and governments.

Dr. Feelgood strikes again!

FOREIGN POLICY

Consider the international ramifications of the Bad News Bias.

In an earlier section we have noted that the true test of the free civilizations is whether they will stand up to defend and promote the values of liberty in a threatened world.

The Bad News Bias may, in some ways, inadvertently diminish the ability of the free nations of the world to do that in circumstances where the survival of freedom is still very much at issue.

Consider first the use of force.

Suppose you were a young military officer or a young diplomat, seeking to understand the way of the world. Think of the string of recent wars and military actions: Afghanistan, Iraq-Iran, El Salvador, the Falklands, and Israel-Lebanon, America-Lebanon, and Grenada. What are the new rules of the road that every geopolitician and military tactician must now learn?

It was said that what was new about these wars had something to do with the devastating French missiles used by Argentina, or with the ingenious Israeli adaptation of American smartware, or with the deficiency of Soviet antiaircraft technology used by Syria.

Wrong. The real lessons that should be taught at West Point or the Fletcher School of Diplomacy ought to be very different. The most important new weapons of war are lightweight television cameras and television satellites. The new rules of warfare concern the way they are used nowadays.

First Rule. Communist countries can wage long, brutal wars and pay very little for it—at home or abroad. As this is published it is approaching five years since the Soviets rolled into Afghanistan. One of their nice tactics, described by French doctors, involves strewing tiny mines, disguised as toys, in Afghan villages. There is about enough explosive in the mine to maim, but not kill, a child. Soviet strategists understand that a child with a gangrenous leg is more of a drain on a society than is a dead child.

Needless to say, the controlled Soviet media do not report this sort of thing at home. Moscow television explains how Afghanistan has been liberated by those heroic Russian troops. Western radio broadcasters (Radio Liberty, Voice of America, BBC, Deutsche Welle) make the case, but the Soviets try to jam the broadcasts, with some success. So far, there is no evidence that the Soviet people have turned against the war. Meanwhile, the Afghans continue to fight well. But the nightly news all over the world usually ignores the conflict. Why? The free press can't get into Afghanistan to view the carnage. And if you can't get television cameras into a country to witness the maimed children, the poison gas, the dead civilians—then what can you show on television?

No access, no horror. No horror, no penalty. And so the partial U.S. grain embargo on the Soviet Union, instituted by an allegedly dovish U.S. President, has been lifted—by an allegedly hawkish U.S. President. And real commercial sanctions were never imposed on the Soviet Union. And the little children keep getting blown up.

Second Rule. Roughly the same guidelines hold for nonfree, non-Communist countries. The Iran-Iraq war has been going on for nearly four years. More than 250,000 people are believed to have been killed. Early in the war, the Iranians developed a new mine detector: young boys, overdosed on the Ayatollah's religious fervor, ran across the battlefield to explode the mines. But there were no television cameras to record the battered bits of young life blown sky-high. *No cameras, no news. No news, no outrage.* No outrage, no great international penalty. In 1983, believe it or not, Iraq—the nation that started the war—still actually hoped to put on pretty ribbons to cover their aggression and host the Conference of Nonaligned Nations. In 1984, Iran—the nation that refuses to end the war—continues trade and diplomatic relations with most nations in the world.

Third Rule. A democracy can wage a quick war if it is on an island—

which enables it successfully to control the news. Leave aside morality and geopolitical considerations for a moment and consider how the lack of coverage changed the tactical nature of two conflicts.

There was plenty of television coverage of the ships leaving England for the Falklands to the tune of "Don't Cry for Me, Argentina." But no foreign correspondents were allowed with the fleet; censorship was tight for the few British reporters with the task force. And so, of course, there were no contemporaneous television tapes of the deaths of the British sailors in the icy sea or on the melting superstructure of aluminum ships. The coverage of the war was devoid of horror. During the course of the conflict, Prime Minister Thatcher's ratings in the public opinion polls went way up! She could stand fast, and prevail. Question: If English television had shown the gore of the war while it was happening, could Mrs. Thatcher have kept the political support necessary to finish the war? Could she have kept that support if the war—and the blood, and the televised horror—had gone on for several months? We don't know the answer to that—after all, it was a very faraway irrelevant little island, and it was all over pretty quickly.

Second case in point: America on Grenada. Journalists were not allowed to accompany the U.S. task force. Indeed, they did not know about the war until after it began. It was several days until the government allowed TV cameras onto the island, by which time the action had already ended in quick victory. During the war a mental hospital was mistakenly shelled and eighteen Grenadans were killed. But there was no blood-and-guts coverage of this incident, or of the death of eighteen U.S. troops in combat. And roughly 80 percent of the American public approved of the operation. Question: If all the horror had been shown up close, if it had been the kind of war that dragged on, for how long would there be 80 percent approval? Fifty percent? Thirty percent? Could a President maintain an effective military position under such circumstances? Perhaps, but at a political cost that would make him think three times before he did it again.

Fourth Rule. This is the crucial one, students. Only at great cost can democracies get involved, even minimally, if the battlefield is in an open country.

As this is written, America has provided military aid and about fifty advisors in the civil war in El Salvador. The U.S. participation is a limited enterprise that seems to this author, at least, highly moral. We are helping a government chosen by free elections that has begun land reform, that has tried with some success to break up the old oligarchy. We are helping to combat Marxist guerrilla forces that have been backed by Nicaragua, Cuba, and the Soviet Union, and who are conducting their campaign by impoverishing the economy of El Salvador, destroying bridges, buses, power plants, all the while saying poverty is the problem.

But the American advisors have been way outnumbered in El Salvador by the press. At times, the Distilled Essence of Media, driven by adversarialism, negativism, liberalism, and smugness, made us appear like conspiratorial, lying, profascist butchers. Months went by while the main thrust of the story was to make the Secretary of State "prove" that the Salvadoran guerrillas were getting help from Nicaragua, Cuba, and the Soviet Union—a proposition patently obvious to even low-grade geopoliticians, although inherently difficult to "prove" in a manner suitable to a court of law. ("I have here, Your Honor, a memo from Brezhnev to Castro that says take over El Salvador immediately . . .") At other times it seemed as if the war was about four murdered American nuns. At all times, the coverage was steeped in what television folks call "bang-bang"—guns going off, dead bodies, spilled guts, flowing blood. Another big story—zounds!—revealed that an American Marine advisor actually carried a rifle.

The Bad News Bias was at work. Television made us look like the bad guys, or at least not like the good guys. Television showed us the ugly, bloody side of warfare, which is naturally repugnant to decent people. Accordingly, it has been very difficult to develop public support—and consequently congressional support—for our legitimate actions in an area of great strategic importance to the U.S.

Or consider Israel's 1982 war in Lebanon. It was the first in history where television had free access to both sides of a war simultaneously. Because Israel and Lebanon are free, strategically important, and usually comfortable countries, they host plenty of television crews. Because a television journalist could get to the front quickly in a Hertz car, because the censorship was porous, much of the horror that any war automatically produces was in everybody's living room the same day. Television could regularly show a sequence of an Israeli artillery battery firing, a shell landing in Beirut, a maimed baby in a hospital, and Yassir Arafat walking with a rent-a-kid explaining how war is hell. Later on, television showed in graphic detail the horror of the massacre in Sabra and Shatilla.

What was missing from these pictures?

An explanation—with equal emotional intensity—of why the war began, of the earlier history of a very bloody Arab *vs* Arab civil war, of how (at least from the Israeli view) the war could reduce the level of violence, and so on. Granted, all that was stated; Israeli spokesmen were heard. But the DEM remained, as it must, with the exploding shells and the dead children. What was missing was context, including the reminder that war is always an ugly business.

And so, for quite a while, Israel was seen as a pariah. International pressure built up. Ultimately, the Israelis pulled back, foiled not by the PLO, but by the DEM. Because they are a free nation, because they provided access to their own and foreign journalists, it became very difficult for Israel to use force as an instrument of policy.*

Or consider America's role in Lebanon from 1982 to 1984. A small number of marines, about 1,600 so-called "peacekeepers," were assigned to police the Beirut airport. Their actual role became broader: to serve as an earnest of the commitment of Western nations attempting to reestablish an independent, democratic, pro-Western government in Lebanon. (The French, Italians, and British also had troops in place.) Part of the marines' role was psychological: as one U.S. government official described it, "it's nice to wake up in the morning next to a marine."

We need not debate here the geopolitical wisdom of this commitment, which was a difficult bet, at best.

What happened?

Moslem forces that opposed the existing, shaky, central Lebanese government pinpointed the U.S. marines as prime targets. There was one big, terrible terrorist hit on the marines: 241 killed in October of 1983. And over a period of eighteen months, a total of twenty-four other marines were killed.

The destruction of the marine barracks was (properly) a huge story, albeit a one-time event. But for our purposes here, it is more relevant to see how the deaths of the other twenty-four marines were treated.

It went something like this:

Day one: a marine gets killed. Television shows his corpse or his coffin—or both—in Beirut. Day two: there is an interview with a

---

* Israel has put the blame on the Western press for this situation. There is some merit in that charge, but it ignores the fact that Israeli journalists were in the forefront of denouncing their own government's goals in Lebanon. It was Israeli journalists who first reported the charges against Defense Minister Ariel Sharon's motives and tactics—perhaps properly so, perhaps not. Public support in Israel began to erode. As the charges intensified and were megaphoned, they were picked up outside Israel as well, and international pressure increased.

grieving buddy, hunkered down in "sitting duck" position in Beirut. Day three: the coffin arrives at Dover Air Force Base. Taps are sounded. Day four: there is a funeral in Muncie. The dead marine's grief-stricken mother is interviewed, tears streaming. Day five: former classmates are heard from. "Joe was really a good guy," we learn. The marine's former high school football coach is asked why the marine was in Beirut, and answers, "I don't know."

Day six: get ready, the process may begin all over again. And so it went, month after month, on television. Twenty-four dead marines played like Vietnam-all-over-again.

Congress goes home for Christmas recess. Members find very distressed constituents asking, "Why are we in Lebanon?" Political pressure builds to remove the marines from Lebanon. It is an election year. Hawks at the Pentagon talk on background to the press, complaining that there is not enough "political will" to continue in Lebanon. The politicians demand a "time limit" on the marine's participation. (Question: why would an adversary bother to negotiate if he knows that if he just sits tight for a while, the balance will shift in his favor?)

Now, that is a hell of a way to run a superpower foreign policy. If it makes sense to have a marine presence in Lebanon, then it makes sense whether or not twenty-four marines are killed—even as "sitting ducks." I do not mean to sound harsh about a tragic situation, but marines are voluntary, professional soldiers, who know what they are getting into when they enlist, and who, in fact, did not complain about their mission in Lebanon. In the real sad world in which we live, professional soldiers are often used as "chips" at the geopolitical poker table. If superpower policy can be eroded at home by a nightly display of the horror of military violence, then those "chips" have been debased in value.

End of new rules.

Now in a simple, moral world all this might be quite desirable. Exposing people to the horror of war on television could force national leaders to stay away from violence as a method of solving disputes. And, surely, free peoples are entitled to know—or to speculate—about the policies, politics, and personalities of their military command structure, from the President or Prime Minister on down. Is Haig really a flake? Is Sharon really a brute? These are legitimate questions when young men's lives are at stake, even if such questions may undermine what used to be called "the war effort."

But the world is not that simple. The new rules of media warfare have established a double standard. Television only forces the free and open societies to abjure the use of force. It only exposes the inner pulls-and-pushes of *our* system. No such pressure or exposure is made by television on the unfree nations. The agent of that double standard is the Bad News Bias—in this case, mostly the impact of repeated close-up horror.

The effect of this is to harm the free nations. For we live in a world where the use of force and, more important, the threat of the use of force are still key elements of the global geopolitical equation. That is unfortunate, but true.

As it stands now, our adversaries can credibly use force in a harsh world; they know they can get away with it if it comes down to it. It is much more difficult for us. Our chips have been debased. We know that they know that. They know that we know that. That means it is easier for them to get their way—which is the object of their activity.

This is not good news. It can lead to more violence in the world if one side believes it can get away with the use of force. And sooner or later, the other side (that's us) will have to do some muscle-flexing to reestablish credibility—even if it is expensive, politically difficult and costs the lives of soldiers.

One more example of the Bad News Bias at work on the international scene: the Central Intelligence Agency.

In 1975, the bad-news/adversarial/liberal/self-righteous lens of modern television focused on the Central Intelligence Agency.

Remember?

This dart gun, Senator, can shoot strychnine in a Commie's ear at thirty paces. Yes, Senator, there was a plan to put itching power in Castro's beard. Yes, Senator, someone came up with a plan to assassinate Lumumba. Yes, Senator, the CIA did use lethal drugs. Yes, Senator, we did intercept mail headed for the Soviet Union. Yes, Senator, it was against the law.

On and on it went, week after week, month after month, dominating the prime-time screen in America and all around the world.

At the time of the hearings the CIA had been operating for almost thirty years. It employed about 18,000 people.

The CIA's errors and mistakes over the years were, by any reasonable standard, rather limited. The Senate hearing revealed that the CIA assassinated no one, and made only half-hearted (and half-assed) attempts (on Castro). The CIA did not overthrow Allende in Chile. The CIA's role in Iran at the time of the Shah's accession to power was very small. One man, a CIA employee, committed suicide several days after being administered LSD without his knowledge.

But the Distilled Essence of Media was something quite different: a runaway gang of spooks, roaming the world in trenchcoats, rubbing out red Commie swine, toppling governments everywhere, undermining the American Constitution. All presented by a Senate committee acting like a political rogue elephant, all reported courtesy of a negative, adversarial, self-righteous, liberal press corps.

Lost in the shuffle, of course, was a sad fact about the modern circumstance: an important part of the competition between the superpowers is waged (as Dean Rusk put it) "in the back alleys of the world." We can either participate in that covert competition or leave it all to the Soviets. Of course, no responsible American government would countenance such a withdrawal. So the upshot was this: we continue with a CIA because we must; we have ridiculed it and humiliated it far out of proportion to any sins it committed; we made it difficult for allied intelligence agencies to cooperate with the CIA (for fear of exposure); we have provided grist for the mills of everyone in the world who seeks to undermine America; we were forced to spend a decade trying to rebuild the confidence and credibility of the CIA and still haven't quite succeeded.

So the Bad News Bias makes it difficult for us to fight our battles overtly (war) or covertly (intelligence).

It also makes it much more difficult for us to participate in what is called "the contest of ideas."

If there is a bad-news tilt in the dissemination of news in America, rest assured that it is picked up—and exaggerated still further—all over the world. If American journalists, talking to Americans, say that poverty is rampant, that big business rips us off, that America is crime-ridden, drug-ridden, sex-ridden, that there is no "proof" that Communists are involved in Central America, that we are the agents of violence in El Salvador, then all that overstatement is sent around the world.

We can live with the domestic material although it surely is not helpful. Despite some anti-Americanism, the American way of life remains the most emulated and admired in the world. And no one seems to be flocking toward the Soviet model voluntarily these days.

But the realm of foreign affairs is trickier. If the world sees the bloody bang-bang TV tape from El Salvador, sees the press playing "Gotcha!" with our Secretary of State because his proof on Soviet involvement had a misplaced semicolon, sees the U.S. as the oppressor—that makes our chore in Central America much more difficult. If, for example, the NATO nations solidly supported our role in the Caribbean area, our task there would be eased immeasurably. But their political activists get the same Bad News Bias that we do, pushing their governments to make pious statements and hyper-moralistic policies that undermine our own. So: the wrong story, or at least the right story pushed out of all proportion, hurts us in our military, intelligence, and diplomatic activity.

Such are some of the wages of the Bad News Bias. There are more.

MEDIA

As noted here, there are some major problems—economic, political, international—that are set in motion if the American people come to believe the bad-news version of reality that they see on their bad-news video screens.

There is another serious problem about the Bad News Bias: it is very bad news for the media itself. In part because of the Bad News Bias—negativism, adversarialism, liberalism, smugness—the American people don't think highly of the press.

How many times have you heard someone say, "Whenever the news is about something I know firsthand, it's wrong."

When the press was critical of being excluded from covering the first few days of the American invasion of Grenada, Max Frankel, the respected editor of the editorial page of the *New York Times* said, "The most astounding thing about the Grenada situation was the quick, facile assumption by some of the public that the press wanted to get in, not to witness the invasion on behalf of the people, but to sabotage it."

When ABC Anchorman Peter Jennings was asked how his mail was running on the issue of press presence on Grenada he said, "99 percent against."

Grenada seemed to be a flash point, but there are long-term numbers to back up these sentiments:

CONFIDENCE IN INSTITUTIONS
"TELEVISION NEWS"

% showing "great deal of confidence"

1973	41%
1974	31%
1975	35%
1977	28%
1978	35%
1979	37%
1980	29%
1981	24%
1982	24%
1983	24%

Source: Harris.

That's for television news. A similar line sketches the fall of "the press" as an entity, except that the figures are even lower, although with bumps in the line. Other Harris polls show that the percentage of the population who think TV news is *"not* fair" has jumped 21 points since 1975. Of course, confidence in many American institutions has fallen, but a 1983 Roper Report poll found that public confidence was falling faster for the press than for any other aspect of life surveyed, and that public confidence in the credibility of the press was the second lowest item, just above the credibility of advertising.

Why is confidence in the press diminishing?

We have seen earlier that most Americans think that the press dwells too much on bad news. A flavor of other aspects of the erosion of confidence was elicited in 1980 by this survey:

ABOUT THE PRESS

"They pay too much attention to bad news."
   71% agree for newspapers, 64% agree for TV.

"Newspapers and television sensationalize the news."
   62% agree for newspapers, 66% agree for TV.

"They are not usually fair."
54% agree for newspapers, 46% agree for TV.

"Too often irresponsible."
50% agree for newspapers, 52% agree for TV.

"News is too violent."
37% agree for newspapers, 48% agree for TV.

Source: Public Agenda Foundation, Yankelovich, Skelly and White.

My, my. Not a bad portrait of a Bad News Bias.

This is a sad state of affairs. I say this not as just another media-basher shedding crocodile tears. Man and boy, I have worked in media: newspapers, television, radio, book publishing—as an editor, reporter, author, publisher, and commentator. With all its ills, our free press is a great ornament of our civilization—probably the true root of our freedom. It cannot be a good situation when the population served by this remarkable free institution thinks ill of it. On general principle, it is a damn shame that this is where we are now.

Somewhat more specifically, consider some of the other wages of the Bad News Bias that the media inflict on themselves.

One constructive function of a free press is to galvanize public concern about real ills in society. But if the anchorman cries wolf every evening, and the American people shrug it off as just so much more negativism—whom can anchormen galvanize?

Or try it the other way. Suppose people were to believe all the bad news pumped out by the Bad News Bias. That would in effect go a long way toward destroying a cardinal precept of public policy: "if it ain't broke don't fix it."

After all, according to the Bad News Bias, everything is broke. The Federal Aviation Administration doesn't enforce safety standards, so planes crash. The Environmental Protection Agency is blind to business violations, so people die of air pollution. If a bridge falls, all bridges are about to fall as the decaying of the American infrastructure proceeds. If there is one instance of police brutality, we are a brutal people. What to do? Everything is broke! Answer: Fix everything!

But you can't fix everything right away. The resources don't exist. Overfixing things that are hardly broke can harm us. Trying to fix everything may mean fixing nothing as arguments break out about priorities.

Do we want to spend another billion on air pollution, if it comes at the expense of, oh, pick any old program, say, food for hungry children?

Do we want to put a heavy negative spotlight on police behavior—to a point where cops become afraid of bad publicity, and are afraid to enforce the law—and somebody's mother gets mugged?

It is not only hungry children and mugged mothers and America that are hurt by this process. The press is hurt in ways that hurt most.

We are speculating in this chapter. What happens when people come to believe that the press is too negative and *not to be believed?* The press begins to become irrelevant. What could be sadder than an irrelevant anchorman?

Or consider the other possibility: that people—and politicians—will sense that the overstated bad news, the bad news that is phony, *is believed* and leads us to faulty decision-making. There is a logical (and unfortunate) remedy for that, one that politicians are drawn to like moth to flame: regulation. Except the drive for regulation in this case would not come from nice liberal do-gooders who want to take particulates out of the air. No sir. These regulators would swing from the other side of the plate, and try to take bad news out of the air.

Give us fair news, they'd say. Report the administration goals accurately, they'd say. Why are we spending taxpayer money on public broadcasting that undermines America, they'd ask. Why can't we squeeze the private broadcasters, they'd ask; after all, they get their license and their access to the air waves from a federal agency. Why can't we squeeze the print media, they'd ask; after all, we subsidize their mailing rates with special postage rates. Tighten up the libel laws, they'd say. Make the press reveal sources, they'd say.

Do not think there is no public constituency for getting tough on the media. Consider:

Question: Do you think the present curbs placed on the press are too strict or not strict enough?

Too strict	17%
About right	32%
Not strict enough	37%
No opinion	14%

Source: Gallup, 1980.

Question: Would you favor or oppose a law that would require
             newspapers to give opponents of a controversial policy
             as much coverage as those in favor of the policy?

Favor	73%
Oppose	17%
Not sure	10%

Source: Public Agenda Foundation, Yankelovich, Skelly and White, 1980.

Control. By government. Not total, not in America. But some. It
could happen.

There is a way out of all this, and it doesn't involve the governmental force-feeding of good news.

Tell it like it is, press!

When the nightly news starts reporting good news as well as bad
news, it will be believed. When the news is credible, we will get more
positive action stimulated by bad news. When our news is more realistic, we will get fewer foolish actions stimulated by phony bad news.

That would be good for all of us. And nobody in government would
dare lay a glove on the press.

SPIRIT

And finally, as we speculate about the future, we ought to face one
overarching question: can the Bad News Bias demoralize us?

When all is said and done, a free society does not have much more
than belief in itself. Many great modern thinkers (Joseph Schumpeter, for one) have understood this and reached a gloomy conclusion—that a society could be healthy enough, but that an "adversary
culture" (as Lionel Trilling called it) or, more recently, a "new class,"
or "elitists," could be so negative about modern democratic life and
its culture that they could (often unwittingly) undermine it, robbing
it of its vigor, vitality and confidence.

Schumpeter wrote about this in 1942, long before television entered
our homes and our lives. But television has bolstered his case many
fold. He was talking about the influence of intellectuals who wrote in
little magazines. But the negative position is now put forward every
night in almost every living room. It is fair to ask: will the Bad News
Bias of television become the Schumpeterian instrumentality that
steals our modern magic away from us?

Will a society that comes to believe it is no longer great have the audacity to send people to the moon and beyond? Will a society that comes to believe nothing works well anymore be able to muster its resources and try to cure cancer? Will a society that is told inferentially every evening that it is no longer proudly riding the wave of history, but is perhaps struggling immorally against the tide, be willing to pay what is necessary to defend its interests and to promote its democratic values? Will a society that believes modernity is a blind alley be prepared to help premodern societies along the road to better health, literacy, communications, economic growth?

Now it may be said—and it is so—that Americans are smart, commonsensical and optimistic, that they are not taken in by the bad news drumbeat, that they know America from their own observations. And so, it may be inferred, video gloom is a mere diversion, water off a duck's back.

There is surely some truth to that—and paradox. I have spent 400 pages here demonstrating that America keeps on moving ahead. We have, so far, survived the staccato trumpet of televised troubles. And yet now, as I end the refrain, I start telling you that we may be in for trouble.

I would maintain these views are not inconsistent. We have been moving ahead mostly in spite of the Bad News Bias. As indicated here, it may already have hurt us in some ways. Logic tells us that the media blues may have a continuing effect upon us, perhaps at compound interest, as a generation grows up with the magic box in the rec room blaring more and more bad news, told more dramatically and more often than ever before.

We don't any of us know the future. But this is a potentially serious problem and we ought to think about it. The argument is about the nature of and future of our civilization.

=====

Luckily for all of us, there is one solid reason to calm down about this real problem. The press is being hassled, and is worrying about the situation.

In late 1983, *Time* magazine did a cover story on the media. The lead headline:

JOURNALISM UNDER FIRE

A Growing Perception of
Arrogance Threatens the
American Press

In December of 1983, Robert C. Maynard, editor and publisher of the *Oakland Tribune* spoke to fellow media bigwigs in Washington on the occasion of the annual Frank E. Gannett Lecture. He spoke of

> . . . immense disaffection between the American public and press
> (that) we must urgently seek to repair lest we find ourselves in great
> peril. . . . we tended after Watergate particularly to increase the
> rate at which we wrote about public officials from a standpoint that
> seemed to suppose that they were guilty of something . . . it appears
> that we are "out to get somebody." The great sense of fair play in
> American society has somehow or another been antagonized by the
> way some of us perform . . . we have tended to be . . . an arrogant
> institution. We don't mind telling the Congress or the President
> and the Court or any number of institutions what they have done
> wrong. We don't mind exposing their secrets when we can get our
> hands on them. But when any of them or anyone else asks us for what
> we have done wrong we are sometimes, dare I say reluctant to discuss
> the subject . . . we project to the public that we can never be
> called into question in matters where we automatically invoke what
> we consider our own right to privacy . . . (we have created) a
> feeling that journalists somehow thought they were holier than
> thou . . . the press as an institution is in trouble.

The Maynard speech and the *Time* cover story came out shortly after the Defense Department's ban on press coverage of the war in Grenada and the favorable public reaction to that ban.

Press soul searching, however, precedes the Grenada fallout. On May 5, 1982, New York *Daily News* editor Michael J. O'Neill delivered a major address to the American Society of Newspaper Editors. Some excerpts:

> While there has been an astonishing growth in the power of the
> media over the last decade or so, I am by no means sure we are using
> it wisely. The tendency has been to revel in the power and wield it
> freely, rather than to accept any corresponding increase in
> responsibility. . . . Individuals and institutions have been needlessly
> hurt when the lure of sensational headlines has prevailed over
> fairness, balance and a valid public purpose . . . (T)he adversarial
> attitude creates barriers to the clear observation and analysis
> necessary for objectivity. It encourages emotional involvement with
> individual personalities and issues. It invites arrogance. It tempts
> reporters to harass officials. Ultimately it undermines credibility
> because people intuitively sense when the press is being unfair . . .

(I)f we are always downbeat—if we exaggerate and dramatize the negatives in our society—we attack the optimism that has always been a wellspring of American progress.

Stanford University journalism professor Elie Abel has written that after Watergate, "much of the Washington press developed an obsession with official dishonesty. Exposure became a sacred mission." Sensing this, Keith Fuller, general manager of the Associated Press, has warned against investigations begun specifically to indict a particular person or organization. "Investigative reporting," he said, "is best when we do not set out to gather the facts to support our own suppositions."

Other media insiders worry about the international implications of these criticisms. In March 1982, Pulitzer Prize-winning journalist Shirley Christian commented in the *Washington Journalism Review* on the subjectivity and blindness of the American press corps' coverage of Nicaragua's Marxist revolution. Under the subtitle, "The Foregone Conclusions of the Fourth Estate," Christian writes that "the story that reporters told—with a mixture of delight and guilt—was the ending of an era in which the United States had once again been proved wrong." In its July 9, 1983, issue, *TV Guide* quotes Howard Stringer, executive producer of CBS Evening News, as follows:

> Stringer does, however, worry about a post-Vietnam cynicism among reporters and is concerned "whether the media, by making comparisons with Vietnam every time we get involved overseas, are making it impossible for the United States to [conduct foreign policy]."

Worry and pressure—from inside and out—are good for free institutions. That, after all, is the media's own maxim about others: "Keep the bastards on their toes."

Now that the media men and women are themselves walking on tippy toes, it might be a good time to have a nice friendly chat.

CHAPTER 52

Cameo:
Cornering the
Anchorman

SUMMARY CONVERSATION

The party at Claude Cleeshay's is coming to an end. There are cigarette butts in half-filled highball glasses.

Let's go off to a corner with Anchorman and wrap this up. After all, the poor fellow has been punched around a bit. He's been called negative, adversarial, liberal, and self-righteous. It's been implied that he harms our economy, our politics, our foreign policy. It's even been claimed that he's harming himself and the media industry.

"Anchorman," we ask, "what do you think?"

"Author, you've given us a bum rap. All you want to do is shoot the messenger who brings the bad news."

"No way, Anchorman. How many messengers do you know who sit around sorting an infinite pile of messages, trying to figure out which ones to deliver and which ones to throw in the wastebasket?"

"Infinite? What are you talking about? Sometimes we're short of news."

"Wrong. There is an infinite quantity of news at any given moment. Think about the 'news hole.' It contracts and expands. In a newspaper it is bigger on Sunday than on weekdays. Is that because there is more news on Sunday? Nope. It is because Sunday papers carry more advertising. So news editors reach into their infinitely high pile and fill the news hole. Same is true for television. Was there more news because ABC developed the concept of 'Nightline'? That added an extra half hour of news every night."

" 'Nightline' did start because there was more news: the Iran hostage crisis was big news."

"But 'Nightline' continued, even expanded, after the hostages were returned. The news hole expanded because people watched the program and liked it, and because advertisers, accordingly, bought commercials."

"What's your point, Author?"

"There was more news all the time. There is still more news today. It will contract or expand as necessary to fit whatever hole is available. One of the big jobs of the media is to select *which* news to deliver. Everyone knows that. But that's not the job of a messenger, that's the job of an editor. An editor can decide that it is news that hexo-bexo-drexo may be carcinogenic. Or he can decide that it is news that people are living longer these days. They're both good stories. But what gets on the air?"

"Author, you're turning into a bore about life expectancy. Don't we have to deliver the bad news about Lebanon and El Salvador and South Vietnam?"

"Sure. But why don't you give equal time to Afghanistan and Iran-Iraq?"

"We can't get our crews there. We can't film what we can't film."

"Fair enough. But you're making my case. You cover our bad news but not their bad news."

"You're giving us a hard time, Author. We run a lot of material that beats up on America, but we're only reporting what academics, politicians, activists, and intellectuals and experts are saying. We don't create these stories. I never heard of hexo-bexo-drexo until some scientist told me about it."

"You're toying with me, Anchor. There are experts out there who will tell you that nuclear power is the cleanest and safest fuel known to man. There are experts out there who will tell you that America is still the profoundly moral force in modern history. There are experts who will tell you that we've made a great deal of headway combating poverty. There are experts who will tell you that we've moved ahead in many ways in education in America in recent years. But are those the experts we see on the nightly news? Not typically. There is an almost infinite pile of academics, politicians, activists, intellectuals, and experts. The ones that appear on television are disproportionately hawking bad news. But what's going on in our time is mostly positive. You're not giving us the straight news, Anchorman."

"You want us to run government handouts? Echo the establishment? We have to challenge that! Who will, if we don't?"

"If you're going to be adversarial, why don't you challenge Ralph Nader's views in the same way? Or challenge the views of the chairman of the National Organization for Women in the same way?"

"Look, Author, we give people what they want. They like scandal, doom-saying, danger, corruption, violence. If we don't give it to them, our competitors give it to them, we lose ratings and go off the air. We can't cover what you call the process of progress. People aren't interested. We're helpless."

"Half true. You're doing an excellent job of making my case. Suppose you are right and that good news doesn't sell. That doesn't refute the notion that there is a Bad News Bias. It proves it. Anyway good news does better in the marketplace than you think. Look at *USA Today*. It covers the good news as well as the bad, but it also handles the process of progress regularly with cute little graphics, and its circulation keeps growing. Same with *U.S. News and World Report*. On television there is Charles Kuralt. Ted Koppel gives it a square shot. So do MacNeil-Lehrer. There are others."

"Author, get serious. How can we cover what you call the process of progress? Are you kidding? I mean, stories about air conditioning as a hallmark of human progress! Nembutal! Boring! Cover more blacks going on to college while black unemployment is soaring? Do regular stories about improved health in less-developed countries? A lot of ZZZs!"

"That's your problem, pal. Those stories are more important than Peter Bourne and Quaaludes. More important than whether someone in the White House called someone in the Justice Department a 'munchkin.' More important than Ed Meese's cufflinks . . . a story which led the evening news on CBS! You're not doing your job, Anchor."

"We do the best we can, where we can. America's no angel. America goes into Vietnam, kills people. We cover it the best we can. Russia goes into Afghanistan. Same difference. We cover that, too. We do the best we can. Dan Rather did a great piece from inside Afghanistan."

"I know. One piece. But look here, Russia invaded Afghanistan. America didn't invade South Vietnam. Russia would like Afghanistan to be a Soviet satellite. We would have liked to see South Vietnam in the community of free nations."

"I can see it coming. You're going to give me that Left-wing crap. We call 'em like we see 'em. Neither fear nor favor. We are adversarial. Someone has to be. That's our job."

"My point exactly. The media are not consciously left of center. But equality of adversarialism yields inequality of results. It says we're as bad as they are. It doubles our badness because our bad news is accessible. But we're not the bad guys. We're the good guys."

"You know what your problem is, Author? You overestimate the power of the press. You say we're adversarial, too negative, too liberal. But in countries with a free, negative, adversarial, Left-tilted press, conservatives keep winning—Reagan, Thatcher, Kohl, Nakasone, Begin. You say we unwittingly foster anti-Americanism, yet the polls you cite show the continued high regard for America around the world. And people hate the Soviet Union. You tell us that Americans are still proud and patriotic. You say—in this book—that America is making so much headway. So what's the problem?"

"We'll get to that, Anchorman. I'd better say something else first. The free press is terrific. The American free press is the best there is. Even on some of the issues I'm concerned about, the press has done great work. I once talked to Georgi Arbatov, a member of the Soviet Politburo, their professional America-watcher. He said to me: 'The dissident story is all hype. It's a few malcontents. Sakharov is a media freak. Your press is making Soviet dissidents into international figures!' Arbatov was on target. That's what happened. A few American journalists in Russia helped the cause of freedom immeasurably. I commend you for it."

"Thank you, Author."

"You're welcome, Anchorman."

"Now that you're being nice, I have to tell you I resented that stuff about the press being self-righteous, smug, arrogant. We're just people."

"Do you think I should apologize?"

"Yes."

"I'll think about it."

"Look, Author, you know what all this boils down to? You say we're selecting unfairly. But who says you're so smart? Who says your vision of the world is right? You've turned into a conservative optimist— and you want everyone to be like you! That's not a free press!"

"Why is it conservative to say the American welfare state has produced such success? That's liberal, Anchorman. Liberals ought to run a political campaign on this book. Besides I'm not an optimist."

"You're not an optimist?"

"The argument is all about who are the realists. I gave you data here, not optimism."

"C'mon, Author, you're playing with me. You say nothing's wrong. That's the title of the book: *The Good News Is the Bad News Is Wrong*. That's strange. How can everything be so good all at once?"

"I didn't say nothing's wrong. Poetic license. I mean most of the bad news is wrong. Crime is terrible in America. Automobile safety is a scandal. Illegitimate birth is a real problem. If you don't think that I think there is a long-range population problem, and a big one, you didn't read this book. But you know, it's not unreasonable to say that most things move in tandem. A successful nation is likely to be successful on most fronts at the same time. It would be bizarre to suggest otherwise. If more people own houses, it's likely that they have better jobs than they had before, and earn more money than they did before. That's why they're able to buy the house."

"Everyone has different statistics. Who says yours are right?"

"Me. I'll tell you what. Read this book. Argue with it. Find experts who will say—aha! He didn't cite this fact or that one; he didn't tell you this statistic or that one. (Although, Anchor, I must tell you I tried to cover as many caveats and counterarguments as I could.) But attack every claim in this book. *And then divide it in half!*"

"Suppose I do?"

"You will still find enormous progress over the last dozen or so years. Women going on to college, getting better jobs. People living longer, healthier lives. Blacks in better jobs, moving into the mainstream. A rich, new infusion of immigrant stock. Environmental progress. More dignity for the elderly. An innovative business community. Strong values. Patriotism. A vigorous, contentious politics."

"Enough already. I read the book. It's very interesting."

"Thanks."

"You're still way too optimistic. You automatically think everything's going to work out super. You think life's a bowl of cherries."

"Who, me?"

"You."

"You've got me wrong, Anchor. People keep screwing up. We know that. Something will go wrong. Count on it. Another recession, more inflation, bigger deficits, deflation—who knows? More turmoil in Central America, Middle East—sure. My point is that we cope with these things, and we usually come out stronger and richer. That's what's happened so far. That's realism. Not optimism."

"How about nuclear war?

"Between the big powers, all-out?"

"Yes."

"Won't happen. I'll bet you."

"Thanks. I win if the world is destroyed."

"You got it."

"Very funny, Author. Your problem is you don't sense any human tragedy."

"The hell I don't. Life is tough. We all go out in a box. There are a lot of sad and sorry people out there. But there are fewer specific miseries than there used to be. All I'm saying is that as a society— all of us put together, on average, and up and down the scale—we're doing better than ever. And you're not covering it."

"Maybe there is a problem. But we're beginning to investigate ourselves. We self-police. You should like that. Anyway, that's the only answer."

"That probably is the only answer. But you may be the worst self-policeman in all history. I hope you investigate other stories better than this one. On this story, you make Inspector Clouseau look like Sherlock Holmes. You concentrate on trivia. You miss the point. Marco Polo returns from China and you grill him to find out if he padded his expense account."

"For instance?"

"For instance, Debategate. It dominated the news week after week. The media pretty well stopped the executive branch from functioning. The smell of character assassination was in the air. That was '-Gating' journalism at its worst. There was no real story there. And what did the media self-policemen concentrate on? That columnist George Will, a public Reagan partisan, didn't publicly announce that he helped candidate Reagan prepare for his debate with Jimmy Carter! Big deal!"

"That's just one example."

"Here's another: Janet Cooke. All that soul searching, all that breast-beating, about an invented child who was supposed to be a heroin addict. But Janet Cooke was just lying. That's not the problem with the press. They don't lie. Or take the CBS television documentary where General William Westmoreland is accused of treachery, deceit, perhaps treason—implying that the Vietnam War was a rip-off and a hustle. What do the media self-policers focus on? The fact that the show's producer taped a phone conversation that he himself was party to. Big deal. That's not the problem."

"And you say the real problem is we don't show good news. You say we're nattering nabobs of negativism. You want blow-dry, happy-time stuff."

"Anchor, are you purposefully trivializing an important argument? That's why the public is getting angry."

"My turn to apologize, Author. It is serious. What do we do about it?"

"I'm glad you asked. You've got two problems as I see it. You've not told the whole truth on the air. With a new dramatic device (television), with so much more time and effort devoted to public affairs, that misreportage may erode our spirit, erode the confidence we have in ourselves."

"I know, I know. And it may be self-fulfilling. You already gave us that list. It reduces our geopolitical power, our economic power, and so on. You probably think it causes dandruff too. What is the other problem?"

"People are really angry about the press."

"I know. You read the polls. I get the mail. You should have seen the mail we got on Grenada."

"I know."

"What's going to happen? What are they going to do—maul the messenger?"

"I hope not. Probably squeeze him a little."

"I bet that breaks your heart, Author."

"I'm pleased with some of it, Anchor. I don't want it to go too much further among people outside the press. That could be dangerous."

"Very."

"Anchorman, just like you. I want an uncensored, undirected, private, tough, critical press corps. I don't like the alternative."

"Me neither. Censorship from the Right. Fascism."

"You said it, not me. Don't worry. It won't come to that. Or anywhere close to it. Remember, I'm a realistic optimist."

"Why won't it? You've scared me. Some optimist! You're telling me we're headed for 1984 in 1984. What can we do to stop it?"

"I'm glad you asked. You've got to do the criticism yourself. But seriously. Sift it out. See which antipress charges make sense. See which don't. Are you tilted to the Left? Are you adversarial? Are you too smug? And mostly—most important—are you too negative? Work on it. It'll be good for you, good for us. And then go back to work and tell it like it is. Then we'll all live happily ever after."

"What are you saying? That we should sit around and read your book about how wonderful things are and have a collective consciousness-raising session about it?"

"That's a good start. That's one of the reasons I wrote it."

"Okay. Good seeing you. Take it easy."

"You too. Drive carefully. I've got to say goodbye to Claude."

ACKNOWLEDGMENTS

This volume deals with a very wide range of topics. The broad rubrics here concern "the quality of life," "the standard of living," "values," "politics" and "media." In tighter focus, the reader will find discussions about premarital sex, cancer, air conditioning, black progress, political action committees, anchormen, the status of women, homelessness, "bang-bang" television journalism, and American attitudes toward foreign policy, just to begin a very long list.

No one is an expert on all these subjects. Accordingly, an author working on a book of this sort relies on many institutional sources. Let me mention two at the outset: the American Enterprise Institute (AEI) and the U.S. Bureau of the Census.

I joined the American Enterprise Institute in 1977 at the invitation of the late William J. Baroody, Sr., at the time AEI's president. He was a most remarkable man, one of whom it can be said with real validity that he changed the nature of the world he left behind.

Someone else will undoubtedly write the full history of "think tanks" in America, tracing their influence on public policy, which is substantial. All I know is that AEI, now ably administered by Bill Baroody, Jr., has gathered together a remarkable group of scholars and fellows, and that it provides a wonderful home for an itinerant free lance like me. It's been quite a rare feeling over the years to be able to walk down the halls and poke my head in on distinguished neighbors who are trying to figure out how the world works.

I should probably list here the whole AEI roster—past and present—because it can be quite a collegial place. But because this volume preaches discipline, I will practice it now by mentioning only those who were of some specific help. (Although of course it is I, not they, who stand behind the opinions expressed here.)

First, of course, are my colleagues on the staff of AEI's *Public Opinion* magazine. They all helped me, and in many ways: Seymour Martin Lipset, Everett Ladd, Karlyn Keene, Victoria Sackett, and Nicola Furlan. Over the two and a half years it took to write this book, three women—Mary Bruun, Mary Buena and Susan Irvings—were research assistants on *Public Opinion* and also labored to organize both me and a manuscript that kept growing longer and longer, while time grew shorter and shorter. They often worked overtime, and their efforts are deeply appreciated.

In addition, these AEI scholars, fellows, and assistants aided me in this effort: Walter Berns, Anne Brunsdale, Marvin Esch, David Gergen, Robert Goldwin, Michael Malbin, Jack Meyer, Michael Novak, Norman Ornstein, Howard Penniman, Austin Ranney, Michael Robinson, Richard Scammon, William Schambra, William Schneider, Tom Skladony, Herbert Stein, Nick Thimmesch, Marshall Tracht, John Weicher, Cicero Wilson, Marvin Kosters, Arthur Burns, and the late William Fellner.

On the administrative side at AEI, particular effort and courtesies were extended by: Evelyn Caldwell, Marie Hackbarth and John Winterson at the AEI Library, as well as by Tait Trussell, Pat Ford, Larry Foust and David Knight.

Karl Zinsmeister served as my research assistant for this book. This is one very intelligent, resourceful, dedicated and interesting young man. I shudder when I think of the hours he put into this project—countless nights and weekends. In many respects this book could not have been done the way it was, in the time it was, without Karl's help.

About the Census Bureau: I first wandered in there in 1962 to write another book, *This U.S.A.* Dick Scammon was the Director of the Bureau at that time and we ended up collaborating on that work, and on others later on, beginning a friendship that remains strong today. The distinguished demographer Conrad Taeuber was the Assistant Director for Population. Herman Miller was the Chief of the Income Division (and later Chief of the Population Division) and he had a very bright young protégé named Roger Herriot.

In any event, I came to work with and know many of the Census experts over the years. They are extremely competent and hardworking professionals. They call them as they see them.

I learned this again working on this book when some Census analysts reviewed certain chapters in an early draft. They let me know with sometimes blunt precision where they thought I might have strayed. Their help, and the help of the remarkable institutional resources they command, was, as always, of inestimable value.

Herriot, the young protégé of yesteryear, became Chief of the Income Division and is now the Chief of the Population Division. He was of particular help. So too was Gordon Green, the very bright young man who succeeded Herriot as head of the income branch, and is now Assistant Chief of the Population Division. Time marches on.

These Census professionals also helped: Suzanne Bianchi, Dan Burkhead, Wendy Bruno, June Cowles, Diana DeAre, William Downs, Carol Fendler, Campbell Gibson, Jerry Jennings, Dwight Johnson, Glenn King, Bob Kominski, Larry Long, Nampeo McKenney, Arthur Norton, Dave O'Neill, Martin O'Connell, Jeffrey Passel, Thomas Palumbo, Adolfo Paez, Steve Rawlings, Steve Rudolph, Paul Ryscavage, Arlene Saluter, Paul Siegel, Cindy Taeuber, Arno Winard, Diane Winter and Arthur Young.

In addition, Census help was provided by Director Bruce Chapman and Acting Director C. L. Kincannon and their staffs, including Helen Fedele, Shelby Weekly and Carolee Bush.

Help from other government agencies came from: Lenna Kennedy, Barbara Ling and Virginia Reno at the Social Security Administration; Doug Robertson and Barbara Sprow at the Bureau of Labor Statistics; Betty Tunstall at the Bureau of Economic Analysis; Larry Suter and Cy Rosen at the National Institute of Education; Sandy Graber at the Internal Revenue Service; Selma Taffel and Barbara Wilson at the National Center for Health Statistics; Howard Snyder at the National Center for Juvenile Justice; Gene Pugliese at the House Immigration Subcommittee; and Myron Uman at the National Academy of Sciences.

Information doesn't come from the government only. My thanks to: Alice McGillivray of the Elections Research Center; Leon Bouvier, Cary Davis and

Carl Haub of the Population Reference Bureau; Deborah Whiteside of the Mortgage Bankers Association; Alberta Henderson, Dr. John Jennings, Jill Schucker and Jeffrey Warren of the Pharmaceutical Manufacturers Association; Reid Gearhart of Dun & Bradstreet, Inc.; Michael Schlain of the New York Stock Exchange; Lawrence Olson of Sage Associates; Maura Clancey of George Washington University; Andrew Brimmer and Felicia Fauntleroy of Brimmer and Co., Inc.; Georgia Alone of Knight-Endey; Kimberly Madden of Ameritrust; Amy MacDonald of Teenage magazine; John Kantner of Johns Hopkins University; John Kaplan of Stanford University; John Oshinski and Steve Chamberlain of the American Petroleum Institute; Sar Levitan of George Washington University; Herbert Alexander of the Citizen's Research Foundation; Edwin Silverberg and Arthur Hollub of the American Cancer Society; Vee Burke of Congressional Research Service; Sol Gordon of Syracuse University; Francine Blough and Andrea Baller of the University of Illinois, Champaign-Urbana; Elizabeth Whelan of the American Council on Science & Health; Richard Young of Indiana University; Frank Furstenberg of the University of Pennsylvania; Ann Robinson and Mary Wreford of the Institute of Social Research, University of Michigan; Scott Hudson of the Employee Benefit Research Institute; Susan Povenmeier of ABC News; June O'Neill and Tom Espenshade of the Urban Institute; Kristin Moore of Child Trends, Inc.; Edwin Harwood of the Hoover Institution; Julian Simon of the University of Maryland and the Heritage Foundation; Penn Kemble of the Institute for Religion and Democracy; Martin Schramm of *The Washington Post,* Daniel Schorr of Cable News Network; Stephen Hess of the Brookings Institute; James Q. Wilson of Harvard University; Dr. Herbert Moscovitz; Joan Brewer of the Kinsey Institute; Sidney Goldstein of Brown University; Jhoon Rhee; Ervin Duggan; Dan Fenn of the Kennedy Library; Steve Miller of Radio Free Europe/Radio Liberty; David Hendin of United Features Syndicate; Ward Chamberlin and Gerry Slater of WETA; Joan Barone of CBS; Anne Marie Amantia of the Population Crisis Committee. I spent a stimulating and productive month at Mishkenat Sh'anunim, a writer's and artist's haven in Jerusalem.

Working with the very skilled editors at Reader's Digest on the magazine condensation of this work was an education in itself. My thanks to Fulton Oursler, Jr., Walter Hunt, Clell Bryant and Richard Hessney.

The people at Simon and Schuster paid special attention to this book, from President Richard Snyder and Publisher Dan Green on down. The copy editing department headed by Sophie Sorkin went through a particularly hectic and thankless task to get this volume out more or less on time.

Robert Asahina edited the book for Simon and Schuster. He is a low-key, indefatigable, incisive fellow whose guidance and commitment are deeply appreciated.

My agent, Jerome Traum of Janklow and Traum, helped out when I needed it.

The late Senator Henry M. Jackson played no direct role in this book, but over the years he influenced my thinking deeply regarding a number of the issues discussed here. He was a great man. Like Bill Baroody, Sr., he changed the world he left behind.

And finally, my family. My father Judah Wattenberg is always of wise counsel as is my sister, Rebecca Schull. My three older children, Ruth, Daniel and

Sarah, have helped me on this project as they always have in so many ways in the past. My youngest daughter, Rachel, is only two months old as this is written, but I am counting on her help in the future. She has a wonderful mother, my wife Diane, to whom this book is dedicated.

Ben Wattenberg
Washington, D.C.
6 June 1984

Index